The Human Right to Water
and International Economic Law

This book discusses the international right to water and the liberalization of water services. It is concerned with the harmonization of the right to water with the legal systems under which liberalization of water services has taken or may take place. It assesses paths of harmonization between international human rights law and international economic law in this specific field.
The issue of the compatibility between the fulfilment of the right to water and the liberalization of water services has been at the heart of a passionate public debate between opponents and advocates of the privatization of the utility. The book provides an unbiased analysis of different international legal regimes under which the liberalization of water services has occurred or is likely to occur, notably international investment law, international trade law and European Union law, in order to assess whether the main features of the right to water can be guaranteed under each of these systems of law and whether there is space for prospective harmonization.
The work will be an invaluable resource for academics, researchers and policy-makers working in the areas of International Human Rights Law, International Economic Law, International Water Law, International Trade Law and EU Law.

Roberta Greco is Adjunct Professor of International Law, University of Rome 'LUMSA', Italy, and Associate attorney at the International Law Firm, Saccucci & Partners, specialized in litigating cases before the European Court of Human Rights.

Roberta Greco

The Human Right to Water and International Economic Law

Routledge
Taylor & Francis Group
LONDON AND NEW YORK

G. Giappichelli Editore

First published 2022
by Routledge
4 Park Square, Milton Park, Abingdon, Oxon OX14 4RN
605 Third Avenue, New York, NY 10017

Routledge is an imprint of the Taylor & Francis Group, an informa business

and by G. Giappichelli Editore
Via Po 21, Torino – Italia

British Library Cataloguing-in-Publication Data
A catalogue record for this book is available from the British Library

Library of Congress Cataloging-in-Publication Data
A catalogue record for this book has been requested

ISBN: 978-0-367-50580-6 (hbk-Routledge)
ISBN: 978-88-921-3351-8 (hbk-Giappichelli)
ISBN: 978-1-003-05040-7 (ebk-Routledge)
ISBN: 978-0-367-61771-4 (pbk-Routledge)

Typeset in Simoncini Garamond
by G. Giappichelli Editore, Turin, Italy

The manuscript has been subjected to a peer review process prior to publication.

This book was completed within the research project on "*Integrated protection of fundamental rights in the face of global challenges: evolutionary trends and reconstructive challenges*" and published with funding from the related LUMSA research group.

To my whole beloved family

CONTENTS

page

List of Abbreviations XI

I. General introduction

1. Setting the scene 1
   1.1. Privatization and liberalization of water services in the wake of water commoditization 4
   1.2. Emergence of a human rights-based approach to water 12
   1.3. Possible conflicting obligations arising from the human right to water and international economic law 15
2. Rationale for the book: a quest for balancing the human rights approach and the trade and investment law approach to water services liberalization 16
3. Area of research: fragmentation of international law 19
4. Research questions 20
5. Model of analysis 21
   5.1. Harmonization by means of conflict prevention 22
   5.2. Harmonization by means of interpretation 23
   5.3. Establishing systemic relationships of priority 28
6. Methodology 36
7. Scope and outline of the book 37

II. The Human Right to Water under International Law

1. Introduction 41
2. The legal basis of the human right to water 47
   2.1. Treaty legal basis 47
      2.1.1. The right to water as a derivative right 51
   2.2. The emergence of a customary human right to water 53
      2.2.1. State practice 60
         2.2.1.1. International treaties 61
         2.2.1.2. Regional instruments 63
         2.2.1.3. Statements by States and conduct within international organizations 66
         2.2.1.4. National constitutions and legislation 68
         2.2.1.5. Domestic case law 73
      2.2.2. States' *opinio juris* 82
      2.2.3. A right in *statu nascendi* or already born? 85

page

2.3. General principles of international law 88
3. The content of the human right to water 89
3.1. The content of the right to water derived from Article 11 ICESCR 89
3.1.1. Subsequent agreement on the interpretation of Article 11 ICESCR 93
3.2. The content of the customary right to water 95
4. The obligations stemming from the human right to water 99
4.1. The nature and content of the obligations 99
4.2. The subjects responsible for their implementation 104
4.3. The territorial extension of the obligations 106
5. The role of international judges and quasi-judicial compliance mechanisms in the identification and formation of the human right to water 112
5.1. International human rights mechanisms 113
5.2. Regional human rights tribunals and compliance mechanisms 114
5.3. International investment tribunals 120
6. Conclusion 120

III. The liberalization of water services under international investment agreements and the human right to water

1. Introduction 123
2. The jurisdiction of investment tribunals to adjudicate violations of the human right to water 128
3. The impact of the human right to water on the merits of investor-State arbitration 131
3.1. The relevant BIT provisions likely to raise concerns from a human rights perspective 131
3.1.1. Expropriation 132
3.1.2. Fair and equitable treatment 134
3.1.3. Full protection and security 137
3.2. Cases lacking clear reference to the human right to water 137
3.2.1. Expropriation 143
3.2.2. Fair and equitable treatment 145
3.2.3. Full protection and security 147
3.3. Cases acknowledging the human right to water 148
3.3.1. Expropriation 155
3.3.2. Fair and equitable treatment 158
3.3.3. Full protection and security 163
3.3.4. The defence of necessity 164
3.4. *Interim* conclusion 165
4. The impact of the human right to water on compensation in investor-State arbitration 167
4.1. Cases lacking clear reference to the human right to water 169

page

4.2. Cases acknowledging the human right to water 169
4.3. *Interim* conclusion 171

5. Harmonizing investment protection with the human right to water 171

5.1. Harmonization by means of conflict prevention 172

5.1.1. Human rights impact assessment 172
5.1.2. Revising domestic rules and stabilization clauses 174
5.1.3. Incorporating human rights considerations in IIAs 176
5.1.4. Drafting a business and human rights treaty 180

5.2. Harmonization by means of interpretation of relevant BITs provisions 182
5.3. Establishing systemic relationships of priority 186

6. The attempts to ground corporate human rights obligations 190
7. Conclusion 194

IV. The liberalization of trade in water services under the GATS and the human right to water

1. Introduction 197
2. The applicability of the GATS to water services 201

2.1. An overview of the GATS 202
2.2. The lack of specific commitments in the water sector 208

3. The compatibility between the GATS and the State's regulatory autonomy in the water services sector 214

3.1. The general GATS provisions likely to raise concern from a human right perspective 216

3.1.1. Domestic regulations 216
3.1.2. Subsidies 220
3.1.3. Monopolies and exclusive service suppliers 222

3.2. The GATS provisions on specific commitments 224

3.2.1. Market access 224
3.2.2. National treatment 226

4. Harmonizing trade in services with the human right to water 229

4.1. Harmonization by means of conflict prevention 229

4.1.1. Scheduling commitments for water services 230
4.1.2. The subordination clause in favor of measures necessary to protect human life and health 234

4.2. Harmonization by means of interpretation of GATS provisions applicable to water services 234

4.2.1. The right to regulate in the public interest and the interpretation of the GATS provisions concerning market access and national treatment 237

4.2.1.1. The interpretation of the market access clause 237
4.2.1.2. The interpretation of the national treatment clause 239

page

4.2.2. The right to regulate in the public interest and the interpretation of the GATS provisions related to public services 242
4.2.2.1. The interpretation of the notion of services supplied in the exercise of governmental authority 244
4.2.2.2. The interpretation of the notion of government procurement for the supply of public services 247
4.2.3. *Interim* conclusion 251
4.3. Establishing systemic relationships of priority 252
5. Conclusion 260

Conclusions

1. Outline of the main findings and responses to the research questions 263
2. Appraisal 266

Selected Bibliography 271

Index 275

Acknowledgements 281

LIST OF ABBREVIATIONS

AComHR	African Commission on Human and Peoples' Rights
AB	Appellate Body
BIT	Bilateral investment treaty
CESCR	Committee on Economic, Social and Cultural Rights
CPC	Central Product Classification
CTE	Committee on Trade and Environment
DSU	Dispute Settlement Understanding
ECHR	European Convention of Human Rights
ECtHR	European Court of Human Rights
ECOSOC	United Nations Economic and Social Council
EU	European Union
FAO	Food and Agricultural Organization
FDI	Foreign Direct Investment
FTA	Free trade agreement
GA	General Assembly
GATS	General Agreement on Trade in Services
GATT	General Agreement on Tariffs and Trade
HRC	Human Rights Committee
HRIA	Human Rights Impact Assessment
IACtHR	Inter-American Court of Human Rights
ICCPR	International Covenant on Civil and Political Rights
ICESCR	International Covenant on Economic, Social and Cultural Rights
ICJ	International Court of Justice
ICSID	International Centre for Settlement of Investment Disputes
IIA	International investment agreement
ILC	International Law Commission
M	Million
MAI	Multilateral Agreement on Investment
MDGs	Millennium Development Goals
NAFTA	North American Free Trade Agreement
Ngo	Non-governmental organization
OAS	Organization of American States
Oecd	Organisation for economic co-operation and development
PCIJ	Permanent Court of International Justice
SADC	Southern African Development Community
TEU	Treaty on European Union
TFEU	Treaty on the Functioning of the European Union

TIP	Treaty with investment provisions
UDHR	Universal Declaration of Human Rights
UN	United Nations
UNCITRAL	United Nations Commission on International Trade Law
UNCTAD	United Nations Conference on Trade and Development
UNDP	United Nations Development Programme
UNECE	United Nations Economic Commission for Europe
UNESCO	United Nations Educational Scientific and Cultural Organization
UNICEF	United Nations Children's Fund
VCLT	Vienna Convention on the Law of Treaties
WFD	Water Framework Directive
WHO	World Health Organization
WTO	World Trade Organization
WWAP	World Water Assessment Programme

Chapter I
GENERAL INTRODUCTION

SUMMARY: 1. Setting the scene. – 1.1. Privatization and liberalization of water services in the wake of water commoditization. – 1.2. Emergence of a human rights-based approach to water. – 1.3. Possible conflicting obligations arising from the human right to water and international economic law. – 2. Rationale for the book: a quest for balancing the human rights approach and the trade and investment law approach to water services liberalization. – 3. Area of research: fragmentation of international law. – 4. Research questions. – 5. Model of analysis. – 5.1. Harmonization by means of conflict prevention. – 5.2. Harmonization by means of interpretation. – 5.3. Establishing systemic relationships of priority. – 6. Methodology. – 7. Scope and outline of the book.

1. Setting the scene

Fresh water is a resource that, unlike other natural resources, has no substitute.[1] It is essential for life and has an impact on human dignity, health, education and ultimately on the enjoyment of all fundamental rights.[2]

Fresh water is also a finite resource. Despite being the most widely occurring substance on the world's surface, fresh water amounts to less than 3 per cent of global water, while the remaining about 97 per cent is saline. Moreover, approximately 70 per cent of the available fresh water is locked up in ice caps and glaciers, while another 30 per cent is ground water and far less than 1 per cent is surface water.[3]

Several factors have contributed to further reducing the availability of freshwater

---

[1] The word "water" in the following sections is meant to indicate "fresh water".

[2] The relationship between access to drinking water, sanitation and the enjoyment of economic, social and cultural rights has been studied by the Special Rapporteur on Water and Sanitation Mr. El Hadji Guissé. See Commission on Human Rights, Sub-Commission on the Promotion and Protection of Human Rights, *Relationship between the enjoyment of economic, social and cultural rights and the promotion of the realization of the right to drinking water and sanitation, Preliminary report* by Mr. El Hadji Guissé, UN Doc. E/CN.4/Sub.2/2002/10, 25 June 2002; *Progress Report*, UN Doc. E/CN.4/Sub.2/2003/WP.3, 11 August 2003; *Final report*, UN Doc. E/CN.4/Sub.2/2004/20, 14 July 2004. See, also, United Nations, Economic and Social Council, Committee on Economic, Social and Cultural Rights, *General Comment No. 15 (2002), The right to water (arts. 11 and 12 of the International Covenant on Economic, Social and Cultural Rights)*, UN Doc. E/C.12/2002/11, 20 January 2003, (hereinafter "General Comment No. 15") para. 6, highlighting that water is required in order to realize many of the Covenant rights, such as the right to food, the right to health, and the right to take part in cultural life.

[3] UNESCO, World Water Assessment Programme (WWAP), *Water for people, water for life: the United Nations world water development report*, New York, 2003, pp. 67-68; A. Rieu-Clarke, R. Moynihan and B-O. Magsig, *UN Watercourses Convention. User's Guide*, Dundee, 2012, p. 73.

resources: *inter alia*, pollution, climate change,[4] and the increasing consumption associated with the growing world population.[5] Over the last century, global population has tripled, and fresh water consumption has increased sixfold.[6]

For the time being, there is no worldwide shortage of fresh water in absolute terms, at least not as far as is required to meet basic human needs.[7] However, there is a problem of *access* to safe drinking water that depends on various causes, notably, the uneven distribution of freshwater and groundwater resources across countries, the allocation of the available fresh water in favor of agricultural and industrial uses rather than for personal and domestic consumption and the prohibitive cost of water infrastructure and services.

Different sectors are in competition for limited water resources. Agriculture is by far the most water consuming, absorbing 69 per cent of annual global water withdrawals, while industry uses at least 19 per cent of the global water and households use account for about 12 per cent.[8]

Freshwater and groundwater resources are also unevenly distributed across countries.[9] For instance, nearly 50 per cent of persons without access to an improved drinking water source lives in Sub-Saharan Africa and one fifth live in Southern Asia.[10] Moreover, differences occur even within countries and between urban and rural areas,[11] where the majority of people without access to an improved drinking water source live.[12]

---

[4] N. Singh, *Climate Change and Human Right to Water: Problems and Prospects*, in N. Singh (ed.), *The Human Right to Water. From Concept to Reality*, Cham, 2016; J.H. Knox, *Climate Change and Human Rights Law*, in *Virginia Journal of International Law*, 2009, p. 163; H. F. M. W. van Rijswick, A. M. Keessen, *Adaptation to Climate Change in European Water Law and Policy*, in *Utrecht Law Review*, 2012, available at: *http://www.utrechtlawreview.org*.

[5] UNESCO, WWAP, *Water for people, water for life*, pp. 10-17 (n 3).

[6] World Bank, *Water Resources Sector Strategy – Strategic Directions for World Bank Engagement,* Washington DC, 2004, p. 5.

[7] According to the Human Development Report: "*the scarcity at the heart of the global water crisis is rooted in power, poverty and inequality, not in physical availability*". United Nations Development Programme (UNDP), *Human Development Report 2006: Beyond Scarcity: Power, Poverty and The Global Water Crisis*, New York, 2006, p. 2.

[8] UNESCO, WWAP, *The United Nations World Water Development Report 2019. Leaving No One Behind. Facts and Figures*, Paris, 2019, p. 2. See, Human Rights Council, *Report of the Special Rapporteur on the human right to safe drinking water and sanitation, Catarina de Albuquerque,* Addendum, *Mission to the United States of America*, UN Doc. A/HRC/18/33/Add.4, 2 August 2011, para. 70.

[9] K. Bourquain, *Freshwater Access from a Human Rights Perspective. A Challenge to International Water and Human Rights Law*, Boston, 2008, p. 3.

[10] UNICEF, WHO, *Progress on Sanitation and Drinking Water*, 2015 Update and MDG Assessment, 2015, See data available at: https://www.who.int/water_sanitation_health/publications/jmp_2015_update_compressed.pdf.

[11] C. de Albuquerque, *Water and sanitation are human rights: why does it matter?*, in L. Boisson de Chazournes, C. Leb, M. Tignino (eds.), *International Law and Freshwater. The Multiple Challenges*, Cheltenham, 2013, p. 48.

[12] UNICEF, WHO, *Progress on Sanitation and Drinking Water*, 2015 Update and MDG Assessment (n 10), p. 4.

The lack of access to fresh water has a different impact on different social groups, with the poorest being hit the hardest.[13] Where settlements either lack water supply or have poor quality water infrastructure, as often occurs in urban slums, people are obliged to resort to private small-scale vendors and hence, to pay higher prices for water.[14]

Human health is strongly affected by the lack of access to safe fresh water. An estimated 1.6 million people die each year from water and sanitation-related diseases, above all from diarrhea caused by unsafe water and poor sanitation.[15] In 2011 alone, diarrhea caused 2 million deaths and 4 billion episodes of illness.[16] This is despite the fact that, according to a WHO-UNICEF report, the best health outcomes are reported where drinking water is supplied on site.[17]

In developing countries, women and children are those most affected by water scarcity. Women usually bear the responsibility of collecting and carrying water for their family. As a consequence, they may spend several hours a day walking to the nearest source of water, which prevents them from employing their time in a more profitable manner. Furthermore, on their way there, they are put at risk of assault and harassment. At the same time, children under the age of 5 are the most vulnerable to water-related disease.[18] Lack of sufficient clean water also impacts their

---

[13] L. Mehta, *Problems of Publicness and Access Rights: Perspectives from the Water Domain*, in I. Kaul, P. Conceição, K. Le Goulven, R. U. Mendoza (eds.), *Providing Global Public Goods: Managing Globalization*, Oxford, 2003, p. 560.

[14] Bourquain, p. 5 (n 9). On the link between poverty, sanitation and water, see Human Rights Council, *Joint Report of the independent expert on the question of human rights and extreme poverty, Magdalena Sepúlveda Cardona, and the independent expert on the issue of human rights obligations related to access to safe drinking water and sanitation, Catarina de Albuquerque,* Addendum. *Mission to Bangladesh* (3-10 December 2009), UN Doc. A/HCR/15/55, 22 July 2010. For instance, it has been estimated that, in Bangladesh, people who live in slums "*have no legal access to water, which means that they pay 10 to 20 times more for it*" (para. 70).

[15] Human Rights Council, *Promotion and protection of all human rights, civil, political, economic, social and cultural rights, including the right to development. Report of the independent expert on the issue of human rights obligations related to access to safe drinking water and sanitation,* Catarina de Albuquerque, UN Doc. A/HRC/12/24, 1 July 2009, pp. 4, 9.

[16] WHO, UN Water, GLAAS Report 2012, *UN-Water Global Analysis and Assessment of Sanitation and Drinking-Water. The Challenge of Extending and Sustaining Services*, p. 7. Available at: http://www.who.int/water_sanitation_health/publications/glaas_report_2012/en/index.html.

[17] UNICEF, WHO, *Progress on Sanitation and Drinking water*, *Update*, Geneva and New York, 2013, p. 9.

[18] According to estimates, approximately 1.5 million children die every year from water-related disease. See Human Rights Council, *Report of the independent expert on the issue of human rights obligations related to access to safe drinking water and sanitation*, *Catarina de Albuquerque*, UN Doc. A/HRC/15/31, 29 June 2010, p. 4; See also WHO, UNICEF report, *Diarrhoea: Why children are still dying and what can be done,* 2009, p. 1, available at: http://whqlibdoc.who.int/publications/2009/9789241598415_eng.pdf. It illustrates that globally diarrhoea, mostly caused by lack of adequate water and sanitation, is the second cause of death among children under five, killing more than AIDS, malaria and measles combined.

right to education. In fact, each year 443 million school days are lost as a result of sickness caused by poor water and sanitation. [19]

Ultimately, the shortage of freshwater also threatens regional peace and security. Tignino argues that "*water has the potential for triggering conflict*" including "*armed hostilities between states*". [20] Hence, the uneven distribution of freshwater resources among countries and across regions cannot be regarded as a matter of domestic concern alone.

Finally, many expert predictions for 2025 are alarming. FAO estimates that "*1.8 billion people will be living in countries or regions with absolute water scarcity, and two-thirds of the world population could be under conditions of water stress*". [21]

1.1. Privatization and liberalization of water services in the wake of water commoditization

Traditionally, water has been considered a public good, [22] but its "*public*" significance has increasingly been challenged. The growing scarcity of water has probably strengthened the case for considering water to be a product, thus fuelling the so-

---

[19] Human Rights Council, *Report of the independent expert on the issue of human rights obligations related to access to safe drinking water and sanitation, Catarina de Albuquerque*, p. 11 (n 18).

[20] M. Tignino, *Water, International Peace, and Security*, in *International Review of the Red Cross*, 2010, pp. 647-648. The author maintains that while disputed waters are not the only source of wars, the scarcity and inequitable allocation of water are among the causes of some armed conflicts, above all in the Middle East. *Ibid.*, p. 651. See, also: M. Tignino, *L'eau et la guerre: éléments pour un régime juridique*, Bruxelles, 2011; I. J. Silverbrand, *The History and Potential Future of the Israeli-Palestinian Water Conflict*, in *Stanford Journal of International Law*, 2008, pp. 221-251.

[21] FAO, *Coping with water scarcity. Challenge of the twenty – first century*, 2007, p. 10, available at: http://www.fao.org/3/a-aq444e.pdf. Similarly, World Bank, *Water Resources Sector Strategy*, p. 5 (n 6): "*[t]he World Commission on Water estimates that water use will increase by about 50 percent in the next 30 years and that an estimated 4 billion people – one half of the world's population – will live under conditions of severe water stress (…) with conditions particularly severe in Africa, the Middle East and South Asia*". See also E. Brown Weiss, *International Law for a Water-Scarce World*, Leiden-Boston, 2013, p. 1; S. C. McCaffrey, *Water, Water Everywhere, But Too Few Drops to Drink: The Coming Fresh Water Crisis and the International Environmental Law*, in *Denver Journal of International Law and Policy*, 2000.

[22] Some scholars even suggest considering water as a global public good, a notion describing a "*non-rivalrous*" good – because its consumption by one person does not prevent others from enjoying the same good or reduce its availability – and one that is "*non-excludable*", as no one can be excluded from its use. Samuelson first theorized the economic notion of global public good. A typical example is the global cultural heritage. In my view, this notion is not entirely applicable to water because people compete for access to water resources and when one gains control over land and waters, others may be excluded from their enjoyment. See R. C. Griffin, D. E. Peck, J. Maestu, *Introduction*, in J. Maestu (ed.), *Water Trading and Global Water Scarcity. International experiences*, Abingdon, 2013, pp. 6-7; Mehta, p.559 (n 13). The author refers to water as an impure public good, p. 561.

called "*commoditization*" of water, understood as the conferment of an economic value to water in order to make it tradable.[23]

Concern about such a process of commoditization has been expressed in several *fora* and by many scholars. Boisson de Chazournes refers to this trend as the "*economization of water*",[24] pointing out that: "*[l]e statut de cette ressource unique soulève naturellement des interrogations, notamment dans la perspective du droit international économique. S'agit-il d'un bien? Doit-on en faire état en termes de service?*".[25]

At present, there are different views on the question of whether water is a public good or a commodity like any other.[26] Advocates of the "*publicness*" of water emphasize the essential and unique role of water for our survival, as well as its religious and symbolic value.[27] Water and ground water are seen as universal resources, common to all human beings, for which no one should have to pay. Opponents of this thesis acknowledge that water is a scarce good and a human need like any other, yet hold that the best way of preserving water is to price it.[28] In this respect, mention is often made of Principle No. 4 of the Dublin Statement on Water and Sustainable Development, which states that "*[w]ater has an economic value in all its competing uses and should be recognized as an economic good*".[29]

---

[23] E. B. Bluemel, *The Implications of Formulating a Human Right to Water*, in *Ecology Law Quarterly*, 2004, pp. 963-967; M. Kothari, *Obstacles to Making Water a Human Right*, in E. H. Riedel, P. Rothen (eds.), *The Human Right to Water*, Berlin, 2006, pp. 149-159.

[24] L. Boisson de Chazournes, *Fresh Water in International Law*, Oxford, 2013, p. 54. The author argues that "*[f]resh water as a natural resource is increasingly seen as a source of profit. This feature is demonstrated in the context of international trade law and of investment law, and may also be perceived in domestic and inter-State negotiations concerning proposed international bulk transfer of water*".

[25] L. Boisson de Chazournes, *Eaux internationals et droit international: vers l'idée de gestion commune*, in L. Boisson de Chazournes, S. M. A Salman (eds.), *Les ressources en Eau et le Droit International, Water Resources and International Law*, Leiden, 2005.

[26] Thompson suggests an alternative vision of water as a *public commodity* which recognizes both "*the 'publicness' of water – its critical roles in advancing life, culture, religion, and supporting ecosystems*" and "*the importance of treating water as a commodity, thus fulfilling the public values of water and maximizing domestic wealth and income*". B. H. Thompson Jr., *Water as a Public Commodity*, in *Marquette Law Review*, 2011, pp. 18, 46.

[27] H. H. G. Savenije, *Why Water Is Not an Ordinary Economic Good, or Why the Girl is Special*, in *Physic and Chemistry of the Earth*, 2002, pp. 741-744; Bluemel, pp. 963-967 (n 23).

[28] It is said that by giving water a high economic value, people will minimize waste and make a more efficient and sustainable use of water, while unpriced and subsidized water, above all for agricultural use, has led to overexploitation of water and groundwater resources, which is at the root of the water-stress situation experienced in several countries. B. Pardy, *The Dark Irony of International Water Rights*, in *Pace Environmental Law Review*, 2011, available at: http://digitalcommons.pace.edu/pelr/vol28/iss3/6.

[29] Dublin Statement on Water and Sustainable Development, adopted on 31 January 1992 at the International Conference on Water and the Environment, 26-31 January 1992, Dublin. Similarly, Agenda 21, Chapter 18, adopted at the United Nations Conference on Environment and

As a matter of fact, water has been subjected to private appropriation and trade, both at a domestic and at an international level. First, the "*publicness*" of water has been challenged by conferring water property rights for ground and surface water.[30] Indeed, although surface water is usually public, some countries have granted ownership of water resources by conferring water rights,[31] which are a set of entitlement rights specifying the right to access, as well as obligations and limits related to the use of these assets.[32] Further, water rights have also been traded in water markets.

In addition to the allocation of transferable water rights, water has also been physically traded as bottled products or as bulk water. Transnational trade in bulk water[33] has been suggested as a way to solve at least the more urgent needs of some countries that, by importing water, can compensate for their lack of water.[34] However, transnational transfer of bulk water has raised concern about its potential environmental and human impact. Indeed, trade in large amounts of water may risk depleting domestic resources or altering the availability of water for local people.[35]

Development, Rio De Janeiro, June 2002, refers to water as a social and economic good. See paras. 18.8; 18.15/16/17; 18.68; 18.76(*f*)(*ii*).

[30] According to some scholars, the traditional concept of property does not properly describe a situation of domain over water. They prefer referring to "*ownership*" of water, understood as the "*control over and the right to use*" water. See A. Hildering, *Water as an Economic Good*, in L. Boisson de Chazournes, S. M. A. Salman (eds.), *Les ressources en Eau et le Droit International, Water Resources and International Law*, Leiden, 2005, p. 209. The granting of water rights is highly controversial. Advocates of the privatization of water resources argue that in regions where water is scarce "*the introduction of enforceable and transferable water rights, for at least a portion of a jurisdiction's water resources, may make a social contribution*" as it may lead to the allocation of water resources for the highest-value uses. Griffin and others, p. 4 (n 22). The World Bank points out that "*[t]he essence of this change is that water rights (of individuals and communities, including traditional users) enjoy the same legal certainty as land and other property rights*". World Bank, *Water Resources Sector Strategy*, pp. 7, 16 and 24 (n 6). Opponents to private water entitlements and markets contend that the conferment of water rights fails to balance reasons of efficiency with those of equity. Concern is expressed for those people who will not be able to pay for the access to water. See Mehta, p. 569 (n 13).

[31] Since the late 1980s, some countries – such as the United States, Brazil, Chile, Mexico, Australia and South Africa (in the 1990s) – have started to subject water to private ownership. World Bank, *Water Resources Sector Strategy*, p. 24 (n 6).

[32] Griffin, p. 4 (n 22); W. Dellapenna, *The Myth of Markets for Water*, in J. Maestu (ed.), *Water Trading and Global Water Scarcity. International Experiences*, Abingdon, 2013, p. 209.

[33] Brown Weiss defines bulk transfer of water as "*removal [of water] by human-made diversions, including canals, tanker ships, trucks, or pipeline*". See E. Brown Weiss, *Water Transfer and International Trade Law*, in E. Brown Weiss, L. Boisson de Chazournes, N. Bernasconi-Osterwalder (eds.), *Fresh Water and International Economic Law*, Oxford, 2005, p. 63 and pp. 66-67.

[34] F. Costamagna, F. Sindico, *The Linkages between Access to Water and Water Scarcity with International Investment Law and the WTO Regime*, in P. Cullet, A. Gowlland-Gualtieri, R. Madhav, U. Ramanathan (eds.), *Water Governance in Motion, towards Socially and Environmentally Sustainable Water Laws*, Cambridge, 2010, pp. 270-271.

[35] Hildering, p. 228 (n 30). In the long run, the exporter country may face a water shortage, and

Commoditization of water is a rather complex phenomenon. Ultimately, it can take place even in a "*virtual*" way. Instead of transporting water by tankers or pipelines, water can be traded after being incorporated into other products.[36] Recently, in fact, attention has been focused on the transfer of so-called "*virtual water*", that is, the water needed to produce certain items – such as agricultural products – and embedded therein.[37] As agriculture is by far the most water-consuming sector, water-stressed countries may prefer importing agricultural products in lieu of producing them locally. However, this makes them dependent on foreign imports. Interestingly, after the food crisis that took place in 2008, countries poor in water resources, along with private investors, started acquiring land abroad where they could grow water-consuming agricultural products for import in order to feed their populations. Woodhouse notes that "*water scarcity is a major driver of international flows of investment in agricultural land*".[38] The problem is that the majority of these land deals have been concluded in Africa, where locals have no enforceable water rights to oppose to foreign investors. Thus, such a trend has exacerbated conflicts over water resources.[39]

Finally, the commoditization process not only concerns water *per se*, but also water services. In the words of Tanzi, the "*compatibility of the 'public good' connotation and the economic relevance of water*" raises the issue of the admissibility of the privatization of water services.[40]

---

hence decide to ban water exports in the public interest. In such a scenario, the question would arise of whether the General Agreement on Tariff and Trade (GATT), which forbids trade restrictions, might prevent such a decision. In fact, if bulk water were considered a tradable good, once it entered into commerce, the GATT rules would become applicable. Therefore, unless the conditions listed under exceptions are met – such as those of art. XX (*b*)(*g*) – the State would be prohibited from banning water exports. In any case, the *status* of bulk water under international economic law is not yet clear and the applicable legal regime is still unsettled. Brown Weiss, p. 63 and pp. 66-67 (n 33).

[36] M. C. Rulli, A. Saviori, P. D'Odorico, *Global Land and Water Grabbing*, in PNAS, 2013, available at: http://www.pnas.org/content/early/2013/01/02/1213163110.full.pdf; M. Antonelli, M. Sartori, *Unfolding the Potential of Virtual Water Concept. What is still under debate?*, MPRA Paper No. 60501, 2014.

[37] M. Antonelli, F. Greco, *L'acqua che mangiamo. Cos'è l'acqua virtuale e come la consumiamo*, Milan, 2013.

[38] P. Woodhouse, *Foreign Agricultural Land Acquisition and the Visibility of Water Resource Impacts in Sub-Saharan Africa*, in *Water Alternatives*, 2012, p. 209; M. K. Scanlan, J. Kehl, *Food and Virtual Water in the Great Lakes States*, Vermont Law School Research Paper No. 15-14, 2014, available at SSRN: https://ssrn.com/abstract=2487418.

[39] L. Cotula, J. Skinner, *Are land deals driving "water grabs"?*, IIED Briefing, 2011, available at http://pubs.iied.org/pdfs/17102IIED.pdf; L. Cotula, *Human Rights, Natural Resource and Investment law in a Globalised World. Shades of Grey in the Shadow of the Law*, Abingdon, 2012; M. Bordignon, R. Greco, G. Lepore, *Water grabbing and water rights: indigenous 'sovereignty' versus State sovereignty?*, in F. Romanin Jacur, A. Bonfanti, F. Seatzu (eds.), *Natural Resources Grabbing: An International Law Perspective*, Leiden-Boston, 2016, pp. 93-115.

[40] A. Tanzi, *Reducing the Gap between International Water Law and Human Rights Law: The UNECE Protocol on Water and Health*, in *International Community Law Review*, 2010, p. 280.

Privatization of water services is a fairly recent phenomenon. Since the late nineteenth century, water services have been managed and supplied by public authorities, who have borne the financial burden of building water infrastructures. Indeed, having sound water services requires significant investment in infrastructure for the collection, treatment, delivery of water, as well as for the connection to water mains. Moreover, high expenditure capacity is also necessary to face the costs of modernization and maintenance of water infrastructure.

These costs have not always been within the means of the public sector alone. Thus, in the last few decades, many countries have started resorting to private operators.[41] The process of privatization of water services began in developed countries in the 1980s and was followed in 1990s by many developing countries,[42] pushed in that direction by international financial institutions, such as the World Bank that, considering public water utilities as excessively costly and inefficient, made lending conditional upon the privatization and liberalization of these utilities.[43]

In developing nations, budgetary constraints, exacerbated by the scarcity of water and increasing urbanization, has generated demand for major investments in new infrastructure, greater water-use efficiency, and more rigorous management of water systems.[44] To match the cost of the service with States' limited expenditure capacity, and to face the complexity of the water sector, public authorities have accepted private contributions both in terms of financial inflow and expertise.[45] It has

---

[41] OECD, *Meeting the Challenge of Financing Water and Sanitation, Tool and Approaches*, Paris, 2011, p. 15: "*[d]espite a high initial asset base, developed countries confront huge costs of modernising and upgrading their systems. The global capital costs of maintaining and developing WSS infrastructure in OECD countries plus the BRICs has been estimated at between 0.35% to 1.2% of their GDP. This corresponds to total projected annual needs of around USD 780 billion by 2015 and USD 1 037 billion by 2025, up from a current estimated expenditure on water infrastructure of USD 576 billion annually. In transition economies, the need for maintaining and upgrading existing infrastructure is combined with sometimes significant needs to expand coverage and address the challenges of poor governance, institutional inefficiency and the deterioration of the asset base*".

[42] Human Rights Council, *Report of the independent expert on the issue of human rights obligations related to access to safe drinking water and sanitation, Catarina de Albuquerque*, p. 4 (n 18).

[43] M. Bronwen, *Water on Tap: Rights and Regulation in the Transnational Governance of Urban Water Services*, Cambridge, 2011, p. 9; A. Olleta, *The World Bank's Influence on Water Privatisation in Argentina: The Experience of the City of Buenos Aires*, in P. Cullet, A. Gowlland-Gualtieri, R. Madhav, U. Ramanathan (eds.), *Water Governance in Motion: Towards Socially and Environmentally Sustainable Water Laws*, New Delhi, 2010; B. Choudhury, *Public Services and International Trade Liberalization: Human Rights and Gender Implication*, Cambridge, 2012, pp.162-164. See Angola, Argentina, Benin, Bolivia, Guinea-Bissau, Ghana, Honduras, Indonesia, Nicaragua, Niger, Panama, Philippines, Rwanda, São Tomé and Príncipe, Senegal, and Yemen.

[44] Thompson Jr., p. 23 (n 26).

[45] E. Reeves, *Water Provision and Design, Build and Operate Schemes: Statement by Dr. Eoin Reeves to the Joint Committee on Environment, Transport, Culture and the Gaeltacht*, 10 January 2012, p. 5: "*[t]he wave of privatization witnessed in the 1990s was significant (...). Most of the privatization witnessed in the 1990s occurred in low and middle-income countries and was at-*

been calculated that, from 1990 to 2002, "*the number of people served by private water suppliers increased sixfold, from approximately 50 million people to over 300 million*".[46]

Although these figures seem large, in reality only about 5 per cent of private investments in infrastructure went into water and sanitation infrastructure.[47] In particular, least developing countries attracted little attention, while investments were concentrated in perceived low-risk economies, such as in Latin America.[48]

The wave of private sector investments in water services reached its peak in 1997,[49] following which it began to decline.[50] Overall, the reversal of privatization in favor of public management was due to early termination of water service concessions.[51] Several factors determined the foreign firms' withdrawal from the water sector including, *inter alia*, the low bids offered compared with the cost of contract obligations and the low rate of returns on private infrastructure investment, above all in developing countries, and the lack of capacity to adapt to changing circumstances (as in Argentina after the 2001 economic crisis). The economic crisis in Argentina has demonstrated the high risk connected to investing in unstable emerging markets. Since then, investments have moved from Latin America to Asia, essentially to China,[52] Eastern Europe and Russia.[53]

---

tributable to the promotion of privatization by the World Bank and donor agencies". Source: http://www.oireachtas.ie/parliament/.

[46] Commission on Human Rights, *Human rights, trade and investment, Report of the High Commissioner for Human Rights*, UN Doc. E/CN.4/Sub.2/2003/9, 2 July 2003, para. 46.

[47] World Bank, *Water Resources Sector Strategy*, p. 44 (n 6).

[48] *Ibid.*

[49] During the period of 1991–97, 90 per cent of total investment was made by five multinational companies: Suez, SAUR, Veolia, Thames Water, and Agbar. P. Marin, *Public-Private Partnerships for Urban Water Utilities: A review of Experiences in Developing Countries – Trends and Policy Options: No. 8*, World Bank & PPIAF, 2009, p. 23.

[50] See, Bronwen, p. 8 (n 43). Examples of reverse privatization include: "*Cochabamba (Bolivia) in 2002, El Alto (Bolivia) in 2003, Manila (Philippines) in 2006, Buenos Aires and Santa Fe (Argentina) in the early 2000s. In Africa, contracts were terminated in Gambia, Mali, Chad, Tanzania and South Africa. Examples from developed countries include the cities of Atlanta (USA) and Halifax (Canada). More recent examples of reversals/terminations include the cities of Paris and Pecs (Hungary) in 2010 as well as Tblisi (Georgia), Almaty (Kazakhstan), Odessa and Kirovograd (Ukraine), and Bukhara and Samarkand (Uzbekistan)*". Reeves, p. 12 (n 45). According to the Independent Expert on the human right to water,"*[s]ome transnational corporations have started to withdraw from developing countries, they are increasingly developing local partnerships, and, in a number of countries, local private actors are also very active*". Human Rights Council, *Report of the independent expert on the issue of human rights obligations related to access to safe drinking water and sanitation, Catarina de Albuquerque* (n 18).

[51] Only 7 per cent of the reversal to public management was due to contract expiration without renewal. Marin, pp. 27-28 (n 49).

[52] Traditionally the Chinese Government had a monopoly in urban water management, but since the 1990s it has opened the water market to private companies (i.e. China Water Industry

Currently, about 90 per cent of water services worldwide are provided by the public sector, and investments still come primarily from public sources, mainly through tax revenue.[54] The amount of people served by private water operators has fallen short of expectations,[55] yet is still increasing due, in part, to the expansion of the customer base of existing contracts.[56]

The process of liberalization and privatization of water services has sparked an intense – often highly ideological[57] – debate. Advocates suggest that private in-

---

Group and Guangdong Investment) including foreign firms (Veolia Environnement and Suez). According to the Chinese specialists, L. Zhong, A. P. J. Mol, T. Fu "*[i]t is premature to conclude whether the various forms of private sector involvement will successfully overcome the major problems (capital shortage, inefficient operation, and service quality) in China's water sector. But at the same time, private sector involvement in water provisioning and waste water treatments seems to have become mainstream in transitional China*", see L. Zhong, A. P. J. Mol, T. Fu, *Public-Private Partnerships in China's Urban Water Sector*, 2008, available at: https://www.ncbi.nlm.nih.gov/pmc/articles/PMC2359833/; The Economist, *Report on water, For want of a drink*, 22 May 2010, available at: www.economist.com/node/16136302; S. Taylor, A. Leung, *China attracts private companies to provide clean water*, in *The New York Times*, 27 March 2008, available at: https://www.nytimes.com/2008/03/27/business/worldbusiness/27iht-water.1.11466317.html.

[53] Marin, pp. 24-25 (n 49); Bronwen, p. 8 (n 43).

[54] OECD, *Meeting the Challenge of Financing Water and Sanitation,* p. 30 (n 41). The public sector is understood as including "*state-owned enterprises, local Governments, municipal companies*". The private water sector remains dominated by several European transnational corporations, such as Veolia, Suez, and RWE. Council for Trade in Services, *Background Note on Environmental Services, Note by the Secretariat*, S/C/W/320, 20 August 2010, p. 8. The document refers also to Agabar, but in May 2010 Suez Environment became the major stakeholder of the Spanish company; D. Hall, E. Lobina, *Water Companies in Europe, Public Services International Research Unit*, University of Greenwich, *mimeo,* 2011. Commission on Human Rights, *Human rights, trade and investment, Report of the High Commissioner for Human Rights*, para. 46 (n 46): "*international private sector investment in the water and sanitation sector has lagged behind other international private sector investments in sectors such as telecommunications, power, gas and hydro (...) [it] makes up some 10-15 per cent of investment in the sector*".

[55] In the early 2000s, data projected a fairly optimistic scenario for private companies. J. Razzaque, *Trading Water: The Human Factor*, in *Review of European Community and International Environmental Law*, 2004, p. 25:"*[t]he proportion of the water sanitation services that are projected to be privatized by 2010 are as follows: Western Europe 20% in 1997 and will increase to 35% in 2010; in Latin America 4% in 1997 and will increase to 60% in 2010; Africa 3% in 1997 and will increase to 33% in 2010; Asia 1% in 1997 and will increase to 20% in 2010*". Likewise, see Commission on Human Rights, *Human Rights, Trade and Investment, Report of the High Commissioner for Human Rights*, para. 46 (n 46), referring for estimates to the World Water Council, *Report of the World Water Panel on Financing Water Infrastructure, Financing Water for All*, 2003, p. 17.

[56] Marin, p. 24 (n 49).

[57] Human Rights Council, *Report of the independent expert on the issue of human rights obligations related to access to safe drinking water and sanitation, Catarina de Albuquerque*, para. 8 (n 18): "*as of 2003, only 5 per cent of world's population was being served by the formal private sector*", thus the dispute about privatization of water services is chiefly ideological. Such figures have been taken from the Asian Development Bank website. H. Gunatilake, M. J. F. Carangal-San Jose, *Privatization revisited: lessons from private sector participation in water supply and sanitation in developing countries*, Economics and Research Department (ERD) Working Paper No. 115, Asian

volvement would improve access to safe drinking water by attracting investments.[58] It is also claimed that foreign private providers possess greater expertise as well as better equipment and technical skills than public suppliers. Thanks to new technologies and skills, private providers may reduce leakages, improve billing and collection and provide more environmentally-friendly services. It is also suggested that performance is improved by the fact that regulatory agencies are more willing to exercise control over private companies than over other Governmental or public bodies. A final view argues that the term privatization has too often been misunderstood due to misleading representations. Privatization refers only to the transfer of control over water utilities, while it does not infringe upon the water resources, whose ownership continues to be vested in public authorities.[59]

Opponents strongly fear the negative impact of privatization policies on the poorest and most vulnerable. The most common concern regards the risk of tariff increases as private providers are granted the right to profit from operating water facilities. According to critics of privatization, the costs for improving, maintaining and running water services risks being shifted to the ultimate users. Private firms and investors are driven by market objectives, so water companies will inevitably seek to maximize their profit by increasing prices. Higher tariffs can reduce water affordability for the less affluent, who might be cut off from the service as a result. Indeed, in some countries the price of water has become so high to consume a significant percentage of poor household income.[60]

Another source of concern is the risk that private companies might not adequately protect water quality or invest sufficiently in the extension and maintenance of water systems in poor or rural areas, where the low rate of return does not cover the cost of the service and makes the investment less profitable than that in wealthy urbanized areas.

Other views stress the special nature of water services, which would prevent opening the market to competition. Indeed, given the extremely high prices of building and maintaining water infrastructure, attempts to introduce competition "*in the market*" have been marginal. For the time being, the only form of competi-

---

Development Bank, 2008, pp. 15-16, available at: https://www.adb.org/publications/privatization-revisited-lessons-private-sector-participation-water-supply-and-sanitatio.

[58] R. B. Al-Hmoud, J. Edwards, *Water Poverty and Private Investment in the Water and Sanitation Sector*, in *Water International*, 2009; T. Slaymaker, P. Newborne, S. Grimm, D. W. te Velde, *Water and GATS: Lots of Smoke but where exactly is the fire?*, in *ODI blog*, 2005, available at:https://www.odi.org/blogs/505-water-and-gats-lots-smoke-where-exactly-fire.

[59] Only England, Wales and Chile have completely divested from water infrastructure, while most countries have opted for softer private involvement in the water sector.

[60] According to the World Bank, the average cost of a water service connection fee is 33% of the average monthly household income in Cambodia; 27% in Bangladesh and 116% in Benin. Source: http://www.worldbank.org/content/dam/Worldbank/Feature%20Story/SDN/Water/Water-TTM-Infographic-WATER-English-FINAL-900px.jpg.

tion in the water sector is over the right to manage the distribution network and to provide the service. In other words, there may be competition "*for*" the market, but not "*in*" the market.[61] As a "*natural monopoly*" – one that is not established by law, but which comes into being in consequence of the high cost of infrastructure that makes its duplication uneconomic – the replacement of a public monopoly with a private one risks leaving the most vulnerable with little alternative in case of market abuse.[62] Prevented from switching to other providers, customers would be obliged to pay the increased price in order to avoid disconnection from the service.[63] Some authors have noted that, since the water industry is a natural monopoly, if a State-owned monopoly turns into private one, structural risks can arise from foreign direct investment in this sector "*with developing countries failing to provide adequate regulatory frameworks or to negotiate appropriate deals with the private sector*".[64]

Another view relies on the history of failed liberalizations, which turned out to be detrimental for the countries that had liberalized the water sector.[65] Concern has been expressed for the unbalanced bargaining power between exporting and importing countries in investment agreements, as well as between powerful corporations and poor States in contracting out the water service. Indeed, in order to attract foreign investment, developing countries have often been too willing to accept constraints on their ability to achieve policy objectives.

Ultimately, the core argument is that water is too important to be left to private economic actors.[66]

1.2. Emergence of a human rights-based approach to water

To balance the "*economization of water*", a human rights-based approach has emerged. This approach does not simply consider water "*a commercial product like*

---

[61] For the sake of completeness it should be underlined that the possibility of introducing competition through privatization, at least in certain segments of the water services chain, exists upon condition of unbundling this network-bound sector.

[62] F. Marrella, *On the Changing Structure of International Investment Law: The Human Right to Water and ICSID Arbitration*, in *International Community Law Review*, 2010, p. 343.

[63] Indeed, water services are often established as a monopoly, despite a recent trend for increasing market competition. In other words, there seems to be a possibility for unbundling this network bound sector. See, in this regard, A. Maziotis, *Breaking Up Water Monopolies: Costs and Benefits*, in *Review of Environment, Energy and Economics*, 6 June 2013, available at: http://papers.ssrn.com.

[64] UNCTAD, *International Investment Agreements in Services*, Geneva, 2005, pp. 3-4

[65] Olleta (n 43).

[66] Savenije, pp. 741-744 (n 27); M. Hallward-Driemeier, *Do Bilater Investment Treaties Attract Foreign Direct Investment? Only a Bit... and They Could Bite*, World Bank Policy Research Working Paper No. 3121, 2003; J. Naegele, *What is Wrong with Full-Fledged Water Privatization?*, in *Journal of Law & Social Challenges*, 2004.

any other", but rather "*a heritage which must be protected, defended, and treated as such*",[67] being essential for the very existence of life, health and human dignity.[68]

The human right to safe drinking water has been recognised and proclaimed by, *inter alia*, the Committee of Economic, Social and Cultural Rights,[69] the General Assembly[70] and the Human Rights Council,[71] in order to stress the special *status* of water, its social and cultural dimension, as well as the role of the State as the main duty bearer for the realization of this right.[72]

Unlike other branches of international law concerned with water, such as international environmental law and international water law, by approaching water issues through the lens of human rights, it is possible to highlight several shortfalls left by the "*economization of water*", *in primis*, the failure to consider social issues connected to water affordability. By increasing water and water service prices, the poorest, above all in developing countries, risk being left without sufficient water. Such a situation occurred, for instance, in early 2000 in Cochabamba, a city in Bolivia where water service prices increased by over 30 per cent in the immediate aftermath of the privatization of the sector, giving rise to public protest.[73]

Moreover, the often-claimed capability of the market to pursue environmental goals, such as the sustainable allocation of water resources, by increasing prices and discouraging waste, has not always proven true. On the contrary, some multinational companies, having acquired the right to exploit water resources in less-developed countries, have caused water pollution and shortages to the detriment of users.[74] Indeed, these companies' expenditure capacity is so high in those countries that they do not suffer from the mounting costs or fines. The appropriation of water resources by foreign private investors is a source of growing concern, at times referred to as "*water grabbing*".[75]

---

[67] See the preamble of the *Directive 2000/60/EC of the European Parliament and of the Council establishing a framework for Community action in the field of water policy*, 23 October 2000, Official Journal of the European Communities L 327, 22 December 2000, p. 1, recital 1.

[68] Savenije, pp. 741-744 (n 27).

[69] General Comment No. 15 (n 2).

[70] General Assembly, res. 64/292, 28 July 2010, UN Doc. A/RES/64/292, 3 August 2010.

[71] Human Right Council, Res. 15/9, 30 September 2010, UN Doc. A/RES/15/9, 6 October 2010.

[72] Human Rights Council, *Report of the independent expert on the issue of human rights obligations related to access to safe drinking water and sanitation, Catarina de Albuquerque*, para. 18 (n 18). The legal sources, status and content of this right will be discussed in detail in chapter two.

[73] *Aguas del Tunari S.A. v. Bolivia*, ICSID Case No. ARB/02/03, 21 October 2005.

[74] A famous case is that of the villagers from Plachimada (Kerala, India), who first protested and then filed a claim with the High Court of Kerala against Coca-Cola for having dissipated and polluted their waters. See *Perumatty Grama Panchayat v. State of Kerala*, High Court of Kerala, India, W.P. (C), 16 December 2003.

[75] The phenomenon of "*water grabbing*" may be defined as "*the take of control by 'powerful actors'– such as States and multinational corporations – of waters in detriment of local communities*

International water law, while considering access to water as a vital human need,[76] does not address the issue of accessibility and affordability of water for human needs. International human rights law, conversely, promotes and protects basic social, economic, and cultural rights, which are recognized to all.[77]

A human rights-based approach presents some important and unique characteristics.[78] In the first place, it empowers individuals with rights and establishes corresponding duties for States. It has been maintained that without the legal leverage of the right to water, economically disadvantaged people disproportionately bear the impact of water scarcity.[79] Moreover, it focuses on non discrimination and quality.[80] Finally, it comprises procedural aspects, such as the right to be informed about matters that infringe upon one's fundamental rights and the right to have access to justice.[81]

---

whose livelihoods depend on these resources". See, S. Duvail, C. Médard, O. Hamerlynck, D. W. Nyingi, *Land and water grabbing in an East African coastal wetland: The case of the Tana delta*, in *Water Alternatives*, 2012, pp. 322-343. Source www.water-alternatives.org; E. Hey, *Virtual water, 'land grab' and international law*, in L. Boisson de Chazournes, C. Leb, M. Tignino (eds.), *International Law and Freshwater. The Multiple Challenges*, Cheltenham-Northampton, 2013.

[76] See, *inter alia*, Convention on the Law of the Non-Navigational Uses of International Watercourses, UN Doc. A/51/869, New York, 11 April 1997, art. 10(2); Convention on the Protection and Use of Transboundary Watercourses and International Lakes, Helsinki, 17 March 1992; Protocol on Water and Health, London, 17 June 1999, art. 6. Some scholars argue for the progressive narrowing of the gap between international water law and human rights law. Leb refers to a process of "*Codification for the protection of vital human needs*". C. Leb, *The right to water in a transboundary context: emergence of seminal trends*, in *Water International*, 2012, p. 648. Tanzi, pp. 267-285 (n 40). See, also, O. McIntyre, *The human right to water as a creature of global administrative law*, in *Water International*, 2012, available at http://www.iwra.org, where the author refers to implicit support for the values inherent to the human right to water.

[77] R. Kolb, *Human Rights and Humanitarian Law*, in *Max Planck Encyclopedia of Public International Law,* 2013, para. 1.

[78] Bourquain, pp. 59-66 (n 9); A. Kuck, *Human Right to Water – Millennium Development Goals: How Do They Go Together in Practice*, in E. H. Riedel, P. Rothen (eds.), *The Human Right to Water*, Berlin, 2006.

[79] R. B. Larson, *The Mirage of the International Human Right to Water*, 12 July 2013.

[80] Mehta maintains that declaring access to water as a human right could "*enhance poor households' dignity and independence and free up the one to four hours a day poor women and children spend collecting water*" and also "*limit the commodification and commercialization of water, because market mechanisms are unlikely to guarantee its provision to all people – and certainly not on a fair basis*". Mehta, p. 568 (n 13).

[81] Among others, A. Uzelac, C. H. van Rhee, *Revisiting Procedural Human Rights. Fundamentals of Civil Procedure and the Changing Face of Civil Justice*, Cambridge, 2017; K. R. Irwin, *Prospects for Justice: The Procedural Aspect of the Right to Life Under the European Convention on Human Rights and Its Application to Investigations of Northern Ireland's Bloody Sunday*, in *Fordham International Law Journal*, 1998, pp. 1822-1859; V. Barral presented at the 2017 Annual Conference of the European Society of International Law (Naples) on the topic "*Water and Procedural Rights – A Comparative Enquiry into the Procedural Dimension of the Right to Water*" arguing in favor of the existence of a right to be informed, to participate and to have access to justice in water related matters.

In the end, a human rights-based approach differs from other perspectives in that it focuses on equality, not simply on the achievement of general targets: non-discrimination in the allocation of water is as important as reaching an overall improvement in access to safe drinking water.[82]

1.3. Possible conflicting obligations arising from the human right to water and international economic law

Normative conflicts between obligations arising from different branches of international law, namely human rights law and international investment and trade law, may arise in case of privatization and liberalization of water services.[83]

While the nature, content and scope of the right to water, together with the ensuing obligations, will be addressed in detail in the following chapter, suffice here to mention that this right holds States parties to the International Covenant on Economic, Social and Cultural Rights ("ICESCR") to guarantee to all a minimum amount of accessible water for personal and domestic uses at an affordable price or, in case of absolute indigence, free of charge.

At the same time, international investment and trade law may require States to prioritize – or to allow private providers to give precedence to – a cost effective management of water services, which does not grant clear guarantees to the less well-off, as it happens in the Cochabamba case mentioned above.[84]

Arbitral tribunals in investment disputes have found themselves adjudicating cases in which these conflicting obligations were clearly invoked by the parties to the disputes.[85] As will be discussed in chapter three, in some cases arbitral tribunals have claimed to balance the obligations stemming from the human right to water and those deriving from investment treaties, but their decisions have fallen short in

---

[82] General Assembly*, Integrating non-discrimination and equality into the post-2015 development agenda for water, sanitation and hygiene*, *Report of the Special Rapporteur on the human right to safe drinking water and sanitation,* UN Doc. A/67/270, 8 August 2012.

[83] For possible normative conflicts between obligations arising from different branches of international law see: M. Lugato, *Trattati di estradizione e norme internazionali sui diritti umani*, Turin, 2006; G. Marceau, *WTO Dispute Settlement and Human Rights*, in *European Journal of International Law*, 2002, p. 753 ff.; J. E. Viñuales, *Foreign Investment and Environment in International Law*, Cambridge, 2012; M. Krepchev, *The Problem of Accommodating Indigenous Law Rights in International Investment Law*, in *Journal of International Dispute Settlement*, 2015, p. 42 ff.

[84] Brown Weiss, 199-204 (n 21).

[85] Suez, *Sociedad General de Aguas de Barcelona, S.A. and Vivendi Universal, S.A. v. Argentine Republic*, ICSID Case No. ARB/03/19, decision on liability, 30 July 2010; *SAUR International v. Argentine Republic*, ICSID Case No. ARB/04/4, Decision on Jurisdiction and Liability, 6 June 2012; *Urbaser S.A. and Consorcio de Aguas Bilbao Bizkaia, Bilbao Biskaia Ur Partzuergoa v. The Argentine Republic*, ICSID Case No. ARB/07/26, Award, 8 December 2016.

reaching a sound harmonization between investment law and human rights law.[86] Likewise, prospective normative conflicts may arise between the obligations derived from the human right to water and those envisaged by the General Agreement on Trade in Services ("GATS"), which will be the focus of chapter four.

These current and prospective legal frictions call for further reflections.

2. Rationale for the book: a quest for balancing the human rights approach and the trade and investment law approach to water services liberalization

The rationale for this book is driven by the contention that liberalization of water services presents both challenges to as well as opportunities for the fulfillment of the human right to water.[87] Both advocates and opponents of the liberalization of the water sector focus on one side of the coin, while each has some grounds and a grain of truth. From an international law perspective, the issue is how to strike a fair balance between foreign private involvement in the water sector and guarantees of availability and affordability of water services.[88] This book endeavors to carry out this task by addressing "*the human rights impairment without sacrificing the wider benefits of freer trade*".[89]

In general terms, international economic law and human rights law may diverge in several respects, yet they can be mutually beneficial. On the one hand, some economic interests have been recognized as human rights.[90] On the other hand, human rights are costly, and the liberalization of trade in services, understood as the open-

---

[86] R. Greco, *The Impact of the Human Right to Water on Investment Disputes*, in *Rivista di Diritto Internazionale*, 2015, pp. 444-485.

[87] Commission on Human Rights, *Liberalization of Trade in Services and Human Rights, Report of the High Commissioner for Human Rights*, UN Doc. E/CN.4/Sub.2/2002/9, 25 June 2002.

[88] Bluemel, p. 980 (n 23). According to the author: "*achieving a financially viable water infrastructure is in tension with a human rights approach to water, but the two are not mutually exclusive*".

[89] A. O. Sykes, *International Trade and Human Rights: An Economic Perspective*, Chicago Working Paper No. 188, 2003, p. 23, available at https://ssrn.com/abstract_id=415802. In this respect, Simma argues that the main problem is to find a strategy within the framework of international investment regime to harmonize investment protection and human rights compliance. B. Simma, *Foreign Investment Arbitration: A Place For Human Rights?*, in *International & Comparative Law Quarterly*, 2011, p. 580.

[90] In this respect, one can mention the right of equal access to public services. See art. 21(2) of the 1948 Universal Declaration of Human Rights, and art. 25(*c*) of the 1966 UN International Covenant on Civil and Political Rights. Some authors even suggest the need to recognize an individual right to freedom of trade across borders, enforceable before domestic tribunals. E.-U. Petersmann, *Human Rights and International Economic Law in the 21st Century: The Need to Clarify their Interrelationships*, in *Journal of International Economic Law*, 2001, pp. 31-33.

ing of national markets, may boost investment, raise the aggregate national income and living standards, and ultimately contribute to enhancing human rights.[91] In particular, for developing countries, a possible way to overcome financial constraints and improve essential services consists in liberalizing these services in order to attract foreign investment necessary to improve or even build essential infrastructure.

The liberalization of water services may also foster investments in this sector and contribute to improving access to drinking water. Currently, there is a gap between what is required by human rights law[92] and what States are capable of achieving, which in part is due to a clear lack of financial resources and expertise.[93] The problem is that water services are "*the most capital-intensive of all the utilities*":[94] large investments are needed to build, modernize and maintain water infrastructure, to replace ageing distribution networks, to extend territorial coverage to unserved areas, to improve the quality of the service and to pay highly specialized personnel. Numerous assessments have documented the large amounts of financing needed for water-related infrastructure in developing countries.[95] Not surprisingly, the majority of people worldwide without access to improved drinking water lives in these countries.[96] In the words of the High Commissioner for Human Rights "*[i]ncreasing investment in the water and sanitation sector is possibly the most pressing issue facing the realization of the right to water today*".[97]

---

[91] Sykes, p. 2 (n 89); Sykes argues that both theory and the available empirical evidence suggest that "*the growth of the trading system generally tends to promote rather than to undermine human rights*" and that, in any case, there is "*[n]o basis for supposing (…) that a more open trading system does systematic damage to human rights in any broad sense*" (*ibid.*, p. 23 and p. 9). On the same line of reasoning, other authors contend that "*a positive relationship exists between the arrival of foreign direct investment (FDI) and development, and that attracting foreign capital is essential to developing countries in order to finance their growth and to improve their access to technologies*". See O. De Schutter, J. Swinnen, J. Wouters, *Introduction*, in O. De Schutter, J. Swinnen, J. Wouters (eds.), *Foreign Direct Investment and Human Development*, Abingdon-New York, 2013, p. 1. According to the authors, the flow of foreign direct investment has been constantly increasing "*from 55 billion US dollars in 1980 to 1,306 US dollars in 2006,*" p. 5; J. R. Paul, *Do International Trade Institution Contribute to Economic Growth and Development?*, in *Virginia Journal of International Law*, 2003.

[92] From a human rights perspective, States must take all the necessary measures to provide each person with "*sufficient, safe, acceptable, physically accessible and affordable water for personal and domestic uses*", General Comment No. 15, para. 2 (n 2).

[93] 785 million people still lack a basic drinking-water service. Data available at: https://www.who.int/news-room/fact-sheets/detail/drinking-water. An improved source of drinking water includes household connections, public standpipes, boreholes, protected dug wells, protected springs and rainwater collections.

[94] Choudhury, p. 131 (n 43).

[95] World Bank, *Water Resources Sector* Strategy, p. 43 (n 6).

[96] WHO/UNICEF, *Joint Monitoring Programme (JMP) for Water Supply, Sanitation and Hygiene*, data available at: http://data.worldbank.org/indicator/SH.H2O.SAFE.ZS.

[97] Commission on Human Rights, *Human rights, trade and investment, Report of the High*

For investment in water services to increase and liberalization to succeed, an effective regulatory system, which provides clear guarantees for both investors and public authorities, is of the utmost importance. It is argued that liberalization of water services can produce positive effects only to the extent that it is accompanied by effective institutions and regulations.[98] A regulatory system consistent with human rights is also required by the Committee on Economic, Social and Cultural Rights ("CESCR"), which is neutral on the issue of the privatization and liberalization of water services, provided that water services are affordable for all, including the most disadvantaged.[99]

From the perspective of international law, parties to international trade and investment agreements have to "*promote and protect human rights during the negotiation and implementation of international rules on trade liberalization*".[100] In this connection, the core concern is to find legal ways allowing States that have decided to liberalize their water service market to maintain the *leeway* necessary to decide how to regulate water services in the public interest without excessive constraints from the foreign private sector. In particular, States must be free to use performance requirements, to introduce new regulations and even to withdraw investment liberalization commitments in the light of experience.[101]

The likeliness that regulation will ensure the enjoyment of essential services such as water depends on several factors, not least the international legal framework under which liberalization is expected to take or has taken place. The liberalization of privatized water services has occurred bilaterally in several countries under the umbrella of a BIT agreement. Unfortunately, some cases have ended up before arbitral tribunals, such as the ICSID, and in several awards a developing country was ordered to pay a high amount in compensation to private investors.[102]

Commissioner for Human Rights, para. 45 (n 46). For instance, investments in water infrastructure can have positive effects on women and children who are often in charge of collecting water in developing countries. Instead, women might employ the time saved in remunerated working activities and children might attend school.

[98] Choudhury, p. 178 (n 43).

[99] General Comment No. 15, para. 27 (n 2). The CESCR limits itself to underlining that the privatization and liberalization of water services do not exempt States from their duties to respect, protect and fulfil the right to water. The duty to protect entails the duty to regulate in order to prevent private companies from interfering with the enjoyment of the right to water, for instance by charging unaffordable tariffs or cutting off the service for arrears due to inability to pay. Under the obligation to fulfil, States are allowed to provide subsidies to those who are unable to pay. In this sense, see Human Rights Council, *Report of the independent expert on the issue of human rights obligations related to access to safe drinking water and sanitation, Catarina de Albuquerque* (n 18).

[100] Commission on Human Rights, *Liberalization of Trade in Services and Human Rights, Report of the High Commissioner for Human Rights*, p. 8, para. 5 (n 87).

[101] Commission on Human Rights, *Human rights, trade and investment, Report of the High Commissioner for Human Rights*, para. 31 (*b*)(*c*)(*d*) (n 46).

[102] For instance, Impregilo, an Italian company that had invested in water service and sanita-

Moreover, liberalization of water services might also take place at an international level under the GATS, when States undertake specific commitments in the water sector. As such a possibility was envisaged during the Doha round of negotiations, it seems important to assess the impact of final commitments for water services on the regulatory power of States, above all the possibility and cost associated with the withdrawal of States' commitments.

Each level of liberalization poses different challenges and offers different opportunities for the fulfillment of the human right to water, both of which merit further study. As stressed by the High Commissioner for human rights: *"[d]ebate is still needed on a number of questions, including (...) interaction [of the right to water] with other areas of international law, including trade and investment law"*.[103]

3. Area of research: fragmentation of international law

This book is part of the strand of research concerning the so-called *"fragmentation of international law"*,[104] a phenomenon that stems from the proliferation and diversification of international regulations, both functionally and geographically defined, together with the expansion of secondary rules concerning enforcement, compliance and dispute settlement. A number of special systems[105] of international law have emerged, each possessing its own principles and norms, together with its own institutions and enforcement systems.[106]

---

tion in Argentina, was awarded compensation for violation of fair and equitable treatment. *Impregilo S.p.A. v. Argentina Republic*, ICSID Case No. ARB/07/17, Award, 21 June 2011.

[103] Human Rights Council, *Report of the United Nations High Commissioner for Human Rights on the scope and content of the relevant human rights obligations related to equitable access to safe drinking water and sanitation under international human rights instruments*, UN Doc. A/HRC/6/3, 16 August 2007, para. 68.

[104] ILC, *Fragmentation of International Law: Difficulties arising from the diversification and expansion of International Law*, Report of the Study Group of the International Law Commission, UN Doc. A/CN.4/L.682, 13 April 2006, (hereinafter, "ILC Report"); J. Pauwelyn, *Fragmentation of International Law*, in *Max Planck Encyclopedia of Public International Law*, 2006, available at: www.mpepil.com; M. Koskenniemi, P. Leino, *Fragmentation of International Law? Postmodern Anxieties*, in *Leiden Journal of International Law*, 2002, p. 553 ff.; M. Craven, *Unity, Diversity and the Fragmentation of International Law*, in *Finnish Yearbook of International Law*, 2003, p. 3 ff.; G. Gruni, *The EU, World Trade Law and the Right to Food. Rethinking Free Trade Agreements with Developing Countries*, Oxford, 2018.

[105] The notion of special systems is meant to address *"a set of primary and secondary rules that covers a whole field of International Law"*. M. Lamour, *Are Human Rights Law Rules 'Special'? Study on Interactions Between Human Rights Law Rules and Other International Law Rules*, in N. Weiß, J.-M. Thouvenin (eds.), *The Influence of Human Rights on International Law*, Cham, 2015, p. 29.

[106] Academics have expressed varied views on the issue of fragmentation of international law, pointing to both the positive and negative aspects, even reaching opposite conclusions. Some see

The problem of this specialization is that each regime tends to exist in isolation both from others and from the general principles and practices of international law. The diversification and expansion of international law is not coordinated by a central legislative body in charge of ensuring the overall coherence and unity of the system. As a result, divergent norms can be adopted under the many special regimes of international law that apply to the same State, leading to "*conflict between rules or rule-systems, deviating institutional practices and, possibly, the loss of an overall perspective on the law*".[107]

As recalled by Hafner: "*fragmentation could generate negative effects by exposing the frictions and contradictions between the various legal regulations and imposing on States mutually exclusive obligations*".[108] Given the lack of coordination among special regimes, conflicting primary rules may generate incompatible obligations. For instance, international commitments to liberalization of trade in water services may jeopardize a State's freedom to regulate in the public interest in compliance with its obligation deriving from the right to water.

Moreover, there is no supreme dispute settlement body that has the competence to implement international norms in a way that is binding on all other international bodies. Thus, owing to the divergence of norms and values of different regimes, bodies belonging to one sub-system can take decisions apt to affect other subsystems. This is, for instance, what might happen if investment tribunals ordered a State to pay a significant amount in compensation for measures taken in the exercise of its regulatory duty to protect the right to water.

While an in-depth analysis of this phenomenon is beyond the scope of the present study, this book addresses the problem of conflicting obligations stemming from international investment and trade rules, and the right to water, taking into consideration the International Law Commission ("ILC")'s work on the fragmentation of international law, together with judicial decisions and the teaching of highly qualified publicists.

4. Research questions

The core research question explored in this book is whether the liberalization of

---

diversity in a positive light, as "*the very precondition of (...) the legalization of world politics*". K. Nicolaïdis, J. L. Tong, *Diversity or Cocophony? The Continuing Debate over New Sources of International Law*, in *Michigan Journal of International Law*, 2004, pp. 1364-1365; G. Abi-Saab, *Fragmentation or Unification: Some Concluding Remarks*, in *New York University Journal of International Law & Politics*, 1999, p. 925.

[107] ILC Report, para. 8 (n 104).

[108] G. Hafner, *Pros and Cons Ensuing from Fragmentation of International Law*, in *Michigan Journal of International Law*, 2004, p. 851.

water services is compatible with the human right to water from the point of view of international law, and if so, to what extent.

In order to answer this question, a number of sub-questions need to be addressed. At the outset, the existence of a human right to water will be discussed as well as its status, content and corresponding obligations.

Secondly, the issue will be addressed of whether, and through which means, it is possible to strike a fair balance between the involvement of private foreign investments in the water sector and guarantees for the availability and affordability of water services. In this connection, it is crucial to assess whether current international investment law leaves States with powers necessary to regulate in the public interest.

Finally, the book enquires on the current international legal framework for trade in services to evaluate if it is sufficiently developed so as to provide guarantees in the case of liberalization of sensitive markets, such as water services. In particular, it is imperative to evaluate whether the prospective liberalization of trade in water services risks being at odds with the obligations stemming from the human right to water.

5. Model of analysis

This section describes an analytical model that will be adopted in chapters three and four – concerning, respectively, private foreign investments in water services, and prospective trade in water services under the umbrella of the GATS – in order to seek harmonization between norms that belong to different special regimes regulating investment protection and trade freedom, on the one hand, and human rights, on the other.

Broadly speaking, I will analyze three ways of harmonization of these different legal regimes. In the first place, there are a number of means for preventing States from undertaking conflicting obligations *ex ante*. In particular, a normative conflict between the right to water and investment and trade rules may be prevented by means of, *inter alia*, specific clauses of subordination or coordination, or general exception clauses.

Secondly, once a dispute has arisen and has been brought before arbitral tribunals or other dispute settlement bodies, the adjudicating bodies may seek to balance the different interests at stake by resorting to interpretative methods. In this respect, due regard will be given to the quest for harmonization of investment and trade rules with the human right to water by use of systemic interpretation of apparently conflicting international rules, as well as recourse to contextual and teleological interpretation.

Finally, in case of a "*genuine*" conflict where interpretation proves to be insufficient, the general rules on the relationship among sources of international law must be applied. In this connection, the case may be made for the prioritization of human rights obligations.[109] It will be ascertained whether the normative conflict may be resolved by attributing priority to international human rights norms in order to challenge the applicability of investment clauses and trade norms on the ground of their incompatibility with the human right to water.

5.1. Harmonization by means of conflict prevention

A normative conflict between international rules belonging to different special systems of law may be avoided by resorting to a number of precautionary steps. The parties to a treaty may commit to taking all measures necessary to free themselves from obligations stemming from a pre-existing treaty by, for instance, opening a negotiation in order to revise their previous commitments or by denouncing the former treaty upon expiry.[110]

More importantly, States parties to a treaty may include conflict clauses, such as of subordination, priority or coordination clauses in the new treaty so as to avoid conflicts of norms. Article 30(2) of the 1969 Vienna Convention on the Law of Treaties ("VCLT" or "the Vienna Convention") refers only to subordination clauses, establishing that the provisions of an earlier treaty prevail over the provisions of a subsequent treaty when the latter "*specifies that it is subject to, or it is not to be considered as incompatible with, an earlier treaty*".[111] However, States parties to a treaty may also establish that its provisions should prevail over other treaty provisions, as is the case of Article 103 of the UN Charter.

Several treaties have included provisions of "*priority*" over other treaties[112] or of "*subordination*" to other treaties.[113] The ILC has listed the clauses that might be in-

[109] The issue is whether the applicability of international trade and investment rules may be challenged to the extent that they deviate from human rights norms establishing *erga omnes* or *erga omnes partes* obligations. P. Picone, *Gli obblighi* erga omnes *tra passato e futuro*, in *QIL*, 2015; P. Picone, *Comunità internazionale e obblighi 'erga omnes'. Studi critici di diritto internazionale*, Naples, 2013; P. Picone, *The Distinction between Jus Cogens and Obligations Erga Omnes*, in E. Cannizzaro (ed.), *The Law of Treaties Beyond the Vienna Convention*, Oxford, 2011, p. 411 ff.; P. Picone, *La distinzione tra norme internazionali di* jus cogens *e norme che producono obblighi* erga omnes, in *Rivista di Diritto Internazionale*, 2008.

[110] B. Conforti, *Consistency among Treaty Obligations*, in E. Cannizzaro (ed.), *The Law of Treaties. Beyond the Vienna Convention*, Oxford, 2011, p. 190; J. B. Mus, *Conflicts between Treaties in International Law*, in *Netherlands International Law Review*, 1998, p. 231.

[111] Vienna Convention on the Law of Treaties, Vienna, 23 May 1969, art. 30(2). K. von der Decken, *Application of Treaties*, in O. Dörr, K. Schmalenbach (eds.), *Vienna Convention on the Law of Treaties. A Commentary*, Berlin, 2018, pp. 546-548.

[112] Convention on the Prevention of Terrorism, Warsaw, 16 May 2005, art. 26(2); Charter of the United Nations, San Francisco, 26 June 1945, art. 103.

[113] UN Convention on Biological Diversity, Rio de Janeiro, 5 June 1992, art. 22(1); Interna-

serted into a treaty in order to avoid normative conflicts,[114] namely: clauses that prohibit the conclusion of incompatible subsequent treaties;[115] clauses that expressly permit subsequent "*compatible*" treaties;[116] clauses in the subsequent treaty providing that it "*shall not affect*" the earlier treaty;[117] clauses in the subsequent treaty providing that among the parties, it overrides an earlier treaty; clauses in the subsequent treaty that expressly abrogate the earlier treaty;[118] clauses in the subsequent treaty that expressly maintain earlier compatible treaties;[119] clauses envisaging that future agreements will abrogate earlier treaties.[120]

However, these clauses may fail to prevent the rise of conflicts[121] for a number of reasons. Notably, conflict clauses bind only parties to the treaty incorporating them and, accordingly, they cannot be invoked against non-States parties in case of conflicting obligations arising from different treaties. Moreover, nothing ensures that the parties to a treaty incorporating a priority clause do not take part in a later treaty including provisions incompatible with those enshrined in the former.[122]

5.2. Harmonization by means of interpretation

Normative conflicts may also be avoided by means of interpretation, a mechanism that in international law "*refers to the process of assigning meaning to texts and other statements for the purposes of establishing rights, obligations, and other consequences relevant in a legal context*".[123] While a number of instruments, documents, judgments, awards, and even unilateral acts may require interpretation, this mainly concerns treaty law, and it is to this specific field that this section refers. Articles 31 and

---

tional Convention for the Suppression of the Financing of Terrorism, New York, 9 December 1999, art. 21.

[114] ILC Report, para. 268 (n 104).

[115] North Atlantic Treaty, 4 April 1949, Washington, art. 8.

[116] United Nations Convention on the Law of the Sea, Montego Bay, 10 December 1982, art. 311(3).

[117] Convention on the High Seas, Geneva, 29 April 1958, art. 30.

[118] United Nations Convention on the Law of the Sea, Montego Bay, 10 December 1982, art. 311(1).

[119] United Nations Convention on the Law of the Sea, Montego Bay, 10 December 1982, art. 311(2).

[120] See Treaty on the Functioning of the European Union (TFEU), as amended by the Treaty of Lisbon, Lisbon, 13 December 2007, art. 351.

[121] J. Klabbers, *Treaty Conflict and the European Union*, Cambridge, 2009, pp. 101-103.

[122] von der Decken, pp. 547-548 (n 111).

[123] M. Herdegen, *Interpretation in International Law*, in *Max Planck Encyclopedia of Public International Law*, 2013.

32 VCLT – which are recognized as expressing customary international law[124] – provide the applicable international norms concerning treaty interpretation.[125]

It is common understanding that interpretation not only aims at establishing a pre-determined meaning, but is also a creative process, whereby the interpreter construes the text by assigning significance to its terms so as to better balance different results.[126] In general terms, while some interpretative techniques (systematic and historical interpretation) aim to establish the meaning of the terms taking into account the original will of the parties, others techniques allow the interpreters to distance themselves from the original meaning attributed to the terms at the time of the conclusion of the treaty and even to depart from the parties' will (systemic and teleological interpretation). Both static and dynamic interpretation may prove useful to balancing conflicting interests and avoiding normative conflicts by means of interpretation, depending on the context.[127]

Dynamic interpretation may take the form of teleological, evolutionary[128] and systemic interpretation. Sometimes the differences among these methods are not clear and authors tend to use them interchangeably.[129] Given that teleological and

---

[124] ICJ, *Application of the Convention on the Prevention and Punishment of the Crime of Genocide (Bosnia and Herzegovina v. Serbia and Montenegro)*, judgment, 26 February 2007, para. 160; ICJ, *Dispute regarding Navigational and Related Rights (Costa Rica v. Nicaragua)*, judgment, 13 July 2009, para. 47; ICJ, *Maritime Dispute (Peru v. Chile)*, judgment, 27 January 2014, para. 57; ILC Report, para. 174 (n 104): "*A minimal conclusion that one can draw from practice and literature is that articles 31 and 32 of the VCLT are always applicable unless specifically set aside by other principles of interpretation*".

[125] C. Focarelli, *Trattato di Diritto Internazionale*, Turin, 2015, pp. 401-420; O. Dörr, *Interpretation of Treaties*, in O. Dörr, K. Schmalenbach (eds.), *Vienna Convention on the Law of Treaties. A Commentary*, Berlin, 2018, pp. 559-651; M. E. Villiger, *The Rules on Interpretation: Misgivings, Misunderstandings, Miscarriage? The 'Crucible' Intended by the International Law Commission*, in E. Cannizzaro (ed.), *The Law of Treaties Beyond the Vienna Convention*, Oxford, 2011, pp. 105-122.

[126] J. Udich, *Human Rights and Interpretation: Limits and Demands of Harmonizing Interpretation of International Law*, in N. Weiß, J.-M. Thouvenin (eds.), *The Influence of Human Rights on International Law,* Cham, 2015, p. 44.

[127] U. Linderfalk, *Doing the Right Thing for the Rights Reason – Why Dynamic or Static Approaches Should Be Taken in the Interpretation of Treaties*, in *International Community Law Review*, 2008, pp. 109-141.

[128] Evolutionary interpretation acknowledges a natural phenomenon: the meaning of terms of a treaty can vary over time due to changes in the domestic and international context and, as a consequence, they must be read in the light of those changes. P.-M. Dupuy, *Evolutionary Interpretation of Treaties*, in E. Cannizzaro (ed.), *The Law of Treaties. Beyond the Vienna Convention*, Oxford, 2011. The European Court of Human Rights and the Inter-American Court of Human Rights tend to consider the respective treaties as "*living instruments*" which "*must be interpreted in the light of present day conditions*". See, among others, *Rees v. the United Kingdom*, 17 October 1986; *Sheffield and Horsham v. the United Kingdom*, 30 July 1998; *Guzzardi v. Italy*, 6 November 1980; *Marckx v. Belgium*, 13 June 1979; *Johnston and others v. Ireland*, 18 December 1986; *Tyrer v. the United Kingdom*, 25 April 1978; *Soering v. the United Kingdom*, 7 July 1979; *Loizidou v. Turkey*, 23 March 1995.

[129] For instance, some authors tend to refer to the evolutionary interpretation and the teleolog-

systemic interpretation are of particular relevance for the present study and will be resorted to in order to solve apparent normative conflicts, it is worth spending a few words on these techniques.

Pursuant to Article 31(1) VCLT, the starting point for interpreting a treaty is looking in good faith at the ordinary meaning of terms [130] in their context and in the light of their object and purpose. [131] This is a single, integrated operation, with no hierarchy among the textual, contextual and teleological elements, which all contribute to shedding light on the ordinary meaning of the words used. [132]

When the interpreter follows a teleological approach, he reads terms in light of both the object of the treaty, namely, the substantive content of the treaty, and its purpose, that is, the aim the parties intended to pursue with the adoption of the agreement. [133] This interpretive technique gives expression to the principle of effectiveness, which seeks to prevent some parts of the treaty from being weakened or becoming redundant. [134] In order to determine the aim of a treaty, the preamble plays a primary role, as it usually establishes the purposes that the parties intended to achieve by concluding the treaty.

In determining the aim of the treaty, the interpreter may enjoy some flexibility in forging the meaning of the terms, and even diverge from the original will of the parties, provided that the parties did not intend to give to the terms a special meaning. It has been argued that when teleological and evolutionary interpretation is applied to human rights treaties, this may increase the overall standard of protection by fostering the underlying values of the treaty. At the same time, it can also contribute to increasing the fragmentation of international law by tending unconditionally to favor human-rights friendly conclusions. [135]

It remains to be seen whether the same proves true in contexts other than human rights treaties, such as the GATS, where explicit reference to public policy ob-

---

ical interpretation as synonyms. See: Udich (n 126); V. P. Tzevelekos, *The Use of Article 31(3)(c) of the VCLT in the Case Law of the ECtHR: An Effective Antifragmentation Tool or a Selective Loophole for the Reinforcement of Human Rights Teleology?*, in *Michigan Journal of International Law*, 2010, p. 622 ff.

[130] The terms of the treaty must be read in accordance with their *ordinary* meaning, unless it is established that the parties intended to give a term a *special* meaning, under VCLT art. 31(4).

[131] VCLT art. 31(1) In addition, there shall be taken into account any subsequent agreement between the parties on the interpretation of the treaty and any subsequent practice in the application of the treaty capable of establishing their agreement on its interpretation. VCLT art. 31(3)(*a*)(*b*); International Law Commission, *Draft conclusion on subsequent agreements and subsequent practice in relation to the interpretation of treaties*, 2018, YBILC, 2018, vol. II, Part Two.

[132] Dörr, p. 580, para. 38 n 125.

[133] *Ibid.*, p. 584, para. 53.

[134] *Ibid.*, p. 584, para. 52.

[135] Tzevelekos, p. 636 (n 129).

jectives is made in the preamble of the Agreement so as to counterbalance the aim of liberalizing trade in services. [136]

An apparent conflict among international rules raising issues of State responsibility might be resolved by giving treaty terms a meaning that corresponds to other rules of international law. Systemic interpretation requires the interpreter to read the treaty in the light of other rules of international law. According to Article 31(3)(*c*) VCLT, "*any relevant rules of international law applicable in the relations between the parties*" should be taken into account, together with the context, in interpreting treaty provisions. [137] The article requires dispute settlement bodies established under different special systems to avoid normative conflicts by interpreting relevant norms systematically, and not as if they existed in a legal vacuum. [138] This method of treaty interpretation is predicated on the premise that the international legal order is a system and that treaties are a creation of this legal system. Accordingly, relevant material sources external to treaties are taken into consideration for interpretative purpose. [139] Thus, the article gives expression to the principle of "*systemic integration*". [140]

The ILC has broadly explored the possibility of resorting to systemic interpretation of international rules belonging to different fields of law in order to avoid or mitigate normative conflicts. In its concluding remarks on the issue of fragmentation of international law, it states that:

> "[t]o hold those institutions [with law-applying tasks] as fully isolated from each other and as only paying attention to their own objectives and preferences is to think of law only as an instrument for attaining regime-objectives. But law is also about protecting rights and enforcing obligations, above all rights and obligations that have a backing in something like a general, public interest. Without the principle of 'systemic integration' it would be impossible to give expression to and to keep alive, any sense of the common good of humankind, not reducible to the good of any particular institution or 'regime'". [141]

---

[136] M. H. Hulme, *Preamble in Treat Interpretation*, in *University of Pennsylvania Law Review*, 2016, pp. 1281-1346.

[137] Dörr, pp. 603-613 (n 125).

[138] In this regard, the Study Group on Fragmentation of International Law, recalled: European Court of Human Rights, *Bankovic v. Belgium and others[dec.]*, 12 December 2001, para. 57; *United States – Standards for Reformulated and Conventional Gasoline*, 29 April 1996, WT/DS2/AB/R, p. 17. In the *Korea – Measures Affecting Government Procurement*, 1 May 2000, WT/DS163/R, para. 7.96, the panel stated that "*customary international law applies generally to the economic relations between the WTO Members. Such international law applies to the extent that the WTO treaty agreements do not 'contract out' from it*".

[139] As explained by Tzevelekos, art. 31(3)(*c*) VCLT "*renders possible the inclusion of sources external but relevant to the norm under interpretation, thus allowing the judge to take into account the broader normative environment*". Tzevelekos, p. 631 (n 129).

[140] ILC Report, para. 423 (n 104). Tzevelekos, p. 631 (n 129).

[141] ILC Report, para. 480 (n 104).

Under Article 31(3)(*c*) VCLT three conditions must be met for an external rule to be taken into account.[142] First, it is to be an international *rule*, not only a principle or a standard. Given the breadth of the terms "*rules* of international law", they are to be understood as including both customary international law as well as other applicable treaty norms. The following chapter will explore the normative status of the right to water in international law in order to establish whether this requirement is met.[143]

Next, such a rule has to be *relevant* to resolve the dispute. According to Simma and Kill "*relevant*" cannot be equated with "*relating to the same subject matter*". More simply, the rule has to provide "*operational guidance*" for the determination of the meaning of the treaty provision.[144] Thus the interpreter can consider rules belonging to other special regimes to the extent that such rules provide guidance in determining the meaning of the provisions under consideration. Chapter three will analyze the case law of investment arbitral tribunals concerning disputes over water services to determine whether the right to water has been considered relevant to ascertaining the meaning of investment treaty provisions.[145]

Finally, the external rule has to be *applicable* in the relations between the *parties*.[146]As put by McLachlan, the problem relates to the meaning of the term "*party*" in cases where the applicable law is a treaty rule. It is questioned whether "*all the parties to the treaty being interpreted*" should also be "*parties to the treaty relied upon as the other source of international law for the interpretation purposes*".[147]

In this respect, we agree with those who read the term "*party*" as referring only to the parties in the dispute who are also parties to the treaty to be taken into account, rather than referring to all parties to both treaties under consideration.[148] The requirement of perfect congruence of the members of multilateral treaties is unduly arduous to satisfy[149] and would devoid the provision of most of its scope. In brief, it would be "*practically impossible ever to find a multilateral context where reference to other multi-*

---

[142] Simma, pp. 584-585 (n 89).

[143] A. Rachovitsa, *The Principle of Systemic Integration in Human Rights Law*, in *International & Comparative Law Quarterly*, 2017, pp. 557-588.

[144] B. Simma, T. Kill, *Harmonizing Investment Protection and International Human Rights: First Steps Towards a Methodology*, in C. Binder, U. Kriebaum, A. Reinisch, S. Wittich (eds.), *International Investment Law for the 21st Century. Essay in Honour of Christoph Schreuer*, Oxford, 2009, pp. 695-696.

[145] See, *SAUR International v. Argentine Republic* (n 85); *Urbaser S.A. and Consorcio de Aguas Bilbao Bizkaia, Bilbao Biskaia Ur Partzuergoa v. The Argentine Republic* (n 85).

[146] In the first place, applicability has been understood as referring to the date on which the treaty is being interpreted. Simma, Kill, p. 696 (n 144).

[147] *Report of the Commission to the General Assembly on the work of its fifty-seventh session*, *YBILC* (2005), Vol. II (Part II), para. 472, p. 88.

[148] Simma, Kill, p 699 (n 144).

[149] ILC Report, para. 471 (n 104).

lateral treaties as aids to interpretation under Article 31(3)(c) would be allowed".[150]

For instance, much discussion has concerned normative conflicts between trade agreements under the umbrella of the WTO and multilateral environmental agreements. Assuming that systemic interpretation operated only when all the parties to the first treaty are also parties to the second treaty would mean *de facto* excluding the possibility of resorting to the principle of systemic integration, given that a perfect coincidence of parties to multilateral treaties is rather unlikely.[151] The same problem might affect the applicability of the right to water in interpreting investment and trade agreements.

Some authors have argued that fundamental human rights might be considered applicable in the relations among all States, regardless of whether there is a treaty obligation in force between the States in question and even if such rules are not formally owed *erga omnes*.[152] This thesis, however fascinating, is not persuasive as it does not explain the legal basis upon which a fundamental human right would by applicable *vis-à-vis* a State if the latter is neither bound by a treaty rule enshrining this norm nor by an existing customary norm. It seems that underlying this argument is an attempt to claim a sort of prevalence of core human rights norms on rules belonging to different branches of international law, such as investment and trade rules, an issue that brings us to the following section.

5.3. Establishing systemic relationships of priority

A conflict of norms across competing special regimes of international law may not always be reconcilable by means of systemic interpretation, as this is (or should be)[153] unable to modify treaty provisions. When the normative conflict is genuine,[154] the State bound by conflicting obligations cannot avoid the breach of some of these and

[150] *Ibid.*, para. 450.

[151] J. Klabbers, *Beyond the Vienna Convention: Conflicting Treaty Provisions*, in E. Cannizzaro (ed.), *The Law of the Treaties Beyond the Vienna Convention*, Oxford, 2011, p. 203.

[152] Simma, Kill, p. 702 (n 144). The authors maintain that severe breaches of economic and social rights have become a matter of community interest and that economic, social and cultural rights "*have taken the first steps away from bilateralism*". Thus, such rights could be applied in the relations among States despite the fact that there may be no treaty obligation between them.

[153] J. d'Aspremont, *The Systemic Integration of International Law by Domestic Courts: Domestic Judges as Architects of the Consistency of the International Legal Order*, in A. Nollkaemper, O. K. Fauchald (eds.), *The Practice of International and National Courts and the (De-)Fragmentation of International Law*, Oxford-Portland, 2012, p. 149. The author refers to the "*possible praetorian manipulations to which the rule enshrined in Article 31(3)(c) of the Vienna Convention can be subject*", quoting in this connection the case ICJ, *Oil Platform*, decision of 6 November 2003.

[154] M. Milanovic, *Norm Conflicts, International Humanitarian Law, and Human Rights*, in O. Ben-Naftali (ed.), *International Humanitarian Law and International Human Rights Law,* Oxford, 2011, p. 102.

questions of international responsibility arise. Confronted with a normative conflict, a State should choose to which rules and obligations it will give priority.

When human rights norms are among the competing rules, the issue is whether prevalence ought to be given to obligations ensuing from human rights norms *vis-à-vis* international obligations stemming from other special regimes of international law.

Several scholars believe that the international legal system grants no priority to human rights norms (be they customary or treaty rules) over other sectoral rules.[155] According to Hafner, apart from Article 103 of the UN Charter and norms of an imperative nature,[156] normative conflicts and inhomogeneous application cannot be avoided, as the international system "*lacks clear legal guidance for the resolution of conflicts of norms*".[157] Likewise, Hennequet contends that no hierarchy exists in international law other than that accorded to *jus cogens* and Article 103 of the Charter.[158] At the same time, the law of State responsibility does not indicate which obligations should be given priority in case of normative conflicts.[159]

The VCLT does not offer a solution to conflicts of treaty provisions and the ensuing obligations owed by a State to other States parties to treaties involving different subjects. Klabbers posits that this is due to the horizontal structure of the international legal order.[160]

The assumption that under the current system of international law there is no possibility of prioritizing some sectoral interest over others,[161] not even in case of multilateral human rights treaties,[162] has been challenged by scholarship for which "*[t]he*

---

[155] See J. Klabbers, A. Peters and G. Ulfstein, *The Constitutionalization of International Law*, Oxford, 2009; B.-O. Bryde, *International Democratic Constitutionalism*, in R. St. J. Macdonald, D. M. Johnston (eds.), *Towards World Constitutionalism: Issues in the Legal Ordering of the World Community*, Leiden, 2005.

[156] Hafner, p. 861 (n 108).

[157] *Ibid.*, p. 854.

[158] E. Hennequet, *Jus Cogens and Human Rights: Interactions Between Two Factors of Harmonization of International Law*, in N. Weiß, J.-M. Thouvenin (eds.), *The Influence of Human Rights on International Law*, Cham, 2015, p. 14: "*[d]espite their universality, human rights are still governed by international law, and under international law as such they do not bear any specific character that would allow them to weigh more than other rules of international law in general. This* status quo *may have changed with the fact that some human rights rules have acquired a* jus cogens *character*".

[159] Kabblers, pp. 98-99 (n 121).

[160] Klabbers, p. 204 (n 151): "*in a horizontal legal order, the solution of treaty conflicts is bound to remain problematic. As long as states remain sovereign equals, as long as treaties are based on the consent of those sovereign equals, and as long as those treaties cannot be regarded as anything other than* res inter alios acta, *the law lacks the instruments to settle treaty conflict in a simple and straightforward way*".

[161] *Ibid.*, p. 205.

[162] Conforti maintains that "*primacy cannot be accorded to some multilateral treaties of great*

unity of international law can provide the basis to reconcile conflicting rules".[163] General international law is deemed to contain principles for establishing relationships of priority between conflicting norms and obligations.

In this connection, the ILC report on fragmentation of international law provides some guidance. The latter refers to the link between general international law and special regimes and states that "*[g]eneral international law contains principles of hierarchy that control the operation of the special regime*" not only in determining jus cogens norms, but also "*in providing resources for determining in case of conflict what regime should be given priority or, at least, what consequences follow from the breach of the requirements of one regime by deferring to another (usually State responsibility)*".[164]

These resources for solving normative conflicts grounded in general international law may be detected in the conflict solution techniques known under the maxims of *lex posterior derogat legi priori*, *lex specialis derogat legi generali*, and *lex superior derogat legi inferiori.* Respectively, these rules attach priority to the most recent rule; to the most specific rule; and to the norm which has the highest *status*.

The relevance of these techniques for establishing priority of human rights obligations over conflicting obligations, such as those deriving from trade and investment law, must be evaluated. I contend that while the *lex posterior* and the *lex specialis* rules do not allow attaching priority to customary and treaty human rights norms as such, the answer as far as the *lex superior* maxim is concerned is more complex.

Starting from the first principle of conflict resolution, it establishes that later law supersedes earlier law.[165] Thus, it is possible that a subsequent treaty prevails over customary law or *vice versa* or that a later treaty supersedes an earlier treaty.

Article 30 VCLT codifies the matter with respect to treaty law,[166] requesting, *in primis*, that for a later treaty to override a prior treaty, both of them have to deal with the "*same subject matter*". According to the ILC, a narrow interpretation would leave most important conflicts outside the scope of Article 30 VCLT,[167] so whether two treaties deal with the "*same subject matter*" must be assessed having regard to "*whether the fulfilment of the obligation under one treaty affects the fulfilment of the obligation of another*".[168]

Article 30 VCLT states that in the situation where all parties to the prior treaty

---

importance, such as, for example, those on human rights (…) since there is no significant practice on the matter". See, Conforti, p. 189 (n 110).

[163] Marrella, p. 359 (n 62).

[164] ILC Report, para. 194 (n 104).

[165] Such a principle does not apply automatically. Indeed, sometimes prior treaties may prevail over subsequent treaties.

[166] Conforti, p. 187 ff. (n 110); Klabbers, p. 192 ff (n 151).

[167] ILC Report, para. 253 (n 104).

[168] *Ibid.*, para. 254.

are also parties to the second, the last one prevails.[169] In case of conflicts between treaties with non-identical parties, as for the relationship between a State party to both treaties and a State party to only one of them, priority is given to the treaty to which both States are parties. Article 30 VCLT casts the problem in terms of State responsibility: the State is internationally responsible for having violated a valid treaty norm. Under this rule, it may well occur that trade and investment treaties are more recent in time and compliance with these must be preferred to that of human rights treaties. The outcome of the application of Article 30 VCLT is that the law of treaties is approached from a neutral point of view, without regard to the substantive norms of the treaties, or, quoting Klabbers, irrespective of the "*the moral or political weight to be attached to their content*".[170]

Turning to the *lex specialis* maxim, it is narrowly defined as a conflict-solution technique covering "*the case where two legal provisions that are both valid and applicable, are in no express hierarchical relationship, and provide incompatible direction on how to deal with the same set of facts. It suggests that instead of the (general) rule, one should apply the (specific) exception*".[171] The above maxim may operate in different situations. It can regulate the relationship between treaties and that between a treaty and a custom.

For the purpose of this study, this technique is hardly applicable to normative conflicts between rules deriving from different special regimes of international law, such as human rights law and trade and investment law, as they do not refer to the same subject matter.[172] As for the relationship between customary norms and treaties, doubts may be cast on whether customary human rights norms can be deemed *lex specialis* in relation to investment or trade treaty rules.[173] Likewise, with respect to two different treaty norms, for a human rights treaty rule to be considered special in relation to rules belonging to investment or trade treaties, the conflicting norms should share the same subject matter,[174] which is unlikely.

Finally, the possible role that the maxim *lex superior derogat legi inferiori* may play in solving conflicts of rules stemming from different branches of international law remains to be considered.

International human rights law, as well as other treaty systems such as international investment law and international trade law, are examples of *lex specialis* that, while known as "*self contained regimes*", contain special primary and secondary rules that are not "*clinically isolated*" from the rest of the legal order.[175] According

---

169 VCLT, art. 30(3).

170 Kabblers, p. 23 (n 121).

171 ILC Report, para. 57 (n 104).

172 Lamour, p. 34 (n 105).

173 *Ibid.*, para. 85 ff.

174 *Ibid.*, para. 116.

175 Self-contained regimes are understood as a "*whole area of functional specialization or teleo-*

to the ILC, general international law provides for: *i*) the conditions of validity for the establishment of a special regime; *ii*) the conditions of operation of said regime; *iii*) and, the consequences of its failure. [176]

As for the conditions of validity, the establishment of a special system of law outside of general international law suffers from some limitations. As the ILC put it, aside from peremptory norms, the special regime *may not* deviate from: *i*) the law benefiting third parties, including individuals and non-State entities; *ii*) general law "*if the obligations of general law are of 'integral' or 'interdependent' nature,* [177] *have erga omnes character or practice has created a legitimate expectation of non-derogation*"; *iii*) treaties that have a public law nature. [178] Therefore, in addition to *jus cogens* norms: "*there may be other types of general law that may not permit derogation*". [179]

Applying these criteria to investment and trade special regimes, the respective treaties should not diverge from, *inter alia*, obligations of general law which are of "*integral*" or "*interdependent*" nature or have *erga omnes* character. Obligations *erga omnes* refers to:

> "a) An obligation under general international law that a State owes in any given case to the international community, in view of its common values and its concern for compliance, so that a breach of that obligation enables all States to take action; or b) An obligation under a multilateral treaty that a State party to the treaty owes in any given case to all the other States parties to the same treaty, in view of their common values and concern for compliance, so that a breach of that obligation enables all these States to take action". [180]

The category of *erga omnes* obligations is procedural in scope, concerning standing in regard to some obligations and the right to invoke responsibility. It does not entail hierarchical superiority over other rules of international law, [181] but "*apper-*

---

logical orientation at a universal scale". See ILC Report, para. 136 (n 104). See also B. Simma, *Self-contained Regimes*, in *Netherlands Yearbook of International Law*, 1985, pp. 112-136; J. Pauwelyn, *Bridging Fragmentation and Unity: International Law as a Universe of Inter-connected Islands*, in *Michigan Journal of International Law*, 2004, pp. 903-916.

[176] ILC Report, para. 194 (n 104).

[177] ILC Report, para. 262 (n 104).

[178] ILC Report, para. 154 (n 104).

[179] ILC Report, para. 108 (n 104). K. Wolfram, *Treaties, Conflicts between*, in R. Bernhardt (ed.), *Encyclopedia of Public International Law*, Amsterdam, 2000, p. 937, p. 939; S. A. Sadat-Akhavi, *Methods of Resolving Conflicts between Treaties,* Leiden, 2003, pp. 213-231.

[180] Institut de Droit International, the Krakow Session, *Obligations and Rights Erga Omnes in International Law,* in *Annuaire de l'Institut de Droit International*, 2005, art. 1. See D. Shelton, *Normative Hierarchy in International Law*, in *American Journal of International Law*, 2006, p. 318; M. Ragazzi, *The Concept of International Obligations* Erga Omnes, Oxford, 1997, pp. 202-203. *Contra* A. Pellet, *Conclusions*, in C. Tomuschat, J.-M. Thouvenin (eds.), *The Fundamental Rules of the International Legal Order*, Leiden, 2006, p. 418.

[181] ILC Report, para. 380 (n 104): "*[t]he* erga omnes *nature of an obligation (…) indicates no clear superiority of that obligation over other obligations*"; J. Vidmar, *Norm Conflicts and Hierarchy*

tains to the area of international enforcement",[182] while peremptory norms relate "*to the hierarchy of rules in the international normative order*",[183] being able to override conflicting norms.

Obligations arising from both general human rights law and human rights treaties can be ascribed, respectively, to the category of obligations *erga omnes* and *erga omnes partes*, as they cannot be reduced to a mere bundle of reciprocal rights owed in a bilateral relationship. On the contrary, they are owed to the international community or the other parties to the treaty as a whole.

From the above considerations, the conclusion can be drawn that, leaving aside human rights rules having the *status* of imperative norms, the fact that they give rise to *erga omnes* obligations does not imply that human rights norms are hierarchically superior to other special rules of international law.

The issue still remains whether any priority of human rights norms can be asserted.

Regional human rights courts have ruled in the affirmative. Human rights norms have developed through regional human rights courts, which have interpreted their respective instituting treaties as "*living instruments*". The Inter American Court of Human Rights ("IACHR") and the European Court of Human Rights ("ECtHR"), by resorting to evolutionary and teleological interpretations of the rights enshrined in their instituting conventions, have increased the standard of human rights protection and fostered the values underlying their respective treaties.[184]

These regional courts, in case of normative conflicts between the obligations owed to a State in force of human rights treaties establishing them and those stemming from other rules of international law, have sometimes given priority to human rights obligations over obligations stemming from other international norms.[185]

In particular, the ECtHR contends that human rights norms enjoy precedence over ordinary instrumental norms, such as bilateral treaty rules. It states:

> "[u]nlike international treaties of the classic kind, the convention comprises more than mere reciprocal engagements between the contracting states. It creates, over and above a network of mutual, bilateral undertakings, objective obligations which, in the words of the Preamble benefit from a 'collective enforcement'".[186]

In the *Al-Saadoon* case, the ECtHR considered States' obligations under the

---

in International Law: Towards a Vertical International Legal System?, in E. De Wet, J. Vidmar (eds.), *Hierarchy in International Law: The Place for Human Rights*, Oxford, 2012, p. 25.

[182] *Prosecutor v. Anto Furundžija*, 10 December 1998, judgment, Case No. IT-95-17/1, Trial Chamber II, 121 *ILR* (2002) p. 260, para. 153.

[183] *Ibid.*

[184] J. Udich (n 126).

[185] ECtHR, *Soering v. The United Kingdom*, 7 July 1979, paras. 87-91; *Al-Saadoon v. The United Kingdom*, 2 March 2010, paras. 128-130.

[186] ECtHR, *Ireland v. United Kingdom*, 18 January 1978, para. 239.

Convention to be "*paramount*" *vis-à-vis* other international obligations,[187] thus excluding the possibilities for Member States to choose which conflicting obligations to respect. Commenting on the ECtHR's judgment, Lugato argues that the Court has recognised the "*supreme*" character of Convention norms from the point of view of their rank and the importance of the ensuing provisions, which follows directly from the object and purpose of the Convention.[188]

The ECtHR's approach assumes that international obligations stemming from the European Convention of Human Rights ("ECHR") have a privileged *status* consisting in their primacy over conflicting obligations. Following this line of reasoning, the "*supreme*" character of the European Convention would require States, in case of normative conflicts among rules belonging to different special regimes, to respect obligations ensuing from the ECHR. As a consequence, although human rights norms do not impact on the validity of other international norms, which remain in force, they cause the latter not to be applied.

While from the point of view of the ECtHR this is plausible,[189] for international law in general such an approach would be justified only in so far as one accepts that certain international obligations, among them human rights, enjoy priority due to their content.

This is the contention of scholars who sustain the *primacy* of human rights law over other treaty rules, for instance over investment norms.[190] Some have argued that, as far as human rights norms are concerned, the conservative approach distinguishing between *erga omnes* obligations and *jus cogens* fails to recognise that human rights rules not possessing *jus cogens* status also preserve "*certain common val-*

[187] ECtHR, *Al-Sadoom v. The United Kingdom* (n 185), para. 140.

[188] M. Lugato, *Obblighi internazionali confliggenti e responsabilità dello Stato parte della Convenzione europea nel caso* Al-Saadoon, in *Rivista di diritto internazionale*, 2011, p. 463.

[189] See, as for the Inter-American Court of Human Rights, *Case of the Sawhoyamaxa Indigenous Community v. Paraguay*, 29 March 2006, para. 140.

[190] G. Aguilar Cavallo, *The Human Right to Water and Sanitation: Going Beyond Corporate Social Responsibility*, in *Utrecht Journal of International and European Law*, 2013, p. 49: "*One of the biggest challenges of public international law remains to strike an adequate balance between international investment treaties and international human rights and environmental obligations, bearing always in mind that investors' rights are conditional rights*". *Contra* Nicolaïdis, Tong, p. 1361 (n 106), who contend that human rights courts, by referring to their conventions as a "*living instrument which must be interpreted in the light of the present-day conditions*", tend to diverge from the original will of States and to move away from the systemic interpretation of international law; Udich (n 126) asserts that in order to pursue the objective of their respective treaties, human rights bodies may threaten the unity of general international law, contributing to the fragmentation of the international legal system; Hennequet, pp. 24-25 (n 158), maintains that aside from some human rights norms possessing imperative character (i.e. the prohibition of torture, inhuman and degrading treatments, the prohibition of genocide), the vast majority of human rights rules do not belong to *jus cogens*, and one should refrain from overly expanding the catalogue of *jus cogens* norms in order to reinforce human rights. Otherwise, the risk is transforming peremptory norms into an empty category.

ues ranked of greater importance to a particular social group"[191] and, as a consequence, enjoy "*hierarchically superior normative status*".[192] Given that human rights rules "*incorporate values bearing substantial moral weight for the community as a whole*", they "*call for the recognition of their normative superiority* vis-à-vis *the classic bilateral or bilateralizable norms of international law*".[193]

This contended normative superiority of human right law would not however resemble that of *jus cogens* norms, as *erga omnes* obligations stemming from human rights norms would not be absolute. The conflicting rules would remain intact and would continue to produce their effects to the extent that they do not disproportionally impede the operation of *erga omnes* rules.[194] The supremacy would only consist in the prioritization of the fulfilment of *erga omnes* obligations *vis-à-vis* "*conflicting bilateral or bilateralizable obligations*".[195] In this way, the approach in Article 30 VCLT is preserved.

From the practice and theory described above, one might infer that human rights norms: *i*) do not threaten the validity of other treaty norms, which remain in force; *ii*) might *de facto* cause the latter to be disapplied; *iii*) the non-application of conflicting norms is not the automatic effect of rules deviating from human rights obligations, but would only occur when the conflicting norms disproportionally affect the fulfilment of human rights obligations.

These conclusions are in line with the request of the High Commissioner for Human Rights to prioritize human rights obligations over obligations stemming from other branches of international law.[196] They would also be coherent with the ILC's reasoning on the issue of fragmentation of international law, since the Commission does not put the prioritization of *erga omnes* obligations in absolute terms, but affirms that among the limitations to which special regimes are subject, the latter "*may not deviate from general law if the obligations of general law (…) have* erga omnes *character*".[197]

Although I find these conclusions persuasive, I analyze in chapters three and four whether this theory of the prioritization of human rights obligations, in part followed by human rights courts,[198] has also been recognized by courts of other

---

[191] Tzevelekos, p. 641 (n 129).

[192] *Ibid.*

[193] *Ibid.*, pp. 642-643.

[194] *Ibid.*, p. 643.

[195] *Ibid.*, p. 644.

[196] Human Rights Council, *Report of the United Nations High Commissioner for Human Rights on the scope and content of the relevant human rights obligations related to equitable access to safe drinking water and sanitation under international human rights instruments*, para. 64 (n 103).

[197] ILC Report, para. 154 (n 104).

[198] ECtHR, *Al-Saadoon v. The United Kingdom* (n 185), para. 140; Inter-American Court of Human Rights, *Case of the Sawhoyamaxa Indigenous Community v. Paraguay*, 29 March 2006, para. 140.

sub-systems, given that each tribunal tends to give priority to the rules pertaining to its own ambit.[199] The sole jurisprudence of human rights courts, inclined as it is to defend its own values, is insufficient to prove such a priority.

From the narrow perspective of this study, the book will examine the practice of international investment tribunals in the context of international investment disputes related to the privatization and liberation of water services. In particular, chapter three will analyze the cases brought before investment tribunals in which the right to water has been claimed and, to some extent, taken into consideration for resolving the dispute. Chapter four will anticipate the possible results of prospective disputes involving trade in water services and the right to water, in the light of the precedents set by international trade bodies.

6. Methodology

The legal framework of this study is quite broad: it covers human rights law, international trade law and investment law with the aim of providing a legal underpinning to the protection of the affordability feature of the right to water in case of privatization and liberalization of water services. Framing the state of the art to this end requires gathering a wide range of documents in order to avoid overlooking pertinent issues.

The methodological approach that has been used in this study is predominantly normative, doctrinal and case law driven. At the outset, secondary sources are considered, such as domestic and international instruments and pertinent publications of international scholars specialized in the different fields of law relevant for this study. In particular, the second chapter focuses on soft law instruments and human rights conventions in order to frame the legal basis of the human right to water. Next, turning the focus to the interplay of the right at issue with international economic law, attention is shifted to international investment treaties and international trade agreements (namely, the GATS). Additionally, primary legal documents are considered, including: domestic judgments; decisions of regional human rights courts; concession contracts for the supply of water services; bilateral investment agreements; WTO panels and Appellate Body decisions interpreting key exceptions to the freedom of trade for the protection of human needs and natural resources; ICSID awards on water service concessions.

The method used to answer the key questions related to the issue of harmonization between the human right to water and investment and trade treaties pursues three main aims, namely: *i*) preventing the emergence of normative conflicts at the

[199] See E. de Wet, J. Vidmar, *Conflicts between International Paradigms: Hierarchy versus Systemic Integration*, in *Global Constitutionalism*, 2013, pp. 196-217.

moment of drafting international economic rules or undertaking commitments to trade liberalization, to the extent that the GATS is concerned; *ii*) suggesting an interpretative approach to international trade and investment rules harmonizing them with human rights norms; *iii*) and finally, on a more general level, investigating potential precedence among rules belonging to different subsystems of international law.

Given that international trade and investment law have tended to disregard human rights issues, and considering the effectiveness of their respective dispute settlement systems, this book focuses principally on ways of preventing normative conflicts prior to undertaking liberalization commitments and on the systemic interpretation of international law, which requires international dispute settlement bodies not to interpret relevant rules according to their own principles and system of law alone, as if they were in a "*legal vacuum*".

7. Scope and outline of the book

The book examines the issue of harmonization of human rights law and other branches of international law through the lens of the human right to water so as to evaluate whether and how this right may be taken into account by law and policy makers in order to prevent normative conflicts, or applied by dispute settlement bodies called to interpret trade and investment treaty clauses in disputes arising from the liberalization of water services. The book is limited in scope in four main respects.

First, although the issue of harmonization of human rights law with other branches of international law may be analyzed in the context of most rights included in the catalogue of human rights law, the research focuses on water, as it essential for the enjoyment of all other rights. In this connection, it should be stressed that the present work deals only indirectly with the right to sanitation. Indeed, although the two rights are often addressed together and considered strictly interconnected, they retain their own specific characteristics.[200] Although the realization of the right to sanitation impacts the right to water, as the management of wastewater may affect water quality, the technical implementation of sanitation services is much more complex than that of water. Moreover, if the right to sanitation were dependant on the right to water, it would cause "*a major drawback for the implementation of the right to water*" because there is not sufficient water to be allocated for water-based sanitation worldwide.[201]

---

[200] Indeed, the UN General Assembly has adopted a resolution by *consensus* which for the first time recognises the distinction between the human right to water and the human right to sanitation. See GA Res 70/169, 17 December 2015, UN Doc. A/RES/70/169, 22 February 2016.

[201] Kuck, p. 180 (n 78).

Second, some authors have suggested various solutions for overcoming the problems related to water services liberalization focusing, *inter alia*, on progressive taxes, subsidies, or other measures tailored to the issue of water. This book does not consider the regulation of water services, a matter left to policy makers and economists. Instead, it focuses on how, from an international legal standpoint, to guarantee that these actors have the leeway necessary to tailor domestic regulatory systems in a way that best suits their countries.

Third, the research focuses on the harmonization of human right law with international trade and investment law, where the potential for normative conflicts seems to be greater. Other branches of international law that can be considered complementary to human rights law (to the extent that the human right to water is concerned) are not addressed: for instance, international environmental law complements the fulfilment of the human right to water by protecting water resources, and thus the availability and quality of water, while international water law addresses issues related to the human access to water in a transboundary water context.[202]

Finally, although the "*commoditization of water*" has taken several forms – among others, the conferment of water rights, the rise of water markets, trade in water as bottled water or bulk waters –, the book focuses on the harmonization of international rules belonging to different special regimes from the narrower point of view of the liberalization and trade of water services.[203] An insight into the normative content of the right to water reveals that sound water services are instrumental for its realization, as all its features greatly hinge upon the regulation of water services, a field in which international law may play a major role. Although some scholars consider that international trade in bulk water might mitigate the shortages in some water-stressed countries, the present research does not address this topic since the role of international trade in water is still marginal, above all if compared with the much wider impact of water services on daily life all across countries.

Following this introduction, chapter two is entirely dedicated to the human right to water. Absent from the so-called International Bill of Rights, this right has recently been recognized by a large number of declarations, resolutions, international and regional treaties and domestic provisions. However, since it has been stressed that "*the lack of normative clarity leads towards an ambiguous and uncertain practical applicability of the human right to water*",[204] the chapter focuses on the legal basis,

[202] Some scholars have already dealt with the complementarity between these different legal regimes. See, for instance, Bulto, T. S., *The Extraterritorial Application of the Human Right to Water in Africa*, Cambridge, 2014; Brown Weiss (n 21).

[203] Moreover, the book deals only with the privatization of water assets, whereas the issue of the private ownership of water resources is not addressed.

[204] S. M. A Salman, *Evolution and Context of International Water Resources Law*, in L. Boisson

normative content and obligations arising from the right to water. In particular, States' obligations are considered in relation to the liberalization of water services since, before undertaking commitments in this direction, States have to assess their impact on human rights in view of avoiding potential conflicts between the resulting obligations under human rights law and economic law. As for the enforceability of the right to water, the chapter illustrates the international, regional and national mechanisms that have already enforced this right.

Chapter three concentrates on the harmonization of the rules of international investment treaties in order to avoid, mitigate or resolve normative conflicts involving the human right to water. Provided that a balance is struck between investors' rights and human rights, foreign investments may be an opportunity to improve the water service and therefore to enhance the access to water. The chapter analyzes possible strategies to make such a harmonization possible, both by way of inclusion of specific clauses in IIAs or by resorting to a systemic interpretation of key provisions of BITs – such as indirect expropriation and fair and equitable treatment – that may affect the enjoyment of the human right to water. As for systemic interpretation, the chapter moves from the analysis of investment arbitral disputes related to the failed liberalization of water services in which the right to water has been invoked by the respondent State in order to justify contested measures. The main source of contrast concerns the leeway left to the host State when it seeks to modify the regulatory environment which existed at the time when the investment was made. The chronological analysis of the investment dispute awards shows a growing consideration for the human right to water and an effort to reach harmonization. However, although the increasing role accorded to the right to water has impacted the tribunals' decisions, tilting the balance in favor of the State's regulatory powers, yet from the point of view of systemic integration of investment law and human rights law, the results achieved by arbitral tribunals are still incomplete, above all when it comes to compensation.

Lastly, chapter four evaluates the potential impact of liberalization of trade in water services within the framework of the WTO General Agreement on Trade in Services in order to prevent "*the implementation of any retrogressive measure that reduces the enjoyment of human rights*".[205] In particular, the chapter provides for an assessment of the compatibility of future commitments to the liberalization of water services under the GATS with the obligations arising from the human right to water. At the moment, water services are exempted from GATS liberalizations as no Member State has yet made specific commitments. However, given that the Agree-

---

de Chazournes, S. M. A Salman (eds.), *Les Ressources en Eau et le Droit International. Water Resources and International Law*, Leiden, 2005, p. 79; S. C. McCaffrey, *The Human Right to Water*, in E. Brown Weiss, L. Boisson de Chazournes, N. Bernasconi-Osterwalder (eds.), *Fresh Water and International Economic Law*, Oxford, 2005.

[205] Commission on Human Rights, *Liberalization of Trade in Services and Human Rights, Report of the High Commissioner for Human Rights*, para. 11 (n 87).

ment is directed at the progressive liberalization of trade in services and that some requests to undertake specific commitments with regard to the sector of management and distribution of water services had been tabled, the current lack of obligations is open to change. The chapter considers whether the Agreement provides sufficient leeway to public regulatory authorities to protect access to water services for the most vulnerable. In fact, the Agreement envisages some exceptions with regard to public services, but their scope is vague. Moreover, the chapter studies whether the GATS grants the necessary flexibility for States to withdraw commitments in order to preserve their power to adjust established rules in response to concrete experience over time, and even to reverse their decision to liberalize and restore public ownership. In this regard, it is questionable whether the compensatory adjustment required in case of modification or withdrawal of commitments, the so-called "*lock-in*" clause envisaged by Article XXI, is compatible with such a need for flexibility. The chapter concludes with appraisal and recommendations. It discourages – for the time being – the opening of trade in water services within the GATS because of the complexity and high degree of accuracy required in scheduling commitments, the uncertainty as to the scope of some of its important rules (*i.e.* those about domestic regulations, subsidies and government procurement), the WTO jurisprudence, and the almost irreversible effects ensuing from mistakes in drafting clauses.

The book concludes with some final remarks and appraisal.

Chapter II

THE HUMAN RIGHT TO WATER UNDER INTERNATIONAL LAW

SUMMARY: 1. Introduction. – 2. The legal basis of the human right to water. – 2.1. Treaty legal basis. – 2.1.1. The right to water as a derivative right. – 2.2. The emergence of a customary human right to water. – 2.2.1. State practice. – 2.2.1.1. International treaties. – 2.2.1.2. Regional instruments. – 2.2.1.3. Statements by States and conduct within international organizations. – 2.2.1.4. National constitutions and legislation. – 2.2.1.5. Domestic case law. – 2.2.2. States' *opinio juris*. – 2.2.3. A right in *statu nascendi* or already born? – 2.3. General principles of international law. – 3. The content of the human right to water. – 3.1. The content of the right to water derived from Article 11 ICESCR. – 3.1.1. Subsequent agreement on the interpretation of Article 11 ICESCR. – 3.2. The content of the customary right to water. – 4. The obligations stemming from the human right to water. – 4.1. The nature and content of the obligations. – 4.2. The subjects responsible for their implementation. – 4.3. The territorial extension of the obligations. – 5. The role of international judges and quasi-judicial compliance mechanisms in the identification and formation of the human right to water. – 5.1. International human rights mechanisms. – 5.2. Regional human rights tribunals and compliance mechanisms. – 5.3. International investment tribunals. – 6. Conclusion.

1. Introduction

Since water resources began to be perceived as scarce and a source of concern, different approaches have been taken to face water-related problems. On the one hand, water has been subjected to private appropriation, priced and treated as a market product. On the other hand, various declarations, resolutions, as well as expert documents, have begun to refer to safe drinking water in terms of human needs and subsequently as a human right.

The first instrument addressing the subject was the 1972 Stockholm Declaration, adopted at the end of the UN Conference on the Human Environment, which recognized that the natural resources of the earth, including water, must be safeguarded for the benefit of present and future generations.[1]

A few years later, the UN Water Conference[2] was held to address specifically water-related issues. Its final report includes the Mar del Plata Action Plan,[3] namely the first instrument to declare that all people *"have the right to drinking water in*

---

[1] Declaration of the United Nations Conference on the Human Environment, Stockholm, 16 June 1972, Principle 2.

[2] United Nations Water Conference, Mar del Plata, 14 – 25 March 1977.

[3] General Assembly, Res. 32/158, 19 December 1977, UN Doc. A/RES/32/158.

quantities and quality equal to their basic needs" and to recommend national policies to "*give priority to the supplying of drinking water for the entire population*".[4]

Following the Action Plan recommendations, the General Assembly launched the International Drinking Water Supply and Sanitation Decade (1981-1990) with the aim of providing safe drinking water and sanitation to unserved urban areas by 1990,[5] and proclaimed 22 March as the World Day for Water.[6]

The Global Consultation on Safe Drinking Water and Sanitation for the 1990s assessed the experiences of the preceding decade. Its conclusions and recommendations, summarized in the New Delhi Statement,[7] showed that notwithstanding the progresses made during the 1980s, one third of the developing countries' populations still lacked safe drinking water and sanitation. Under the slogan "*[s]ome for all rather than more for some*", the Statement called upon States to achieve universal coverage of safe drinking water and sanitation by the end of the century, suggesting principles for improving water management and increasing investments.[8]

Further international conferences dealt with the need to optimize the use of fresh-water resources and to guarantee access to safe drinking water and sanitation to all. In 1992, two major conferences took place, the International Conference on Water and the Environment and the Rio Conference on Environment and Development, which respectively gave rise to the Dublin Statement on Water and Sustainable Development[9] and to Agenda 21.[10] Principle No. 4 of the Dublin Statement is often recalled for having affirmed, on the one hand, that "*[w]ater has an economic value in all its competing uses and should be recognized as an economic*

---

[4] Mar del Plata Action Plan, United Nations Water Conference, Mar del Plata, 14-25 March 1977, pp. 63-64.

[5] General Assembly, Res. 35/48, 10 November 1980, UN Doc. A/RES/35/18.

[6] General Assembly, Res. 47/193, 22 December 1992, UN Doc. A/RES/47/193, 22 February 1993.

[7] New Delhi Statement, adopted at the Global Consultation on Safe Drinking Water and Sanitation for the 1990s, New Delhi, 10-14 September 1990, and then transmitted to General Assembly, UN Doc. A/C.2/45/3, 11 October 1990.

[8] The four Guiding Principles read as follows: "*1. Protection of the environment and safeguarding of health through the integrated management of water resources and liquid and solid wastes; 2. Institutional reforms promoting an integrated approach and including changes in procedures, attitudes and behaviour, and the full participation of women at all levels in sector institutions; 3. Community management of services, backed by measures to strengthen local institutions in implementing and sustaining water and sanitation programmes; 4. Sound financial practices, achieved through better management of existing assets, and widespread use of appropriate technologies*".

[9] Adopted at the International Conference on Water and the Environment, 26-31 January 1992, Dublin. Note by the Secretary-General of the Conference transmitting the report of the Conference on Water and the Environment, UN Doc. A/CONF151/PC/112.

[10] Agenda 21, Chapter 18, *Report of the United Nations Conference on Environment and Development*, Rio de Janeiro, 3-14 June 1992, A/CONF.151/26/Rev.1, Resolution adopted by the Conference, resolution 1, annex II.

good" and, on the other, that "*it is vital to recognize first the basic right of all human beings to have access to clean water and sanitation at an affordable price*".[11] In a similar way, Agenda 21 established that "*[i]n developing and using water resources, priority has to be given to the satisfaction of basic needs and the safeguarding of ecosystems*".[12] The problem of freshwater scarcity was later addressed by the General Assembly in the Programme for the further implementation of Agenda 21, which underlined the urgent need for actions against the unsustainable use patterns of freshwater and increasing stress in water supplies.[13]

In the 1990s, water issues were often linked to the push for development. Principle No. 2 of the Cairo Principles, adopted at the end of the 1994 UN International Conference on Population and Development, recognised the right of all human beings to an adequate standard of life, including water and sanitation.[14] The General Assembly affirmed, for the first time, that the promotion of the right to food and clean water "*constitutes a moral imperative for national Government and for international community*".[15] The Sub-Commission on Prevention of Discrimination and Protection of Minorities entrusted Mr. El Hadji Guissé with the task of drafting a report on the promotion of the realization of the right to drinking water and sanitation. The Report ended up by recommending further in-depth study on the relationship between the enjoyment of economic, social and cultural rights, the right to development and the question of access to drinking water and sanitation.[16]

---

[11] Dublin Statement on Water and Sustainable Development, International Conference on Water and the Environment, Dublin, 26-31 January 1992.

[12] Agenda 21, para. 18.8 (n 10). See also para. 18.47.

[13] General Assembly, Res. S-19/2, annex, Programme for the Further Implementation of Agenda 21, 19 September 1997. See Section III, paras. 34-35 and also Section III, para. 27(*b*) where the quest for eradicating poverty requires, *inter alia*, to provide universal access to basic social services including clean water and sanitation.

[14] *Programme of Action, Report of the United Nations International Conference on Population and Development*, Cairo, 5-13 September 1994, chapter I, resolution 1, annex, UN publication, Sales No. E.95.XIII.18. See also the Habitat Agenda, issued at the end of the second UN Conference on Human Settlements. The Habitat Agenda Goals and Principles, Commitments and the Global Plan of Action, adopted at the II Habitat conference, Istanbul, 3-14 June 1996.

[15] General Assembly, Res. 54/175, 17 December 1999, UN Doc. A/RES/54/175, 15 February 2000, para. 12(*a*).

[16] Commission on Human Rights, Sub-Commission on Prevention of Discrimination and Protection of Minorities, *The realization of economic, social and cultural rights, The right of access of everyone to drinking water and sanitation services, working paper by Mr. El Hadji Guissé, Special Rapporteur, under Sub-Commission resolution 1997/18*, UN Doc. E/CN.4/Sub.2/1998/7, 10 June 1998. By Decision 2002/105, 22 April 2002, the Commission on Human Rights (taking note of Resolution 2001/2, *Promotion of the realization of the right to drinking water and sanitation*, E/CN.4/Sub.2/RES/2001/2, 10 August 2001), approved the appointment of Mr. Guissé as Special Rapporteur to conduct a study on the relationship between the enjoyment of economic, social and cultural rights and the right to water. See E. Filmer-Wilson, *The Human Rights-Based Approach to Development: The Right to Water*, in *Netherlands Quarterly of Human Rights*, 2005.

At the turn of the century, the Millennium Declaration set goals – the so-called Millennium Development Goals ("MDGs") – to be reached within defined time limits.[17] The target for water and sanitation (MDG No. 7.3) required halving the population without sustainable access to safe drinking water and basic sanitation by 2015.[18] The target for access to water was achieved five years ahead of schedule.[19]

However, this was only a partial goal as, by the end of 2015, approximately 663 million people still lacked access to improved water sources,[20] including 159 million people relying on surface water to meet their drinking-water needs.[21] Moreover, further efforts were needed in terms of equality and non-discrimination,[22] as the MDG No. 7.3 focused only on overall attainment and did not specifically require the extension of access to fresh water to the most marginalized and disadvantaged citizens.[23]

The recognition of the right to water – in legal terms – came in the early 2000s when the UN Committee of Economic, Social and Cultural Rights ("Committee" or "CESCR") issued its well-known General Comment No. 15,[24] identifying the legal

---

[17] In 2000, the Heads of State and Government gathered in New York at the UN Millennium Summit set eight Millennium Development Goals. See General Assembly, *United Nations Millennium Declaration*, UN Doc. A/RES/55/2, 8 September 2000.

[18] The target for water and sanitation (7.C) comes under the environmental Goal 7, "*Ensure Environmental Sustainability*". Initially, the target referred only to safe drinking water, but in 2002, at the Johannesburg World Summit for Sustainable Development, it was expanded as to include also basic sanitation. United Nations, *Report of the World Summit on Sustainable Development*, Johannesburg, 26 August – 4 September 2002. A. Kuck, *Human Right to Water – Millennium Development Goals: How Do They Go Together In Practice?*, in E. H. Riedel, P. Rothen (eds.), *The Human Right to Water*, Berlin, 2006, pp. 173-180.

[19] UNICEF, WHO, *Progress on Drinking Water and Sanitation, 2012 Update*, 2012, p. 4. On the contrary, the goal has not been met for sanitation as 2 billion people still lack access to basic sanitation facilities. See UNICEF, WHO, *Progress on household drinking water, sanitation and hygiene/ 2000-2017*, New York, 2019, p. 32, available at: https://washdata.org/.

[20] An improved source of drinking water includes household connections, public standpipes, boreholes, protected dug wells, protected springs and rainwater collectors.

[21] UNICEF, WHO, *Progress on Sanitation and Drinking Water, 2015 Update and MDG Assessment*, Geneva-New York, 2015, p. 25.

[22] Human Rights Council, Res. 24/18, 27 September 2013, UN Doc. A/HRC/RES/24/18, 8 October 2013, para. 3.

[23] C. de Albuquerque, *Water and sanitation are human rights: why does it matter?*, in L. Boisson de Chazournes, C. Leb, M. Tignino (eds.), *International Law and Freshwater. The Multiple Challenges*, Cheltenham– Northampton, 2013, p. 52. See also UN General Assembly, *Integrating non-discrimination and equality into the post-2015 development agenda for water, sanitation and hygiene, Report of the Special Rapporteur on the human right to safe drinking water and sanitation*, UN. Doc. A/67/270, 8 August 2012.

[24] Committee on Economic, Social and Cultural Rights, *General Comment No. 15 (2002), The right to water (arts. 11 and 12 of the International Covenant on Economic, Social and Cultural Rights)*, UN Doc. E/C. 12/2002/11 (2002), 20 January 2003 (hereinafter, "General Comment No.

basis of such a right in Articles 11(1) and 12(1) of the International Covenant on Economic, Social and Cultural Rights ("ICESCR"), respectively concerning the right to an adequate standard of living and the right to the highest attainable standard of physical and mental health.

A few years later, the Sub-Commission on the Promotion and Protection of Human Rights requested the Special Rapporteur on the right to water to prepare draft guidelines intended to assist governments, international agencies and members of civil society working in the water and sanitation sector in the implemention of the right to drinking water and sanitation.[25] The Draft guidelines for the realization of the human right to water took for granted the existence of such a right[26] and defined water resources a common heritage.[27]

Worthy of mention are also the 2006 *Human Development Report – Beyond scarcity: Power, poverty and the global water crisis*, issued by the UN Development Programme, for stressing the importance of recognizing and implementing the right to water,[28] and the 2007 High Commissioner for Human Rights' Report, focusing on the scope and content of the obligations related to the right to water and sanitation.[29]

15"). See, *inter alia*: E. Riedel, *The Human Right to Water and the General Comment No. 15 of the Committee of Economic, Social and Cultural Rights*, in E. H. Riedel, P. Rothen (eds.), *The Human Right to Water*, Berlin, 2006, pp. 19-36; S. M. A. Salman, *Evolution and Context of International Water Resources Law*, in L. Boisson de Chazournes, S. M. A. Salman (eds.), *Les Ressources en Eau et le Droit International. Water Resources and International Law*, Leiden, 2005, pp. 78-80; S. C. McCaffrey, *The Human Right to Water*, in E. Brown Weiss, L. Boisson de Chazournes, N. Bernasconi-Osterwalder (eds.), *Fresh Water and International Economic Law*, Oxford, 2005; H. F. M. W. van Rijswick, *Searching for the Right to Water in the Legislation and Case Law of the European Union*, in H. Smets (ed.), *Le droit à l'eau potable et à l'assainissement en Europe. Implementing the right to drinking water and sanitation in 17 European countries*, Paris, 2012, p. 119.

25 Sub-Commission on the Promotion and Protection of Human Rights, Decision 2004/107, 9 August 2004.

26 Special Rapporteur of the UN Commission on Human Rights, Sub-Commission on the Promotion and Protection of Human Rights, *Guidelines for the realization of the right to drinking water and sanitation*, UN Doc E/CN.4/Sub.2/2005/25, 11 July 2005, second recital of the Preamble and para. 1(1). The Sub-Commission adopted the above Guidelines and submitted them to the Human Rights Council for consideration and adoption. Resolution 2006/10, *Promotion of the Right to Drinking Water and Sanitation, Report of the Sub-Commission on the Promotion and Protection of Human Rights*, Fifty-eighth session, subsequently adopted by the Human Rights Council, UN Doc. A/HRC/Sub.1/58/L.11, 24 August 2006.

27 See the eighth recital of the Preamble, *Guidelines for the realization of the right to drinking water and sanitation*, para. 4(3) (n 26). The Special Rapporteur affirmed that in case of conflicts over the use of water, priority should be given to personal and domestic uses.

28 United Nations Development Programme, *Human Development Report 2006 – Beyond scarcity: Power, poverty and the global water crisis*, New York, 2006.

29 Human Rights Council, *Report of the United Nations High Commissioner for Human Rights on the scope and content of the relevant human rights obligations related to equitable ac-*

In 2008, the Human Rights Council appointed an Independent Expert on the issue of human rights obligations related to access to safe drinking water and sanitation[30] who was tasked, *inter alia*, with: carrying out thematic research; collecting good practices;[31] providing recommendations to governments, the United Nations and other stakeholders; submitting annual reports to the Human Rights Council and to the General Assembly;[32] and undertaking country visits.[33]

The highest acknowledgment of the right to water came in 2010, when it was explicitly recognized by both the General Assembly[34] and the Human Rights Council.[35]

In 2012, twenty years after the Rio Conference, States confirmed their commitment to the human right to water and sanitation at the Conference on Sustainable Development.[36]

In 2015, the General Assembly affirmed that the right to sanitation, while closely related to the human rights to safe drinking water, is a distinct right with specific features that warrant special treatment in order to address the challenges in its implementation.[37]

---

cess to safe drinking water and sanitation under international human rights instruments, UN Doc. A/HRC/6/3, 16 August 2007. The report was requested by the Human Right Council, Decision UN Doc. HRC/2/104, 27 November 2006.

[30] Human Rights Council, Res. 7/22, 28 March 2008, UN Doc. A/HRC/RES/7/22. Mr. Léo Heller is the current Special Rapporteur on the human rights to safe drinking water and sanitation. He was appointed in November 2014 and his mandate was renewed in 2016 for three more years (December 2017-December 2020). See Human Rights Council, Res. 33/10, 28 September 2016, UN Doc. A/HRC/RES/33/10, 5 October 2016. Catarina de Albuquerque was the former Special Rapporteur.

[31] Human Rights Council, *Report of the Special Rapporteur on the human right to safe drinking water and sanitation, Catarina de Albuquerque, Addendum, Compilation of good practices*, UN Doc. A/HRC/18/33/Add.1, 29 June 2011.

[32] Human Rights Council, 1 October 2009, UN Doc. A/HRC/12/8, 12 October 2009, para. 7.

[33] The Independent experts have visited various countries, including: Bangladesh, Botswana, Costa Rica, Egypt, El Salvador, India, Japan, Kenya, Kiribati, Mexico, Namibia, Portugal, Senegal, Slovenia, Tajikistan, Thailand, Tuvalu, United States of America, Uruguay.

[34] General Assembly, Res. 64/292, 28 July 2010, UN Doc. A/RES/64/292, 3 August 2010.

[35] Human Rights Council, Res. 15/9, 30 September 2010, UN Doc. A/HRC/RES/15/9, 6 October 2010. For an early comment on this resolution see A. Olmo, *Diritto all'acqua potabile e alle misure igienico-sanitarie*, in *Diritti Umani e Diritto Internazionale*, 2011, pp. 178-182. For further developments see: Human Rights Council, Res. 16/2, 24 March 2011, UN Doc. A/HRC/RES/16/2, 8 April 2011; Res. 18/1, 28 September 2011, UN Doc. A/HRC/RES/18/1, 12 October 2011; Res. 24/18 (n 22).

[36] *Report of the United Nations Conference on Sustainable Development*, Rio de Janeiro, 20-22 June 2012, UN Doc. A/CONF.216/16, para. 121: "*[w]e reaffirm our commitments regarding the human right to safe drinking water and sanitation, to be progressively realized for our populations with full respect for national sovereignty*".

[37] General Assembly, Res. 70/169, 17 December 2015, UN Doc. A/REA/70/169, 22 February 2016.

Finally, the 2030 Agenda for Sustainable Development, a set of 17 goals and numerous targets to be reached by 2030, included "*Goal 6 – Ensure availability and sustainable management of water and sanitation for all*", which requires States to achieve "*universal and equitable access to safe and affordable drinking water for all*".[38]

Against this (soft law) background, section 2 sets forth the legal basis of the human right to water. Following the line traced by General Comment No. 15 cited above, it argues in favor of the existence of a "*derivative*" right to water, where Articles 11 and 12 ICESCR are taken as its main treaty sources. In addition, the section seeks to assess the *status* of the right to water in general international law. Section 3 focuses on the content of the derivative human right to water under the ICESCR, as it posits that State parties to this treaty have agreed on the definition of the right to water given by the CESCR. Subsequently, the section seeks to shed light on the content of the customary right to water on the assumption that it may diverge from the right flowing from Articles 11 and 12 ICESCR. Section 4 deals with the nature and content of the obligations arising for States from the right to water and with their territorial extension. Before drawing conclusions in section 6, section 5 illustrates the decisions of international judges and quasi-judicial compliance mechanisms as a subsidiary means for the interpretation of the human right to water.

2. The legal basis of the human right to water

The human right to safe drinking water has been recently recognized and proclaimed.[39] However, neither the International Bill of Rights nor regional human rights conventions include any *explicit* provisions on the right to water and its customary nature is widely debated. This section aims at assessing the legal foundation of the right to water by looking at the sources of international law as listed in Article 38 of the Statute of the ICJ.

2.1. Treaty legal basis

International bodies and scholars have inferred the human right to water from a number of core treaty rights whose enjoyment is strictly related to access to water,[40]

---

[38] General Assembly, Res. 70/1, 25 September 2015, UN Doc. A/RES/70/1, 21 October 2015. See also the attached Declaration of States reaffirming their "*commitments regarding the human right to safe drinking water and sanitation*", para. 7.

[39] See, *inter alia*, General Assembly, Res 64/292 (n 34); Human Rights Council, Res. 15/9 (n 35).

[40] S.C. McCaffrey, *A Human Right to Water: Domestic and International Implications*, in *The Georgetown International Environmental Law Review*, 1992; I. T. Winkler, *The Human Right to Water. Significance, Legal Status and Implication for Water Allocation*, Oxford-Portland, 2012, pp.

such as the right to life, to an adequate standard of living conditions, to dignity, to food,[41] and to health.[42]

The CESCR has found the legal foundation of the right to water in the CESCR. Although General Comment No. 15, like all General Comments, is not legally binding for States parties to the ICESCR, it provides *authoritative* interpretation of the provisions enshrined in the Covenant and will be often referred to in this chapter as guidance for establishing the legal basis, as well as the content and the ensuing obligations of the right at issue.[43]

According to General Comment No. 15, the right to water is a right emanating from, and indispensable for, the realization of the right to an adequate standard of living enshrined in Article 11(1) ICESCR, which reads as follows:

> "[t]he States Parties to the present Covenant recognize the right of everyone to an adequate standard of living for himself and his family, including adequate food, clothing and housing, and to the continuous improvement of living conditions. The States Parties will take appropriate steps to ensure the realization of this right, recognizing to this effect the essential importance of international cooperation based on free consent".[44]

It is argued that the word "*including*" used in Article 11 is meant to indicate a non-exhaustive list of rights necessary for securing an adequate standard of living, also considering that water is among "*the most fundamental conditions for survival*".[45]

38-55; M. Dubuy, *Le Droit à l'Eau Potable et à l'Assainissement et le Droit International*, in *Revue Général de Droit International Public*, 2012, p. 292; E. Brown Weiss, *International Law for a Water-Scarce World*, Leiden-Boston, 2013, pp. 214-222; P. Thielbörger, *The Right(s) to Water. The Multi-Level Governance of a Unique Human Right*, Berlin-Heidelberg, 2014, pp. 117-120; D. Misiedjan, *Towards a Sustainable Human Right to Water. Supporting Vulnerable People and Protecting Water Resources*, Cambridge, 2019, pp. 54-81; R. B. Larson, *Water, Worship, and Wisdom: Indigenous Traditional Ecological Knowledge and the Human Right to Water*, in *ILSA Journal of International & Comparative Law*, 2012, pp. 43-67; R. B. Larson, *Holy Water and Human Rights: Indigenous Peoples Religious Rights Claims to Water Resources*, in *Arizona Journal of Environmental Law & Policy*, 2011, pp. 81-109.

[41] Winkler disagrees with the authors who consider the right to water as belonging to the right to food, as the right to food would only encompass drinking water and not water for other basic needs, such as personal hygiene. Winkler, p. 46 (n 40).

[42] E. Brown Weiss, *The Evolution of International Water Law*, in *Recueil des Cours de l'Académie de droit international de la Haye*, 2007, pp. 323-331.

[43] For an early comment on General Comment No. 15 see: P. Gleik, *Implementing the Human Right to Water*, in E. H. Riedel, P. Rothen (eds.), *The Human Right to Water*, Berlin, 2006, pp. 143-147.

[44] General Comment No. 15, para. 3 (n 24).

[45] *Ibid.* Tully has strongly criticised the reasoning of the Committee in General Comment No. 15 for having inferred the right to water from the right to an adequate standard of living. S. Tully, *A Human Right to Access Water? A Critique of General Comment No. 15*, in *Netherlands Quarter-*

In addition, the Committee pointed out that the right to water is strictly linked to the right to the highest attainable standard of health, protected under Article 12(1) ICESCR, and to the rights to adequate housing and food.[46] In this respect, the Committee interpreted the right to water as a "*derivate*" right, which can be embedded in a number of other fundamental rights, especially the right to health, since safe drinking water is essential to prevent infectious disease.[47]

Finally, the Committee held that the right to water "*should also be seen in conjunction with other rights enshrined in the International Bill of Human Rights, foremost amongst them the right to life and human dignity*".[48] While the Committee is only allowed to provide authoritative interpretation of the ICESCR, the reported statement goes further, including also civil and political rights among the rights to be taken into consideration when establishing the legal foundation of the right to water.

In this connection, several authors have inferred the right to water from civil and political rights, *in primis* the right to life enshrined in Article 6 of the International Covenant on Civil and Political Rights ("ICCPR").[49]

Winkler and Thielbörger suggest that the right to water may be understood as acceding to both civil and political as well as economic and social rights.[50] Winkler argues that the right to have access to a minimum amount of water belongs to the human right to life, enshrined in Article 6 ICCPR, while the right to enjoy a greater amount of water for personal and domestic uses belongs to economic and social rights, which can be subject to progressive realization.[51]

The present author shares the view that the right to water can be considered a facet of the right to life, as well as of the right to an adequate standard of living, the right to the highest attainable standard of health, and further rights according to the

---

ly of Human Rights, 2005, p. 37. According to him, by inferring new rights from art. 11 ICESCR, the Committee exercises excessive discretion, circumvents the procedure for amending the Covenant under art. 29 ICESCR and undermines the principle of legal certainty.

[46] General Comment No. 15, para. 3 (n 24).

[47] The same view was also held by the Commission for Human Rights who affirmed that "*access to a sufficient amount of safe, clean water for personal and domestic use and adequate nutrition is fundamental to the realization of the right of everyone to the enjoyment of the highest attainable standard of health*". Commission for Human Rights, Resolution on the right of everyone to the enjoyment of the highest attainable standard of physical and mental health, UN Doc. E/CN.4/RES/2005/24, 15 April 2005, para. 17.

[48] General Comment No. 15, para. 3 (n 24).

[49] International Covenant on Civil and Political Rights adopted and opened for signature, ratification and accession by General Assembly resolution 2200A (XXI) of 16 December 1966, entry into force 23 March 1976, art. 6. See, K. Bourquain, *Freshwater Access from a Human Rights Perspective. A Challenge to International Water and Human Rights Law*, Boston, 2008, pp. 125-134; Winkler, pp. 50-55 (n 40); Brown Weiss, pp. 214-222 (n 40); Thielbörger, pp. 117-120 (n 40); P. Thielbörger, *Re-Conceptualizing the Human Rights to Water: A Pledge for a Hybrid Approach*, in *Human Rights Law Review*, 2015, pp. 228-234; Misiedjan, pp. 56-59 (n 40).

[50] Winkler, pp. 38-55 (n 40); Thielbörger, pp. 117-120 (n 40).

[51] Winkler, p. 139 (n 40).

circumstances.[52] Undoubtedly, lack of fresh water for human consumption is likely to endanger human survival, and the right to life is an inherent right to be protected through positive efforts,[53] including measures aimed at providing at least a minimum amount of water for the sake of survival. However, access to a safe and sufficient amount of fresh water is also necessary to prevent diseases that, even if not life threatening, can endanger human health. In this respect, the right to water is a precondition of the right to health. Furthermore, a sufficient amount of accessible and affordable water is needed for personal and domestic hygienic requirements, which fall under the purview of the right to an adequate standard of living.

We cannot but conclude that the right to water finds its legal basis in treaty law in so far as access to safe water in sufficient quantity is necessary to fulfill a number of fundamental rights entrenched in existing international human rights treaty law, such as the right to an adequate standard of living, the right to health, the right to food or the right to life.

However, it follows from this premise that if the right to water is understood as instrumental to the realization of relevant rights in a specific context, it risks being recognized only partially and with different content in relation to the given circumstances. For instance, the right to life only encompasses drinking water necessary for human survival and not water for other basic needs, such as personal hygiene. The same holds true with respect to the right to food. In this connection, Cavallo states:

> "[i]f the right to water is considered to derive from different human rights, this could lead to the guarantee of different quantities of water. For instance, one quantity of water is necessary to protect the right to life, while another quantity for a life with dignity, and another quantity for the right to food, and yet another quantity for the right to health".[54]

The recognition of the right to water as an independent right, the author argues, "*would give more clarity and consistency to states' obligations*".[55]

Along the same line of thought, Weiss argues that:

> "[t]he recognition of the right to water as an independent and freestanding right may be the most potent outcome (…) An independent right to water would not be limited by the objectives of its parent right, but could accommodate those uses and other uses".[56]

---

[52] Thielbörger, pp. 232-234 (n 49); Misiedjan, pp. 54-72 (n 40).

[53] Human Rights Committee, General Comment No 6: art. 6 (Right to Life), 30 April 1982.

[54] J. Murillo Chávarro, *The Human Right to Water. A Legal Comparative Perspective at the International, Regional and Domestic Level*, Cambridge, 2015, p. 53.

[55] *Ibid.*, p. 54.

[56] Brown Weiss, p. 223 (n 40).

However, the proposition of an existing independent right to water cannot be shared for the reasons explained in the following sub-section.

2.1.1. The right to water as a derivative right

The Committee on Economic Social and Cultural Rights was ambiguous in its General Comment No. 15 as to the nature of the right to water and, more specifically, as to whether it was to be intended as a derivative or a self-standing right. The professed connection with the rights to the highest attainable standard of health, to adequate housing and food,[57] and to life and human dignity[58] speaks in favor of a derivative right, as derivative rights are the offspring of their "mother" rights. On the contrary, the Committee, by referring to the right to water as both "*emanating from*" and "*indispensable for*" the fulfillment of the right to an adequate standard of living, seems to describe a self-standing right, separable from the "mother" right.[59] While the right to water is a *conditio sine qua non* for the attainment of an adequate standard of living ("*indispensable for*"), its scope would be independent of the latter right by way of emanation.

Initially, the General Assembly also referred to the right to water as an independent right "*essential for the full enjoyment of life and all human rights*".[60]

However useful it would be to proclaim an independent right to water, neither General Comment No. 15 nor General Assembly resolution No. 64/292 have explained the legal basis of this alleged free-standing right.

As for General Comment No. 15, inferring an independent right from another treaty right (i.e. the right to an adequate standard of living) may amount to circumventing States' consent. While interpreting a treaty provisions extensively, for instance by resorting to teleological or evolutionary interpretation, is in line with the Committee's mandate, it would exceed this mandate to consider States bound by an independent rule not explicitly mentioned by the same treaty.

With regard to General Assembly resolution No. 64/292, a number of States pointed out in the explanations of their vote that they considered the right to water as a component of the right to an adequate standard of living,[61] of the right to the enjoyment of the highest attainable standard of health,[62] and of the right to

---

[57] General Comment No. 15, para. 3 (n 24).

[58] General Comment No. 15, para. 3 (n 24).

[59] See also E. B. Bluemel, *The Implications of Formulating a Human Right to Water,* in *Ecology Law Quarterly*, 2004, pp. 968-972. According to her, General Comment No. 15 does recognize the human right to water as an independent human right.

[60] General Assembly, Res. 64/292, para. 1 (n 34).

[61] General Assembly, Sixty-fourth session, 108th plenary meeting, 28 July 2010, UN Doc. A/64/PV.108, explanation of vote by Germany (p. 6); Spain (p. 7); Hungary (p. 7); Norway (p. 10); United Kingdom (p 12); Mexico (16).

[62] *Ibid.*, Norway (p. 10) p. 16, Mexico (16); Venezuela (p. 20).

life.[63] Egypt made it clear that it voted in favor of the resolution "*based on the understanding that it does not create new rights or sub-categories of human rights different from those stipulated in the internationally agreed human rights instruments*".[64] The United Kingdom abstained, as it denied that at the time there was "*sufficient legal basis under international law to either declare or recognize water or sanitation as free-standing human rights*".[65]

It is noteworthy that, only a few months later, the Human Rights Council took a different stand, emphasizing the nature of the right to water as a "*derivative*" right.[66]

Moreover, the same General Assembly overturned its previous position and in subsequent resolutions expressly stated that the rights to water and sanitation are "*derived from the right to an adequate standard of living and are inextricably related to the right to the highest attainable standard of physical and mental health, as well as to the right to life and human dignity*".[67]

States parties to the ICESCR, which are required to report to the CESCR on the measures adopted to implement the ICESCR, have started to provide information about the steps undertaken towards the progressive realization of the human right to water under the purview of the right to an adequate standard of living conditions.[68]

---

[63] *Ibid.*, Norway (p. 10), Colombia (p. 14); Venezuela (p. 20).

[64] *Ibid.*, Egypt (p. 10).

[65] *Ibid.*, United Kingdom (p. 12).

[66] Human Rights Council, Res. 15/9, para. 3 (n 35). It is held that the right to water "*is derived from the right to an adequate standard of living and inextricably related to the right to the highest attainable standard of physical and mental health, as well as the right to life and human dignity*".

[67] General Assembly, Res. 72/178, 19 December 2017, UN Doc. A/RES/72/178, 29 January 2018.

[68] See recently: ECOSOC, *Initial Report Submitted by Cabo Verde under articles 16 and 17 of the Covenant, due in 1995*, date received: 6 November 2017, UN Doc. E/C.12/CPV/1, 27 December 2017, paras. 178-184; ECOSOC, *Consideration of reports submitted by States parties under Articles 16 and 17 of the International Covenant on Economic, Social and Cultural Rights*, Fifth periodic reports of States parties due in 2015, Mauritius, date received: 19 July 2017, Un. Doc. E/C.12/MUS/5, 13 September 2017, paras. 110-112; ECOSOC, *Sixth periodic report submitted by Denmark under articles 16 and 17 of the Covenant, due in 2018*, date received: 31 May 2018, UN. Doc. E/C.12/DNK/6, 15 November 2018, para. 170; ECOSOC, *Fourth periodic report submitted by Israel under Articles 16 and 17 of the Covenant, due in 2016*, date received: 30 July 2018, UN Doc. E/C.12/ISR/4, 14 January 2019, paras. 195-204; ECOSOC, *Third periodic report submitted by Senegal under Articles 16 and 17 of the Covenant, due in 2003*, date received: 9 November 2018, UN Doc. E/C.12/SEN/3, 27 November 2018, paras. 140-151; ECOSOC, *Fourth periodic report submitted by Switzerland under Articles 16 and 17 of the Covenant, due in 2015*, date received: 21 February 2018, UN Doc. E.C.12/CHE/4, 26 June 2018, para. 267; ECOSOC, *Third periodic report submitted by Benin under Articles 16 and 17 of the Covenant, due in 2010*, date received: 15 November 2018, UN Doc. E/C.12/BEN/3, 21 November 2018, paras. 53-57; ECOSOC, *Fourth periodic report submitted by Azerbaijan under Articles 16 and 17 of the Cove-*

The theoretical underpinning and the practical reasons illustrated above argue in favor of admitting the derivative nature of the right to water. Considering the right to water as a derivative right implies that States are legally bound to respect it each time it impinges upon the enjoyment of other rights enshrined in a treaty or a customary norm. Unfortunately, this indirect protection remains confined within the scope of the specific provisions under consideration.

Against this conclusion, Thielbörger suggests an integrated approach, under which the right to water is "*a synthesis of different rights* [the right to life, to the highest attainable standard of health and to adequate living conditions], *thereby creating a new derivative right*".[69] The author posits that this hybrid right is made up of different layers, one connected to the availability of water and deriving from the right to life, another linked to the quality of water and stemming from the right to health, and the third related to the accessibility of water and drawing from the right to adequate standard of living conditions.

While this theory would overcome the difficulties of singling out a clear and univocal content for the right to water, it creates a new (independent) right made of various layers borrowed from different rights, whose full content would not be enforceable in all venues. For instance, the lack of affordability of water services could not be claimed before the Human Rights Committee, as this aspect falls outside the purview of the right to life.

I contend that the shortcomings connected to the "*derivative*" nature of the right to water would be overcome only if a legal foundation establishing an independent right was found in general international law. Against this background, the following section deals with the existence of a customary human right to water.

2.2. The emergence of a customary human right to water

Having concluded in favor of the derivative *status* of the right to water under both the International Covenant on Economic, Social and Cultural Rights and the International Covenant on Civil and Political Rights, this section explores the *status* (if any) of the right to water in general international law. One may question the practical relevance of this exercise, given that the right to water has already been acknowledged, at least, as a right protected under the ICESCR, which counts 169 State parties, and under the ICCPR, that counts 172 State parties.

However, the existence of a customary human right to water does matter for a number of reasons. In the first place, its content would be the same in any circum-

nant, due in 2018, date received: 27 December 2018, UN Doc. E/C.12/AZE/4, 29 January 2019, para. 144; ECOSOC, *Third periodic report submitted by Bosnia and Herzegovina under Articles 16 and 17 of the Covenant, due in 2018*, date received: 11 March 2019, UN Doc. E/C.12/BIH/3, 24 April 2019, paras. 172-173. For previous practice, see Murillo Chávarro, pp. 84-93 (n 54).

[69] Thielbörger, p. 115 (n 40).

stance, while deriving the right to water from other treaty rights entails that its boundaries are always different in connection with the embedding right taken into consideration in any given case.

Moreover, the right to water would also bind those States that are not parties to the ICESCR or the ICCPR.

Finally, borrowing an argument from Simma and Alston, a number of national constitutions incorporate customary international law in national law automatically (without the need for express law, the so-called incorporation doctrine), and with higher rank than domestic law.[70] Accordingly, conflicting domestic legislations cannot derogate from customary international law. On the contrary, national constitutions often provide that treaty law become part of national law with the same rank of domestic statutes, which have the potential to derogate from conflicting international treaty rules. In this perspective, a customary right to water would be granted higher rank in those legal systems incorporating customary rules with a rank higher than domestic legislations and, accordingly, would prevail over domestic statutes.

Recently, the emergence of a *customary* human right to water under international law has started to be debated and has gathered much attention from scholars maintaining different and even opposing views. While some authors have acknowledged the customary *status* of the right to water,[71] others have denied it,[72] and still others have taken a cautious approach.[73]

---

[70] B. Simma, P. Alston, *The Sources of Human Rights Law: Custom, Jus Cogens, and General Principles*, in *Australian Year Book of International Law*, 1988, pp. 85-86.

[71] R. Bates, *The Road to the Well: An Evaluation of the Customary Right to Water*, in *Review of European Community & International Environmental Law*, 2010, pp. 282-293; C. Cinelli, *Gli Obblighi Positivi degli Stati in Materia di Investimenti Stranieri e la Privatizzazione del 'Nuovo' Diritto Umano all'Acqua*, in A. Di Stefano e R. Sapienza (eds.), *La Tutela dei Diritti Umani e il Diritto Internazionale*, Naples, 2011; H. Smets, *Le droit de l'homme à l'eau et à l'assainissement est finalment reconnu*, in *Revue Juridique de l'Environnement*, 2011, pp. 79-89; G. Aguilar Cavallo, *The Human Right to Water and Sanitation: Going Beyond Corporate Social Responsibility*, in *Utrecht Journal of International and European Law*, 2013, pp. 39-64; S. De Vido, *The Right to Water as an International Customary Norm: The Implications in Climate Change Adaptation Measures*, in *Carbon and Climate Law Review*, 2012, pp. 224-225; Thielbörger, pp. 234-243 (n 49); L.-Y. Huang, *Not Just Another Drop in the Human Rights Bucket: The Legal Significance of a Codified Human Right to Water*, in *Florida Journal of International Law*, 2008, the author calls for a *jus cogens status* for the right to water, pp. 364-366.

[72] See, *inter alia*, Tully, p. 43 (n 45); Brown Weiss, p. 310 (n 42); Brown Weiss, p. 214 (n 40); O. McIntyre, *The human right to water as a creature of global administrative law*, in *Water International*, 2012, online on http://www.iwra.org; Misiedjan, p. 81 (n 40); P. Thielbörger, *Re-Conceptualizing the Human Right to water: A Pledge for a Hybrid Approach*, in *Human Rights Law Review*, 2015, pp. 236-243; F. M. Palombino, *Il diritto all'acqua. Una prospettiva internazionalistica*, Florence, 2017, p. 71; S. C. McCaffrey, *The Human Right to Water: A False Promise?*, in *University of the Pacific Law Review*, 2016, p. 227.

[73] F. Marrella, *On the Changing Structure of International Investment Law: The Human Right to Water and ICSID Arbitration*, in *International Community Law Review*, 2010, pp. 337-338; B.

Those who deny the customary *status* of the right to water argue that, for such a right to exist, States must have corresponding legal duties. Since implementing the human right to water requires legal and technical expertise, as well as significant financial resources beyond the reach of most developing countries,[74] these kinds of obligations cannot be accomplished.[75] For instance, Bluemel disputes the recognition of an independent right to water in terms of financial costs to be borne by States. In the short run, the author suggests referring to the concept of water needs with the aim of progressively reaching the full recognition of water rights.[76]

The criticism regarding the financial burdens arising from the right to water is not persuasive. First, in general terms, the same criticism might be directed against all economic, social and cultural rights and would amount to denying the customary nature of most of them. On the contrary, it is acknowledged that States are not obliged to implement the full content of these rights immediately, but to take steps towards their full realization.[77]

In addition, if we accept the derivative nature of the right to water, financial difficulties would in any case be faced by most States parties to the 1966 International Covenants.

Among the scholars who acknowledge the growing consensus on the right to water, but still consider the corresponding practice insufficient, some have referred to the right to water as customary law "*in statu nascendi*",[78] while others deem it to be a "*right of unique* status", that is a right whose *status* is posited *"somewhere between that of a derivative right and an independent right"*.[79]

H. Thompson Jr., *Water as a Public Commodity*, in *Marquette Law Review*, 2011, pp. 33-34; Chávarro maintains that, while the right to water has been "*unmistakably recognised at the international level (...), there is no consensus regarding the manner in which this right is recognised*", whether as an independent or a derivative right. Murillo Chávarro, pp. 124-125 (n 54); F. Staiano, La *progressiva emersione di un diritto umano e fondamentale all'acqua in sistemi di diritto internazionale e costituzionale: principi generali e prospettive di implementazione*, in *Federalismi.it*, 2013.

[74] S. C. McCaffrey, K. J. Neville, *Small Capacity and Big Responsibilities: Financial and Legal Implication of a Human Right to Water for Developing Countries*, in *The Georgetown International Environmental Law Review*, 2008.

[75] Salman, pp. 78-80 (n 24).

[76] Bluemel, pp. 1004-1005 (n 59). In this connection, see also D. Ziganshina, *Rethinking the Concept of the Human Right to Water*, in *Santa Clara Journal of International Law*, 2008, pp. 113-128.

[77] McCaffrey, p. 114 (n 24); Gleick, pp.146-147 (n 43).

[78] Winkler, p. 277 (n 40); G. Aguilar Cavallo, *The Human Right to Water and Sanitation: From Political Commitments to Customary Rule*, in *Pace International Law Review Online Companion*, 2012, p. 200; Misiedjan, p. 80 (n 40).

[79] A. Cahill-Ripley, *The Human Right to Water – A Right of Unique Status: The Legal Status and The Normative Content of the Right to Water*, in *International Journal of Human Rights*, 2005, p. 391. According to Piccone, the *status* of the right to water is unclear. In fact "*[t]he dynamism of soft law sources has produced a spill-over of the right to water from the ICESCR context to custom-*

Whether or not a customary human right to water exists is to be ascertained "*as evidence of a general practice accepted as law*".[80] The double requirement of *diuturnitas* and *opinio juris* has been reiterated by the International Law Commission ("ILC") in its work on the identification of customary international law,[81] is shared by the majority of scholars,[82] and by international courts and tribunals.[83]

This traditional approach on how custom is created has been challenged over

---

ary law but the transition is not yet concluded. This situation defines the right to water as a right of unique status, somewhere between a derivative and an independent right". A. Piccone, *The right to safe drinking water for consumption and preparation of foodstuffs*, in A. M. G. Lupone, C. Ricci, A. Santini (eds.), *The right to safe food towards a global governance*, Turin, 2013, pp. 78-79. See, also, Bates, pp. 283-293 (n 71).

[80] Statute of the International Court of Justice, San Francisco, 26 June 1945, art. 38(1)(*b*). The issue of the formation and identification of customary international law is under consideration by the International Law Commission (ILC). In 2011, at its sixty-third session, the ILC decided to include the topic "*Formation and evidence of customary international law*" in its long-term programme of work. See, Report of the ILC, Sixty-third session, 26 April-3 June and 4 July-12 August 2011, New York, UN Doc. A/66/10, paras. 365-367. At its sixty-fourth session (2012), the ILC included the topic in its current programme of work and appointed Sir Michael Wood as Special Rapporteur. See, Report of the ILC, Sixty-fourth session, 7 May-1 June and 2 July-3 August 2012, New York, UN Doc. A/67/10, para. 19. At its sixty-fourth session (2012), the ILC also requested that the Secretariat prepare a memorandum identifying elements in the previous work of the Commission that could be particularly relevant to the topic. See Memorandum by the Secretariat, UN Doc. A/CN.4/659, 14 March 2013. At its sixty-fifth session, in 2013, the Commission decided to change the title of the topic to "*Identification of customary international law*". The work of the ILC on the subject is in progress. See, *Identification of Customary International Law, Text of the draft conclusions as adopted by the Drafting Committee on second reading*, seventieth session, New York, 30 April-1 June and Geneva, 2 July-10 August 2018, UN Doc. A/CN.4/L.908, 17 May 2018.

[81] ILC, *Identification of Customary International Law* (n 80), Conclusion 2 – Two constituent elements: "*[t]o determine the existence and content of a rule of customary international law, it is necessary to ascertain whether there is a general practice that is accepted as law (*opinio juris*)*".

[82] B. Conforti, *Diritto Internazionale*, Naples, 2018, p. 40; N. Ronzitti, *Introduzione al Diritto Internazionale*, Turin, 2016, pp. 172-173; C. Focarelli, *Trattato di Diritto Internazionale*, Turin, 2015, pp. 263-265; T. Treves, *Diritto Internazionale. Problemi Fondamentali*, Milan, 2005, pp. 225-226; P. Dumberry, *The Formation and Identification of Rules of Customary International law in International Investment Law*, Cambridge, 2016, p. 301; M. Dixon, *Textbook on International Law*, Oxford, 2013, pp. 32-38; M. N. Shaw, *International Law*, Cambridge, 2017, p. 55.

[83] ICJ, *North Sea Continental Shelf, Federal Republic of Germany v. Denmark; Federal Republic of Germany v. Netherlands*, Judgment, 20 February 1969, para. 77; *Jurisdictional Immunities of the State, Germany v. Italy*, Judgment, 3 February 2012, para. 55; *Case concerning the Continental Shelf, Libyan Arab Jamahiriya v. Malta*, Judgment, 3 June 1985, para. 27; *Legality of the Threat or Use of Nuclear Weapons*, Advisory Opinion, 8 July 1996, para. 64; *Case Concerning Military and Paramilitary Activities In and Against Nicaragua, Nicaragua v. United States of America*, Judgment, 27 June 1986, para. 183. It is noteworthy that the *Nicaragua case* has been sharply criticized for having *de facto* walked away from the traditional theory of customary international law, having grounded the existence of a rule on non-intervention on UN resolutions. See A. D'Amato, *Trashing Customary International Law*, in *American Journal of International Law*, 1987, pp. 101-105.

the years by a number of scholars, who have focused alternatively on the prevalence of practice or of *opinio juris*,[84] and also by international tribunals.[85] Some authors have even suggested various combination of the two elements of customary international law, accepting the possibility to lower the threshold necessary for ascertaining a consistent and uniform *usus* when *opinion juris* is well established.[86]

In the field of human rights law, the customary nature of human rights norms and the role of the *opinio juris* in their formation have been widely debated.[87] Some have argued that the subjective element should weight more in this field of international law as it touches upon fundamental moral issues.[88]

According to Lepard, States' practice "*is not by itself an essential independent requirement for recognition of a norm as customary law*" but only "*important evi-*

---

[84] A. E. Roberts, *Traditional and Modern Approaches to Customary International Law: A Reconciliation*, in *The American Journal of International Law*, 2001, pp. 757-791; R. B. Baker, *Customary International Law in the 21st Century: Old Challenges and New Debates*, in *European Journal of International Law*, 2010, pp. 173-204; J. d'Aspremont, *Customary International Law as a Dance Floor: Part II*, in *ejiltalk.org*, 2014; B. Cheng, *United Resolutions on Outer Space: 'Instant' International Customary Law?*, in *Indian Journal of International Law*, 1965, pp. 23-48; B. Cheng, *The Future of General State Practice in a Divided World*, in R. St. J. Macdonald, D. M. Johnston (eds.), *The Structure and Process of International Law*, The Hague, 1983, p. 513, pp. 531-532.

[85] The International Criminal Tribunal for the former Yugoslavia (ICTY) has maintained the existence of customary humanitarian norms even where State practice was inconsistent or scant, by attaching a greater role to *opinio juris*. ICTY Trial Chamber, *Prosecutor v. Kupreškić*, ICTY case No. IT-95-16-T, 14 January 2000, para. 527; ICTY Appeals Chamber, *Prosecutor v. Tadić*, ICTY case No. IT-94-1, Decision on the Defence Motion for Interlocutory Appeal on Jurisdiction, 2 October 1995, para. 99. The International Court of Justice has inferred obligations for States non-parties to humanitarian conventions based on the premise that some rules of these conventions are "*so fundamental to the respect of the human person and 'elementary considerations of humanity'* (…)", that they are "*to be observed by all States whether or not they have ratified the conventions that contain them*". ICJ, *Legal Consequences of the Construction of a Wall in the Occupied Palestinian Territory*, Advisory Opinion, 9 July 2004, para. 157. The International Court of Justice recalls here a passage of its Advisory Opinion on the *Legality of the Threat or Use of Nuclear Weapons*, para. 79. See P. De Sena, *Prassi, consuetudine e principi nel campo dei diritti dell'uomo. Riflessioni internazionalistiche*, in *Ragion pratica*, 2014, pp. 511-539.

[86] F. L. Kirgis, *Custom on a Sliding Scale*, in *American Journal of International Law*, 1987, pp. 146-151; Roberts, pp. 757-791 (n 84).

[87] B. Simma, P. Alston, *The Source of Human Rights Law: Custom, Jus Cogens, and General Principles*, in *Australian Year Book of International Law*, 1989, pp. 89-90; A. D'Amato, *Human Rights as Part of Customary International Law: A Plea for Change of Paradigms*, in *Georgia Journal of International & Comparative Law*, 1995, pp. 47-98; J. J. Paust, *The Complex Nature, Sources and Evidences of Customary Human Rights*, in *Georgia Journal of International & Comparative Law*, 1996, pp. 147-164; R. B. Lillich, *The Growing Importance of Customary International Human Rights Law*, in *Georgia Journal of International & Comparative Law*, 1995, pp. 1-30.

[88] B. D. Lepard, *Toward a New Theory of Customary International Human Rights Law*, in B. D. Lepard (ed.), *Reexamining Customary International Law*, Cambridge, 2017, p. 233 ff.; A. W. Shavers, *Using Customary International law to Improve Women's Lives*, in B. D. Lepard (ed.), *Reexamining Customary International Law*, Cambridge, 2017, p. 266 ff.

dence" of *opinio juris.*[89] The latter is defined as the States' belief that a norm should be law instead of their belief that a norm is already law.[90] Moreover, in assessing States' belief that a norm is binding, the interpreter should evaluate whether and to what extent such norm "*is consistent with certain fundamental ethical principles in contemporary international law*".[91] Finally, this theory of customary international law claims to articulate a role for ethics – where traditional doctrine is said to have failed – and to have solved "*some of serious problems with recognizing many human rights standards as customary law*".[92]

The present author believes that these new theories risk transforming moral aspiration in "*fake custom*",[93] incapable of generating any State commitments or, even less, State compliance. I agree with the conclusion of Simma and Alston that by attaching a prominent role to *opinio juris* over *usus* the risk is turning the process of creation of customary rules into a rhetorical exercise.[94] *Extra*-legal factors risk influencing legal assessment, with little gain, as the practice of States would not be overturned by scholars' theories on a given customary rule.

As for the contended need to introduce ethical reasoning into the determination of customary international law,[95] this author finds that a full and convincing demonstration that what is *morally* binding is, or should be, *legally* binding for this sole reason, has not been provided. Indeed, it is doubted that this assumption would offer concrete benefit, beyond responding to scholars and judges' ethical ambitions, as, once again, the principle of effectiveness is not taken in due consideration.

What can be conceded to this theory is that fundamental ethical principles may influence States' belief of what is legally binding and, accordingly, induce States to

---

[89] Lepard, pp. 252-253 (n 88).

[90] Lepard states: "*a rule or principle ought to be considered customary law if states generally believe that it is desirable, now or in the future, to make the rule or principle legally authoritative for all members of the global community of states*". *Ibid.*, p. 252.

[91] *Ibid.*

[92] *Ibid.*, p. 253.

[93] I borrow this expression from Tesón, who defines fake custom as "*the practice of claiming customary status for rules notwithstanding the fact that these rules cannot be traced back to any plausible rule of recognition*". F. R. Tesón, *Fake Custom*, in B. D. Lepard (ed.), *Reexamining Customary International Law*, Cambridge, 2017, p. 86.

[94] Simma, Alston, pp. 89-90 (n 87).

[95] Tesón, p. 104 (n 93) ("*So I do not suggest that lawyers should avoid value choices. I suggest, instead, that lawyers and courts should acknowledge that often diplomatic history [in the form of state practice] is normatively indeterminate and that rules should be defended on* their merits, *and not by feigning positivistic support for them*") and pp. 109-110 ("*Rejecting fake custom does not mean adopting the positivistic thesis of the separation between law and morality. On the contrary, an honest account of international obligation allows us to recognize norms that do not meet the test for custom but are nonetheless indispensable to a minimally justified international order and, for that reason, legally binding even in the absence of positivist support*").

undertake practices from a sense of legal right or obligation. In other words, while both elements remain essential to shape customary international law, States' belief of what is legally due in the field of international human rights law may be influenced by moral belief. This would also explain the language used by international tribunals when identifying specific customary international law, such as the prohibition of genocide. [96]

Along the same line of reasoning, the present author is not persuaded by the "*reflective interpretive approach*" to customary international law of Roberts, according to whom when State practice (relevant for the formation of customary rules) is not sufficiently clear (uniform and widespread) and may give rise to different possible interpretations, this practice must be read in line with the supporting *opinio juris.* [97] Needless to say, this exercise would allow interpreters to infer the existence of a customary rule more easily by reducing the need to rely on consistent, uniform and general practice.

Building on Roberts' theory, Thielbörger argued that in the case of the right to water, despite the absence of a sufficiently uniform State practice, "*the strong* opinio juris *that states have over the last years repeatedly expressed*" allows one to interpret the non-clear practice in favor of the recognition of the customary nature of the right to water. [98]

Once again, the present author is not persuaded to abandon the traditional view that State practice must be general, namely "*sufficient widespread and representative, as well as consistent*", for a customary international law to come into existence. [99] If practice is not widespread and uniform across States, *opinio juris* cannot fill this gap in order to infer a given customary right because the risk is, once again, to assume the existence of a "*customary*" norm that is not sufficiently established in the international legal order and that, for this reason, will not be complied with by States. This in the end is the position of the ICJ and of the ILC, in addition to that of what appears to be the prevailing doctrine.

In light of the above considerations, the present section will follow the traditional double requirement approach, as I share the view that both elements are essential in equal manner. State practice is relevant for ensuring the effectiveness of the assumed customary rule, so as not to infer non-existing rules, however morally desira-

---

[96] ICJ, *Reservations to the Convention on the Prevention and Punishment of the Crime of Genocide*, Advisory Opinion, 28 May 1951. According to the ICJ, the object of this Convention was "*to confirm and endorse the most elementary principles of morality*", p. 12. This passage was then quoted by the ICJ in the 2015 judgment; *Application of the Convention on the Prevention and Punishment of the Crime of Genocide, Croatia v. Serbia*, Judgment, 3 February 2015, para. 84.

[97] Roberts, pp. 757-791 (n 84).

[98] Thielbörger, p. 243 (n 49).

[99] ILC, *Identification of Customary International Law* (n 80), Conclusion 8 – The practice must be general.

ble they are. *Opinio juris* allows interpreters to avoid confusing legal norms with behaviour reiterated as a matter of courtesy or social and moral requirements.[100] Accordingly, the following sub-sections will investigate the existence of a customary right to water by looking to State practice as well as to State *opinio juris*.

2.2.1. State practice

As for evidence of the constitutive elements of international customs, according to international tribunals' *dicta,*[101] authoritative scholars' writings,[102] and the work of the ILC,[103] State practice can be found, *inter alia*, in treaties and States' conduct in connection with treaties;[104] States' statements (including, policy statements, press releases, the opinions of governmental legal advisers, official manuals on legal questions, codes and guidelines, comments by governments on ILC drafts and corresponding commentaries, pleading by States involved in international litigations),[105] diplomatic acts and correspondence;[106] States' conduct within international organizations or conferences,[107] such as declarations and statements in connection with resolutions adopted by international organizations,[108] in particular, declarations at the General Assembly, or during intergovernmental conferences, i.e. votes, explanations given to justify their votes, interpretative declarations, reservations, the work of the ILC;[109] legislative and administrative acts,[110] decisions of national courts;[111] practice of the executive branch (decisions; orders to military forces).

---

[100] Focarelli, p. 265 (n 82).

[101] ICJ, *Fisheries Case, United Kingdom v. Norway*, Judgement, 18 December 1951; *North Sea Continental Shelf*, paras. 70-78 (n 83); *Case Concerning Military and Paramilitary activities in and against Nicaragua*, paras. 182-185 (n 83); *Legality of the Threat or Use of Nuclear Weapons*, paras. 64-73 (n 83); *Jurisdictional Immunities of the State*, para. 55 (n 83).

[102] See, among others, J. Kammerhofer, *Uncertainty in the Formal Sources of International Law: Customary International Law and Some of Its Problems*, in *European Journal of International Law*, 2004, pp. 523-553; T. Treves, *Customary International Law*, in *Max Planck Encyclopaedia of Public International Law*, 2006, online at: www.mpepil.com,; C. Focarelli, *Diritto Internazionale I. Il sistema degli Stati e i valori comuni dell'umanità*, Padua, 2012; Shaw, pp. 60-62 (n 82).

[103] ILC, *Identification of Customary International Law* (n 80), Conclusion 6 – Forms of practice.

[104] *Ibid.*

[105] ICJ, *Jurisdictional Immunities of the State*, para. 55 (n 83).

[106] ILC, *Identification of Customary International Law* (n 80), Conclusion 6 – Forms of practice.

[107] *Ibid.*

[108] T. Treves, para. 43 (n 102).

[109] ICJ, *Jurisdictional Immunities of the State*, para. 55 (n 83).

[110] ILC, *Identification of Customary International Law* (n 80), Conclusion 6 – Forms of practice.

[111] ICJ, *Case concerning the Arrest Warrant of 11 April 2000, Democratic Republic of Congo v. Belgium*, Judgment, 14 February 2002, para. 58; *Jurisdictional Immunities of the State*, para. 77 (n 83); ILC, *Identification of Customary International Law* (n 80), Conclusion 6 – Forms of practice.

Practice of international organizations cannot be equated to the practice of the States parties to the organization. However, it is relevant for providing evidence of the existence of customary rules [112] and in certain cases it can also "*contributes to the formation, or expression, of rules of customary international law*". [113]

The following sub-sections will scrutinize State practice with respect to the right to water. It will look at States' participation in international and regional agreements recognizing the right at issue, at the judgments of national courts faced with a claim concerning the right to water, at the legislation of those States which have enacted the right to water, at the claims of States acting for the protection of such a right before arbitral and judicial tribunals, at the statements States made in the context of the adoption of international resolutions, recommendations and declarations on the right to water. [114]

2.2.1.1. International treaties

As already pointed out, no international human rights treaty recognizes access to safe drinking water and sanitation as an independent human right. The absence of any reference to water within the International Bill of Rights may be related to the lack of concern for water resources, which were not perceived as scarce at the time when the Bill was drafted.

In the following years, the growing scarcity of water has led to greater awareness of its invaluable role. The right to water has thus been explicitly acknowledged in a number of treaties with respect to the most vulnerable and disadvantaged people, such as women, children and persons with disabilities. These agreements, taken together, may be regarded as practice subsequent to the International Covenants, which has interpretative value as a supplementary means of interpretation of the ICESCR under Article 32 of the Vienna Convention on the Law of Treaties ("VCLT"). This subsequent practice can thus provide further guidance in establishing the meaning of the treaty, but it does not fall under Article 31(*a*)(*b*) VCLT, as it does not establish an agreement of the Parties and does not regard the application of the treaty. [115]

---

[112] ICJ, *Legality of the Threat or use of Nuclear Weapons*, para. 70 (n 83); Focarelli, pp. 267-268 (n 82); Dumberry, p. 258 and pp. 261-267 (n 82).

[113] ILC, *Identification of Customary International Law* (n 80), Conclusion 4.2 – Requirement of practice and Conclusion 12.2 – Resolution of international organizations and intergovernmental conferences.

[114] ICJ, *Jurisdictional Immunities of the State,* para. 55 (n 83).

[115] ILC, Report, seventieth session, 30 April-1 June and 2 July-10 August 2018, UN Doc. A/73/10, Chapter IV, *Subsequent Agreements and Subsequent Practice in Relation to Interpretation of Treaties*, Draft Conclusions and Commentaries adopted on second reading, Commentary to Conclusion 4. Definition of subsequent agreement and subsequent practice, p. 30, para. 12; O. Dörr, *Article 32, Supplementary means of Interpretation*, in O. Dörr, K. Schmalenbach (eds.), *Vienna Convention on the Law of Treaties. A Commentary*, 2018, p. 627, para. 27.

In detail, the Convention on the Elimination of All Forms of Discrimination Against Women refers to the human right to water of rural women. Article 14(2)(*h*) requires States parties to take all appropriate measures to eliminate discrimination against women in rural areas and to ensure their enjoyment of adequate living conditions in relation to, *inter alia*, water supply. As mentioned in the first chapter, problem of access to safe drinking water and sanitation can increase inequality, notably between men and women, as limited access to water tends to disproportionately affect women's health, physical and psychological integrity, privacy and access to education. For instance, as collecting and carrying water is a woman's burden in most developing countries, a gender gap has been observed in school attendance by young girls. Moreover, when water sources are distant from their home, women collecting water are vulnerable to harassment and assault.

The Convention on the Rights of the Child links water to health, as the lack of water and hygiene is among the main reasons for the high rate of infant mortality in developing countries. Article 24(2)(*c*) establishes that States parties shall pursue the full implementation of the right to health and, in particular, shall take appropriate measures to combat disease and malnutrition through, *inter alia*, the provision of adequate clean drinking-water.

Under the Convention on the Rights of Persons with Disabilities, water needs are considered necessary for the achievement of an adequate standard of living and social protection. Article 28(2)(*a*) provides that States parties shall take appropriate steps to safeguard and promote the realization of the rights of persons with disabilities, including measures aimed at ensuring equal access to clean water services.

The use of water for human purposes is also protected under international humanitarian treaty law, even if the relevant provisions are not expressed in human rights terms.[116] For instance, the Geneva Convention Relative to the Treatment of Prisoners of War,[117] and the Geneva Convention Relative to the Protection of Civilian Persons in Time of War[118] require the detaining Powers to supply, respectively, prisoners of war and internees with sufficient drinking water and sufficient water for their daily personal toilet and for washing their personal laundry.

International water law recognizes the prominent role of drinking water in the allocation of water resources. For instance, the Convention on the Law of the Non-navigational Uses of International Watercourses ("UN Watercourses Convention") establishes that in the event of a conflict over different uses of a shared international

---

[116] Among other provisions, see: arts. 54 and 55 of Additional Protocol No. I to the Convention of Geneva of 1949, 1977; art. 5 (*b*) and 14 of Additional Protocol No. II to the Convention of Geneva of 1949, 1977; Statute of the International Criminal Court, art. 8, para. 2(*b*).

[117] Arts. 20, 26, 29, 46 of the Geneva Convention (III) relative to the Treatment of Prisoners of War, 1949.

[118] Arts. 85, 89 and 127 of the Geneva Convention (IV) relative to the Treatment of Civilian Persons in Time of War, 1949.

watercourse, special regard must be given to "*vital human needs*".[119] According to the Statement of Understanding accompanying this Convention, in determining vital human needs "*special attention is to be paid to providing sufficient water to sustain human life, including both drinking water and water required for production of food in order to prevent starvation*".[120]

2.2.1.2. Regional instruments

At the regional level, attention to water-related issues varies among continents. To limit the analysis to treaty provisions, the African Convention on the Conservation of Nature and Natural Resources establishes that the Parties shall "*endeavour to guarantee for their populations a sufficient and continuous supply of suitable water*".[121]

The human right to water has also been taken into account in regional watercourse conventions, such as the Charter of Waters of the Senegal River,[122] the Water Charter of the River Niger Basin[123] and the Water Charter for the Lake Chad Basin.[124]

Special attention has been given to the most water-vulnerable groups, namely children and women. The African Charter on the Rights and Welfare of the Child provides for the obligation of the States parties to implement the right to health of every child, and for this sake, to take measures to ensure the provision of adequate drinking water.[125] Women's needs have also been considered by the Protocol to the African Charter on Human and Peoples' Rights on the Rights of Women in Africa, which requires States parties to "*provide women with access to clean drinking water*".[126]

---

[119] Convention on the Law of the Non-navigational Uses of International Watercourses, UN Doc. A/51/869, New York, 11 April 1997, art. 10(2). The Convention, codified by the ILC, enshrines customary international principles dealing with transboundary waters, such as the equitable and reasonable utilization of transboundary waters, the duty not to cause harm and to cooperate.

[120] *Statements of Understanding Pertaining to Certain Articles of the Convention*, Report of the Sixth Committee convening as the Working Group of the Whole, para. 8.

[121] See African Convention on the Conservation of Nature and Natural Resources, Algiers, 15 September 1968, entered into force 9 October 1969, revised at Maputo, in 2003, art. 7(2) of the revised version.

[122] Charter of Water of the Senegal River (Charte des eaux du fleuve Sénégal), 28 May 2002, art. 4.

[123] Water Charter of the Niger River Basin (Charte de l'eau du bassin du Niger), 30 April 2008, arts. 1, 4, 9.

[124] Water Charter of the Lake Chad Basin (Charte de l'eau du Bassin du lac Tchad), 30 April 2012, art. 72, ratified by: Cameroon, Chad, Niger and Nigeria.

[125] Organisation of African Unity, African Charter on the Rights and Welfare of Child, Doc. CAB/LEG/24.9/49, 1990, entered into force on 29 November 1999, art. 14(2)(*c*).

[126] African Union, Protocol to the African Charter on Human and Peoples' Rights on the Rights of Women in Africa, 11 July 2003, Maputo, art. 15.

Although some Asian States, such as India, suffer from water scarcity, no regional treaty provision relating to Asia refers to the right to water.

As for the Organization of American States ("OAS"), its member States do not share a common view of the right to water. While South American countries have attached greater value to its recognition,[127] Canada and the United States of America have been among the most sceptical on this right. This lack of a coherent view might explain the absence of binding instruments. The right to access water services might be inferred from the right of all "*to have access to basic public services*", included in the Protocol of San Salvador,[128] to which, however, Canada and the United States of America are not parties.

The Arab Charter of Human Rights enshrines the right to water within the right to the highest attainable standard of physical and mental health. In this context, it requires that States parties shall take steps to "*[e]nsure basic nutrition and clear water for everybody*".[129]

Turning to Europe, the Protocol on Water and Health (hereinafter "the London Protocol")[130] to the Convention on the Protection and Use of Transboundary Watercourses and International Lakes[131] is undoubtedly one of the most valuable and ad-

---

[127]After the uprising which took place in 2000 following the privatization of water services in Cochabamba (Bolivia), a declaration was adopted stating that "*[w]ater is a fundamental human right and a public trust to be guarded by all levels of Government, therefore, it should not be commodified, privatized or traded for commercial purposes.*" Cochabamba Declaration, 8 December 2000. Recently, the Panama Declaration of the Latin American and Caribbean States adopted at the third Latin American and Caribbean Conference on Sanitation, 29-31 May 2013, reiterated "*la voluntad y compromise politico para alcanzar la universalizatción del derecho human al agua y los servicios de saneamiento integral de los gobiernos de América Latina*" (see p. 2, para. *ii*). See A. Berti Suman, *The Human Right to Water in Latin America. Challenges to Implementation and Contribution to Concept*, in *Brill Research Perspectives in International Water Law*, 2018.

[128]Additional Protocol to the American Convention on Human Rights in the Area of Economic, Social and Cultural Rights, San Salvador, 17 November 1998, art. 11.

[129]Arab Charter of Human Rights, Tunis, 22 May 2004, entered into force on 15 March 2008, art. 39(2)(*e*). State parties: Algeria, Bahrain, Iraq, Jordan, Lebanon, Libya, Palestine, Qatar, Saudi Arabia, Syria, United Arab Emirates, Yemen.

[130]United Nation Economic Commission for Europe, Protocol on Water and Health to the UNECE Convention on the Protection and Use of Transboundary Watercourses and International Lakes, London, 17 June 1999. The so-called London Protocol counts twenty-six States parties including: Albania, Azerbaijan, Belarus, Belgium, Bosnia and Herzegovina, Croatia, Czech Republic, Estonia, Finland, France, Germany, Hungary, Latvia, Lithuania, Luxembourg, Netherlands, Norway, Portugal, Republic of Moldova, Romania, Russian Federation, Serbia, Slovakia, Spain, Switzerland, Ukraine.

[131]Convention on the Protection and Use of Transboundary Watercourses and International Lakes, Helsinki, 17 March 1992, entered into force on 6 October 1996. The Convention is binding upon European States and has been recently opened to accession of all Members of the United Nations. See Amendments to Articles 25 and 26 of the Convention on the Protection and Use of Transboundary Watercourses and International Lakes, Madrid, 28 November 2003, entered into force on 6 February 2013.

vanced treaties for the implementation of the right to water. Its overall objective is to promote the protection of human health and well-being through improving water management and preventing, controlling and reducing water-related diseases. [132]

The London Protocol is the first regional agreement to have required States to provide "*[a]ccess to drinking water for everyone*" [133] in a non-discriminatory manner. [134] To achieve such aim, the Protocol lists a number of measures, including the publication of "*national and/or local targets*" covering, *inter alia*, the quality of drinking water supplied and "*[t]he area of territory, or the population sizes or proportions, which should be served by collective systems for the supply of drinking water*". [135]

Tanzi argues that although the Protocol makes no explicit reference to the human right to water, it is "*a concrete tool for the implementation of the human right to safe drinking water and sanitation*", as it "*explicitly translates into binding treaty law pertaining to water law most, if not all, of the emerging body of the human right to water*". [136] The London Protocol, continues the author, in fact meets almost all the minimum core obligations that the General Comment No. 15 has inferred from Articles 11 and 12 ICESCR in relation to access to water. [137]

Unlike the Convention, the Protocol is not open to non-UNECE States, [138] which would have rendered it the first universal instrument establishing the right to water.

The European Union is not fully committed to ensuring the right to water. The main concern of the EU is water quality, [139] while binding EU provisions ignore ques-

---

[132] Protocol on Water and Health, art. 1 (n 130). A. Tanzi, L. Iapichino, *The Added Value of the UNECE Protocol on Water and Health for the Implementation of the Right to Drinking Water and Sanitation*, in H. Smets (ed.), *Le droit à l'eau potable et à l'assainissement en Europe. Implementing the right to drinking water and sanitation in 17 European countries*, Paris, 2012, pp. 161-175.

[133] *Ibid.*, art. 6, para. 1.

[134] *Ibid.*, art. 5, para. 1.

[135] *Ibid.*, art. 6, para. 2.

[136] A. Tanzi, *Reducing the Gap between International Water Law and Human Rights Law: The UNECE Protocol on Water and Health*, in *International Community Law Review*, 2010, p. 271. Of the same view is C. Leb, *The Right to Water in a Transboundary Context: Emergence of Seminal Trends*, in *Water International*, 2012, p. 648.

[137] A. Tanzi, p. 272 (n 136). Tanzi analyzed the main provisions of the Protocol in the light of General Comment No. 15 to show how they reflect the requirements set by the CESCR.

[138] One explanation of the different treatment reserved to the Protocol compared to the Convention is that the two instruments do not share the same Member States, as the Protocol is open for signature by UNECE countries that have not yet ratified the Water Convention.

[139] Council Directive 98/83/EC, 3 November 1998 on the quality of water intended for human consumption, OJ L 330, 5 December 1998, p. 32; Directive 2000/60/EC of the European Parliament and of the Council of 23 October 2000, establishing a framework for Community action in the field of water policy, OJ L 327, 22 December 2000, p. 1 ("WFS"). The consolidated version of the amended Directive is available at: https://eur-lex.europa.eu/legal-content/EN/TXT/?uri=CELEX:02000L0060-20141120.

tions of physical availability and economic affordability. In particular, at the European Union level, it is for national or local authorities to confront water related problems, [140] given that, unlike other network industries, the water service sector is still largely regulated by Member States. This lack of regulation is at odds with the regulatory trend addressing other network industries, such as electricity, gas, postal services and transport, whose respective services have already been harmonized and liberalized.

Similarly, in the context of the Council of Europe, no binding provision refers to the human right to water. However, the European Court of Human Rights ("ECtHR") has inferred such a right from other rights enshrined in the European Convention of Human Rights ("ECHR", see, section 5.2 below). [141]

2.2.1.3. Statements by States and conduct within international organizations

States have expressed their recognition of the right to water and their commitment towards its implementation at the end of several international conferences [142] and in numerous declarations or statements. [143]

Moreover, States involved in international litigation concerning investment disputes arisen from the privatization of water services have often claimed they had acted for the protection of the right to water. [144]

---

[140] Such an approach is in line with the provision of the London Protocol, art. 5(*f*): "*Action to manage water resources should be taken at the lowest appropriate administrative level*".

[141] As regards soft law references to the human right to water, see: Council of Europe, Parliamentary Assembly, Res. 1693(2009), 2 October 2009; Council of Europe, Parliamentary Assembly, Res. 1809(2011), 15 April 2011; Council of Europe, Recommendation Rec(2001)14, Committee of Ministers to Member States on the European Charter on Water Resources, adopted by the Committee of Ministers on 17 October 2001.

[142] See, among others, Mar del Plata Action Plan (n 4); Dublin Statement on Water and Sustainable Development (n 11); *Report of the United Nations Conference on Sustainable Development* (n 36); *Programme of Action, Report of the United Nations International Conference on Population and Development* (n 14).

[143] See, *inter alia*, declarations and/or statements by groups of States: Declaration of the first Africa-South America Summit, Abuja, Nigeria, 30 November 2006, para. 18; Message From Beppu, 1st Asia-Pacific Water Summit, Beppu, Japan, 3-4 December 2007; The Delhi Declaration, adopted at the Third South Asian Conference on Sanitation, 16-21 November 2008, New Delhi, India; Sharm el-Sheikh Final Document, adopted by the Movement of Non-Aligned Countries (XV Summit of the Heads of State and Government of the Non-Aligned Movement), Sharm el Sheikh, Egypt, 11-16 July 2009, para. 393; ASEAN Human Rights Declaration, Phnom Penh, Cambodia, 18 November 2012, art. 28(*e*); Chiang Mai Declaration, adopted at the second Asia-Pacific Water Summit, Chiang Mai, Thailandia,14-20 May 2013.

[144] In this regard, see chapter III, *Suez, Sociedad General de Aguas de Barcelona, S.A. and Vivendi Universal, S.A. v. Argentine Republic*, ICSID Case No. ARB/03/19; *Suez, Sociedad General de Aguas de Barcelona SA and Interagua Servicios Integrales de Agua SA v. Argentine Republic*, ICSID No ARB/03/17; *Aguas Cordobesas, S.A., Suez, and Sociedad General de Aguas de Barcelona, S.A. v. Argentine Republic*, ICSID No. ARB/03/18; *Impregilio S.p.A. v. Argentina Republic*, ICSID Case No. ARB/07/17; *SAUR International v. Argentine Republic*, ICSID Case no. ARB/04/4; *Ur-*

As for States' conduct within international organizations, the General Assembly has adopted several resolutions on the right to water. As anticipated, the General Assembly recognised for the first time the right to water in 2010,[145] but the resolution was not adopted by *consensus*: 41 States abstained (including Australia, Canada, China, Israel, the United Kingdom and the United States), 122 voted in favor, and none voted against. However, in 2013 and 2015, subsequent resolutions on the right to water were adopted by *consensus*.[146] Oddly, the 2017 resolution on the right to water[147] received three abstentions (New Zealand, South Africa and Turkey) and one contrary vote (Kyrgyzstan).[148] Notwithstanding this fluctuating attitude, the explanation of votes shows no objection to the recognition of the right to water as such (see section 2.2.2 below).

At the UN level, the Human Rights Council has adopted several resolutions recognising the right at issue,[149] while at the regional level, resolutions and declarations on the right to water have been adopted by the OAS,[150] the European Union,[151] and the Council of Europe.[152]

---

baser S.A. and Consorcio de Aguas Bilbao Bizkaia, Bilbao Biskaia Ur Partzuergoa v. The Argentine Republic, ICSID Case No. ARB/07/26.

[145] General Assembly, Res. 64/292 (n 34).

[146] General Assembly, Res. 68/157, 18 December 2013, UN Doc. A/RES/68/157, 12 February 2014; Res 70/169, 17 December 2015, UN Doc. A/RES/70/169, 22 February 2016.

[147] General Assembly, Res. 72/178 (n 67).

[148] General Assembly, Seventy-second session, Third Committee, 49th meeting, UN Doc. A/C.3/72/SR.49, 18 January 2018, paras. 15-45.

[149] See, *inter alia*: Human Rights Council, Res. 15/9, para. 3 (n 35); Res. 16/2, 24 March 2011, UN Doc. A/HRC/16/2, 14 November 2011; Res. 18/1, 28 September 2011, UN Doc. A/HRC/18/1, 12 October 2011; Res. 24/18 (n 22).

[150] OAS, Declaration of Santa Cruz + 10, 5 December 2006; Inter-American Meeting on Economic, Social, and Environmental Aspects Related to the Availability of and Access to Drinking Water, AG/RES. 2347 (XXXVII O/07), 5 June 2007; Water, Health, and Human Rights, AG/RES. 2349 (XXXVII O/07), 5 June 2007; The Human Right to Safe Drinking Water and Sanitation, AG/RES. 2760 (XLII-O/12), 5 June 2012; Declaration of Panama, 29-31 May 2013.

[151] European Parliament, Written Declaration on the protection of water as a public asset, 0086/2010, 10 November 2010; European Parliament resolution on the 4th World Water Forum, 15 March 2006, OJ C 291 E/294; European Parliament resolution on the Commission Communication on Water Management in Developing Countries and Priorities for EU Development Cooperation (COM(2002)132-C5-0335/2002-2002/2179(COS))(2003); European Parliament resolution of 12 March 2009 on 5th World Water Forum, 2010/C 87 E/31; European Parliament resolution of 15 March 2012 on 6th World Water Forum, 2013/C 251 E/18; Council of the European Union, Declaration by the High Representative, Catherine Ashton, on behalf of the EU to commemorate the World Water Day, Brussels, 22 March 2010, 7810/10 (Presse 72) P12.

[152] Council of Europe, Committee of Ministers, Recommendation Re(2001)14 of the Committee of Ministers on the European Charter on Water Resources, 17 October 2011, para. 5: "*Everyone has the right to a sufficient quantity of water for his or her basic needs. International human rights instruments recognise the fundamental right of all human beings to be free from hunger and to*

2.2.1.4. National constitutions and legislation

As noted by the CESCR, the right to water "*has been constitutionally entrenched by a number of States and has been subject to litigation before national courts*".[153] In addition, several countries have adopted specific legislation that, although not formulated in human rights terms, regulates specific aspects of water and sanitation – notably the quality of water, water service pricing policies and subsidies, prioritization among different water uses or disconnection.

It has been estimated that since 2002, when the General Comment No. 15 was adopted, the number of States recognizing the human right to water has doubled.[154] Although exact figure are difficult to provide, the following overview of countries' legal commitments to respect the right to water may show the extent of the phenomenon.

Africa counts the highest number of States – Algeria,[155] Angola,[156] Democratic Republic of Congo,[157] Gambia,[158] Eritrea,[159] Ethiopia,[160] Kenya,[161] Madagascar,[162] Mauritania,[163] Morocco,[164] Mozambique,[165] Niger,[166] South Africa,[167]

---

an adequate standard of living for themselves and their families. It is quite clear that these two requirements include the right to a minimum quantity of water of satisfactory quality from the point of view of health and hygiene. Social measures should be put in place to prevent the supply of water to destitute persons from being cut off"; Committee of Ministers, European Water Charter, Strasbourg, 6 May 1968; Parliamentary Assembly, Resolution 1963 (2009), Water: a strategic challenge for the Mediterranean Basin, Strasbourg, 2 October 2009.

[153] General Comment No 15, para. 55 (n 24).

[154] According to Ripley, as of 2009, 55 States have given explicit recognition and legal entitlements to the right to water in their national domestic legislation and 34 States have adopted domestic legislation dealing with one or more aspects of the right at issue. See Cahill-Ripley, *The Human Right to Water and Its Application in the Occupied Palestinian Territories*, Oxford-New York, 2011, p. 184, nt. 880.

[155] Law No. 05-12, 4 August 2005, Official Journal of Algeria No. 60, art. 3.

[156] Water Law No. 6/02.21, 11 February 2002, art. 10.

[157] Constitution of the Democratic Republic of the Congo, 18 February 2006, art. 48.

[158] Constitution of the Republic of Gambia, 16 January 1997, art. 216(4).

[159] Constitution of Eritrea, 23 May 1997, art. 8(3).

[160] Constitution of the Federal Democratic Republic of Ethiopia, 21 August 1995, art. 90(1).

[161] Constitution of Kenya, 27 August 2010, art. 43(1)(*d*).

[162] Water Code, Law No. 98– 029, 20 January 1998, art. 37.

[163] Water Code, Law No. 2005-030, art. 2(2) and art. 37.

[164] Morocco Water Law, Law No. 10-95, 1995; Draft Text of Constitution, adopted at the Referendum of the 1st July 2011, Le Bulletin Officiel n. 5964 bis du 28 Chaâbane 1432, 30 July 2011, art. 31.

[165] Mozambique Water Act, art. 26.

[166] Order No. 2010-09, 1 April 2010, concerning the Niger Water Code, art. 4: "*[l]a présente ordonnance reconnaît à chaque citoyen le droit fondamental d'accès à l'eau*".

[167] Constitution of the Republic of South Africa, 4 December 1996, art. 27(1)(*b*).

South Sudan,[168] Tanzania[169]; Uganda,[170] Zimbabwe[171] – that have recognized, implicitly or explicitly, at a constitutional or a legislative level, the human right to water.

In South America, some States – Bolivia,[172] Brazil,[173] Colombia,[174] Ecuador,[175] Mexico,[176] Paraguay,[177] Uruguay,[178] Venezuela[179] – have explicitly enshrined the right to water into their constitutions. Others have provided legal safeguards to the right at issue by means of legislative provisions or judicial interpretation, namely: Argentina,[180] Dominican Republic,[181] Guatemala,[182] Honduras,[183] Nica-

---

[168] South Sudan's Constitution, 7 July 2011, art. 35(2).

[169] Water Utilization Act, 22 October 1974, as revised in 1993, art. 10.

[170] Constitution of the Republic of Uganda, 8 October 1995 – as amended by the Constitution Act, 2000, Act No. 13 of 2000, the Constitution Act, 2005, Act No. 11/2005 and the Constitution Act, 2005, Act No. 21/200 – art. XIV(*b*).

[171] The Constitution of Zimbabwe, Amendment (No 20), Act, 2013, 22 May 2013, Section 77.

[172] The Constitution of the Plurinational State of Bolivia, 7 February 2009, art. 16(1); art. 20(1)(3).

[173] Law No. 11445, 5 January 2007, art. 9.III establishes the service holder's duty to draft policy to: "*adopt benchmarks for assuring essential public health services, including the minimum per capita volume of water for public supply, in compliance with national rules regarding water potability*".

[174] The Political Constitution of Colombia, amended on 1 April 2005, arts. 334, 361, 366 and 368.

[175] The Constitution of the Republic of Ecuador, 20 October 2008, art. 12. See also arts: 3, 15, 32, 66, 264, 281, 375, 314, 411. The privatization of water services is unconstitutional under art. 282 and art. 318.

[176] The Political Constitution of the United States of Mexico, 5 February 1917, last amended on 9 February 2012, art. 4.

[177] Law on Water Resources, Law No. 3239, 10 July 2007, arts. 3, 4, 16, 22. art. 16 reads as follow: "*Every natural person has a right to access to a minimum quantity of drinking water per day that is sufficient for the satisfaction of their basic needs. The minimum quantity of water per person per day shall be established by regulation by the Ministry of Public Health and Social Welfare*". Available at http://www.waterlex.org/waterlex-legal-database/index.php?r=legalDocument/customView&id=149.

[178] The Constitution of Uruguay, as amended on 26 November 1989, 26 November 1994, 8 December 1996 and 31 October 2004, art. 47. In addition, Law No. 18610, Política Nacional de Aguas. Se Establecen los Principios Rectores, published on 28 October 2009, D.O. No. 27845, art. 2: "*[t]odos los habitantes tienen derecho al acceso al agua potable y al saneamiento. El Estado actuará propendiendo al efectivo ejercicio de tales derechos*". See R. Moshman, *The Constitutional Right to Water in Uruguay*, in *Sustainable Development Law & Policy*, 2005.

[179] The Constitution of the Bolivarian Republic of Venezuela, 15 December 1999, arts. 127, 304.

[180] Ley De Gestión Ambiental Del Agua De La Ciudad Autónoma De Buenos Aires, law No. 3295, 11 January 2010, art. 3: "*[l]a ciudad garantiza a todos sus habitantes el acceso al agua potable en cantidad y calidad suficientes para usos personales y doméstico como derecho humano fundamental*".

[181] The Constitution of the Dominican Republic, 26 January 2010, arts. 15 and 61(1).

[182] The Constitution of the Republic of Guatemala, 31 May 1985, as amended by the Legislative Decree No. 18-93 of 17 November 1993, art. 127.

[183] The Constitution of the Republic of Honduras, 20 January 1982, as amended on 2013, art. 145.

ragua,[184] Panama,[185] Paraguay,[186] Peru.[187]

With respect to the United States of America, the former Special Rapporteur on the right to water highlighted that, despite the lack of a federally recognized right to safe drinking water and sanitation, "*individual states have taken the initiative to consecrate this right*".[188] For instance, the states of Massachusetts and Pennsylvania were mentioned as having enshrined the right to water into their constitutions, and California, for having introduced a bill that recognizes the human right to water.

In 2009, Quebec has adopted a law establishing the collective character of water resources, which entitles each physical person to the right to access to drinking water for personal use and hygiene.[189]

In Asia, express references to the right to water are included in the Constitutions of the Maldives[190] and Nepal,[191] while implied references are enshrined in the Water Code of Kazakhstan.[192] Indirect guarantees might be ensured by means of the constitutional provisions – see Armenia,[193] Bangladesh,[194] Indonesia,[195] Laos,[196] Pakistan,[197] Philip-

[184] The Political Constitution of the Republic of Nicaragua, 19 November 1986, amended in 1990, 1995, 2000, 2005, 2007, arts. 89 and 105. See also National Water Law No. 620 and Enabling Regulation, 15 May 2007, fourth preambular paragraph: "*access to water is a right associated with life and human health, and must be guaranteed to the Nicaraguan people by the State*".

[185] The Political Constitution of Panama, 11 October 1972, as amended in 2004, arts. 110 (4), 118, 258 and 259.

[186] Law on Water Resources, Law No. 3239, 10 July 2007, arts. 3, 4 and 16.

[187] Decreto Supremo No. 001-2010-AG, Aprueban Reglamento de la Ley No. 29338, Ley de Recursos Hídricos, 31 March 2009, Titulo Preliminar, art. III.

[188] Human Rights Council, *Report of the Special Rapporteur on the human right to safe drinking water and sanitation, Catarina de Albuquerque, Addendum, Mission to the United States of America*, UN Doc. A/HRC/18/33/Add.4, 2 August 2011, para. 9. The Special Rapporteur refers respectively to: Constitution of the Commonwealth of Massachusetts, art. XCVII; and Constitution of the Commonwealth of Pennsylvania, art. 1, sect. 27; California Legislature, 2011–12 regular season, Assembly Bill No. 685 introduced by Assembly Member Mike Eng.

[189] Loi affirmant le caractère collectif des ressources en eau et favorisant une meilleure gouvernance de l'eau et des milieux associés, 1 June 2019, Chapitre C-6.2, Section I.2.

[190] The Constitution of the Republic of Maldives, 7 August 2008, art. 23.

[191] The Constitution of Nepal, 28 February 2016, art. 33.

[192] Kazakhstan Water Code, No. 481, 9 July 2003, arts. 9 and 90. See C. Arce, *Water – A Human Right out of Reach? Experiences from the Middle East*, in E. H. Riedel, P. Rothen (eds.), *The Human Right to Water*, Berlin, 2006.

[193] The Constitution of the Republic of Armenia, 5 July 1995, amended in 2005, art. 31.

[194] The Constitution of Bangladesh, 4 December 1972, as modified up to the 17 May 2004, art. 15.

[195] The Constitution of the Republic of Indonesia of 1945 last amended in 2002, art. 33(3).

[196] The Constitution of the Lao People's Democratic Republic, 15 August 1991, art. 19.

[197] The Constitution of the Islamic Republic of Pakistan, 10 April 1973, amended on 31 July 2004, art. 38.

pines[198] – requiring, *inter alia*, the provision of basic necessities for an adequate standard of living. Despite facing alarming water stress, China does not recognize the right in question within its Constitution. However, recent policies[199] and laws[200] are showing a more sensitive approach towards the protection of water resources and the provision of water supply for the public interest, in particular for drinking and domestic uses.

Equally, Middle Eastern countries, notwithstanding water scarcity, rarely include provisions addressing water related issues in their constitutions and legislations.

As for Europe, Slovenia is the first EU country to have amended its Constitution in order to recognise the human right to water.[201] A number of domestic legal systems protect the quality of water, as well as its availability and accessibility (Finland,[202] France,[203] Germany,[204] Italy).[205] Others infer the right to water from the

---

[198] The Constitution of the Republic of the Philippines, 2 February 1987, art. 2, section 9.

[199] A local NGO, the IPE (Institute of Public and Environmental Affairs), has developed the China Water Pollution Map, a public database which gives information on water pollution and water discharges, together with a list of violators at national, provincial and municipal levels. The advantage of this database is that it allows a comparative analysis of discharge. The database aims at encouraging public participation and strengthening law enforcement in order to protect water resources. The IPE is directed by Ma Jun, a writer, environmental consultant, and journalist, specialized in environmental matter. His book, China's Water Crisis, originally published in1999, dealt with the China's environmental crisis.

[200] Water Law of the People's Republic of China, adopted on 21 January 1988, revised on 29 August 2002 (Order No. 74 of the President of the People's Republic of China of 29 August 2002), arts. 48, 28 and 76. See R. Soprano, *China and the Recognition and Protection of the Human Right to Water*, in P. Davide Farah, E. Cima (Eds), *China's Influence on Non-Trade Concerns in International Economic Law*, gLAWcal Book Series, New-York-London, 2016, pp. 331-340.

[201] Constitution Act Amending Chapter III of the Constitution of the Republic of Slovenia, 17 November 2016, art. 70(*a*) (Right to Drinking Water), which states that "*everyone has the right to drinkable water*" and that "*water resources represent a public good that is managed by the state (…) not a market commodity*".

[202] Finland, Water Services Act (119/2001), as amended up to 979/2015.

[203] Loi sur l'eau et les milieu aquatiques n. 2006-1772, 30 December 2006, LEMA, consolidated version of 14 July 2010. Art. 1 modified rt. L210-1 (V) of the Environmental Code of 4 October 2006.

[204] In its comments submitted on 4 May 2007 pursuant to the Decision No. 2/204 of the Human Rights Council of 27 November 2006, the Federal Republic of Germany listed several legal acts that mirror aspects of the human right to water, including: Social Security Code XII, Section 17, access to water and beverages is a component of social assistance; Several federal laws secure the quality of drinking water, namely the Drinking Water Ordinance (Trinkwasserverordnung); Ordinance about Mineral Water (Mineral– und Tafelwasserverordnung); Disease Protection Act (nfektionsschutzgesetz), section 37; Ordinance concerning general conditions for water supply (Verordnung über allgemeine Bedingungen für die Versorgung mit Wasser), which deal with water quality standards and quantity of water supply; German Water Resources Act (Wasserhaushaltsgesetz), whose primary objective is to protect drinking water. These comments are available at: https://www2.ohchr.org/english/issues/water/contributions/Germany.pdf.

[205] In Italy, most of the provisions related to the supply of water are enshrined in the environ-

right to dignity, to an adequate standard of living and to a healthy environment (Belgium,[206] Portugal,[207] Spain,[208] Ukraine)[209]. The United Kingdom provides guarantees against the disconnection of water services for "*any dwelling which is occupied by a person as his only or principal home*", irrespective of non-payment of charges.[210] In Italy, where the provision of water services can be interrupted for

mental code, D. Lgs. 3 April 2006, No. 152, art. 73. The Italian water supply system is high fragmented; the national territory is divided into integrated water services ("servizi idrici integrati"), which each Region then groups into the so-called "ATO" ("Ambito Territoriale Ottimale") that are in turn managed by special entities created by the Italian Regions, which have to guarantee the quality of the service, the availability of water as well as the equal treatment of consumers. Italy has not yet inserted the human right to water in its domestic law, and still considers this right as functional to the fulfillment of other rights. S. Urbinati, *Il diritto all'acqua e all'accesso ai servizi igienici è riconosciuto in modo incompleto nel diritto italiano come anche nel diritto internazionale e nel diritto europeo*, in *Diritto comunitario e degli scambi internazionali*, 2015, p. 29; S. Urbinati, *L'état de la reconnaissance du droit de l'homme à l'eau potable et à l'assainissement en Italie*, in H. Smets (ed.), *Le droit à l'eau potable et à l'assainissement en Europe. Implementing the right to drinking water and sanitation in 17 European countries*, Paris, 2012, pp. 525-556; C. Iannello, *Il Diritto all'acqua. L'appartenenza collettiva della risorsa idrica*, Naples, 2012; A. Vigorito, *La gestion de l'eau en Italie et les influences du droit del'union européenne*, in A. Oriolo, A. Vigorito (eds.), *"L'EAU", questions juridiques et économiques concernant la gestion, l'utilisation et la protection des "ressources hydriques": perspectives compares et internationales*, Rome, 2012.

206 Belgian Constitution, 7 February 1831, current text of 17 February 1994 last amended in 2012, art. 23. In Belgium, a Walloon Regional Decree sets forth that "*[e]veryone has the right to access drinking water in quality and quantity sufficient for nutrition, domestic needs and health*". Decree regarding the water cycle and instituting a public water provider, Wallon Regional Council, 15 April 1999, art. 1(2). Similarly, a Decree of Flanders states that: "*every subscriber has the right to a minimum uninterrupted supply of (…) water for domestic uses in order to live a life in human dignity*". Decree regulating the right to a minimum supply of electricity, gas and water, Parliament of Flanders, 19 December 1996, art. 3. Moreover, the Decree of the Flemish Council of 20 December 1996, amending the 1933 Law on the Protection of Drinking Water, art. 34, also requires all water providers to provide 15 m3 of tap water per annum, per person, free of charge.

207 The Constitution of the Portuguese Republic, 2 April 1976, amended in 2005, art. 81(*n*).

208 Autonomy Statute of the Community of Valencia, 2006, art. 17; Autonomy Statute of the Community of Catalunya, 2006, arts. 27, 30.1, 42(1). The Autonomy Statute of the Community of Valencia also refers to the right of the people of Valencia to the provision of sufficient water. Autonomy Statute of the Community of Valencia, 2006, art. 17; Autonomy Statute of the Community of Catalunya, 2006, art. 27, 30(1), 42.1. Source: http://www.ielrc.org/water/doc_hr2.htm.

209 Constitution of Ukraine, 28 June 1996, amended in 2010, arts. 48 and 50 stating, respectively, the right to an adequate standard of living and to the right to a healthy environment. Domestic law establishes citizens' right to potable water and, to this end, entrusts bodies of executive power and of local self-government with ensuring the provision of drinking water "*of quality and quantities complying with the requirements of sanitary regulations and state standards*". Law of Ukraine on ensuring the sanitary and epidemic safety of the population, Law No. 4004 –XII of 24 February 1994, as amended by Law N 3037-III of 7 February 2002.

210 Water Industry Act 1991, chapter 56, section 61, read in conjunction with Schedule 4A (amended by Sch. 4A inserted (30.6.1999) by 1999 c. 9, ss. 1(2), 17(2), Sch. 1). See also S. Hendry,

non-payment of the invoices, a water bonus has recently been introduced, providing for fifty liters of free water per day per person to less well-off families.[211] French law also refers to the right to have access to potable water at reasonable economic conditions for all.[212] A number of provisions are enshrined in the Netherlands' Drinking water law concerning water quality, affordability, access to information and accountability which, taken together, provide guarantees for the fulfillment of the human right to water.[213]

2.2.1.5. Domestic case law

Years ago, the former Special Rapporteur on the human right to water encouraged States to enact accountability mechanisms at a national level, in particular administrative and judicial remedies, for submitting complaints against natural or legal persons responsible for delivering water and sanitation services when they fail to fulfill their obligations. The Rapporteur also called for the establishment of monitoring bodies, such as independent institutions, human rights commissions or regulatory agencies, to verify the implementation of obligations concerning the human right to water and sanitation.[214]

In line with this call, the High Commissioner for Human Rights has observed that there is an ongoing trend towards greater recognition of the right at issue. He noted that:

> *"a number of domestic courts have adjudicated certain aspects of human rights obligations in relation to access to safe drinking water – notably in relation to the pollution of water resources and disconnections – or have derived a right to access safe drinking water from the enjoyment of other human rights, such as the right to life or the right to a healthy environment".*[215]

The Human Right to Water in Scotland, in H. Smets (ed.), *Le droit a l'eau potable et à l'assainissement en Europe. Implementing the right to water and sanitation in 17 European countries*, Paris, 2012.

[211] For details, see the document available at https://www.autorita.energia.it/allegati/docs/17/470-17.pdf.

[212] Loi sur l'eau et les milieu aquatiques n. 2006-1772, 30 December 2006, art. L210-1 (V): "*[l]'eau fait partie du patrimoine commun de la nation. Sa protection, sa mise en valeur et le développement de la ressource utilisable, dans le respect des équilibres naturels, sont d'intérêt général. Dans le cadre des lois et règlements ainsi que des droits antérieurement établis, l'usage de l'eau appartient à tous et chaque personne physique, pour son alimentation et son hygiène, a le* droit d'accéder à l'eau potable *dans des conditions économiquement acceptables par tous. Les coûts liés à l'utilisation de l'eau, y compris les coûts pour l'environnement et les ressources elles-mêmes, sont supportés par les utilisateurs en tenant compte des conséquences sociales, environnementales et économiques ainsi que des conditions géographiques et climatiques*".

[213] Drinking Water Law, 19 July 2009, art. 2. See also arts. 8(3), 9, 21(3), 45-46.

[214] Special Rapporteur of the UN Commission on Human Rights, Sub-Commission on the Promotion and Protection of Human Rights, Guidelines for the realization of the right to drinking water and sanitation, para. 9 (n 26).

[215] Human Rights Council, *Report of the United Nations High Commissioner for Human Rights*

This sub-section describes several major rulings to show how domestic courts have started to enforce the right to water. A comprehensive description of all judicial and non-judicial cases[216] that have addressed water rights abuses is beyond the reach of the present study.

Widely known is the South African case law concerning violations of the right to water. In the *Bon Vista Mansions* case,[217] residents of the Bon Vista Mansions, a block of flats in Johannesburg, sued the Southern Metropolitan Local Council for having been disconnected from the water supply system due to non-payment of water charges.

In the judgment on interim measures, the High Court of South Africa stated that "*[t]he state must take reasonable legislative and other measures, within its available resources, to achieve the progressive realisation of this right [to water]*".[218] Interestingly, the Court argued that the matter under consideration was connected "*very directly to the duty to 'respect' the right of access to water*"[219] and interpreted the content of such a duty to respect in the light of international law.[220] Moreover, it ruled that "*water supply may not be discontinued if it results in a person being denied access to basic water services for non-payment, where that person proves, to the satisfaction of the relevant water services authority, that he or she is unable to pay for basic services*".[221]

The Court found that the local Council's disconnection of the residents from the water supply, by depriving the consumers of an existing access, was *prima facie* a breach of the State's constitutional duty to respect the right of access to water.[222]

---

on the scope and content of the relevant human rights obligations related to equitable access to safe drinking water and sanitation under international human rights instruments, para. 43(*d*) (n 29). In this connection, see I. Winkler, *Judicial Enforcement of The Human Right To Water, Case Law From South Africa, Argentina and India*, in *Law, Social Justice & Global Development Journal*, 2008.

[216] As regards alternative dispute resolution mechanisms, various national laws provide for remedies that allow water users to submit complaints. For instance, the Australian Utilities Act provides for a Consumer Council that protects users' rights, and Finland's Water Services Act institutes an ombudsman who ensures compliance with water laws.

[217] *Residents of Bon Vista Mansions v. Southern Metropolitan Local Council*, Case No. 01/12312, 5 September 2001 (High Court of South Africa 2001). See, J. Kothari, *The Right to Water: A Constitutional Perspective*, 2006, p. 10, available at: http://www.ielrc.org/activities/workshop_0612/content/d0607.pdf.

[218] *Ibid.*, para. 11.

[219] *Ibid.*, para. 13.

[220] *Ibid.*, para. 14.

[221] *Ibid.*, para. 26.

[222] The Court applied Section 4(3) of the South African Water Services Act (Act No. 108 of 1997) in order to establish that the disconnection procedure had not been conducted in a 'fair and equitable' manner, as the local Council had failed to provide notice of its intention to terminate the supply.

The Court hence ordered the local Council to restore the water supply to Bon Vista Mansions.[223]

Another landmark ruling from South Africa is the one rendered in the *Mazibuko* case,[224] in which the Constitutional Court was called to interpret section 27(1) of the Constitution, ruling that everyone has the right to have access to sufficient water.[225] In particular, the Court had to establish whether: *i)* the City of Johannesburg's Free Basic Water policy of supplying 25 litres per person per day was in compliance with section 27 of the Constitution; *ii)* the installation of pre-paid meters in a poor area of the City, Phiri in Soweto, was lawful, given that such meters halted the supply of water once the monthly free basic water ration had been consumed, unless credit was purchased.

Requested to determine the exact amount of free water per month to be considered "*sufficient for dignified life*", the Court ruled that the constitutional provision does not require the State to provide each person with any particular amount of free water.[226] The content of the right to water was to be determined case by case on the basis of the social and economic context, as the Constitution only "*requires the state to take reasonable legislative and other measures progressively to achieve the right of access to sufficient water within available resources. It does not confer a right to claim 'sufficient water' from the State immediately*".[227]

As for the pre-paid water meters, the Court found that this system was not unlawful as it did not amount to disconnection, but only to a temporary suspension of the supply of water once the free monthly water allowance was consumed without the purchase of further credit.

This ruling has been criticized for being a regression in the fulfillment of the human right to water, as the installation of prepaid meters has effects similar to cut-offs.[228] Such criticism can be shared only on the grounds that, from the perspective of international law, the judgment at issue sets forth an inaccurate and thus misleading principle. While it is true that the right to water must be achieved progressively and does not entitle everyone to immediate access to water sufficient to meet all

---

223 *Ibid.*, para. 35.

224 *Lindiwe Mazibuko and Others v. City of Johannesburg and Others*, Case No. CCT 39/09 [2009], ZACC 28, 8 October 2009 (Constitutional Court of South Africa, 2009).

225 Constitution of the Republic of South Africa, 4 December 1996, 4 February 1997.

226 The Court built upon its previous decision in *Government of the Republic of South Africa & Others v. Grootboom*, Case CCT 11/00, 4 October 2000.

227 *Lindiwe Mazibuko and Others v. City of Johannesburg and Others*, para. 57 (n 224).

228 See P. Danchin, A *Human Right to Water? The South African Constitutional Court's Decision in the Mazibuko* Case, in *EJIL: Talk!*, 2010, available at: https://www.ejiltalk.org/a-human-right-to-water-the-south-african-constitutional-court%E2%80%99s-decision-in-the-mazibuko-case/; Thielbörger, p. 49 (n 40); M. Langford, A. Russell, *'Global Precedent' or 'Reasonable No More'? The Mazibuko Case*, in *The Journal of Water Law,* 2008.

human needs, the State still bears a core obligation to "*ensure access to the minimum essential amount of water, that is sufficient and safe for personal and domestic uses to prevent disease*".[229]

It may be argued that since the City of Johannesburg fulfilled this obligation by providing a basic amount of water free of charge to all, the Court was concerned with not invading the field of other State powers by upholding requests exceeding the minimum. It is for the legislative and executive powers to adopt measures aimed at giving content to the right set forth in the Constitution in order to respond to basic social and economic needs, while constitutional judges must limit themselves to assessing such measures against the test of reasonableness,[230] a test that the City's Free Basic Water policy passed.

It is noteworthy that the case law following the *Mazibuko* judgment shows that this constitutional ruling has not affected the judicial implementation of the right to water by lower courts, which have continued to hold that the disconnection of water services is in violation of the human right to water.[231]

Other African courts have also adjudicated on the right to water.[232] In the *Matsipane Mosethanyane* case,[233] the appellants were members of the Basarwa community, an ancestral community settled in the Central Kalahari Game Reserve ("CKGR"), a national park in Botswana. The residents of the CKGR had access to water through a borehole installed, but never used, by a local company. The borehole engine was maintained and provided with fuel by a public entity, the Ghanzi District Council. In 2002, the management policy of the Reserve changed. The Government determined that permanent settlements, such as that of the Bosarwa, were not compatible with the purposes of the CKGR and sought to resettle the appellants and other communities outside the Reserve. To induce the community to leave the CKGR, the Government dismantled and removed the pump of the borehole. As a consequence, the Basarwa community suffered from an alarming lack of water that seriously undermined their health.

The Court of first instance upheld the appellants' request to remain within the CKGR, but denied their demand to have the borehole restored because the Community lacked the administrative waters rights for the groundwater withdrawal.

---

[229] General Comment No. 15, para. 37(*a*) (n 24).

[230] *Ibid.*, para. 66. See also paras. 67, 71 and 78 ff.

[231] See *City of Cape Town v. Strümpher* (104/2011) [2012] ZASCA 54 (30 March 2012) (Supreme Court of Appeal in South Africa 2012); *Mushoriwa v. City of Harare,* HH 195-14 HC 4266/13, 30 April 2014 (High Court in Zimbabwe 2014).

[232] B. R. Dinokopila, *The right to water in Botswana: A Review of the Matsipane Mosetlhanyane Case*, in *African Human Rights Law Journal*, 2011.

[233] Court of Appeals of the Republic of Botswana, *Matsipane Mosetlhanyane and Other v. Attorney General*, Civil Appeal No. CACLB-074-10, High Court Civil Case No. MAHLB-000393-09, 27 January 2011.

Appealing to the Court of Appeal of Botswana, the claimants requested the permission to use, at their own expenses, the existing borehole for domestic purposes. The Court of Appeal stated that the *Matsipane* case is "*a harrowing story of human suffering and despair caused by a shortage of water in the harsh climatic conditions of the Kalahari Desert where the appellants and their 'Basarwa' community live*".[234] Referring to the right to water as recognized by the Committee on Economic, Social and Cultural Rights in the General Comment No. 15 and by the UN General Assembly in the 2010 resolution,[235] the Court of Appeal reversed the previous judgment, stating that the Government's refusal to grant the locals permission to use the borehole in the CKGR for domestic purposes amounted to degrading treatment, in violation of section 7(1) of the Constitution of Botswana. In the end, the Court of Appeal ruled that the applicants had the right to re-commission the borehole at Mothomelo in the CKG Reserve and also to drill other boreholes inside the Reserve.

An approach similar to that of the South African Constitutional Court was taken by the Israeli Supreme Court in the ruling on the *Abdallah Abu Massad* case.[236] This case concerned the refusal by the Israeli Water Authority to grant a connection to the water network to Bedouins living in unrecognized villages in the Negev desert, due to the fact that their houses lacked building permits. Bedouins who did not want to move to town were offered two options for obtaining access to water: purchasing water in water centers adjacent to their village or applying for a private water connection on humanitarian considerations.[237] Some Bedouins, whose applications for a private connection were refused, lodged an appeal with the Water Tribunal and, subsequently, with the Supreme Court.[238]

The Supreme Court established that the right to water derived from "*the constitutional right to human dignity*"[239] and from "*the principles of international law*".[240] However, it underlined that such a right is "*not an absolute right*",[241] but a relative one that must be balanced with competing interests. According to the Court, "*insofar as the right to water is realized in its basic form, as part of the right for minimal existence with dignity (...) the opposing interests and values might gain greater*

[234] *Ibid.*, para. 4.

[235] *Ibid.*, para. 19(1)(2).

[236] *Abdallah Abu Masad and others v. Water Commissioner and Israel Lands Administration*, Appeal No. 9535/06, [2011] (Supreme Court Civil 2011). S. L. Murthy, M. Williams, E. Baskin, *The Human Right to Water in Israel: A Case Study of the Unrecognized Bedouin Villages in the Negev*, in *Israel Law Review*, 2013, p. 25.

[237] *Ibid.*, para. 1.

[238] *Ibid.*, paras. 9-12.

[239] *Ibid.*, para. 23.

[240] *Ibid.*, para. 25. The Court referred to arts. 11 and 12 ICCPR as interpreted in the General Comment 15.

[241] *Ibid.*, para. 24.

weight".[242] In order to assess whether the right balance between individuals' right to water and the general interest is struck, the Court must apply a test of reasonableness and proportionality.[243]

The Court concluded that there had been a violation of the Bedouins' right to water due to the implementation of the State planning policy concerning access to water sources for unrecognized Bedouin villages,[244] but, at the same time, it found that the State had balanced the Bedouins' right to water against the State's interest in an ordered planning policy. Thus, by applying the test of reasonableness and proportionality on an individual basis, *vis-à-vis* several applicants, the Court upheld the Water authority's decision to deny connection to the water network, given that they have alternative means of accessing water resources. On the contrary, with respect to other applicants, the Court ordered additional investigations on the level of reasonable access to water sources in order to ensure minimal access, as well as reconsideration of the possibility of private connections to water sources on humanitarian grounds.[245]

As in the *Mazibuko* case, the Court resorted to the test of reasonableness to evaluate the measures adopted,[246] a test grounded, *inter alia*, on the assessment of the guarantee of minimum access to water for those most in need.

Equally, courts of the Netherlands have recognized the right to water as derived from the right to an adequate standard of living and the right to health (Articles 11 and 12 ICESCR) and subjected its implementation to the test of reasonableness and fairness on the grounds that it is not an absolute right. Relying on General Comment No. 15, which provides that: "*[t]he direct and indirect costs and charges associated with securing water must be affordable, and must not compromise or threaten the realization of other Covenant rights*", a court concluded that the right to water does not entail an absolute right to a free supply of water as claimed by the applicants. Therefore, disconnection from the water network is allowed in case of arrears, provided that the water company shows that it has made all reasonable efforts to persuade the consumer to pay and has informed him of the risk of disconnection in default of payment.[247] No mention was made to the case in which a person is unable to pay for the supply of water.

---

[242] *Ibid.*, para. 24.

[243] *Ibid.*, paras. 24, 39, 43-46.

[244] *Ibid.*, para. 44.

[245] *Ibid.*, para. 55.

[246] In line with the Constitutional Court of South African and the Israeli Supreme Court, the Peruvian Constitutional Tribunal also acknowledged the right to water but did not consider it as an absolute right. See *Eduardo Antonio Malca Vasquez v. Cajamarca*, file No. 01985-2011-PA-TC, Lima, 22 September 2011.

[247] Den Bosch Court of Appeal, HD 200.018.358 [2010] Gerechtshof ('s-Hertogenbosch) LJN BL6583, PRG (2010) 70, paras. 4.5, 4.8, 4.10, 4.11.

Indian jurisprudence[248] has played a central role in enforcing the right to water.[249] Although the right to water is not explicitly guaranteed by the Indian Constitution, the Indian Supreme Court and the High Courts have broadly interpreted the right to life, provided for in Article 21 of the Constitution, as encompassing the right to water.[250]

One of the first cases, *F.K. Hussain v. Union of India*,[251] concerned the coral isles of Lakshdweep, a place with limited water resources, where large scale withdrawals risked depleting water sources and causing the intrusion of salt water in the aquifers. The Kerala High Court held that "*[t]he right to sweet water, and the right to free air, are attributes of the right to life, for, these are the basic elements which sustain life itself*". Therefore, the Court ruled that exploitation of water resources was to be limited and human needs prioritised.

The *Perumatty Grama Panchayat* case has received worldwide attention.[252] In 2000, the Panchayat of Plachimada (the Council of elders of the village), in the Palakkad district of Kerala, gave a licence to a Coca-Cola plant to commence production. During the first two years, the Coca-Cola plant exploited groundwater resources to such an extent as to drain up several wells and to leave local people without a sufficient supply of drinking water or water to meet agricultural needs. Moreover, Coca-Cola had polluted the water with toxic waste, causing health problems to the locals. In 2003, when the district medical officer informed the residents that

---

[248] See, *inter alia*, *M.C. Mehta v. Union of India and others*, 12 January 1988, 1988 SCR(2) 530 (Supreme Court of India 1988); *Vellore Citizens Welfare Forum v. Union of India and others*, 28 August 1996 (Supreme Court of India 1996).

[249] Bluemel, pp. 980-983 (n 59).

[250] Indian Constitution, art. 21: "*No person shall be deprived of his life or personal liberty except according to procedure established by law*". See judgements: Supreme Court of India, *M.C. Mehta v. Union of India*, 1987 AIR 1086, 20 December 1986; Supreme Court of India, *Charan Lal Sahu v. Union of India*, 1990 AIR 1480, 22 December 1989; Kerala High Court, *Attakoya Thangal v. Union of India*, 1990 KLT 580, 17 September 2002, recognizing the right of people to clean water in connection with the right to life enshrined in art. 21; Supreme Court of India, *Subhash Kumar v. State of Bihar and Others*, 1991 AIR 420, 9 January 1991; Supreme Court of India, *Vellore Citizens Welfare Forum v. Union of India*, 1996 AIR 2715, 28 August 1996; High Court of Allahabad, *S. K. Garg v. State of Uttar Pradesh and Others*, 1999,AIR All 41, 28 May 1998; Supreme Court of India, *M. C. v. Union of India*, 2004 12SCC118, 18 March 2004, stating that groundwater is a social asset and citizens have the right to the use of air, water and earth as protected under art. 21 of the Constitution. See, P. Cullet, *Water Law – Evolving Regulatory Framework*, in P. Cullet, A. Gowlland-Gualtieri, R. Madhav, U. Ramanathan (eds.), *Water Governance in Motion: Towards Socially and Environmentally Sustainable Water Laws*, New Delhi, 2010, pp. 31, 34, 48-51; S. Muralidhar, *The right to water: An overview of the Indian Legal Regime*, in E. H. Riedel, P. Rothen (eds.), *The Human Right to Water*, Berlin, 2006.

[251] High Court of Kerala, *F.K. Hussain v. Union of India*, AIR 1990 Ker 321, 26 February 1990, para. 7.

[252] High Court of Kerala, *State Perumatty Grama Panchayat v. State of Kerala*, 2004 (1) KLT 731, 16 December 2003. See, V. Shiva, *Globalization's New War*, New Delhi, 2005.

water was no longer potable, the adivasi women protested, kicking off a massive popular movement against the Coca-Cola plant, which gained global support. In the aftermath of the uprising, the local Council withdrew the license for the Coca-Cola plant, which, as a result, was forced to close.

However, in December of the same year, the Company challenged the Village Council's decision before the High Court of Kerala State. The latter ordered the company to stop withdrawing groundwater, stating that "*the State is the trustee of all natural resources which are by nature meant for public use*",[253] thus it "*has got a duty to protect ground water against excessive exploitation and the inaction of the State in this regard will be tantamount to infringement of the right to life of the people guaranteed under Article 21 of the Constitution of India*".[254] The company appealed and since then a long judicial battle has been fought.[255]

Other national courts have dealt with the matter of water quality. Noteworthy is a recent case, *Alberto Castilla et al v. Colombia*,[256] in which the Colombian Constitutional Court clearly declared the unconstitutionality of Article 173 of the National Development Plan ("NDP")[257] on the ground that it breached, *inter alia*, the human right to water. The NDP, while banning agricultural activities, the exploration or exploitation of non-renewable natural resources and the construction of hydrocarbon refineries in the páramos, allowed mining and hydrocarbon activities, for which the licenses had been previously granted. Studies, however, had proved that mining and hydrocarbon activities were likely to have a serious negative impact on the ecosystem, potentially threatening the right to water of the residents, taking into consideration the fact that the *páramo* is a fragile ecosystem and that it provides most of Colombia's drinking water.

The Constitutional Court first reiterated its jurisprudence on the right to water,[258]

---

[253] *Ibid.*, para. 34.

[254] Similarly, see Supreme Constitutional Court, *C M. C. v. Union of India*, 2004(12) SCC118. The Supreme Court of India here recognised that groundwater is a common good and citizens have the right to the use water according to art. 21 of the Constitution.

[255] Supreme Court of India, *Perumatty Grama Panchayat v. State of Kerala and Others*, Appeal Civil 3538-3539 of 2010; Supreme Court of India, *Perumatty Grama Panchayat v. M/S Hindustan Coca Cola P. Ltd. & Others*, Appeal Civil 3540 of 2010. Both are connected to *Perumatty Grama Panchayat v. State of Kerala and Others*, Appeal Civil 4033 of 2009. Supreme Court of India, *Perumatty Grama Panchayat v. M/S Hindustan Coca Cola P. LTD. & Others*, Special Leave Petition (Civil) 25046 of 2005, connected to Special Leave Petiton (Civil) 15680-15681 of 2005. Info available at: http://courtnic.nic.in/supremecourt/causedisp.asp.

[256] *Alberto Castilla et al v. Colombia*, C-035 of 2016, 8 February 2016 (Constitutional Court of Colombia 2016).

[257] Art. 173, Law No. 1753 of 9 June 2015 "*Por la cual se expide el Plan Nacional de Desarrollo 2014-2018 'Todos por un Nuevo país*".

[258] See, *inter alia*, *Hernán Galeano Díaz contra Empresas Públicas de Medellín E.S.P*, T-616 of 2010, 5 August 2010 (Colombian Constitutional Court 2010); *María del Socorro Soto contra la Al-*

according to which it is a fundamental right that seriously impacts the enjoyment of other rights, such as the right to a dignified life, health and the environment. Next, it recalled the corresponding obligation of the state to guarantee the availability, accessibility and quality of the resource. Finally, the Court concluded that the *páramo* ecosystem was not properly protected by the challenged law and that such a deficit of protection affected the fundamental right to water.[259]

In the *Menores Comunidad Paynemil* case,[260] the Argentine Court of Appeal found an oil company guilty of having polluted the waters of the indigenous Paynemil Community. Since the Community relied on these waters for their daily needs, the Court also found the Government responsible for having violated its obligation to protect and, subsequently, for having failed to tackle the pollution problem. The Government was thus required to provide 250 liters of water per person per day to the members of Community, without regard to their ability to pay.[261]

Similarly, in Latin America, the right to water has been enforced in a number of cases concerning water service disconnections and indigenous peoples' rights. In the *Quevedo Miguel Angel y Otros* case,[262] several poor households of the City of Cordoba were disconnected from the water supply network due to their non-payment of water tariffs. The families concerned lodged a complaint with the First Instance Court of Argentina, requesting to be provided with 200 liters of water per family per day. The Court stated that, since the provincial law established the right of everyone to receive adequate services, and given that water services are essential services, the State was responsible for providing drinking water irrespective of the consumers' ability to pay.[263] Moreover, the Court deemed insufficient to meet health and hygienic basic requirements the provision of 50 liters of water per family

---

caldía Municipal de La Tebaida, Quindío, y la Empresa Sanitaria del Quindío S.A. E.S.P, T-614 of 2010, 5 August 2010 (Colombian Constitutional Court 2010); *María Inés Hernández y otros contra el Acueducto Metropolitano de Bucaramanga y la Alcaldía del municipio de San Juan Girón*, T-916 of 2011, 7 December 2011 (Colombian Constitutional Court 2011); *Lucas Hernández Alba y otros contra los municipios de Apulo y otros*, T-312 of 2012, 26 April 2012 (Colombian Constitutional Court 2012).

[259] *Alberto Castilla et al v.* Colombia, para. 164, n. 41 (n 256).

[260] *Menores Communidad Paynemil s/accion de amparo*, Expte. 311-CA-1997. Sala II. Camara de Aplicaciones en lo Civil, Neuquen, 19 May 1997.

[261] See also Primera Instancia y 8 Nominación en lo Civil y Comercial, *Marchisio José Bautista y Otros*, Acción de Amparo (Expte. No. 500003/36), Ciudad de Córdoba, 14 October 2004. The court ordered the municipality to adopt all necessary measures to improve the functioning of the sewage treatment plant and minimize the effects of untreated wastewater that was contaminating the drinking water of the community of Chacras de la Merced. *Report of the Independent Expert on the issue of human rights obligations related to access to safe drinking water and sanitation*, UN Doc. A/HRC/12/24, 1 July 2009, p. 13.

[262] *Juez Sustituta de Primera Instancia y 51 Nominación en lo Civil y Comercial: Quevedo Miguel Angel y Otros c/ Aguas Cordobesas S.A.*, Acción de Amparo, Ciudad de Córdoba, 8 April 2002.

[263] *Ibid.*, para. VII.

per day granted to non-paying users under the concession agreement. Accordingly, it ordered the State to supply at least 200 liters of water per household per day.

Finally, in Europe domestic courts have also contributed to the implementation of the right to water. In Belgium, the Constitutional Court has upheld the legislation of the Brussels-Capital Region, which allows water distribution companies to invoice the bill to the owner of a house if the tenant is unable to pay it.[264] In this way, tenants cannot be denied the right to the supply of drinking water. The Constitutional Court also upheld the Regulation of Flanders, which entitles every person to a minimum amount of drinking water per year free of charge.[265]

2.2.2. States' *opinio juris*

Opinio juris is the subjective element necessary for the formation of customary rules.[266] It is a belief that a given practice "*is rendered obligatory by the existence of a rule of law requiring it*".[267]

Evidence of States' *opinio juris* may be found in their statements, as well as in their explanations for their vote in connection with resolutions adopted by an international organization or at an intergovernmental conference.[268] For instance, a vote by a State in favor of a UN General Assembly resolution can provide evidence of its *opinio juris*.[269] Additionally, decisions of national courts have been considered evidence of States' *opinio juris*.[270]

The value of General Assembly resolutions for the establishment of customary rules is disputed. Opinions diverge as to whether they may provide evidence for establishing the existence of a rule or the emergence of an *opinio juris*. It is however generally agreed that they may also contribute to the development of customary law.

---

[264] Ruling No. 9/1996, 8 February 1996. See http://www2.ohchr.org/english/issues/water/contributions/Belgium.pdf.

[265] Ruling No. 36/98, 1 April 1998. See http://www2.ohchr.org/english/issues/water/contributions/Belgium.pdf.

[266] ILC, *Identification of Customary International Law* (n 80), Conclusion 9.1 – Requirement of acceptance as law.

[267] ICJ, *North Sea Continental Shelf*, para. 77 (n 83).

[268] ILC, *Identification of Customary International Law* (n 80), Conclusion 10.2 – Forms of evidence of acceptance as law.

[269] ICJ, *Case Concerning Military and Paramilitary Activities In and Against Nicaragua*, para. 188 (n 83).

[270] ICJ, *Jurisdictional Immunities of the State*, para. 77 (n 83); ILC, *Identification of Customary International Law* (n 80), Conclusion 10 – Forms of evidence of acceptance as law; H. Lauterpacht, *Decisions of Municipal Courts as a Source of International Law*, in *British Year Book of International Law*, 1929, pp. 84-85; I. Wuerth, *National Court Decisions and* Opinio Juris, Conference Paper, Duke – Geneva Institute in Transnational Law, University of Geneva, 2013, available at https://law.duke.edu/cicl/pdf/opiniojuris/panel_3-wuerth-national_court_decisions_and_opinio_juris.pdf, p. 1.

According to the International Court of Justice, to ascertain whether a General Assembly resolution may serve the scope of providing evidence of States' *opinio juris* "*it is necessary to look at its content and the conditions of its adoption; it is also necessary to see whether an* opinio juris *exists as to its normative character. Or a series of resolutions may show the gradual evolution of the* opinio juris *required for the establishment of a new rule*".[271]

The present author acknowledges that scholars have maintained different positions as for the role of States' statements and UN General Assembly resolutions in the formation of customary rules.[272] While, according to some, these are evidence of State practice,[273] others deny such a role[274] and consider them as a possible proof of States' *opinio juris.*[275] A convincing intermediate position is to regard States' statements and UN General Assembly resolutions as evidence of both State practice and *opinio*, according to the circumstances.[276] As Dumberry well stated, "*there is no valid reason why so-called double-counting should be avoided at all cost*".[277] Indeed, "*while the fact that a State* says something *constitutes an element of State practice, the content of what the state is* actually saying *can also represent its* opinio juris".[278]

In line with this conclusion, I do not avoid double-counting and consider as relevant *opinio juris* the acknowledgements made by States of the right to water in various declarations and statements,[279] as well as expressed in their explanations of vote cast within the international organizations that have adopted resolutions on the matter.

---

[271] ICJ, *Legality of the Threat or Use of Nuclear Weapons*, para. 70 (n 83).

[272] Roberts, p. 758 (n 84); Kammerhofer, pp. 525-532 (n 102); A. T. Guzman, *Saving Customary International Law*, in *Michigan Journal of International Law*, 2005, pp. 152-153.

[273] Shaw, p. 61 (n 82); M. Akehurst, *Custom as a Source of International Law*, in *British Yearbook of International Law*, 1976, pp. 1-53. See also ICJ, *Nuclear test case, Australia v. France*, Judgment, 20 December 1974, para. 49; ICJ, *Nuclear test case, New Zealand v. France*, Judgment, 20 December 1974, para. 49.

[274] A. D'Amato, *The Concept of Custom in International Law*, New York, 1971, p. 88; d'Aspremont (n 84).

[275] M. E. Villiger, *Customary International Law and Treaties. A Manual on the Theory and Practice of the Interrelation of Sources*, The Hague, 1997, p. 24, p. 51; See also: ICJ, *Legality of the Threat or Use of Nuclear Weapons*, para. 70 (n 83); ILC, *Identification of Customary International Law* (n 80), Conclusion 10.2 – Forms of evidence of acceptance as law (*opinio juris*).

[276] Dumberry, p. 317 (n 82); ILA, *Final Report of the Committee on the Formation of Customary (General) International Law, Statement of Principles Applicable to the Formation of General Customary International Law*, 2000, pp. 14-15.

[277] Dumberry, pp. 317-321 (n 82).

[278] *Ibid.*, pp. 318-319. Villiger, p. 23 (n 275).

[279] See, *inter alia*, declarations and/or statements by a group of States: Declaration of the first Africa-South America Summit, para. 18 (n 143); Message From Beppu (n 143); The Delhi Declaration (n 143); Sharm el-Sheikh Final Document, para. 393 (n 143); ASEAN Human Rights Declaration, art. 28(*e*) (n 143); Chiang Mai Declaration (n 143).

In this connection, as anticipated in section 2.2.1.3, the 2010 General Assembly resolution on the right to water was adopted with 41 abstentions.[280] However, the reasons for abstaining focused principally on the lack of transparency in the drafting process, which resulted in a resolution that did not reflect the views of all the voting States.[281]

Paradigmatic of the modification of States' attitude towards the recognition of the right to water are Canada's statements. While it abstained from voting in favor of the 2010 General Assembly resolution on the ground that it was premature, as at that time "*there was no consensus among States regarding the basis, scope and content of a possible right to water*",[282] two years later, at the end of the UN Conference on Sustainable Development held in Rio de Janeiro in 2012, Canada posited not only that it recognized such a right as "*implicit under article 11 of the International Covenant on Economic, Social and Cultural Rights*", but also singled out its content.[283]

The absence of any refusal in principle to the recognition of the right to water was made clear by the subsequent resolution of the General Assembly on the right to water, which was adopted in 2015 by *consensus*.[284] It explicitly embraced the definition of this right provided by the CESCR in General Comment No. 15. In this connection, the United States of America once again expressed their disagreement, but did not vote against it.[285]

The General Assembly subsequently adopted a resolution on the right to water[286]

---

[280] General Assembly, Res. 64/292 (n 34).

[281] See the explanation of vote by the United States of America, p. 8 (n 61). The U.S.A.'s major complaints against the resolution regarded the way it was drafted, specifically that this took place not "*in a transparent, inclusive manner*", and the fact that its legal implications "*have not yet been carefully and fully considered*".

[282] General Assembly, explanation of vote by Canada, p. 17 (n 61).

[283] Annex to the letter dated 22 June 2012 from the Permanent Representative of Canada to the United Nations addressed to the Secretary-General of the United Nations Conference on Sustainable Development, Explanation of position, 22 June 2012, UN Doc. A/CONF.216/12, 17 July 2012. Canada affirmed that the right to water was interpreted as: "*the right to a sufficient quantity and safe quality of reasonably affordable and accessible water for personal and domestic uses (i.e., for drinking, cooking and for personal and household hygiene), and to basic sanitation that is safe and hygienic. Water and sanitation services should be physically and economically accessible on an equal and non-discriminatory basis*".

[284] General Assembly, Res 70/169 (n 146).

[285] Official Records of the General Assembly, Seventieth Session, Third Committee, 55th meeting, UN Doc. A/C.3/70/SR.55, 24 November 2015, para. 144. The South African delegation did not sponsor the draft resolution as it did not take adequately into account the link between sanitation and water needs (para. 133). Moreover, South Africa (para. 134) and India (para. 139) expressed reservations on the human rights-based approach to development taken in the resolution. However, no State party to the ICESCR has refuted the definition of the right to water given by the General Assembly.

[286] General Assembly, Res. 72/178 (n 67).

in 2017 with the abstention of New Zealand, South Africa and Turkey and the contrary vote of Kyrgyzstan. While Turkey gave no explanation, South Africa openly expressed appreciation for the decision to address the issue of water and sanitation under a human rights perspective, but criticised the absence of clear progressive language.[287] Kyrgyzstan mainly complained that the wording of paragraph 9 of the resolution allowed for the inference of extraterritorial obligations from the right to water, while it accepted commitments arising from this right only within its own territory.[288]

In general terms, it seems that the extensive number of votes in favor of the General Assembly resolutions on the right to water, together with the accompanying explanations of vote, represent evidence of the States' belief in the existence of a human right to water.

In addition, the growing number of decisions of national courts acknowledging the right to water (see above section 2.2.1.5) confirms the same conclusion, showing a consistent evolution of the *opinio juris* required for the establishment of a customary human right to water.

2.2.3. A right in *statu nascendi* or already born?

The bar to proving the existence of a customary international rule is high, so high that it is said that "*everyone fails*".[289] The time-consuming and complex search for evidence of State practice and *opinio juris* dissuades us from undertaking this exercise and even the ICJ has often avoided carrying out a proper investigation into the two elements of custom, relying essentially on evidence such as the work of the ILC, previous decisions of international tribunals or General Assembly resolutions.[290]

However burdensome it may be to provide proof of State practice and *opinio juris* in respect of the right to water, the present author has endeavoured to carry out an objective analysis on the formation of a customary human right to water and it is time to draw some conclusions on its customary *status*.

Starting from the analysis of State practice, at the outset it should be recalled that for a customary rule to come into existence, complete consistency in States' be-

---

[287] General Assembly, para. 38 (n 148).

[288] *Ibid.*, para. 20. Another amendment to the draft resolution was technical in nature and concerned an alleged different translation of some words of the twenty-sixth preambular paragraph. *Ibid.*, para. 19.

[289] According to Roberts "*[a]lmost no one actually 'finds' custom. Instead, arbitrators, academics and counsel typically refer to other sources that supposedly have already 'found' custom.*" See A. Roberts, *Custom, Public Law and the Human Rights Analogy*, in *EJIL: Talk!*, 14 August 2013.

[290] P. Tomka, *Custom and the International Court of Justice*, in *Law and Practice of International Courts and Tribunals*, 2013, p. 197; D'Amato, pp. 101-103 (n 83); A. Alvarez-Jimenez, *Methods for the Identification of Customary International Law in the International Court of Justice's Jurisprudence: 2000-2009*, in *International & Comparative Law Quarterly*, 2011, pp. 681-712; Tesón, pp. 99-102 (n 93).

haviour is not expected. The fact that approximately 663 million people still lack access to improved water sources does not imply, *per se*, that no customary rule on the human right to water has come into being.

As recalled by the ICJ, for a rule to be established as customary, it is not necessary to ascertain that the corresponding practice is "*in absolutely rigorous conformity with the rule*".[291] On the contrary, it is sufficient that the practice of States consistent with the right at issue is "*extensive and virtually uniform*",[292] and that where inconsistent behaviours are adopted, they are justified on some grounds.

The overall practice of States with respect to the human right to water is directed at making efforts to progressively achieve access to water worldwide. Indeed, since the Millennium Development Goal on water and sanitation was set, the percentage of people worldwide with access to water has progressively increased and the goal was reached wide before the scheduled time.

There is widespread involvement of States in international conventions recognizing the right to water for certain categories of people.[293] Moreover, although the ICESCR does not expressly encompass the right to water, States parties to this treaty have acknowledged that it requires them to respect the right to water as embedded in the right to an adequate standard of living and in the right to the highest attainable standard of health (see below section 3). In addition, several regional treaties have been adopted, which enshrine the right to water.[294] Overall, the vast majority of the international community is party to a treaty that provides for the right at issue.

---

[291] ICJ, *Case Concerning Military and Paramilitary activities in and against Nicaragua,* para. 186 (n 83).

[292] ICJ, *North Sea Continental Shelf,* para. 74 (n 83).

[293] The Convention on the Elimination of All Forms of Discrimination against Women counts 188 Parties; the Convention on the Rights of the Child has 194 Parties; and, the Convention on the Rights of Persons with Disabilities has 144 Parties (see: https://treaties.un.org).

[294] The African Convention on the Conservation of Nature and Natural Resources counts 32 Parties (See: https://www.ecolex.org/details/treaty/african-convention-on-the-conservation-of-nature-and-natural-resources-tre-000492/); Charte de l'eau du bassin du Niger, Signatories: Burkina Faso, Benin, Cameroon, Ivory Coast, Guinea, Mali, Niger, Nigeria and Chad, entered into force on 19 July 2010; the African Charter on the Rights and Welfare of Child has been ratified by 47 States (Source: http://acerwc.org/the-african-charter-on-the-rights-and-welfare-of-the-child-acrwc/ratifications/); the Protocol to the African Charter on Human and Peoples' Rights on the Rights of Women in Africa has been ratified by 28 States (see, http://www.achpr.org/instruments/women-protocol/); Additional Protocol to the American Convention on Human Rights in the Area of Economic, Social and Cultural Rights has 16 ratifications (see, http://www.oas.org/juridico/english/sigs/a-52.html); Protocol on Water and Health, counts 26 Parties (see, https://treaties.un.org/Pages/ViewDetails.aspx?src=TREATY&mtdsg_no=XXVII-5-a&chapter=27&lang=en); The Arab Charter on Human Rights adopted in 2004 counts 12 Parties (see, http://unipd-centrodirittiumani.it/en/spilli/Ratification-and-signature-status-of-the-Arab-Charter-on-Human-Rights-2004/147).

Around sixty States (to the author's knowledge), amounting for almost one third of the international community, have enacted the right to water at constitutional level or have regulated various aspects of water management and the provision of water services at the legislative level, implicitly recognizing at least some aspects of the right to water.

States have also claimed to have acted for the protection of the right to water in several *fora*, in particular before investment arbitral tribunals in order to justify measures adopted *vis-à-vis* investors in the context of the privatization of water services (see chapter three).[295]

Moreover, numerous cases decided by domestic courts are evidence of State practice consistent with the right to water. To mention but a few, reference may be made to the African,[296] South American,[297] and Indian[298] jurisprudence. Interestingly, to the author's knowledge, States have never denied the existence of the right at issue before domestic and international tribunals.

Additionally, States have expressed their consent to the recognition of the right to water in several declarations[299] and in a number of statements concluding international conferences.[300] Various resolutions on the human right to water have also

---

[295] In this regard, see, *inter alia*, chapter III, *Suez, Sociedad General de Aguas de Barcelona, S.A. and Vivendi Universal, S.A. v. Argentine Republic* (n 144); *Suez, Sociedad General de Aguas de Barcelona SA and Interagua Servicios Integrales de Agua SA v. Argentine Republic* (n 144); *Aguas Cordobesas, S.A., Suez, and Sociedad General de Aguas de Barcelona, S.A. v. Argentine Republic* (n 144); *Impregilio S.p.A. v. Argentina Republic* (n 144); *SAUR International v. Argentine Republic* (n 144).

[296] High Court of South Africa, *Residents of Bon Vista Mansions v. Southern Metropolitan Local Council* (n 217); Supreme Africa's Constitutional Court, *Mazibuko v. City of Johannesburg* (n 224); Court of Appeals of the Republic of Botswana, *Matsipane Mosetlhanyane and Other v. Attorney General* (n 233).

[297] *Juez Sustituta de Primera Instancia y 51 Nominación en lo Civil y Comercial: Quevedo Miguel Angel y Otros c/ Aguas Cordobesas S.A.* (n 262); *Menores Communidad Paynemil s/accion de amparo* (n 260).

[298] High Court of Kerala, *F.K. Hussain v. Union of India*, para. 7 (n 251); High Court of Kerala, *State Perumatty Grama Panchayat v State of Kerala* (n 252).

[299] See, *inter alia*, declarations and/or statements by a group of States: Declaration of the first Africa-South America Summit, para. 18 (n 143); Sharm el-Sheikh Final Document, para. 393 (n 143); Message From Beppu (n 143); The Delhi Declaration (n 143); Chiang Mai Declaration (n 143); European Parliament, Written Declaration on the protection of water as a public asset (n 151); European Parliament resolution on the Fourth World Water Forum (n 151); European Parliament resolution on the Commission Communication on Water Management in Developing Countries and Priorities for EU Development Cooperation (n 151); European Parliament resolution of 12 March 2009 on 5th World Water Forum (n 151).

[300] See, among others, Mar del Plata Action Plan, Preamble (n 4); Dublin Statement on Water and Sustainable Development (n 11); *Report of the United Nations Conference on Sustainable Development* (n 36); *Programme of Action, Report of the United Nations International Conference on Population and Development* (n 14).

been adopted by *consensus* by the General Assembly[301] and the Human Rights Council.[302]

In particular, General Assembly resolutions show the gradual evolution of the *opinio juris* required for the establishment of a customary human right to water. While the first General Assembly resolution on the right to water was adopted with 122 votes in favor and 41 abstentions, the 2013 and 2015 resolutions were adopted by *consensus*. Looking at the conditions of their adoption, the characterization of these General Assembly resolutions as a manifestation of States' *opinio juris* may be accepted.

Finally, with respect to the period of time necessary for a rule to be considered a general rule of international law, the passage of a considerable amount of time is not a *conditio sine qua non*, as long as States' behaviour is consistent and widespread.[303] In this connection, the passage of a short period of time since the early recognition of the right to water is not in itself an impediment to the formation of a new customary rule.[304]

In light of the foregoing examination, the present author concludes that there is a rather "*extensive and virtually uniform*" practice of States with respect to the right to water accompanied by the acceptance that it is socially and legally due, which allows one to argue for the existence of a customary self-standing norm.

However, this conclusion needs to be further specified because uncertainties remain as to the scope and content of the customary right to water.[305]

2.3. General principles of international law

Concerning the third source of international law listed in Article 38 of the Statute of the ICJ, I share the view that general principles of law recognized by civilized nations are principles of justice and legal reasoning accepted and developed by States

---

[301] General Assembly, Res 64/292 (n 34); Res. 70/169 (n 146); Res. 72/178 (n 67).

[302] See, *inter alia*: Human Rights Council, Res. 15/9, para. 3 (n 35); Res. 16/2 (n 149); Res. 18/1 (n 149); Res. 24/18 (n 22).

[303] ICJ, *North Sea Continental Shelf*, para. 73 (n 83).

[304] *Ibid.*, para. 74: "*an indispensable requirement would be that within the period in question, short though it may be, State practice (...) should have been both extensive and virtually uniform in the sense of the provision invoked; – and should moreover have occurred in such a way as to show a general recognition that a rule of law or legal obligation is involved*".

[305] Cannizzaro distinguishes between the issue of ascertaining the existence of a norm from that of establishing its content. E. Cannizzaro, *Unità e pluralità dei metodi di accertamento del diritto consuetudinario*, in P. Palchetti (ed.), *L'incidenza del Diritto Non Scritto sul Diritto Internazionale ed Europeo*, Naples, 2016, pp. 24-28. Notwithstanding the large number of instruments dealing with water rights, scholars underline that "*the lack of normative clarity*" on that issue "*leads towards an ambiguous and uncertain practical applicability of the human right to water*". Salman, pp. 78-80 (n 24). See also McCaffrey, p. 79 (n 24).

in *foro domestic.*[306] These principles – such as, for instance, *ne bis in idem* or *nemo iudex in re sua* – are common to most domestic legal systems and applicable on a subsidiary basis, absent treaty and customary norms.[307] In this perspective, the right to water cannot be framed in this autonomous source of law.[308]

3. The content of the human right to water

This section analyzes the content of the human right to water as both a derivative right enshrined in the right to an adequate standard of living under Article 11 ICESCR and strictly related to the right to the highest attainable standard of health pursuant to Article 12 ICESCR, and as a customary norm. The present author suggests in fact that the content of the two norms does not coincide.

3.1. The content of the right to water derived from Article 11 ICESCR

General Comment No. 15 defines the human right to water as the entitlement of everyone to "*sufficient, safe, acceptable, physically accessible and affordable water for personal and domestic uses*".[309] As mentioned in the previous sections, the CESCR inferred this right from the right to an adequate standard of living, enshrined in Article 11(1) ICESCR,[310] and considered it as "*inextricably related to the right to the highest attainable standard of health*" prescribed by Article 12(1) ICESCR.[311]

Moreover, as anticipated in sections 2.1 and 2.1.1, the right to water has been derived from a number of other rights, such as the right to life, to human dignity, to food and housing and, as a consequence, its content as a derivative right is bound to vary according to the embedding right invoked each time. For the sake of this section, the content of the right to water is derived from the right to an adequate

---

[306] *Contra*, Misiedjan, p. 81 (n 40). Misiedjan relies on Simma and Alston, who outlined a different concept of general principles of international law in the field of human rights law, namely principles grounded on general acceptance and recognition rather than on State practice. Simma, Alston, pp. 102-108 (n 70).

[307] Focarelli, pp. 325-331 (n 82). Authors have formulated different theories on general principles of international law, ranging from those who deny their autonomous legal *status* and consider them as customary norms *sui generis* (Conforti, p. 51 (n 82) to those who link general principles of international law to natural law (Focarelli, p. 327, nt. 159 (n 82).

[308] Thielbörger and Misiedjan reached the same conclusions (that the right to water cannot be framed as a general principle of international law), but following a different line of reasoning, notably that the right to water is not sufficiently reflected in national constitutions and legislations. Thielbörger, pp. 86-87 (n 40); Misiedjan, p. 81 (n 40).

[309] General Comment No. 15, para. 2 (n 24).

[310] *Ibid.*, para. 3.

[311] *Ibid.*, para. 3.

standard of living, as this is the widest in scope. It not only covers life-threatening situations or situations capable of affecting health conditions or access to food, but also less serious circumstances in which human well-being is jeopardized without reaching such thresholds of gravity.[312] For this purpose, General Comment No. 15 will be taken as the landmark document describing the content of the right at issue.

The definition of the right to water places emphasis on its use for human consumption, while it is silent *vis-à-vis* other usages, such as agricultural or industrial purposes. Accordingly, the latter are exempted from the scope of the derivative right to water and in case of conflicting uses, water is to be allocated with priority for personal and domestic needs.

Personal uses include drinking water and personal hygiene. Domestic uses refer to cooking, washing of clothes and household hygiene.[313] Other uses to be given priority are those necessary to prevent starvation and disease.[314]

The first General Assembly resolution on the right to water referred to "*the right to safe and clean* drinking *water and sanitation*",[315] without providing any definition of this right, a circumstance that led some authors to infer that the UN body meant to exclude some personal and domestic uses from the scope of the right.[316] However, subsequently the General Assembly adopted the definition of the right to water provided by the ICESCR, clearing the uncertainty concerning the extension of the right to water to personal and domestic needs.

According to General Comment No. 15, the right to water implies both the freedom from third parties' interference in its enjoyment (such as arbitrary disconnection from or contamination of waters) and individual and collective entitlements, *inter alia*, to a system of water supply.[317]

The Committee distinguishes three substantive features of the right at issue, namely the availability, quality and accessibility of water,[318] which must be ensured both for present and future generations.[319]

Availability is defined as the supply of a sufficient and continuous amount of wa-

---

[312] For instance, it would be difficult to conceive of an individual communication submitted to the HRC complaining of a violation of the right to life due to the absence of sufficient water for domestic hygiene.

[313] General Comment No. 15, para. 12 (*a*) (n 24).

[314] *Ibid.*, para. 6.

[315] General Assembly, Res. 64/292 (n 34).

[316] Dubuy, p. 297 (n 40).

[317] General Comment No. 15, para. 10 (n 24). Several scholars have commented on the substantive features of the right to water as singled out by the CESCR. Among others: Brown Weiss, pp. 191-209 (n 40); Murillo Chávarro, pp. 19-29, (n 54); T. S. Bulto, *The Extraterritorial Application of the Human Right to Water in Africa*, Cambridge, 2014, pp. 55-56.

[318] General Comment No. 15, para. 12 (n 24).

[319] *Ibid.*, para. 11. Brown Weiss speaks in this respect of the "*intergenerational aspect of the right to water*". Brown Weiss, pp. 205-209 (n 40).

ter for personal and domestic uses. It requires both the physical availability of freshwater in a given territory and the possibility to enjoy a sufficient supply in a regular manner.[320] To quantify the amount of water needed to comply with the right to water, reference should be made to the World Health Organization Guidelines. The WHO/UNICEF Joint Monitoring Programme suggests that "*reasonable access*" consists of "*the availability of at least 20 liters per person per day from a source within one kilometer of the users' dwelling*", but such figures are the bare minimum necessary to meet basic hygiene and consumption requirements.[321] Between 50 and 100 liters of water per person per day is recommended to meet all personal and domestic needs, depending on many factors, such as health status, work, climate conditions and cultural requirements.[322] The right to water immediately entitles everyone to a limited amount of water considered strictly necessary to prevent disease.[323] An adequate amount of water, which goes beyond the minimum requirement, must be provided progressively in order to reach the full realization of the right at stake.[324] According to Winkler, the human right to water extends over several levels of intensity, ranging from its core obligations to its complete fulfillment. The core obligations consist of the right to an amount of drinking water for survival and for hygienic needs. A second level also includes water for personal and domestic needs, such as cooking. A third level encompasses the complete fulfillment of the right to water. Finally, all other kinds of water use, including filling swimming pools or watering golf courses, are not comprised in the human right to water.[325]

The requirement of *quality* refers to the safety of drinking water which must be free from micro-organisms, chemical substances or radiological hazards that can undermine human health.[326]

Accessibility refers to physical, economic and non-discriminatory dimensions.

---

[320] General Comment No. 15, para. 12 (*a*) (n 24).

[321] WHO/UNICEF, Global Water Supply and Sanitation Assessment, 2000, p. 85. As for sanitation, it "*was defined to include connection to a sewer or septic tank system, pour-flush latrine, simple pit or ventilated improved pit latrine, again with allowance for acceptable local technologies*". Source: www.who.int. See: G. Hutton, L. Haller, World Health Organization, *Evaluation of the costs and benefits of water and sanitation improvements at the global level*, Geneva, 2004; G. Howard, J. Bartram, *Domestic Water Quantity, Service Level and Health*, Doc. WHO/SDE/WSH/03.02, Geneva, 2003. Howard and Bartram estimate that 7.5 liters per capita per day is the basic minimum amount of water necessary (drinking water plus water for food preparation) to meet the requirements of most people under most conditions, p. 9. See also P. H. Gleick, *The Human Right to Water*, in *Water Policy*, 1998, pp. 487-503.

[322] Howard, Bartram, Executive summary (n 321).

[323] General Comment No. 15, para. 37(*a*) (n 24).

[324] *Ibid.*, para. 17.

[325] Winkler (n 40).

[326] General Comment No. 15, para. 12(*b*) (n 24). See the WHO Guidelines for Drinking-Water Quality, fourth edition, 2011, available at: http://www.who.int/water_sanitation_health/publications/2011/dwq_guidelines/en/index.html.

Water must be *physically* accessible by everyone within or in close proximity to the household, educational institution and workplace. This requirement is met even when water and sanitation facilities are available in the immediate vicinity of these places.[327] Moreover, water and water facilities and services should be *affordable*, meaning that the costs and charges associated with securing water and sanitation must not compromise the users' ability to pay for other basic needs, such as food, housing, education and health.[328] From a human right perspective, the cost recovery principle – referring to the charges required in order to cover costs associated with the connection to the mains and the delivery of water – has to be interpreted in a manner consistent with the right to access to a basic amount of safe drinking water, even in the case of inability to pay.[329] Access to water must also be *equitable* – understood as without discrimination among different users – especially the most vulnerable and marginalized people.[330]

Finally, in addition to these substantive aspects, the CESCR refers also to a procedural dimension of the right to water, consisting in the right to receive information,[331] to participate in public decisions related to water and to have access to justice in water-related issues. Any action likely to interfere with an individual's right to water must not be adopted before providing the affected people with all the relevant information, as well as with the opportunity to be consulted, and to lodge an appeal against the proposed measures.[332]

The right to participate in the decision-making process must be ensured as a part of any policy, programme or strategy concerning water,[333] and in particular when water services are operated by third parties.[334] The States' obligation to adopt and implement national water strategies and plans of action on the basis of a participatory process is listed among the core non-derogable obligations of immediate ef-

---

[327] General Comment No. 15, para. 12(*c*)(*i*) (n 24); Human Rights Council, *Report of the United Nations High Commissioner for Human Rights on the scope and content of the relevant human rights obligations related to equitable access to safe drinking water and sanitation under international human rights instruments*, para. 26 (n 29).

[328] General Comment No. 15, para. 12(*c*)(*ii*) (n 24); Human Rights Council, *Report of the Special Rapporteur on the human right to safe drinking water and sanitation,* para. 47 (n 188).

[329] Brown Weiss refers to flexible pricing schemes, which allow utilities to recover the water services cost without denying access to water to the poorest segments of society. Brown Weiss, p. 203 (n 40).

[330] General Comment No. 15, para. 12 (*c*)(*iii*) (n 24); Human Rights Council, *Report of the United Nations High Commissioner for Human Rights on the scope and content of the relevant human rights obligations related to equitable access to safe drinking water and sanitation under international human rights instruments*, para. 22 (n 29).

[331] General Comment No. 15, para. 12 (*c*)(*iv*) (n 24).

[332] *Ibid.*, para. 56.

[333] *Ibid.*, para. 48.

[334] *Ibid.*, para. 24.

fect.[335] In case of denial of the right to water, persons or groups affected must have access to effective judicial or other remedies at both a national and an international level.[336]

The procedural dimension of the right to water has been attracting growing attention[337] following its adjudication before human rights bodies,[338] contributing to enhance the achievement of the substantive dimension of this right.

To what extent does the description of the main features of the right to water provided for in General Comment No. 15 correspond to the content of the derivative right under consideration? Ultimately, General Comment No. 15 is an authoritative interpretation, but still not binding for the State parties to the ICESCR. In the following section, I submit that the definition of the right to water included in General Comment No. 15 is agreed to a large extent by State parties to the ICESCR and corresponds to the content that those States have accepted as binding by way of a subsequent agreement on the interpretation of the ICESCR.

3.1.1. Subsequent agreement on the interpretation of Article 11 ICESCR

As mentioned in the previous sub-section, the CESCR has defined the right to water as the entitlement of everyone to "*sufficient, safe, acceptable, physically accessible and affordable water for personal and domestic uses*".[339] Subsequently, the General Assembly has acknowledged the definition of the right to water enshrined in General Comment No. 15 and made it its own.[340]

In the framework of the work of the ILC on subsequent agreements and practice in relation to the interpretation of treaties, the ILC has taken the view that General Comment No. 15 offers an "*illustration of the way in which an agreement of the parties may come about*".[341] It is maintained that pronouncements of expert treaty bod-

---

[335] *Ibid.*, paras. 37(*f*) and 40.

[336] *Ibid.*, para. 55.

[337] O. McIntyre, *The Role of the Public and the Human Right to Water*, in M. Tignino, K. Sangbana (eds.), *Public Participation and Water Resources Management: Where Do We Stand in International Law*, Paris, 2015, pp. 139-146; J. Razzaque, *Public Participation in Water Governance*, in J. W. Dellapenna, J. Gupta (eds.), *The Evolution of the Law and Politics of Water*, Dordrecht, 2009, pp. 355-369.

[338] L. Boisson De Chazournes, *Le droit à l'eau et la satisfaction des besoins humains: notions de justice*, in D. Alland, V. Chetail, O. de Frouville, J. E. Viñuales (eds), *Unité et Diversité du Droit International: Ecrits en l'honneur du Professeur Pierre-Marie Dupuy/Unity and Diversity of International Law: Essays in Honour of Professor Pierre-Marie Dupuy*, Leiden, 2014, pp. 978-980.

[339] General Comment No. 15, para. 2 (n 24).

[340] General Assembly, Res. 70/169 (n 146); General Assembly, Res. 72/178 (n 67).

[341] ILC, *Subsequent Agreements and Subsequent Practice in Relation to Interpretation of Treaties*, p. 111, para. 14 (n 115). It is noteworthy that the ILC did not hold that the findings of international treaty bodies, such as the CESCR, are to be considered subsequent practice *per se*, but

ies, such as General Comment No. 15, may give rise to, or refer to, a subsequent agreement or subsequent practice by parties on the interpretation of the treaty pursuant to Article 31(3)(*a*)(*b*) VCLT.[342]

Admittedly, according the ILC, it may prove difficult to establish the existence of an agreement of *all* parties to a treaty that a given pronouncement of an expert treaty body does express the interpretation to be given to that treaty. However, it is held that a possible way to overcome this problem is by considering the resolutions of organs of international organizations, in particular General Assembly resolutions, that refer to pronouncements of expert treaty bodies as implying an agreement of the parties regarding the interpretation of a treaty.[343]

In this respect, the ILC notes that in 2015 General Assembly adopted by *consensus* a resolution that defines the human right to water in the same terms employed by the CESCR in General Comment No. 15.[344] However, the ILC suggests that the adoption of the resolution by *consensus*, i.e. without a vote, may not *per se* reflect unanimity of opinion on the substantive matter. Therefore, whether the General Assembly resolution constitutes an agreement of all parties to the ICESCR accepting the interpretation contained in the CESCR pronouncement is to be ascertained.[345]

In this connection, it is notable that only the United States, which is not a party to the ICESCR, dissented from the consensus by disagreeing on the definition of the right to water that the General Assembly borrowed from General Comment No. 15.[346] On the contrary, no State party to the ICESCR contested this definition.[347]

---

that they may reflect or give rise to a subsequent agreement or subsequent practice. S. Kadelbach, *The International Law Commission and the role of subsequent practice as a means of interpretation under Articles 31 and 32 VCLT*, in *QIL*, 2018, pp. 13-14.

[342] ILC, *Subsequent Agreements and Subsequent Practice in Relation to Interpretation of Treaties*, Conclusion 13 (n 115). Pronouncements of expert treaty bodies, p. 111, para. 12.

[343] *Ibid.*, Commentary to Conclusion 13, p. 111, para. 13.

[344] *Ibid.*, para. 14. See General Assembly, Res. 70/169 (n 146).

[345] O. Dörr, *Interpretation of Treaties*, in O. Dörr, K. Schmalenbach (eds.), V*ienna Convention on the Law of Treaties. A Commentary*, Berlin, 2018, p. 594-594, paras. 75-76. A subsequent agreement under art. 31(3)(*a*) does not need to be in treaty form but may also be an informal agreement or understanding, provided that the parties "*intended their understanding to be the basis for an agreed interpretation*". In this connection, the agreement may also take the form of a decision of a treaty organ, if such a decision is taken unanimously or at least, the parties to the treaty that did not vote have implicitly accepted the decision.

[346] Official Records of the General Assembly, para. 144 (n 285). The South Africa delegation did not sponsor the draft resolution as it did not take adequately into account the link between sanitation and water needs (para. 133). Moreover, South Africa (para. 134) and India (para. 139) have expressed reservations on the human rights-based approach to development taken in the resolution. However, no State party to the ICESCR has refuted the definition of the right to water given by the General Assembly.

[347] *Ibid.* The South Africa delegation did not sponsor the draft resolution as it did not take adequately into account the link between sanitation and water needs (para. 133). Moreover, South

In 2017, the General Assembly adopted a further resolution on the right to water, which reiterates the same definition enshrined in General Comment No. 15 and in its previous resolution.[348] This time the resolution was not adopted by *consensus* but with the negative vote of Kyrgyzstan and the abstention of New Zealand, South Africa and Turkey.[349] All of them are States parties to the ICESCR. Turkey and New Zealand did not attach an explanation of vote, while Kyrgyzstan and South Africa did.

Kyrgyzstan mainly complained about the possible extraterritorial obligations arising from the right to water. It proposed an amendment, which was rejected, to paragraph 9 of the draft resolution so as to render it clear that States' responsibilities do not extend "*to territory of other Member States*".[350] South Africa, after having expressed appreciation for the maintenance of a human rights perspective in addressing the issues of water and sanitation, explained its abstention on the grounds that the resolution separated those rights from the right to development and did not employ a progressive language.[351]

Once again, no State party to the ICESCR contested the definition of the right to water provided for in General Comment No. 15, reiterated in the General Assembly resolutions.[352] In light of the above considerations, the present author does not deem it incautious to conclude that the definition of the right to water given by the CESCR and reiterated in subsequent General Assembly resolutions, first adopted by consensus and then without dispute among States parties to the ICESCR, has gathered the agreement of the parties to the ICESCR.

3.2. The content of the customary right to water

Ascertaining the content of the customary human right to water is a rather complex undertaking.

At the outset, a theoretical premise needs to be made. I acknowledge the existence of scholarship that supports the notion that general international norms, especially human rights norms, may arise out of States' wide participation in interna-

Africa (para. 134) and India (para. 139) expressed reservations on the human rights-based approach to development taken in the resolution.

348 General Assembly, Res. 72/178 (n 67).

349 General Assembly, paras. 15-45 (n 148).

350 *Ibid.*, para. 20.

351 *Ibid.*, para. 38.

352 The United States voted in favor but "*dissociated itself from paragraph 2 of the resolution, as the definition of the right to water and sanitation was based on the views of the Committee on Economic, Social, and Cultural Rights and the Special Rapporteur only and such language did not appear in an international agreement or reflect any international consensus*". *Ibid.*, para. 44.

tional treaties.[353] Addressing this issue, Baker suggests that the well known passage of the ICJ in the *North Sea Continental Shelf* judgment – stating that a "*widespread and representative participation in the convention* [on the Continental Shelf] *might suffice of itself*" to establish a customary norm[354] – has contributed to lowering the threshold necessary to establish the existence of a customary norm.[355] From this passage, the author argues, a non-traditional scholarship has arisen claiming that international conventions "*actually generate international legal norms*",[356] and that "*human rights norms by virtue of their inclusion in widely ratified international conventions were seamlessly transmuted into customary international law*".[357]

It seems that the ICJ passage in the *North Continental Shelf* case has been misinterpreted. In this case the Court suggested three ways in which treaty and custom may interact, namely: *i*) a treaty may codify a pre-existent customary norm; *ii*) a treaty may crystallize an emerging customary norm; and, finally, *iii*) a treaty may boost the formation of a customary norm providing model behaviour, which if complied with by States over a period of time (however short) may give rise to new customs. After having ruled out that the principle of equidistance enshrined in Article 6 of the Geneva Convention on the Continental Shelf codified an existing rule of international law or crystallized such a rule, the Court examined whether a customary norm had came into being since the adoption of the Geneva Convention by means of its impact on the subsequent practice of States. The Court warned that "*this result is not lightly to be regarded as having been attained*".[358]

Thus, the ICJ passage under discussion seems rather to exclude that a treaty rule seamlessly transmutes into a customary norm, as the sole participation to treaties *per se* is insufficient to generate general international law. This participation is only one

---

[353] D'Amato, pp. 47-98 (n 87); A. D'Amato, *The Concept of Human Rights in International Law*, in *Columbia Law Review*, 1982, pp. 1127-1135.

[354] ICJ, *North Sea Continental Shelf*, para. 73, p. 43 (n 83).

[355] In particular, according to Baker, the Court required only "*widespread and representative*" participation in a given treaty for the purpose of establishing the existence of a customary norm; it did not even request the favorable *opinio juris* of, at least, the majority of the international community. Baker, p. 179 (n 84).

[356] *Ibid.*, p. 180.

[357] *Ibid.*

[358] ICJ, *North Sea Continental Shelf*, p. 42, para. 71 (n 83): "*In so far as this contention is based on the view that Article 6 of the Convention has had the influence, and has produced the effect described, it clearly involves treating that Article as a norm-creating provision which has constituted the foundation of, or has generated a rule which, while only conventional or contractual in its origin, has since passed the general* corpus *of international law, and is now accepted as such by the* opinio juris, *so as to have become binding even for countries which have never, and do not, become parties to the Convention. There is no doubt that this process is a perfectly possible one and does from time to time occur: it constitutes indeed one of the recognized methods by which news rules of customary international law may be formed. At the same time this result is not lightly to be regarded as having been attained*".

among a number of factors needed to establish the existence of a customary rule.[359] Put differently, a widely ratified treaty may be the *occasio legis*, generating a customary international norm by way of subsequent practice, but in order to reach this conclusion other evidence must be found.

Turning to the case under examination, the issue is whether the customary right to water has the same content as the derivative right to water, given that the ICESCR has been widely ratified and the contracting States have agreed upon the definition of such a right given in General Comment No. 15.

For the reasons expressed above, I am of the opinion that the sole acceptance of the derivative nature of the right to water from the ICESCR, however widespread, as an aspect of the rights under Articles 11 and 12 ICESCR, does not allow as such to conclude that the content of the treaty right and that of the customary norm perfectly overlap, as other evidence needs to be found.

The United States of America has consistently rejected the definition of the right to water given by international bodies, such as the CESCR and the General Assembly. Among the statements made in the context of the adoption of the above-mentioned General Assembly resolutions, they have reiterated their doubts over the right in question. Explaining the reasons for their abstention from voting in favor of the 2010 resolution on the right to water, the United States' representative, Mr. John F. Sammis, declared that it: *"describes a right to water and sanitation in a way that is not reflective of existing international law; as there is no 'right to water and sanitation' in an international legal sense as described by this resolution"*.[360]

Subsequently, the United States did not object nor vote in favor of later General Assembly resolutions on the right to water, but always on the understanding that the reference to the right to water is derived from the economic, social and cultural rights contained in the ICESCR to which they are not a party[361] and, in any case, dissociating themselves from the *consensus* on the definition of the right to water based on paragraph 2 of General Comment No. 15, as such language "*did not appear in an international agreement or reflect any international consensus*".[362]

The United States does not reject the existence of a right to water *per se*, but contests the content attached to such a right and the ensuing obligations as stated by General Comment No. 15.

As for other States that are not parties to the ICESCR, the vast majority voted in

---

[359] *Contra* D'Amato, 1982, p. 1129 (n 353): "*I do not claim that this evidence [of customary law] can be found subsequent to, or apart from, the conventions, but rather that the conventions themselves constitute or generate customary rules of law*".

[360] General Assembly, p. 8 (n 61).

[361] Official Records of the General Assembly, paras. 141-142 (n 285); General Assembly, para. 42 (n 148).

[362] Official Records of the General Assembly, para. 144 (n 285); General Assembly, para. 44 (n 148).

favor of the General Assembly resolutions on the right to water.[363] Cuba expressed its keen enthusiasm for the first GA resolution,[364] while Côte d'Ivoire, Micronesia, South Sudan, Vanuatu were among the sponsors of the following ones.[365] South Sudan[366] and Mozambique[367] inserted the right to water into their constitutions and legislation and Botswana's courts applied this right domestically.[368] The reported practice of the rest of non-State parties to the ICESCR[369] is scant.

However, the strong objection of the United States to the definition of the right to water enshrined in para. 2 of the General Comment No. 15, together with the absence of a reported practice among most States that are not parties to the ICESCR, suggest caution is needed in affirming that the content of the customary right to water mirrors that of the derivative right.

In addition, the fact that most States of the international community have agreed on the interpretation of Article 11(1) ICESCR and, to this end, accepted to be bound to a derivative right to water with a given content, does not *per se* entail that the subsequent practice has been or will be perfectly consistent with the accepted treaty rule. In other words, while the agreement of 170 States on the existence of a derivative right to water constitutes evidence of States' *opinio juris* critical for establishing the existence of customary right to water, the same cannot be said for the content of this right. The practice subsequent to such an agreement (which I assume was taken by means of the 2015 GA resolution on the right to water, adopted by *consensus*, which defined for the first time the right to water) needs to be monitored in the years to come.

For the time being, at a minimum it can be acknowledged that the content attached to the customary right to water entitles everyone not to be deprived of access to drinking water. In this connection, the customary right to water mirrors the corresponding derivative right, as it establishes freedom from interference in its enjoyment (and the corresponding duty to respect, see section 4.1 below). This minimum core content can be easily agreed upon, as negative obligations do not constrain

---

363 General Assembly, explanation of vote by Cuba, p. 9 (n 61); General Assembly, para. 39 (n 148).

364 General Assembly, explanation of vote by Cuba, pp. 18-19 (n 61).

365 Official Records of the General Assembly, para. 113 (n 285); General Assembly, para. 17 (n 148).

366 South Sudan's Constitution, 7 July 2011, art. 35(2).

367 Mozambique Water Act, art. 26.

368 Court of Appeals of the Republic of Botswana, *Matsipane Mosetlhanyane and Other v. Attorney General* (n 233).

369 States that are not parties to the ICESCR are: Andorra, Bhutan, Botswana, Brunei, Comoros, Cuba, East Timor, Côte d'Ivoire, Kiribati, Kosovo, Malaysia, Micronesia, Mozambique, Nauru, Palau, Saint Kitts and Nevis, Saint Lucia, Singapore, South Sudan, Taiwan, Tonga, Vanuatu, Vatican City.

State budgets and do not require the adoption of positive measures. The same was held by the investment arbitral tribunal in the *Urbaser* case, when it took for granted the obligation to abstain from committing acts violating the right to water.[370] Denying such an assumption would mean refuting the very existence of a customary right to water.

I do not exclude the possibility that positive obligations may derive from this customary right, as in situations where there is a lack of drinking water sufficient for human life and health, but I believe that the entitlement to any further guarantees must be explored in the years to come.

4. The obligations stemming from the human right to water

Given the uncertainties that surround the content of the customary right to water, aside from the prohibition to interfere with the enjoyment of access to water, it seems premature to draw further conclusions on the ensuing obligations. Therefore, we turn to analyse the obligations based in the derivative right to water as a component of the right to an adequate standard of living under Article 11 ICESCR and as strictly linked to the right to the highest attainable standard of health, enshrined in Article 12 ICESCR.

In brief, this section investigates three questions: it seeks to shed light on the nature and content of the obligations at issue; it asks who is responsible for their implementation; and last, it enquiries on the possible extraterritorial extension of the duties to be fulfilled.

4.1. The nature and content of the obligations

A preliminary issue is whether the obligations stemming from the derivative right to water are of immediate effect or of progressive realization. In fact, the nature of the obligations ensuing from the derivative right to water does not allow us to apply this dichotomy *sic et simpliciter*, as both kinds of obligations must be respected at once.

In general terms, the distinction between civil and political rights – meant to be immediately enforceable – and economic, social and cultural rights – considered to be subject to progressive realization – appears blurred,[371] as the latter category also

---

[370] *Urbaser S.A. and Consorcio de Aguas Bilbao Bizkaia, Bilbao Biskaia Ur Partzuergoa v. The Argentine Republic* (n 144), Award, 8 December 2016, para. 1210.

[371] Among others: M. A. Baderin, M. Ssenyonjo, *International Human Rights Law. Six decades after the UDHR and Beyond*, Farnham-Burlington, 2010; M. J. Dennis, D. P. Stewart, *Justiciability of Economic, Social, and Cultural Rights: Should There Be an International Complaints Mechanism to Adjudicate the Rights to Food, Water, Housing, and Health*, in *American Journal of International*

recognizes that it is incumbent upon every State party to the ICESCR "*a minimum core obligation to ensure the satisfaction of, at the very least, minimum essential levels of each of the rights*".[372] This distinction has no special implications for the nature of States' obligations stemming from the right to water.[373]

The CESCR posits that the full content of the human right to water belongs to the category of economic, social and cultural rights, specifically the right to an adequate standard of living and the right to health. However, States are not discharged from complying with certain immediate obligations, among which the CESCR singles out the duties:

> "(a) To ensure access to the minimum essential amount of water, that is sufficient and safe for personal and domestic uses to prevent disease; (b) To ensure the right of access to water and water facilities and services on a non-discriminatory basis, especially for disadvantaged or marginalized groups; (c) To ensure physical access to water facilities or services that provide sufficient, safe and regular water".[374]

According to the CESCR, no derogation from these core obligations is allowed.[375] By the same token, Winkler refers to "*[t]he concept of minimum core obligations*", which "*requires that the minimum core of the right to water is realized for everyone immediately, and States have to show that they have undertaken every effort to achieve this*".[376]

Tanzi maintains a different approach. According to the author, under international law, the right to water has some direct effects deriving from the States' due diligence obligations on the matter. Individuals suffering for lack of access to water should be considered "*entitled to bring a case before a domestic court or international competent court*" except when "*the lack of access to an adequate amount of safe water would occur despite all appropriate action and efforts having been undertaken by the State in point in order to supply adequate quantity and quality of water*".[377] In brief, the author argues that "*in the present state of international law, the obligation for States correspondent to*

Law, 2004, pp. 462-515; R. Pisillo Mazzeschi, *Sulla natura degli obblighi internazionali di tutela e promozione dei diritti economici, sociali e culturali*, in F. Bestagno (ed.), *I diritti economici, social e culturali, Promozione e tutela nella comunità internazionale*, Milan, 2009, pp. 6-9; A. Facchi, *Breve storia dei diritti umani*, Bologna, 2007, pp. 125-127; A. Cassese, *I diritti umani oggi*, Rome-Bari, 2005, p. 215; F. Costamagna, *Realizzazione progressiva dei diritti economici, sociali e culturali e miglior utilizzo delle risorse disponibili*, in *Diritti Umani e Diritto Internazionale*, 2008, p. 167.

[372] Committee on Economic, Social and Cultural Rights, General Comment No. 3, The nature of States Parties' obligations, art. 2, para.1, UN Doc. E/1991/23, 14 December 1990, para. 10.

[373] See Cinelli, pp. 482-488 (n 71).

[374] General Comment No. 15, para. 37 (n 24).

[375] *Ibid.*, para. 40: "*State party cannot justify its non-compliance with the core obligations*".

[376] Winkler, p. 215 (n 40).

[377] Tanzi, p. 277 (n 136).

the human right to water is one of due diligence",[378] namely an obligation to take, in good faith, all the necessary and feasible steps towards the realization of this right. A failure in this sense amounts to a violation of the right to water by omission. In practical terms, it may be difficult to establish when the due diligence obligation is infringed: setting targets or benchmarks may prove useful to this end.

Following this line of reasoning, the obligation to provide a minimum amount of water to all for the sake of survival is not an obligation of result, as the CESCR suggests, but an obligation of means. Provided that a strict threshold is applied to demonstrate that all efforts have been made to comply with the minimum requirement obligations, I consider that the stand of Tanzi is more balanced. In view of the water shortages that affect and will sharply impact water availability in some developing countries in the forthcoming years, States that make all possible efforts to avoid water crises, and still fail to do so due to circumstances beyond their control, should not be held responsible for not having supplied a minimum amount of water.

Turning to the content of the obligations at issue, the human right to water sets out obligations similar to those provided for by human rights law, namely the duties to respect, protect and fulfill.[379] The duty to respect requires States to refrain from engaging in any practice or activity that denies or limits equal access to adequate water, for example by: arbitrarily interfering with customary or traditional arrangements for water allocation; unlawfully diminishing or polluting water; limiting access to water services; or destroying water infrastructure during armed conflicts.[380] In order to address infringements, States have to set "*effective judicial or other appropriate remedies providing adequate reparation, including restitution, compensation, satisfaction or guarantee of non-repetition*".[381] In addition, States have to refrain from entering trade and investments treaties when they are aware of possible conflicting obligations stemming from such treaties.[382]

The State's duty to protect the enjoyment of the right to water from interference by third parties[383] is probably the most problematic in terms of compliance. States

---

[378] *Ibid.*, p. 277.

[379] Guidelines on Violations of Economic, Social and Cultural Rights, 22-26 January 1997, para. 6. I. T. Winkler, *Respect, Protect and Fulfill: the Implementation of the Human Right to Water in South Africa*, in P. Cullet, A. Gowlland-Gualtieri, R. Madhav, U. Ramanathan (eds.), *Water Governance in Motion: Towards Socially and Environmentally Sustainable Water Laws*, New Delhi, 2010, pp. 415-444.

[380] General Comment No. 15, para. 21 (n 24).

[381] Human Rights Council, *Report of the United Nations High Commissioner for Human Rights on the scope and content of the relevant human rights obligations related to equitable access to safe drinking water and sanitation under international human rights instruments*, para. 36 (n 29).

[382] CESCR, *General Comment No. 24 (2017) on State obligations under the International Covenant on Economic, Social and Cultural Rights in the context of business activities*, UN Doc. E/C.12/GC/24, 10 August 2017, paras. 13, 29.

[383] The term "third parties" refers to individuals, groups or corporations.

have to adopt all measures necessary to prevent non-State actors from denying equal access to adequate water, and from polluting water resources or from acquiring them by inequitably extracting from "*natural sources, wells and other water distribution systems*".[384]

With regard to the provision of water services, the human right to water does not dictate the way water and sanitation services have to be provided.[385] States are free to choose the policy they deem appropriate,[386] including privatization. However, when water services are operated or controlled by private stakeholders, States must prevent them from compromising the users' right to have access to the service.[387] Put differently, "*the delegation of the delivery of safe drinking water and/or sanitation services to a third party does not exempt the State from its human rights obligations*".[388] On the contrary, the State remains "*the primary duty-bearer*"[389] for the realization of the right to water.

Tanzi makes a further distinction. Interestingly, according the author, when water services are delivered by a State-owned company, the State is directly legally accountable, but when these services have been privatized the State is "*legally accountable for the conduct of its organs in charge of controlling and preventing that activities under its jurisdiction will not be in breach of international law*".[390] However, "*irrespective of whether water services are operated by state or private entities under their jurisdiction (…) the State will be accountable as to whether its different organs live up to the international due diligence obligations*".[391]

---

[384] General Comment No.15, para. 23.

[385] The former independent expert on the human right to safe drinking water made recommendations and clarifications both on the human rights obligations of States and the human rights responsibilities of non-State service providers in the delivery of water and sanitation services. Human Rights Council, *Report of the independent expert on the issue of human rights obligations related to access to safe drinking water and sanitation, Catarina de Albuquerque*, UN Doc. A/HRC/15/31, 29 June 2010.

[386] Human Rights Council, *Report of the United Nations High Commissioner for Human Rights on the scope and content of the relevant human rights obligations related to equitable access to safe drinking water and sanitation under international human rights instruments*, paras. 48, 52 (n 29).

[387] General Comment No. 15, para. 24 (n 24). Thielbörger argues that irrespective of its adverse impact on the quality or the accessibility of water, entering into an agreement or a contract likely to lower the standard of water services amounts to a violation of the States' duty to respect, that is to refrain from any interference with the enjoyment of the human right to water by individuals within their jurisdiction. P. Thielbörger, *The Human Right to Water versus Investors Rights: Double Dilemma or Pseudo-conflict?*, in P. M. Dupuy, F. Francioni, E. Petersmann (eds.), *Human Rights in International Investment Law and Arbitration*, Oxford, 2009, p. 495.

[388] Human Rights Council, Res. 15/9, para. 6 (n 35).

[389] Human Rights Council, *Report of the independent expert on the issue of human rights obligations related to access to safe drinking water and sanitation,* para. 18 (n 385).

[390] Tanzi, p. 281 (n 136).

[391] *Ibid.*

On the same line, it has been argued that the State's duty to protect varies according to the model of privatization chosen for the water sector. When a State exercises close control over a company that is considered its mere agent, corporate acts may be directly attributed to the State. In this case, the State's duty to protect is a standard of result. On the contrary, when States have no control over the company, they should "*not be held responsible for corporate-related human rights abuse* per se, *but may be considered in breach of their obligations where they fail to take appropriate steps to prevent it and to investigate, punish and redress it when it occurs*".[392] As a consequence, in this case, the State's duty to protect is a standard of conduct.

In the words of the Human Rights Commissioner, when water services are operated by private providers, establishing State responsibility is more complex as States have to adopt specific measures that take into account the involvement of non-State actors and prevent abuses.[393] In the first place, States must put in place a regulatory system requiring private suppliers to provide sufficient, accessible and safe water.[394] Under such a system, States must retain the flexibility to regulate and control the provision of water.[395] Moreover, to be effective, the regulatory system must include genuine public participation.[396] Besides adopting and implementing regulatory frameworks, States have to monitor and enforce those regulations. Finally, they have to ensure effective remedies, accessible accountability mechanisms[397] and the imposition of penalties for non-compliance.[398]

Finally, the obligation to fulfill, the last of the above-mentioned tripartite obligations, requires positive efforts to be undertaken by States in order to facilitate, promote and provide the right to water. Facilitating the enjoyment of such a right implies that States have to take positive measures to assist individuals and communities. Promoting the right to water requires States to "*take steps to ensure that there is appropriate education concerning the hygienic use of water, protection of water sources and methods to minimize water wastage*".[399] States are obligated to directly provide the means necessary when individuals or a group are unable, for reasons beyond

---

[392] Human Rights Council, *Report of the Special Representative of the Secretary-General on the issue of human rights and transnational corporations and other business enterprises*, UN Doc. A/HRC/11/13, 22 April 2009, para. 14.

[393] Human Rights Council, *Report of the independent expert on the issue of human rights obligations related to access to safe drinking water and sanitation,* para. 16 (n 385).

[394] Special Rapporteur of the UN Commission on Human Rights, Sub-Commission on the Promotion and Protection of Human Rights, *Guidelines for the realization of the right to drinking water and sanitation*, lett. *e*), para. 2.3 (n 26).

[395] General Comment No.15, para. 44(*b*) (n 24).

[396] *Ibid.*, para. 24.

[397] Human Rights Council, Res. 15/9, para. 8 (n 35).

[398] General Comment No. 15, para. 24 (n 24).

[399] *Ibid.*, para. 25.

their control, to realize that right themselves by the means at their disposal.[400]

When water services are provided by private parties, the obligation to fulfill requires States to take measures in order to ensure that these services are affordable for all, "*including socially disadvantaged groups*"[401] and people living in rural and deprived urban areas.[402] In addition, as will be better illustrated in the following chapters, before undertaking commitments for liberalizing the water services market – for instance by entering into investment agreements at a bilateral level or negotiating their international commitments at the GATS level – States must make a prior assessment of the resulting impacts on the human right to water in view of avoiding potential conflicts between the obligations arising from human rights law and international economic law.[403]

In order to fulfill the right to water, procedural obligations are also envisaged, such as those necessary to ensure access to information concerning safe drinking water and sanitation issues, and participation in related decision-making processes.[404]

4.2. The subjects responsible for their implementation

In line with the ICESCR, General Comment No. 15 places the obligations deriving from the human right to water upon States and does not refer to any direct obligation to be complied with by third parties, such as individuals, groups or corporations. Section VI of the General Comment addresses international organizations and UN agencies concerned with water, and only requires their cooperation with States to implement the right to water at a national level.

Some years after the adoption of General Comment No. 15, the Human Rights Council addressed the issue of private companies' responsibilities for the fulfillment of the human right to water and the corresponding duties of States to prevent third-party infringement.[405] Responsibilities of business enterprises in this respect have also been dealt with by the General Assembly, which has called upon non-State ac-

---

[400] *Ibid.*, para. 25.

[401] *Ibid.*, para. 27.

[402] *Ibid.*, para. 26. The Committee's standing for non-discrimination claims has been endorsed by Winkler, p. 217 (n 40).

[403] General Comment. No. 15, para. 44(*c*)(*vii*) (n 24).

[404] *Ibid.*, para. 48. This issue was dealt with in a comprehensively manner during the Conference "*Public Participation and Water Resources Management: Where do We Stand in International Law?*", Geneva, 13 December 2013. L. Boisson de Chazournes, *Fresh Water in International Law*, Oxford, 2013, pp. 162-167.

[405] Human Rights Council, Res. 15/9, paras. 7, 9 (n 35). The international responsibility of transnational corporations in respect to human rights is beyond the scope of the present work and will not be addressed in full. However, see chapter three, section 6.

tors to cooperate with States in order to both investigate allegations of abuses of the right to water and to detect and remedy such abuses.[406] This quest for cooperative commitments comes into play once infringements have already occurred, while no direct obligation of non-State actors to prevent breaches has been invoked.

So far, no binding instrument has established corporate human rights responsibilities.[407] In this connection, the Human Right Council has appointed an open-ended intergovernmental working group on transnational corporations and other business enterprises ("IGWG") with respect to human rights, which received the mandate to draft an international legally binding instrument to regulate the activities of transnational corporations and other business enterprises.[408] In 2018, the IGWG discussed a draft legal instrument, the so-called Zero draft,[409] and in July 2019 a revised draft was issued.[410] It maintains a State-centric approach by imposing obligations on States parties to ensure that persons within their jurisdiction undertake due diligence obligations to evaluate the impact of their business activities on human rights.

The issue is rather complex and cannot be fully addressed in this context. Suffice it to say that the adoption of this treaty, as presently drafted, seems to bring few additional safeguards in terms of compliance with the human right to water, given

---

[406] General Assembly, Res. 72/178, para. 5 (n 67).

[407] Only guiding principles dealing with the human rights obligations of multinational corporations and other business enterprises. See Human Rights Council, Report of the Special Representative of the Secretary General on the issue of human rights and transnational corporations and other business enterprises, *Guiding Principles on Business and Human Rights: Implementing the United Nations 'Protect, Respect and Remedy' Framework*, UN Doc. A/HRC/17/31, 21 March 2011 (hereinafter "Guiding Principles on Business and Human Rights"); OECD, *OECD Guidelines for Multinational Enterprises*, 2011. The Human Rights Council has promoted the implementation of the Guiding Principles on Business and Human Rights by, *inter alia*, establishing a Working Group on the issue of human rights and transnational corporations and other business enterprise, and a Forum on Business and Human Rights under the guidance of this Working Group "*to discuss the trends and challenges in the implementation of the Guiding Principles*": Human Rights Council, *Resolution on Human Rights and transnational corporations and other business enterprises*, UN Doc. A/HRC/RES/17/4, 6 July 2011. Subsequently, the Human Rights Council extended the mandate of the Working Group for a period of three years, see Human Rights Council, Res. 35/7, 22 June 2017, UN Doc. A/HRC/RES/35/7, 14 July 2017.

[408] Human Rights Council, Res. 26/9, 26 June 2014, UN Doc. A/HCR/RES/26/9, 14 July 2014. Since 2015, the IGWG dedicates annual sessions to negotiating this treaty.

[409] *Zero Draft, Legally binding Instrument to Regulate, in International Human Rights Law, the Activities of Transnational Corporations and Other Business Enterprises*, 16 July 2018 (hereinafter "Zero Draft"), available online at: https://www.ohchr.org/Documents/HRBodies/HRCouncil/WGTransCorp/Session3/DraftLBI.pdf. See also the *Draft Optional Protocol to the Legally Binding Instrument to Regulate, in International Human Rights Law, the Activities of Transnational Corporations and Other Business Enterprises*, annexed to the Zero Draft.

[410] OEIGWG Chairmanship Revised Draft, 16 July 2019, available at: https://www.ohchr.org/Documents/HRBodies/HRCouncil/WGTransCorp/OEIGWG_RevisedDraft_LBI.pdf.

that States parties to the ICESCR are already vested with the duty to protect people within their jurisdiction from corporate abuses of the right to water.

4.3. The territorial extension of the obligations

According to General Comment No. 15, the obligations arising from the right to water as enshrined in Articles 11 and 12 ICESCR may be divided into "internal", which parties owe to individuals or groups within the territory and subject to their jurisdiction,[411] and "international", which they are bound to perform towards third States.[412]

States' obligations towards third countries might be framed within the duty to cooperate and assist, established by Article 2(1), Article 11(1) and Article 23 ICESCR, albeit not without controversy.[413]

---

[411] General Comment No. 15, paras. 20-29 (n 24). According to the Special Rapporteur for the realization of the right to drinking water and sanitation, Governments should make all efforts to guarantee the right to water, above all to persons without any basic access to it, by *inter alia*: recognizing such a right under relevant laws; refraining from interfering with its enjoyment; and, ensuring that private persons and organizations do not interfere with its enjoyment. Special Rapporteur of the UN Commission on Human Rights, Sub-Commission on the Promotion and Protection of Human Rights, *Guidelines for the realization of the right to drinking water and sanitation*, para. 2.3 (n 26).

[412] General Comment No. 15, paras. 30-36 (n 24). The legal basis of the extraterritorial obligations stemming from economic, social and cultural rights can be traced back to arts. 55 and 56 of the UN Charter and to the International Covenant on Economic, Social and Cultural Rights, art. 2(1). For a definition of extraterritorial obligations, see the ETO Consortium, *The Maastricht Principles on Extraterritorial Obligations of States in the Area of Economic, Social and Cultural Rights*, Heidelberg, January 2013, Principle 8: "*a) obligations relating to the acts and omission of a State, within or beyond its territory, that have effects on the enjoyment of human rights outside of that State's territory; and b) obligations of a global character that are set out in the Charter of the United Nations and human rights instruments to take action, separately, and jointly through international cooperation, to realize human rights universally*". See M. Milanovic, *Extraterritorial Application of Human Rights Treaties: Law, Principles, and Policy*, Oxford, 2013; M. Langford, W. Vandenhole, M. Scheinin, W. Van Genungten (eds.), *Global Justice, State Duties: The Extraterritorial Scope of Economic, Social and Cultural Rights in International Law*, Cambridge-New York, 2013; M. Gondek, *The Reach of Human Rights in a Globalising World: Extraterritorial Application of Human Rights Treaties*, Antwerp, 2009. For an in-depth analysis of the matter, see Bulto (n 317); T. S. Bulto, *Towards Rights-Duties Congruence: Extraterritorial Application of the Human Right to Water in the African Human Rights System*, in *Netherlands Quarterly of Human Rights*, 2011; A. Cahill-Ripley, *Protecting Rights in the Face of Scarcity: The Right to Water*, in M. Gibney and S. Skogly (eds.), *Universal Human Rights and Extraterritorial Obligations*, Philadelphia, 2010; A. F. S. Russell, S. C. McCaffrey, *Tapping Transboundary Waters: Implications of the Right to Water for States Sharing International Watercourse*, in Langford, M., Russell, A. F. S. (eds.), *The Human Right to Water. Theory, Practice and Prospects*, Cambridge, 2019.

[413] In this regard see M. Craven, *Some Thoughts on The Emergent Right to Water*, in E. H. Riedel, P. Rothen (eds.), *The Human Right to Water*, Berlin, 2006, pp. 39-41.

According to the CESCR, international obligations arising for States from the human right to water consist in the same tripartite division recalled for internal obligations. The obligation to respect requires States to refrain from interfering with the enjoyment of the right to water in other countries.[414] In this connection, States should avoid international and regional agreements concerning investment and trade liberalization that may curtail or inhibit a country's capacity to ensure the full realization of the right to water.[415]

The obligation to protect requires States to take steps in order to prevent their citizens and companies from violating the right to water of individuals and communities in other countries.[416]

Finally, the obligation to fulfill as understood by the Committee is more nuanced. It requires States, in particular those that are economically developed, to facilitate the realization of the right to water in other countries "*[d]epending on the availability of resources (...) for example through provision of water resources, financial and technical assistance, and provide the necessary aid when required*".[417]

The Committee's view can be shared only in part. It is my understanding that some extraterritorial obligations to refrain from interfering with the enjoyment of the right to water abroad exist.[418] Such interference might occur both in times of peace, for instance by polluting, over-utilising or diverting transboundary watercourses, and during armed conflict, i.e. by limiting access to water resources or destroying water services and infrastructure.[419]

In general terms, the obligations to respect and protect are based on a widely recognized customary international law rule, according to which States bear the duty – corresponding to the Latin maxim *sic utere tuo ut alienum non laedas* – to ensure that activities within their jurisdiction do not cause significant harm to the environment of other States or areas beyond their jurisdiction, including transboundary watercourses.[420] While they are free to exploit their own natural re-

---

[414] General Comment No. 15, para. 31 (n 24).

[415] *Ibid.*, para. 35; CESCR, *General Comment No. 24 (2017) on State obligations under the International Covenant on Economic, Social and Cultural Rights in the context of business activities*, para. 29 (n 382).

[416] *Ibid.*, para. 35.

[417] *Ibid.*, para. 34.

[418] R. Greco, *The Silala Dispute: Between International Water Law and the Human Right to Water*, in *QIL*, 2017.

[419] General Comment No. 15, para. 21 (n 24).

[420] *Trail Smelter Arbitration, United States v. Canada*, Award, 16 April 1938 and 11 March 1941, at 1965; ICJ, *Corfu Channel, United Kingdom of Great Britain and Northern Ireland v Albania*, Judgment, 9 April 1949, at 22; ICJ, *Legality of the Threat or Use of Nuclear Weapons*, para. 29 (n 83); ICJ, *Case concerning Pulp Mills on the River Uruguay, Argentina v. Uruguay*, Judgment, 20 April 2010, at 56, para. 101. For the customary *status* of this rule, see: Commentary to art. 16 of ILA, The Berlin Rules on Water Resources, Berlin, 2004, p. 22; S. M. A. Salman, *The Obligation*

sources,[421] States must respect the obligations not to cause significant harm to other watercourse States.[422]

This customary rule has been incorporated in various instruments that provide for the States' duty to take into consideration the environmental impact of proposed measures outside their territories in order to avoid transferring the harmful effects of their activities to other States.[423] *In primis*, reference can be made to the UN Watercourses Convention, which establishes that watercourse States must take all necessary measures to prevent significant harm to other watercourse States when using an international watercourse.[424]

In addition to the duty not to cause harm, the customary rule requiring equitable and reasonable utilization of water resources is codified in the UN Watercourses Convention. According to this rule, watercourse States shall participate in the use, development and protection of an international watercourse in an equitable and reasonable manner, taking into account "*the population dependent on the watercourse in each watercourse State*".[425] Furthermore, in the event of a conflict between uses of an international watercourse, special regard must be given to the requirements of *vital human needs*,[426] such as drinking water.[427]

---

not to Cause Significant Harm, in L. Boisson De Chazournes, M. M. Mbengue, M. Tignino, K. Sangbana (eds.), *The UN Convention on the Law of the Non-Navigational Uses of International Watercourses, a Commentary*, Oxford, 2018, pp. 114-119.

[421] Art. 2(7) of the Charter of the United Nations. V. Nanda, G. Pring, *International Environmental Law and Policy for the 21st Century*, Leiden-Boston, 2012; P. Birnie, A. Boyle, C. Redgwell, *International Law & Environment,* Oxford, 2009; P. Cullet, pp. 27-31 (n 250).

[422] See ILA, The Berlin Rules on Water Resources, Berlin, 2004, art. 10.2: "*States shall not cause a significant adverse effect on the rights of or uses in another basin State*"; P. M. Dupuy, *Le Droit à L'Eau, Un Droit International?*, EUI Working Papers, 2006, pp. 7-8.

[423] Declaration of the United Nations Conference on the Human Environment, Principle 21 (n 1); Rio Declaration on Environment and Development, Rio de Janeiro, 1992, Principle 2; Convention on Cooperation for the Protection and Sustainable Use of the Danube River, Sofia, 1994, art. 5; ILA, The Berlin Rules on Water Resources, art. 16 (n 422); AU, Revised African Convention on the Conservation of Nature and Natural Resources (2003), art. 7(1)(*b*); Revised Protocol on Shared Watercourses in the Southern African Development Community (SADC) (2000), art. 4(2)(*b*).

[424] Convention on the Law of the Non-navigational Uses of International Watercourses, art. 7 (n 119). See A. Tanzi, M. Arcari, *The United Nations Convention on the Law of International Watercourses: A Framework for Sharing,* The Hague, 2001; S. C. McCaffrey, *The Law of International Watercourses: Non-Navigational Uses*, Oxford, 2007; O. McIntyre, *Environmental Protection of International Watercourses under International Law*, Farnham, 2007; A. Rieu-Clarke, R. Moynihan, B. Magsig, *UN Watercourses Convention User's Guide*, Dundee, 2012; Salman (n 420); L. Boisson De Chazournes, M. M. Mbengue, M. Tignino, K. Sangbana (eds.), *The UN Convention on the Law of the Non-Navigational Uses of International Watercourses, a Commentary*, Oxford, 2018.

[425] *Ibid.*, arts. 5, 6.

[426] *Ibid.*, art. 10.2.

[427] S. M. A. Salman, S. McInenrney-Lankford, *The Human Right to Water: Legal and Policy Di-*

These provisions, read together, allow the interpreter to infer an obligation of co-riparian States not to use the national portion of international watercourses in a manner likely to cause (or let non-state actors cause) significant harm to the vital human needs of people living in other riparian States, for instance by seriously polluting shared waters or by diverting transboundary watercourses.[428]

The above conclusion is corroborated by Article 21 of the UN Watercourses Convention, which requires contracting States to "*prevent, reduce and control the pollution of an international watercourse that may cause significant harm to other watercourse States or to the environment, including harm to human health or safety*".[429]

The Convention on the Protection and Use of Transboundary Watercourses and International Lakes ("UNECE Water Convention")[430] also requires States parties to take appropriate legal, administrative, economic, financial and technical measures to prevent, control and reduce any transboundary impacts, such as watercourse pollution.[431] To this end, riparian States must cooperate to develop harmonized policies, programmes and strategies[432].

The Protocol on Water and Health to the UNECE Water Convention,[433] which "*introduces a social component into cooperation on water management*",[434] gives special attention to the prevention of extraterritorial damages to water resources used, *inter alia*, as sources of drinking water.[435] Indeed, the parties to the Protocol must pursue the aim of providing access to water for everyone within a framework of an integrated water-management system.[436] They are thus not free to endanger the right to water of people subject to the jurisdiction of other States parties.

By becoming parties to treaties establishing the duty not to cause transboundary water harm, States accept the duty to adopt measures to prevent activities within their jurisdiction from damaging shared water resources abroad, above all if the water concerned is used for vital human needs, such as drinking water.

Extraterritorial obligations towards third-States in respect of their populations' human right to water can thus be traced back to these international water law rules.

---

mensions, World Bank, Washington, 2004, pp. 12-13; Tanzi, Arcari, p. 139 (n 424); C. Cinelli, *A New Human Rights-Based Approach to the UN Watercourses Convention*, in *International Water*, 2013.

[428] See Bulto, pp. 208-215 (n 317);

[429] Convention on the Law of the Non-navigational Uses of International Watercourses, art. 21 (n 119).

[430] Convention on the Protection and Use of Transboundary Watercourses and International Lakes (n 131).

[431] *Ibid.*, arts. 2.1, 3.1.

[432] *Ibid.*, art. 2.6.

[433] Protocol on Water and Health (n 130).

[434] See the UNECE website: https://www.unece.org/env/water/pwh_text/text_protocol.html.

[435] Protocol on Water and Health, arts. 1 and 4(2)(*c*) and 5(1)(*c*) (n 130).

[436] *Ibid.*, arts. 11-12.

In addition, States bear extraterritorial obligations concerning the human right to water in time of armed conflicts.[437] Article 29 of the UN Watercourses Convention subjects the usage of international watercourses and related installations to the applicable principles and rules of international humanitarian law.

Humanitarian law protects access to water during international armed conflicts. In particular, water is considered a civil good necessary for the survival of the civil population.[438] Article 54(2) of the I Protocol to the Geneva Convention on the protection of victims of international armed conflicts prohibits attacks directed against goods necessary for the survival of the civil population, including drinking water installations. Articles 35(3) and 55 of this Protocol prohibit causing extensive, lasting and serious damage to the environment, while rivers, lakes and groundwater are considered civil goods subject to the relative guarantees. In brief, military operations during international armed conflicts are constrained in so far as the protection of access to water is concerned.

In this connection, the former Special Rapporteur on the human right to water has recalled the denial by Israel of access to water in the Occupied Palestinian Territory,[439] as referred to by two treaty bodies, namely CESCR and the Human Rights Committee ("HRC").[440]

The CESCR, in its concluding observations on the report submitted by Israel, has drawn the attention of the State party to its General Comment No. 15 in order to reiterate its recommendation "*to ensure the availability of sufficient and safe drinking water and adequate sanitation for Palestinians living in the Occupied Palestinian Territory, including through the facilitation of the entry of necessary materials to rebuild the water and sanitation systems in Gaza*".[441]

---

[437] General Comment No. 15, para. 22 (n 24).

[438] M. Tignino, *L'Eau Source et Victim des Conflits: Les Norms Applicables*, in N. Kridis (ed.), *Maintien de la Paix et de la Sécurité Internationales et la Gestion des Ressources en Eau*, Tunis, 2018, p. 34.

[439] The issue of water shortages and human rights violations in the occupied Palestinian territories was addressed also by the International Court of Justice in its Advisory Opinion on the construction of a wall. The Court referred to a report of the Secretary-General, according to which 8 localities had so far been separated from primary water sources, and a report of the UN Special Rapporteur on the Right to Food, which states that by constructing the wall Israel would have annexed most of the western aquifer system, providing for 51 per cent of the West Bank's water resources. ICJ, *Legal Consequences of the Construction of a Wall in the Occupied Palestinian Territory*, para. 133 (n 85).

[440] Human Rights Council, *Report of the Special Rapporteur on the human right to safe drinking water and sanitation, Catarina de Albuquerque, Common violations of the human rights to water and sanitation*, UN Doc A/HRC/27/5530, 30 June 2014, pp. 20-21.

[441] UN Committee on Economic, Social and Cultural Rights, *Consideration of reports submitted by States parties under articles 16 and 17 of the Covenant. Concluding observations of the Committee on Economic, Social and Cultural Rights*, UN Doc E/C.12/ISR/CO/3, 16 December 2011, para. 29.

The HRC has also expressed concern about the water shortages affecting the Palestinian population of the West Bank "*due to prevention of construction and maintenance of water and sanitation infrastructure, as well as the prohibition of construction of wells*" and recommended Israel to "*allow the construction of water and sanitation infrastructure, and wells*".[442]

While occupied territories cannot simply be equated to third States, as the occupying States have special responsibilities toward them, the arguments of the former Special Rapporteur on the human right to water inferring obligations from the right to water during armed conflicts deserve attention.

At the same time, it cannot be overlooked that some States have expressed a radically different view on the matter of their external obligations stemming from the human right to water. For instance, Canada,[443] Argentina,[444] Guatemala,[445] and Kyrgyzstan[446] have explicitly denied that the ICESCR permits a reading of its provisions as imposing international obligations on States in order to guarantee the right to water beyond their own territory and people.

In this respect, the binding nature of the extraterritorial obligation to fulfill in respect of the human right to water may be called into question. After all, the CESCR itself has expressed the obligation to fulfill in careful terms, making its implementation dependent "*on the availability of resources*".[447]

In this connection, a further difference might be drawn between the obligation to cooperate and the one to provide assistance. Several transboundary water treaties provide for a duty to cooperate in the management of shared resources[448] and some authors have even argued in favor of the emergence of a duty to cooperate in the management of global water resources as an obligation *erga omnes* imposed on all States.[449]

---

442 HRC, *Consideration of reports submitted by States parties under article 40 of the Covenant. Concluding observations of the Human Rights Committee*, UN Doc. CCPR/C/ISR/CO/3, 3 September 2010, para. 18.

443 Official Records of the General Assembly, para. 146 (n 285); Official Records of the General Assembly, Seventieth Session, Third Committee, 49th meeting, UN Doc. A/C.3/68/SR.49, 20 January 2014, para. 117. See Craven, p. 39 (n 413), recalling the position taken by the Canadian representative in a debate within the UN Commission on Human Rights. UN Doc. E/CN.4/2003/SR.56, p. 10, para. 48.

444 Official Records of the General Assembly, para. 148 (n 285); Official Records of the General Assembly, para. 41 (n 443).

445 General Assembly, explanation of vote by Guatemala, p. 10 (n 61).

446 General Assembly, para. 20 (n 148).

447 General Comment No. 15, para. 34 (n 24).

448 See, for instance, the Protocol on Water and Health, arts. 6(1), 2 and 5(*b*) (n 130), requiring the achievement and maintenance of high levels of protection against water-related disease and cooperation in this regard by developing water-management plans in transboundary contexts, and arts. 11-12, requiring international cooperation in adopting actions aimed to achieving its objectives, including the attainment of access to water.

449 P. Wouters, D. Tarlock, *The third wave of normativity on Global Water Law. The duty to*

The obligation to provide assistance is far weaker considering the current lack of clear provisions, together with the contrary position expressed by some States, which makes it difficult to infer a duty to implement the right to water abroad.[450]

5. The role of international judges and quasi-judicial compliance mechanisms in the identification and formation of the human right to water

Judicial decisions of international courts and tribunals are "*subsidiary means for the determination of rules of law*".[451] International tribunals are tasked, *inter alia*, with the duty to ascertain the existence and content of international customary rules. The decisions of international tribunals may be a source for ascertaining the existence of a given right, provided that they deal with the matter in an analytical manner. According to Treves, given that, by agreement, States confer on international courts and tribunals the authority to settle disputes among them, judgments of international courts may be indirectly regarded to be "*manifestations of the practice of States that have agreed to confer on them such authority and the mandate to apply international – including customary – law*".[452]

Although "*[a]lmost all international dispute settlement bodies have dealt with water issues*"[453] in various contexts, including investment protection, human rights, or trade policies, for the purpose of the present chapter, the analysis will be confined to human rights disputes, while other mechanisms outside the human rights context[454] will be in part addressed in the following chapters.

The human rights-based approach to water has provided legal remedies to individuals who have suffered from a violation of the right to water, making States accountable for their violations.[455] The present section offers an overview of some

---

cooperate in the peaceful management of the world's water resources: an emerging obligation erga omnes*?*, in *Water Law*, 2013.

450 *Contra*, Bulto, pp. 191-208 (n 317).

451 Statute of the International Court of justice, art. 38, para. 1(*d*) (n 80).

452 T. Treves, paras. 53-54 (n 102).

453 Boisson de Chazournes, p. 247 (n 404).

454 For instance, the review mechanism established under the Protocol on Water and Health (n 130).

455 The effectiveness of legal entitlements rests on "*access to effective judicial or other appropriate remedies at both national and international levels*" and on the ensuing right to "*adequate reparation, including restitution, compensation, satisfaction or guarantees of non-repetition*". General Comment No. 15, para. 55 (n 24) refers to General Comment No. 9 (1998) on the domestic application of the Covenant, para. 4, and to Principle 10 of the Rio Declaration on Environment and Development. In this respect, see also Human Rights Council, *Joint report on of the independent expert on the question of human rights and extreme poverty, Magdalena Sepúlveda Cardona, and the*

important cases that have addressed remedies sought against the violations of the right to water at regional and international levels.

5.1. International human rights mechanisms

As for international human rights bodies, the Human Rights Committee has rarely enforced aspects of the human right to water. In a few relevant cases, the HRC has ruled that the deprivation of water and food to detainees amounted to cruel and inhuman treatment (Article 7 ICCPR), as well as to a violation of human dignity (Article 10(1) ICCPR).[456]

Furthermore, it is worth recalling the case *Poma v. Perù*, in which the HRC resorted to Article 27 of the Covenant – establishing the right of a minority to enjoy their culture – in order to give justice to the complainant's right to water. Ángela Poma Poma, a Peruvian citizen descendant of the Aymara people, claimed to have been deprived of the enjoyment of local natural resources due to the Government's implementation of a water diversion project that had considerably reduced the availability of water for human and animal consumption, depriving her family and community of their livelihood.[457] According to the Committee, raising animals is an essential element of the culture of the indigenous community to which the claimant belonged. By diverting waters, the State had caused the death of the community's livestock, thus breaching the claimant's right to enjoy her own culture.

The HRC also protected the right to water of a group of Roma people living in informal settlements by referring to the right to adequate housing enshrined in Article 17 ICCPR. In the case *Liliana Assenova Naidenova and others v Bulgaria*,[458] several Roma who had built unlawful houses on municipal land were served with an eviction order and, in order to force them to leave, their water services were cut off. The HRC requested the adoption of interim protection measures to re-establish water supply, given that cutting off the water supply to the community "*could be considered as indirect means of achieving eviction*",[459] and is a measure amounting to an unlawful interference with the right to enjoy one's home.

Looking to future developments in the field, the CESCR may have an important say in further defining the content of the right to water and the ensuing obligations.

---

independent expert on the issue of human rights obligations related to access to safe drinking water and sanitation, Catarina de Albuquerque, UN Doc. A/HRC/15/55, 22 July 2010, paras. 48, 53.

[456] *Essono Mika Miha v. Equatorial Guinea*, UN Doc. CCPR/C/51/D/414/1990, Communication No. 414/1990, IHRL 2259 (UNHRC 1994), 8 July 1994, para. 6.4.

[457] *Poma Poma v. Perù*, UN Doc. CCPR/C/95/D/1457/2006, Communication No. 1457/2006, IHRL 3331 (UNHRC 2009), 27 March 2009.

[458] *Liliana Assenova Naidenova and others v. Bulgaria*, UN Doc. CCPR/C/106/D/2073/2011, Communication No. 2073/2011, IHRL 2070 (UNHCR 2011), 30 October 2012.

[459] *Ibid.*, para. 10.

The new mechanism of accountability set forth by the Optional Protocol to the ICESCR,[460] allows the Committee to receive individual communications concerning violations of the rights enshrined in the ICESCR. Although the right to water is not explicitly provided for in the Covenant, given that the Committee has interpreted Articles 11 and 12 ICESCR as encompassing it, one can make the case that individuals or groups of individuals are in a position to submit a communication against the infringement of the right to water, for instance due to an excessive increase in water tariffs or undue disconnection from water services. In light of its General Comment No. 15, it is likely that the Committee will find it admissible and worthy of consideration.

5.2. Regional human rights tribunals and compliance mechanisms

Despite the lack of explicit regulation of the right to water in their respective instituting conventions – namely, the European Convention on Human Rights, the American Convention on Human Rights and the African Convention on Human and Peoples' Rights – regional human rights bodies have dealt, explicitly or implicitly, with water rights related issues by resorting to a wide interpretation of, in particular, the rights to private and family life, the right to life and the right to health.

The European Court of Human Rights, despite some criticism,[461] has never openly mentioned the right to water in its judgments.[462] However, in several cases, the Court has interpreted some Conventional rights, such as Article 3 ECHR (prohibition of torture and inhuman and degrading treatment), Article 6 ECHR (right to a fair trial)[463] and Article 8 ECHR (right to respect for private and family life) consistently with the human right to water.[464]

---

[460] Optional Protocol to the International Covenant on Economic, Social and Cultural Rights, adopted by the General Assembly, UN Doc. A/RES/63/117, 10 December 2008, New York. It was opened to signature on 24 September 2009 and entered into force on 5 May 2013. Currently, 24 States are parties to the Protocol (see, https://treaties.un.org/Pages/ViewDetails.aspx?src=TREATY&mtdsg_no=IV-3-a&chapter=4&lang=entitolo:Protocole&clang=_en http://indicators.ohchr.org/). For detailed information about the Protocol see M. Odello, F. Seatzu, *The UN Committee on Economic, Social and Cultural Rights: The Law, Process and Practice*, Abingdon, 2013, chapters two and three.

[461] F. M. Palombino, *Il diritto umano all'acqua nella prospettiva della Corte europea dei diritti dell'uomo: in margine al caso Otgon*, in *Rivista di Diritto internazionale*, 2017, pp. 149-154.

[462] See P. Steichen, *Le droit à l'eau dans la jurisprudence de la Cour européenne des droits de l'homme*, in H. Smets (ed.), *Le droit à l'eau potable et à l'assainissement en Europe. Implementing the right to drinking water and sanitation in 17 European countries*, Paris, 2012, pp. 69-75.

[463] See ECtHR, *Zander v. Sweden*, 25 November 1993; *Fisher v. Austria*, 26 April 1995; *Butan and Dragomir v. Romania*, 14 May 2008.

[464] P. Steichen (n 462); K. F. Braig, *The European Court of Human Rights and the right to clean water and sanitation*, in *Water Policy*, 2018; A. Saccucci, *La protezione dell'ambiente nella giurisprudenza della Corte europea dei diritti umani*, in G. Cataldi, A. Caligiuri, N. Napolitano (eds.), *La tutela dei diritti umani in Europa*, Padua, 2010.

In cases concerning precarious conditions of detention, in which the very *availability* of sufficient water for drinking and personal hygiene was contested, the Strasbourg Court has found violations of the prohibition of degrading treatment.[465]

In several other cases, the Court ascribed the infringement of the right to water to the category of environmental damages that, by meeting a certain minimum threshold of gravity, affect private and family life, triggering the applicability of Article 8 ECHR.[466] In this respect, the element that drew the attention of the Court has frequently been the lack of water quality due to the State's failure to prevent polluting water activities.

For example, in the *Zander* case, the claimants, Mr. and Mrs. Zander, claimed that their water well had been polluted by industrial activities and that they had been denied judicial remedies against such abuses.[467] The claimants owned a property adjacent to a land where a private company was granted a licence to deliver and treat waste. The licence was issued despite the excessive levels of cyanide found in the local water and the risk that the company's activities would have caused further pollution. Given the unsafe quality of the local waters, the landowners requested the Licensing Board to oblige the company to supply drinking water free of charge. The Licensing Board in charge of giving permission to the company, dismissed the owners' claims, assessing that the activities on the dump were unlikely to further pollute their water and that the measures requested were unreasonable.[468] Against this decision, the applicants appealed to the Government, which dismissed the appeal. Finally, Mr. and Mrs. Zander filed a claim with the Commission on Human Rights for having been denied the right to judicial review of the decision authorizing the company's activities. The European Court upheld the claims of violation of the right to a fair trial, as it found that Swedish law did not allow the applicants to have the Government's decision reviewed by a court. The applicants were thus recognized the right to bring their claims against the company's polluting activities before domestic judicial bodies.

The *Tătar* case[469] concerns two Romanian citizens resident in Baia Mare, a neighborhood nearby a mining activity of gold extraction responsible for having caused serious pollution of the local air, soil and both surface and groundwater. The mining company was allowed to use hazardous substances, such as sodium cyanide,

---

[465] See ECtHR, *Melnik v. Ukraine*, 28 March 2006; *Viorel Burzo v. Romania*, 30 June 2009; *Kadiķis v. Latvia*, 4 May 2006; *Marian Stoicescu v. Romania*, 16 July 2009; *M.S.S. v. Belgium and Greece* [GC], 21 January 2011.

[466] See ECtHR, *Otgon v. The Republic of Moldova*, 25 October 2016; *Tătar v. Romania*, 27 January 2009; *Dubetska and others v. Ukraine*, 10 February 2011; *Lopez Ostra v. Spain*, 9 December 1994; *Taşkin and others v. Turkey*, 10 November 2004; *Giacomelli v. Italy*, 2 November 2006.

[467] ECtHR, *Zander v. Sweden* (n 463).

[468] *Ibid.*, para. 10.

[469] ECtHR, *Tătar v. Romania* (n 466).

despite the risk of surface and groundwater contamination. On January 2000, a breach in a dam caused a significant ecological disaster: polluted water containing sodium cyanide spilled into nearby rivers and, through the Danube, poured into the Black Sea. Even Hungary and Serbia-Montenegro were affected.

The case was brought before the European Court, which found the respondent State responsible for having failed to fulfill its obligations under Article 8 of the Convention, namely, to secure the applicants' rights to respect for their private and family life[470]. The Court stated that under Article 8 of the Convention, States have to take all the necessary measures to protect private and family life, including the provision of a legal framework capable of preventing damages to human health and environment. Critically, the Court sanctioned the State's lack of adequate environmental regulations.[471] Moreover, despite the absence of a causal link of probability, the Court found sufficient evidence of the existence of a foreseeable and serious risk to the health and well-being of the applicants. Therefore, the State was found responsible for its failure to meet its obligations to protect private and family life and, more generally, the enjoyment of a healthy and safe environment.[472]

In the *Dzemyuk* case,[473] the State allowed the construction of a cemetery on a plot of land in close proximity to the applicant's house, in breach of environmental and health laws and regulations, causing the bacteriological contamination of the applicant's well, the sole source of water for his personal and household needs. The Court considered that the pollution had risen to a sufficient degree of seriousness so as to affect the applicant's "*quality of life*" and to trigger the application of Article 8 ECHR, and that the State had breached its positive obligations to protect the applicant from third party interference in the enjoyment of his private life.

The pending case *Hudorovič*[474] also deserves consideration. In this case, the applicants, inhabitants of informal Roma settlements, have complained against the lack of access to drinking water and sanitation public utilities. In its communication to Slovenia, the Court asked the Government to provide its observations on the following questions: *i*) whether Article 3 ECHR and/or Article 8 ECHR had been violated on account of the living conditions of the applicants, due to "*the lack of safe drinking water and sanitation in the settlements which have long been tolerated by the competent authorities*"; and *ii*) whether the Government had adopted "*a normative framework through which it committed to provide to its inhabitants, and especially to members of vulnerable groups such as the Roma, access to safe drinking water*

---

[470] *Ibid.*, para. 125.

[471] *Ibid.*, para. 87.

[472] *Ibid.*, para. 107.

[473] ECtHR, *Dzemyuk v. Ukraine*, 4 September 2014, paras. 30-32.

[474] ECtHR, *Hudorovič v. Slovenia*, communicated on 8 April 2015 (last accessed 10 February 2020).

and sanitation". These questions clearly assume the existence of *positive obligations* on the part of States to set forth a legal and administrative framework capable of providing access to safe drinking water and sanitation.

The Inter-American Court of Human Rights ("IACtHR") has similarly found violations of Article 5(2) of the American Convention (prohibition of cruel, inhuman and degrading treatment) on account of the detention conditions of the applicants who complained, *inter alia*, of lack of adequate access to water for personal consumption and hygiene.[475]

Moreover, the Court has ruled in several cases related to the human right to water of indigenous people, a right believed to emanate "*from their relationship with traditional lands and the natural resources thereof*".[476] The Court has held that the right to water of indigenous communities is part of their right to life and the right to property, respectively enshrined in Article 4 and Article 21 of the American Convention on Human Rights.[477]

In this context, the Inter-American Court has openly referred to the General Comment No. 15.[478] In two similar cases, the *Yake Axa indigenous community* case[479] and the *Sawhoyamaxa* case,[480] indigenous communities complained of the lack of access to natural resources, including water. At the end of the 19th century, Paraguay transferred the property of traditional indigenous lands to private owners, forcing members of the communities to resettle in distant lands where they faced precarious living conditions. At the beginning of the 90s, the Communities began to reclaim the lands that they considered their ancestral homelands and some members settled alongside the roads bordering these lands, living in destitute conditions, without basic services or access to clean water. The Court found that Paraguay had affected the right of its members to a decent life by failing to provide the indigenous communities with communal property where they would have access to natural resources, necessary to obtain clean water and other means of subsistence to preserve their way of life.[481] The Court ordered the State to establish a fund to be used for

---

[475] IACtHR, *López Álvarez v. Honduras*, 1 February 2006; *Vélez Loor v. Panamá*, 23 November 2010.

[476] Human Rights Council, *Report of the Special Rapporteur on the human right to safe drinking water and sanitation,* para. 65 (n 188).

[477] IACtHR, *Caso Villagrán Morales y Otros v. Guatemala* (Caso de los "Niños de la Calle"), 19 November 1999, para. 144; *Saramaka People v. Suriname*, 28 November 2007, para. 126; *Xákmok Kásek Indigenous Community v. Paraguay*, 24 August 2010, para. 195.

[478] IACtHR, *Sawhoyamaxa Indigenous Community v. Paraguay*, 29 March 2006, para. 164 nt. 216.

[479] IACtHR, *Yakye Axa Indigenous Community v. Paraguay*, 17 June 2005, paras. 50.15.

[480] IACtHR, *Sawhoyamaxa Indigenous Community v. Paraguay*, paras. 153, 178 (n 478).

[481] IACtHR, *Yakye Axa Indigenous Community v. Paraguay*, para. 168 (n 479); *Sawhoyamaxa Indigenous Community v. Paraguay*, para. 164 (n 478).

providing drinking water and sanitation to the members of the Community on the lands that were to be given to them,[482] and, as long as the Community remained landless, to supply them immediately with sufficient drinking water for consumption and personal hygiene.[483]

When read through the lens of the human right to water, in both cases an issue of *availability* and physical *accessibility* of water resources was raised and in both cases the State, by denying the property of the ancestral lands to indigenous communities, breached its obligations to respect, protect and fulfill, and thus to prevent any interference, including from third parties, in the enjoyment of the right to water of indigenous communities and to provide alternative access to water resources.

In the case *Mayagna (Sumo) Awas Tingni Community*, the Court derived the right to freely dispose of natural resources, including water resources, from the right to property of indigenous people on their ancestral lands.[484] The Court found a violation of the "*right of the members of the Mayagna Awas Tingni Community to the use and enjoyment of their property*" as the State "*granted concessions to third parties to utilize the property and resources located in an area*"[485] which was held by the indigenous community. The Court established that for indigenous communities lacking deed title on ancestral land, *de facto* possession of the land is sufficient to obtain official recognition and registration of their property rights. The Court also referred to Article 89(3) of the Nicaraguan Constitution, according to which the State recognizes the communal forms of land ownership of the Community of the Atlantic Coast and recognizes the use and enjoyment of the waters and forests on their communal lands.[486]

On a different note, the *Kichwa De Sarayaku Indigenous Community* case concerned the State's responsibility for having granted a contract for oil exploration and exploitation to a private company in the ancestral land of the Sarayaku Community, without their prior consultation and against their will. The Commission found that the State had violated Article 4 of the Convention, as the detonation of explosives had destroyed the forests, water sources and underground rivers needed to provide drinking water to the community, putting at risk the life and survival of the Community's members.[487] The Court agreed with the Commission and held that the State had failed to guarantee the right to life by allowing a permanent situa-

---

[482] IACtHR, *Sawhoyamaxa Indigenous Community v. Paraguay,* para. 224 (n 478).

[483] *Ibid.*, para. 230; *Yakye Axa Indigenous Community v. Paraguay*, para. 221 (n 479).

[484] IACtHR, *Mayagna (Sumo) Awas Tingni Community v. Nicaragua*, 31 August 2001. See, S. J. Anaya, C. Grossman, *The Case of the Awas Tingni v. Nicaragua: A New Step in the International Law of Indigenous Peoples*, in *Arizona Journal of International & Comparative Law*, 2002, pp. 1-15.

[485] *Ibid.*, para. 153.

[486] *Ibid.,* para. 117.

[487] IACtHR, *Pueblo Indígena Kichwa De Sarayaku v. Ecuador*, 27 June 2012, para. 233.

tion of risk, which threatened the life and physical integrity of the Sarayaku Community's members.[488]

It is noteworthy that the Inter-American Commission on Human Rights has also dealt with water related issues. For instance, the Commission published a country report on the human rights situation in Ecuador in which it found that inhabitants were exposed to toxic by-products of oil exploitation in their drinking and bathing water, which jeopardized their human rights to life and health.[489]

Finally, the African Commission on Human and Peoples' Rights ("AComHR") has often regarded the right to water as inherent in the right to health embedded in Article 16 of the African Charter on Human and Peoples' Rights, according to which everyone has the right to enjoy the best attainable state of physical and mental health, and States parties have to take the measures necessary to protect their peoples' health.[490]

The AComHR has given broad consideration to the accessibility aspects of the human right to water in relation to the States' duty to provide basic water services. In the case *Free Legal Assistance Group*, the claimants reported severe violations of human rights committed by Zaire (now Democratic Republic of Congo) from the late 1990s to the early 2000s, including the Government's failure to supply drinking water services. The African Commission considered such a failure as an infringement of the right to health under Article 16 of the African Charter.[491]

In the well-known *Ogoni* case, the African Commission found that the Government of Nigeria was responsible for having breached, among other provisions, the right to health and the right to a clean environment (Article 24 of the African Charter)[492] due to the actions of a State oil company, which had disposed of toxic waste in local waterways and contaminated the water, soil and air with oil spills, causing severe environmental pollution and serious health problems to the community residing in the Niger River Delta basin. Despite similarities with the *Kichwa De Sarayaku Indigenous Community* case, here the violation of the duty to respect may be found given that the Government of Nigeria was the major shareholder of the polluting company that had not refrained from unlawfully polluting water.

In the case *Sudan Human Rights Organisation & Centre on Housing Rights and Evictions (COHRE)*, the complainants accused the Republic of Sudan of having

---

488 *Ibid.*, para. 248.

489 Inter-American Commission on Human Rights, *Report on the Situation of Human Rights in Ecuador*, OEA/Ser.L/V/II.96, Doc. 10 rev. 1, 24 April 1997, para. 88.

490 T. S. Bulto, *The human right to water in the corpus and jurisprudence of the African human rights system*, in *African Human Rights Law Journal*, 2011.

491 AComHR, *Free Legal Assistance Group and Others v. Zaire*, 11 October 1995, para. 47.

492 AComHR, *Social and Economic Rights Action Center & the Center for Economic and Social Rights v. Nigeria*, 27 May 2002, paras. 50-54. See F. Coomans, *The Ogoni Case Before the African Commission on Human and Peoples' Rights*, in *International & Comparative Law Quarterly*, 2003, p. 1077.

bombed water wells in the Darfur region, among other atrocities.[493] In particular, they submitted that conduct such as poisoning wells and denying access to water sources violated the right to water as recognized by General Comment No. 15 and implicitly guaranteed under the right to life (Article 4), the right to health (Article 16) and the right to development (Article 22) of the African Charter.[494] The Commission recommended that the State take all necessary measures to restore water services.[495]

5.3. International investment tribunals

International investment tribunals, while vested with the power to settle international investment disputes, have recently started to address issues exceeding their traditional jurisdiction, including human rights and environment-related matters.[496] Interestingly, among these issues, the human right to water has been one of the most discussed.[497] Chapter three will focus extensively on the case law in this area.[498]

6. Conclusion

Human rights come to the fore when States begin to perceive certain individual interests as essential. For a long time, water was taken for granted, resulting in its omission from the traditional human rights instruments, such as the Bill of Rights.

More than three decades ago, a number of factors including pollution, climate change, growing world population and privatization policies contributed to a reconsideration of the value of water. Since then, a growing number of declarations, statements of States made in the framework of international organizations or con-

---

[493] AcomHR, *Sudan Human Rights Organisation & Others v. Sudan*, 27 May 2009; *Centre on Housing Rights and Evictions (COHRE) v. Sudan*, 27 May 2009.

[494] *Ibid.*, paras. 124-126.

[495] *Ibid.*, para. 229.

[496] See, among others, P.-M. Dupuy, E.-U. Petersmann, F. Francioni (eds.) *Human Rights in International Investment and Arbitration*, Oxford, 2009; F. Balcerzak, *Investor-State Arbitration and Human Rights*, Leiden-Boston, 2017.

[497] Marrella, pp. 335-359 (n 73); R. Greco, *The Impact of the Human Right to Water on Investment Disputes*, in *Rivista di Diritto Internationale*, 2015, pp. 444-486.

[498] *Suez, Sociedad General de Aguas de Barcelona, S.A. and Vivendi Universal, S.A. v. Argentine Republic* (n 144); *Suez, Sociedad General de Aguas de Barcelona SA and Interagua Servicios Integrales de Agua SA v. Argentine Republic* (n 144); *Aguas Cordobesas, S.A., Suez, and Sociedad General de Aguas de Barcelona, S.A. v. Argentine Republic* (n 144); *Impregilio S.p.A. v. Argentina Republic* (n 144); *SAUR International v. Argentine Republic* (n 144); *Urbaser S.A. and Consorcio de Aguas Bilbao Bizkaia, Bilbao Biskaia Ur Partzuergoa v. The Argentine Republic* (n 144).

ferences, resolutions, international and regional treaties, as well as domestic laws have approached water as a human right.

General Comment No. 15 gave an important impulse for drawing attention to the right at issue. It identified a conventional legal basis of the right to water in the ICESCR. By means of interpretation, the CESCR has inferred the right to water from, *inter alia*, the right to attain an adequate standard of living and the right to the highest attainable standard of physical and mental health. Moreover, it has clarified its content and the related obligations to be fulfilled by States.

States parties to the ICESCR have subsequently agreed on the derivative nature of the right to water as a right embedded in that of an adequate standard of living, pursuant to Article 11 ICESCR, and strictly linked to the right to health, under Article 12 ICESCR. Moreover, they reached an agreement on the definition of the right to water given by the Committee by voting in favor of the General Assembly resolutions, which made this definition their own. In respect of those States, the right to water may be invoked as a derivative right as defined by the CESCR.

Although only a short time has passed since the first recognition of the right to water, State practice in this connection has grown in a consistent and widespread manner, accompanied by a sense of legal obligation, which is evidence of the existence of a customary human right to water. However, while the *status* of the right to water under international general law can be held to be no longer unclear, its content is still embryonic and on a path of development.

Moreover, the obligations ensuing from the right to water, as based in both treaty and custom, should be further explored, above all in respect of their extraterritorial extension.

The current chapter is intended to provide a legal understanding of the right to water, necessary before investigating the relations and possible conflicts among this right and rights stemming from other legal fields, in order to explore possible avenues for avoiding or resolving potentially conflicting obligations likely to affect the progressive realization of the right at issue.

In this connection, the following chapters will analyze the different international legal regimes under which the liberalization of water services has occurred or is likely to occur – notably international investment law and international trade law –, in order to assess whether the main features of the right to water can be guaranteed under each of these systems and whether there is space for prospective harmonization of conflicting obligations.

Chapter III

THE LIBERALIZATION OF WATER SERVICES UNDER INTERNATIONAL INVESTMENT AGREEMENTS AND THE HUMAN RIGHT TO WATER

SUMMARY: 1. Introduction. – 2. The jurisdiction of investment tribunals to adjudicate violations of the human right to water. – 3. The impact of the human right to water on the merits of investor-State arbitration. – 3.1. The relevant BIT provisions likely to raise concerns from a human rights perspective. – 3.1.1. Expropriation. – 3.1.2. Fair and equitable treatment. – 3.1.3. Full protection and security. – 3.2. Cases lacking clear reference to the human right to water. – 3.2.1. Expropriation. – 3.2.2. Fair and equitable treatment. – 3.2.3. Full protection and security. – 3.3. Cases acknowledging the human right to water. – 3.3.1. Expropriation. – 3.3.2 Fair and equitable treatment. – 3.3.3. Full protection and security. – 3.3.4. The defence of necessity. – 3.4. *Interim* conclusion. – 4. The impact of the human right to water on compensation in investor-State arbitration. – 4.1. Cases lacking clear reference to the human right to water. – 4.2. Cases acknowledging the human right to water. – 4.3. *Interim* conclusion. – 5. Harmonizing investment protection with the human right to water. – 5.1. Harmonization by means of conflict prevention. – 5.1.1. Human rights impact assessment. – 5.1.2. Revising domestic rules and stabilization clauses. – 5.1.3. Incorporating human rights considerations in IIAs. – 5.1.4. Drafting a business and human rights treaty. – 5.2. Harmonization by means of interpretation of relevant BITs provisions. – 5.3. Establishing systemic relationships of priority. – 6. The attempts to ground corporate human rights obligations. – 7. Conclusion.

1. Introduction

States parties to the ICESCR have agreed to interpret Articles 11 and 12 ICESCR as encompassing the human right to drinking water,[1] which entitles all to "*sufficient, safe, acceptable, physically accessible and affordable water for personal and domestic uses*",[2] and, accordingly, to take all measures necessary to provide this water. However, according to the UN World Water Development Report in 2019, approximately 844 million people still lacked basic drinking water services,[3] while around

[1] For the purpose of this chapter, reference to the right to water must be intended as referred to the derivative right, unless otherwise stated, as the content and the obligations stemming from the customary right to water need to be further clarified in the years to come (see chapter two, section 3.2.).

[2] Committee on Economic, Social and Cultural Rights, General Comment No. 15 (2002), *The right to water (arts. 11 and 12 of the International Covenant on Economic, Social and Cultural Rights)*, UN Doc. E/C. 12/2002/11 (2002), 20 January 2003, para. 2 (hereinafter "General Comment No. 15").

[3] UNESCO, WWAP (World Water Assessment Programme), *The United Nations World Water Development Report 2019: Leaving No One Behind,* Paris, 2019, p. 18 (nt. 5). Basic drinking

one third of the global population, 2.1 billion people, did not use a "*safely managed drinking water service*".[4]

As discussed in chapter one, this gap is in part due to lack of financial resources and expertise, given that water infrastructure is among the most expensive to build and maintain, and water services management requires highly specialised personnel. Some States, even resorting to the maximum of their available resources, may still fall short in meeting their human rights obligations. Foreign private investment may be critical to provide States with the economic inflows and technical skills needed to this end.[5]

Liberalization, understood as opening the domestic market to foreign investments, may boost private investments. Several States have undertaken investment liberalization policies unilaterally by issuing domestic investment law, bilaterally by signing bilateral investment agreements (BITs), and multilaterally by adopting multilateral trade and investment treaties. Currently, there are more than 3,300 international investment agreements (IIAs),[6] including BITs and other treaties with investment provisions (TIPs).[7] The majority of BITs have been signed between developing and developed countries. However, recent BITs have been concluded by developing countries among themselves.[8]

The conclusion of investment treaties has a dual purpose. From the point of view of the State that hosts foreign investors (host State), it encourages investments by offering guarantees of a friendly investment environment (trustworthy climate), while from the perspective of the national state of the investors (home State), it protects investors from possible interference they may suffer abroad. By creating a clear legal framework for investment, the host State commits itself to safeguarding investors' rights and to granting the necessary stability for the success of the investment. Moreover, IIAs provide for investor-to-State dispute settlement mechanisms, which allow national investors of the foreign State to file complaints with, for instance, the International Centre for the Settlement of Investment Disputes ("ICSID")[9] or un-

---

water service indicates that the collection time for improved drinking water does not exceed 30 minutes for a round trip, including queuing.

[4] *Ibid.*, nt. 4. Safely managed drinking water services is understood as drinking water from an improved water source, located on premises, that is available and safe. Improved source refers to, *inter alia*: "*piped water, boreholes or tube wells, protected dug wells, protected springs, rainwater, and packaged or delivered water*".

[5] For an overview of the subject matter, see Commission on Human Rights, *Human rights, trade and investment, Report of the High Commissioner for Human Rights*, E/CN.4/Sub.2/2003/9, 2 July 2003.

[6] UNCTAD, *World Investment Report 2017*, 2017, p. 111.

[7] UNCTAD, *Investment Policy Framework for Sustainable Development*, 2015, p. 16.

[8] UNCTAD, *World Investment Report 2011*, 2011, p. 100.

[9] ICSID is an autonomous international arbitration institution established under the Convention on the Settlement of Investment Disputes between States and Nationals of Other States, signed in Washington DC on 18 March 1965, entered into force on 14 October 1966.

der the Arbitration Rules of the United Nations Commission on International Trade Law ("UNCITRAL").[10]

It has been contended that the bargaining power of host and home States in concluding investment treaties is excessively uneven. Developing countries are in desperate need of capital flows to support their economy, whereas foreign investors have a wide range of choices as to where to invest. Developing States are in competition for bilateral or multilateral investment agreements,[11] persuaded that in so doing they will gain an advantage over their neighbours in attracting investments.

In a sort of race towards the conclusion of BITs, countries have been willing to accept agreements curtailing their regulatory power. The very content of the obligations undertaken may have not been clear to developing States if they lacked the necessary expertise to assess models of investment proposed by investing countries.[12] In theory, IIAs may include exceptions to investors' rights for the protection of the public interest (*inter alia*, the environment, public order, national security, as well as human rights), but recourse to this possibility has been rare.[13] These shortcomings may curtail the States' regulatory leeway to adopt measures in the public interest, including measures necessary to guarantee the human right to water of population served by liberalized water services, if they affect investors' rights.

Although at present, no global investment agreement exists,[14] several features are widely common to all IIAs. Aside from the provisions establishing the scope of

---

[10] The United Nation Commission on International Trade Law adopted the UNCITRAL Arbitration Rules, a set of rules concerning the procedure before arbitral tribunals. They were settled on 28 April 1976 and revised in 2010.

[11] Moreover, in order to attract investments, some countries have issued domestic investment laws providing consent to arbitration of investor-State disputes. Such provisions may be claimed by all investors worldwide, whether a BIT exists or not. On the other hand, they may be easily changed by means of a subsequent law.

[12] Investment models are samples of BIT which have been prepared by same States or International Organizations.

[13] J. Wouters, S. Duquet, N. Hachez, *International Investment Law: The Perpetual Search for Consensus*, in O. De Schutter, J. Swinnen, J. Wouters (eds.), *Foreign Direct Investment and Human Development. The Law and Economics of International Investment Agreements*, London, 2012, p. 48; D. Kalderimis, *Investment Treaties and Public Goods*, in *Transnational Dispute Management*, 2009, p. 16.

[14] The OECD endorsed a Multilateral Agreement on Investment ("MAI"), but it was a failure. In the meanwhile, the WTO Working Group on the Relationship between Trade and Investment received the mandate to clarify certain aspects of a possible future international investment agreement. Further, WTO ministers agreed that negotiations on a multilateral framework for investment would have commenced at the Fifth WTO Ministerial Conference in Cancún, Mexico, in September 2003 so long as it was on the basis of an explicit consensus decision by WTO members. As no agreement on this topic was reached, the initiative was halted in 2004. See, Decision adopted by the WTO General Council on 1 August 2004 on the Doha Agenda Work Programme, DOC. WT/L/579, 2 August 2004. Source: http://www.wto.org/english/tratop_e/dda_e/draft_text_gc_dg_31july04_e.htm.

the treaty and providing for the market access rule, we can mention: the "*most favored nation*" clause and the "*national treatment*" clause, which safeguard foreign investors against discrimination; the ban of expropriation except for public reasons and subject to compensation; the ban of performance requirements;[15] the provisions of fair and equitable treatment and full protection and security of foreign investment; the guarantees of free transfer of funds and investments; the umbrella clause; and, finally, the dispute settlement mechanism allowing foreign investors to sue States before national courts and international investment tribunals.[16]

Arbitrators have given divergent interpretations of similar BITs provisions, thus undermining the predictability of the obligations undertaken by both investors and States. Uncertainty over the outcome of a dispute risks affecting developing countries which – risking to bear the cost of arbitration – may be discouraged from taking measures in the public interest likely to raise claims of indirect expropriation or unfair treatment.[17]

Within this framework, some issues have emerged. First, drafting IIAs in univocal pro-investors terms is not essential for encouraging investments.[18] It should be kept in mind that the flow of investments depends on several factors, such as the political stability of the country at issue, its legal and administrative background, the education and training of local personnel, the level of corruption, the cost of work and local tax burden.[19] Second, the possibility of resorting to arbitration in order to enforce the safeguard clauses included in BITs is not the sole driver for investments. Third, a better understanding of the respective rights and duties of host and home countries would help to address the increasing number of investment disputes. Fourth, before committing to investment treaties, developing countries should assess whether and to what extent their power to act for the public interest would be impaired.[20]

---

[15] Performance requirements aim at introducing special measures to promote domestic development, for instance assuring certain level of employment or the utilization of local products.

[16] Some authors argue that despite these common features, it cannot be assumed that such a network of bilateral agreements has generated customary international law. See, Wouters and others (n 13).

[17] It cannot be overlooked that "*the overwhelming majority of cases (85 per cent) have been brought by investors from developed countries*". UNCTAD, *Recent Developments in Investor-State Dispute Settlement (ISDS)*, IIA Issues No. 1, 2014, p. 8, available at http://unctad.org/en/PublicationsLibrary/webdiaepcb2014d3_en.pdf.

[18] See M. Hallward-Driemeier, *Do Bilateral Investment Treaties Attract Foreign Direct Investment? Only a Bit ... and They Could Bite*, World Bank Policy Research Working Paper No. 3121, 2003.

[19] It has been argued that: "*it is now well established that FDI flows are encouraged where the country of destination respects civil and political rights, and therefore preserves social and political stability*". O. De Schutter, *The Host State: Improving the Monitoring of International Investment Agreements at the National Level*, in O. De Schutter, J. Swinnen, J. Wouters (eds.), *Foreign Direct Investment and Human Development. The Law and Economics of International Investment Agreements*, London, 2012, p. 160.

[20] It has been noted that structural risks can arise from FDI in the water industry. State-owned

When it comes to water services,[21] cases of conflicts between obligations[22] under international investment law and human rights law, not avoidable by means of systemic interpretation, are likely to occur as investments in water and sanitation sectors are strictly related to the enjoyment of human rights.[23] In these situations, interpreters may have to decide whether to apply certain provisions rather than others and which obligations should receive priority.

In this connection, the High Commissioner for Human Rights has expressed concerns regarding the relationship between the obligations of States under BITs and in relation to access to safe drinking water. According to him:

> "Some of the current proceedings before the ICSID opposing private water companies to States, draw attention to the potential impact that obligations arising from bilateral investment treaties can have on the duty of States to regulate companies in the context of private provision of water or sanitation services. It remains unclear whether and how the obligations of Governments under international human rights instruments will be taken into account in ICSID judgements".[24]

Problems arising from the liberalization and privatization of water services have been dealt with by different bodies belonging to different special regimes, namely human rights law and investment law.[25] Chapter two analyzed disputes related to

---

monopolies may be converted into private ones. In this context, developing countries need "*to provide adequate regulatory frameworks or to negotiate appropriate deals with the private sector*". UNCTAD, *International Investment Agreements in Services*, Geneva, 2005, pp. 3-4.

[21] A. M. Daza Vargas, *Protection of Foreign Investment and the Implications for Regulation of Water Services and Resources: Challenges for Investment Arbitration*, in *The Journal of Water Law*, 2010.

[22] The notion of conflict adopted here is the one suggested by the Report of the International Law Commission (ILC) on the fragmentation of international law: "*a situation where two rules or principles suggest different ways of dealing with a problem*". International Law Commission, *Fragmentation of International Law: Difficulties Arising from the Diversification and Expansion of International Law, Report of the Study Group of the International Law Commission*, UN Doc. A/CN.4/L.682, 13 April 2006 (hereinafter "ILC Report"), para. 25.

[23] In particular, when public-owned utilities are privatized and liberalized, some concerns arise "*due to the differences of approach in service provision between public and private service providers and their different responsibilities towards the promotion and protection of human rights*". Commission on Human Rights, *Human rights, trade and investment,* para. 11 (n 5).

[24] Human Rights Council, *Annual report of the United Nations High Commissioner for Human Rights and reports of the Office of the United Nations High Commissioner for Human Rights and the Secretary-General – Report of the United Nations High Commissioner for Human Rights on the scope and content of the relevant human rights obligations related to equitable access to safe drinking water and sanitation under international human rights instruments*, A/HRC/6/3, 16 August 2007, para. 63.

[25] Sometimes, special regimes of international law are referred to as "*self-contained regime*". According to the ILC, the notion of "*self-contained regime*" has been used with different meanings, namely: "*a special set of secondary rules that determine the consequences of a breach of certain primary rules; any interrelated cluster (set, regime, subsystem) of rules on a limited problem together*

the supply of water that have been adjudged by human rights treaty bodies and regional courts. The present chapter focuses on several investment disputes that arose from failed attempts by States to liberalize water services, where investors have claimed the violation of their rights before investment arbitral tribunals due to the measures adopted by the respondent State to protect the right to water of the population under its jurisdiction. It also discusses the relationship and possible integration of human rights law and investment law in the context of the liberalisation and privatisation of water services.

The chapter proceeds as follows: the next section concerns the possible jurisdiction of investment arbitral tribunal to adjudicate claims concerning human rights, and specifically the human right to water. Section 3 describes the impact of the right to water on the merits of investor-State arbitration. It starts by describing the main provisions usually included in investment agreements that are likely to raise concerns from a human rights perspective. Then, it analyzes investment arbitral case law concerning water service privatisation, in which the right to water has been addressed, either implicitly or directly. Assuming that privatization policies may have an impact on the host State's regulatory powers, this section aims at assessing whether the emergence of the right to water has influenced investment tribunals' reasoning and their final decisions on liability. Then, section 4 evaluates whether the same trend is followed by the arbitral tribunals in their decisions on compensation. After evaluating possible trends in disputes arising from water services privatisation, section 5 focuses on the harmonization of human rights and investment special regimes. It considers ways to avoid normative conflicts or, once they have arisen, techniques for managing them. Section 6 briefly inquires into the legal basis for corporate human rights obligations. Finally, the last section draws some conclusions.

2. The jurisdiction of investment tribunals to adjudicate violations of the human right to water

It is acknowledged that autonomous human right claims are beyond the jurisdiction of investment arbitral tribunals,[26] whose competence is limited in scope *ratione per-*

---

with the rules for the creation, interpretation, application, modification, or termination – in a word, administration – of those rules"; and, "'*branches of international law' – that are also assumed to function in the manner of self-contained regimes, claiming to be regulated by their own principles*". In this chapter this notion is understood in its wider meaning, as different branches of international law. See, ILC Report, para. 152 (n 22).

[26] C. Reiner, C. Schreuer, *Human Rights and International Investment Arbitration*, in P.-M. Dupuy, F. Francioni, E.-U. Petersmann (eds.), *Human Rights in International Investment Law and Arbitration*, Oxford, 2009, pp. 83-84; B. Simma, T. Kill, *Harmonizing Investment Protection and International Human Rights: First Steps Towards a Methodology*, in C. Binder, U. Kriebaum, A. Reinisch, S. Wittich (eds.), *International Investment Law for the 21st Century. Essay in Honour of Christoph Schreuer*, Oxford, 2009, p. 679.

sonae to investors and *ratione materiae* to matters related to investments.[27] Nonetheless, the possibility for States to raise counterclaims exists,[28] and this has become the focus of growing interest for its potential connection with human rights.[29]

In this connection, Argentina's counterclaim in the *Urbaser* case,[30] which alleged violation of human rights obligations by investors, has gathered widespread attention[31], as it was the first time an arbitral tribunal found it had the competence to adjudicate a human rights counterclaim.

Argentina challenged the claimants' failure to comply with the terms of a concession contract concerning the provision of water and sewage services and, as a consequence, to abide by their obligations under the human right to water.[32] The Republic argued that the concessionaire had omitted to invest in the improvement and expansion of the water network, thus undermining the right to water of the residents. The region where the concession was awarded was one of the poorest areas in Argentina, characterized by extremely low coverage of water and sewerage services. For these reasons, it was essential for the Province that the investors complied with their obligation to make investments in expanding the infrastructure and guaranteeing access to water services.

---

[27] F. Balcerzak, *Investor-State Arbitration and Human Rights*, Leiden-Boston, 2017.

[28] *Saluka Investment B.V. v. Czech Republic*, UNCITRAL, Decision on Jurisdiction over the Czech Republic's Counterclaim, 7 May 2004; *Limited Liability Company Amto v. Ukraine*, SCC Case No. 080/2005, Final Award, 26 March 2008, para. 118; *RSM Production Corporation v. Grenada*, ICSID Case No. ARB/05/14, Award, 13 March 2009, para. 266; *Antoine Goetz & Consorts et S.A. Affinage des Metaux v. Republic of Burundi*, ICSID Case No. ARB/01/2, Award, 21 June 2012, para. 281; *Occidental Petroleum Corporation and Occidental Exploration and Production Company v. The Republic of Ecuador*, ICSID Case No. ARB/06/11, Award, 5 October 2012, paras. 854-69.

[29] E. Burova, *Jurisdiction of Investment Tribunals Over Host States' Counterclaims: Wind of Change?*, in *Kluwer Arbitration Blog*, 2017, available at: http://kluwerarbitrationblog.com/2017/03/06/jurisdiction-of-investment-tribunals-over-host-states-counterclaims-wind-of-change/.

[30] *Urbaser S.A. and Consorcio de Aguas Bilbao Bizkaia, Bilbao Biskaia Ur Partzuergoa v. The Argentine Republic*, ICSID Case No. ARB/07/26, Award, 8 December 2016.

[31] E. Guntrip, Urbaser v. Argentina: *The Origins of a Host State Human Rights Counterclaim in ICSID Arbitration?*, in *EJIL:* Talk!, 2017, available at https://www.ejiltalk.org/urbaser-v-argentina-the-origins-of-a-host-state-human-rights-counterclaim-in-icsid-arbitration/; M. Krajewski, *Human Rights in International Investment Law: Recent Trends in Arbitration and Treaty-Making Practice*, in *Yearbook on International Investment Law & Policy 2017*, Oxford, 2019, available at SSRN: https://ssrn.com/abstract=3133529; K. Crow, L. Lorenzoni Escobar, *International Corporate Obligations, Human Rights, and the* Urbaser *Standard: Breaking New Ground?*, in *Boston University International Law Journal*, 2018, available at: https://ssrn.com/abstract=2984987; U. Kriebaum, *The Right to Water Before Investment Tribunals*, in *Brill Open Law*, 2018, pp. 16-36, available at: file:///C:/Users/Robeta/Downloads/[23527072%20%20Brill%20Open%20Law]%20The%20Right%20to%20Water%20Before%20Investment%20Tribunals.pdf

[32] *Urbaser S.A. and others v. The Argentine Republic*, Award (n 30), para. 36. For a description of the main facts of this case, see section 3.3 below.

The tribunal's reasoning warrants attention. The arbitrators grounded their jurisdiction on the arbitration agreement governed by the Spain-Argentina BIT. Article X of the BIT allows both the investor and the host State, without distinction, to submit a dispute to an international arbitral tribunal.[33] Unlike other BITs, which limit the scope of the parties' consent to arbitrate to claims submitted by the investor only, the BIT under consideration is neutral in this regard, leaving both investors and the host State free to submit a dispute to arbitration and, *a fortiori,* free to lodge a counterclaim.[34] The tribunal dismissed the argument that an investor may subsequently limit the scope of the arbitral jurisdiction to its claims alone by means of its acceptance to arbitrate the investment dispute. Since the arbitration agreement governed by the BIT provides for the possibility of raising a counterclaim, the investors' consent to arbitration cannot restrict the arbitral tribunal's jurisdiction to their claims only.[35]

In addition, the jurisdictional clause in the BIT does not limit the scope of the arbitral tribunal's jurisdiction *ratione materiae* to disputes concerning breaches of the BIT only. On the contrary, any claim, based *prima facie* on a dispute related to an investment covered by the BIT, can be adjudicated, even if the breaches claimed are human rights violations.[36]

Having established its jurisdictional competence, the tribunal went on to consider the law applicable to the dispute under the BIT. It held that the relevant BIT provisions protected not only the rights granted to investors, but also the States' rights,[37] which can be grounded on other sources of international law.[38] Indeed, the BIT rules on the applicable law referred also to the general principles of international law. This reference excludes the possibility of construing the investment treaty as a set of rules in isolation from general international law.[39] In this connection, Article 31(3)(*c*) of the Vienna Convention on the Law of Treaties ("VCLT") requires treaty provisions to be read in harmony with other rules in international law, including those relating to human rights law,[40] to which the right to water belongs.[41]

Scholars agree that a cause of action may be grounded on rules of international law extraneous to investment law, including human rights law, provided that the

---

[33] *Ibid.*, para. 1143.

[34] *Ibid.*, para. 1144.

[35] *Ibid.*, paras. 1145-1148.

[36] *Ibid.*, paras. 1152-1154.

[37] *Ibid.*, paras. 1183-1187.

[38] *Ibid.*, para. 1191.

[39] *Ibid.*, para. 1189.

[40] *Ibid.*, paras. 1200, 1204.

[41] *Ibid.*, para. 1205.

arbitration clause conferring jurisdiction is drafted in terms wide enough to encompass all breaches that affect investments and not only breaches of the BIT. [42]

3. The impact of the human right to water on the merits of investor-State arbitration

This section analyses a selection of ICSID awards and decisions concerning failed attempts to privatise water services. [43] Each award/decision deals with a selection of BIT clauses and for each clause this section consider the interpretation given by arbitral tribunals in order to establish whether or not the adjudicating bodies have endorsed a human rights-oriented interpretation.

In particular, this section evaluates if and to what extent respondent States and *amicus curiae* have successfully invoked the human right to water before investment tribunals, looking at the weight that has been attached to the human rights defence in the tribunals' decisions on the merits.

The arbitral interpretation of the main BIT provisions described in the following section will be analyzed against some *parameters*, namely, disputed elements such as the weight to be given to the intent or to the effect of expropriatory measures, or the role to be played by the investor's legitimate expectations in the fair and equitable treatment clause.

In order to show a possible evolution in the arbitral jurisprudence, [44] relevant cases will be presented following the chronological order of publication of the respective awards, beginning with the least recent in which a clear reference to the human right to water is absent and concluding with the latest publicly available, where the right to water was widely acknowledged.

3.1. The relevant BIT provisions likely to raise concerns from a human rights perspective

Several recurring provisions enshrined in BITs are meant to protect foreign investments and to limit States' police power. Among them, some clauses – such as those

---

[42] Balcerzak, pp. 111-113 (n 27); U. Kriebaum, *Foreign Investment & Human Rights – The Actors and Their Different Roles*, in *Transnational Dispute Management*, 2013, p. 12.

[43] The cases analyzed in this section are emblematic of a trend of human rights-friendly interpretation of BIT provisions. In addition to these, other investment disputes concerning failed water services privatization are: *Aguas del Tunari S.A. v. Republic of Bolivia*, ICSID Case No. ARB/02/03; *Suez, Sociedad General de Aguas de Barcelona SA and Interagua Servicios Integrales de Agua SA v. Argentine Republic*, ICSID No ARB/03/17; and *Impregilo S.p.A. v. Argentina Republic*, ICSID Case No. ARB/07/17.

[44] All of the following arbitrations have been conducted under the ICSID.

concerning expropriation, fair and equitable treatment ("FET") and full protection and security ("FPS") – may undermine the fulfillment of human rights obligations.

The more such provisions are broadly expressed and interpreted, the less leeway the host State is left with to regulate in the general interest. Recently, some arbitral tribunals have resorted to systemic interpretation of existing provisions in order to balance investors' rights with the State's regulatory powers. Sections 3.2 and 3.3 will analyze whether and to what extent arbitrators have interpreted investment treaty norms by taking human rights considerations into account, in particular the right to water.

Before turning to examine this case law, it seems appropriate to first offer an overview of the key BIT provisions whose interpretation has been at the heart of disputes between investors and host States.

3.1.1. Expropriation

Under the principle of sovereignty, States have the right to expropriate foreign property within their territory.[45] Investors run the risk of losing their investments, but this risk is counterbalanced by customary international rules protecting assets held by foreign nationals in accordance with "*a minimum standard of protection*" for aliens, however indefinite this standard may be.[46]

In addition, IIAs set some limitations to the host State's right to expropriate, particularly with regard to the pre-conditions and consequences of expropriation. As for preconditions, the most common is that expropriation must be justified by a public purpose and must not be discriminatory. Among the consequences, States have to provide compensation for losses suffered by investors. The agreement may even specify that the compensation must be "*prompt, adequate and effective*" (the so-called *Hull* formula). Usually, compensation for a lawful expropriation is calculated in relation to the fair market value of the investment.

While formal expropriation undoubtedly falls under the scope of this rule and thus requires the payment of said compensation, another concept has been more problematic, namely that of "*indirect expropriation*".[47] This refers to situations in

---

[45] F. M. Palombino, *Il Trattamento 'Giusto e Equo' degli Investimenti Stranieri*, Bologna, 2012; J. M. Cox, *Expropriation in Investment Treaty Arbitration*, Oxford, 2019; C. McLachlan, L. Shore, M. Weiniger, *International Investment Arbitration. Substantive Principles*, Oxford, 2017, pp. 259-412; G. Sacerdoti, *General Interests of States in International Investment Law*, Cambridge, 2014.

[46] Dumberry refers to "*[a] firmly established rule*" of customary international law "*with an imprecise content*". See P. Dumberry, *The Formation and Identification of Rules of Customary International Law in International Investment Law*, Cambridge, 2016, pp. 96-110; I. Marboe, *Calculation of Compensation and Damages in International Investment Law*, Oxford, 2017, p. 85: "*the existence and extent of an international minimum standard for the treatment of aliens is one of the most controversial issues*".

[47] See McLachlan and others, pp. 381-386, paras. 8.71-8.85 (n 45).

which a State adopts measures that interfere with investors' rights, without a formal taking of title, to such an extent as to amount to a *de facto* expropriation. In other words, notwithstanding the maintenance of formal title, investors are deprived of the possibility of managing their investment in a profitable manner. Indirect expropriation may give rise to the international responsibility of the host State and to the duty to provide reparation.

The High Commissioner for Human Rights underlines that:

> "[t]here is mounting concern that tribunals adjudicating investor-to-State disputes are increasingly interpreting expropriation provisions broadly in a way that could threaten States' ability and willingness to introduce new regulations to protect the environment and human rights. It is important to safeguard the ability to introduce new measures to promote and protect human rights within interpretations of expropriation provisions".[48]

Arbitral tribunal case law shows that investors frequently claim to have been indirectly expropriated in order to be awarded compensation for the losses incurred. On the contrary, States usually deny in such cases that any expropriation has taken place, contending that the contested measures served a public purpose, were within their regulatory powers and, as a consequence, did not gave rise to any duty to compensate the investors for their alleged losses.

The definition of "*indirect expropriation*" is needed to distinguish between legitimate, non-compensable measures and measures that have effects equivalent to expropriation. Arbitrators have adopted two main approaches in interpreting the notion of indirect expropriation. Under the "sole *effect* doctrine", some tribunals have taken into account the effect of the States' measures only, without any consideration for their motivations. In the *Metalclad* case, it was held that:

> "[t]he Tribunal need not decide or consider the motivation or intent of the adoption of the Ecological Decree. Indeed, a finding of expropriation on the basis of the Ecological Decree is not essential to the Tribunal's finding of a violation of NAFTA Article 1110. However, the Tribunal considers that the implementation of the Ecological Decree would, in and of itself, constitute an act tantamount to expropriation"[49].

On the contrary, in order to establish whether an expropriation has occurred, other tribunals have also considered the *purpose* pursued by States. For instance, some have applied the "*public powers doctrine*", according to which the legitimate public purpose that characterizes the measures adopted by the public authorities

---

[48] Commission on Human Rights, *Human rights, trade and investment*, p. 3 (n 5).

[49] See, in this regard, *Metalclad v. United Mexican States*, ICSID Case No. ARB(AF)/97/1, Award, 30 August 2000, para. 111; *Siemens v. Argentina*, Award, 6 February 2007, para. 270.

prevents these measures from being considered an expropriation. The *Methanex* case is often referred to as an example in point.[50]

The controversial issue is then whether States are liable for paying compensation when they adopt measures in the exercise of their powers to regulate in the general interest. This kind of dispute would arise, for instance, if a State adopted regulations that were aimed at protecting and fulfilling the right to water, but which were considered by the investor as amounting to an indirect expropriation.

Faced with an inconsistent case law on the matter,[51] the present section seeks to assess whether a coherent approach has been adopted in the context of water services disputes. It will consider how arbitral tribunals have judged regulations designed to protect water quality and affordability. In particular, it will discuss if these tribunals have been influenced by human rights considerations and have accordingly endorsed the "*public powers doctrine*". The following sub-sections 3.2.1. and 3.3.1. will provide an overview of water investment disputes in order to draw some conclusions.

3.1.2. Fair and equitable treatment

The fair and equitable treatment clause obliges States to guarantee a certain standard of treatment to foreign investors, yet the content of this standard is rather vague.[52] Indeed, this clause is usually referred to in order to fill gaps left by other, more specific, treaty provisions. Moreover, it is invoked when evidence does not support a claim of expropriation. Judicial bodies have sought to clarify the meaning of the FET clause, but they offered inconsistent interpretations.[53]

According to a narrow interpretation, FET clauses reflect the customary international minimum standard of treatment of aliens. Although the content of the international minimum standard is not well defined,[54] it is intended to include at least

---

[50] *Methanex Corporation v. United States of America*, Final Award of the NAFTA Tribunal, 3 August 2005. See Wouters and others, p. 57 (n 13).

[51] For instance, in *Saluka Investments B.V. v. The Czech Republic*, Partial Award, 17 March 2006, UNCITRAL (1976), para. 262, it was held that State had not committed an expropriation and was not liable to pay compensation when it adopted regulations that were within its police powers. On the contrary, in *Compañia del Desarrollo de Santa Elena S.A. v. Republic of Costa Rica*, ICSID Case No. ARB/96/1, Award 17 February 2000, at para. 72, the Tribunal considered it irrelevant that the contested measures were undertaken to serve environmental purposes.

[52] I. Knoll-Tudor, *The Fair and Equitable Treatment Standard and Human Rights Norms*, in P.-M. Dupuy, F. Francioni, E.-U. Petersmann (eds.), *Human Rights in International Investment Law and Arbitration*, Oxford, 2009.

[53] See, Wouters and others, pp. 52-54 (n 13). Different definitions of the FET clause have been given in: *Técnicas Medioambientales Tecmed S.A. v. The United Mexican States*, ICSID Case No. ARB(AF)/00/2, Award, 29 May 2003, paras. 155-156; *Waste Management, Inc. v. United Mexican States*, ICSID Case No. ARB(AF)/00/3, Award, 30 April 2004, para. 98.

[54] M. Paparinskis, *The International Minimum Standard and Fair and Equitable Treatment*, Oxford,

the prohibition of gross misconduct or manifest injustice by the State.

Respondent States usually endorse this reading as it puts few constraints on their public policy powers. Moreover, it has been approved by the NAFTA[55] Free Trade Commission[56] in its binding interpretation of Article 1105(1) of NAFTA, which states: "*[e]ach Party shall accord to investments of investors of another Party treatment in accordance with international law, including fair and equitable treatment and full protection and security*".

The Commission contended that:

> "[a]rticle 1105(1) prescribes the customary international law minimum standard of treatment of aliens as the minimum standard of treatment to be afforded to investments of investors of another Party"

and that:

> "[t]he concepts of 'fair and equitable treatment' and of 'full protection and security' do not require treatment in addition to or beyond that which is required by the customary international law minimum standard of treatment of aliens".[57]

Furthermore, some treaties have expressly linked FET to customary international law.[58]

On the other side, the UNCTAD deems that the FET clause is not synonymous with the international minimum standard.[59] In cases where investment treaties did not refer to general international law, some arbitrators have interpreted the FET clause as separate from the general standard of international customary law.[60] They have argued that this clause provides for a higher level of protection of investors' rights and, conversely, for a greater limitation of the regulatory power of the host State. Broadly interpreted, this clause can be read as to virtually bar any regulation likely to affect investments.

2013, p. 171 ff. The author refers to the modern standard of administration of justice and of protection of property.

[55] North American Free Trade Agreement, 8-17 December 1992, entered into force on 1 January 1994. It was adopted by Canada, Mexico and USA.

[56] The Commission, made up of representatives of the States parties, has the power to adopt a binding interpretation (NAFTA, art. 1132(2).

[57] Free Trade Commission, *Note of Interpretation*, 31 July 2001, paras. 1-2.

[58] Among others: French Model BIT, art. 3; Canada 2004 Model BIT, art. 5; United States 2012 Model BIT, art. 5 and Annex A.

[59] UNCTAD, *Fair and Equitable Treatment*, IIA issues paper series, Geneva, New York, 1999, p. 40, available at: https://unctad.org/en/Docs/psiteiitd11v3.en.pdf.

[60] *Tecmed Tecnicas Medioambientales S.A. v. The United Mexican States*, Award (n 53), paras. 155-156.

A controversial point is then to establish the exact content of the clause at issue. Some principles may be helpful to this end. *In primis*, arbitral tribunals often refer to the "*legitimate expectation*" of investors. However, this notion has also been read in different ways.

Investors tend to invoke the interpretation set out in the often-cited award *Tecmed v. Mexico*, where the tribunal seemed to disapprove any change in policy and regulation that could potentially affect foreign investment. It was contended that:

> "[t]he foreign investor expects the host State to act in a consistent manner, free from ambiguity and totally transparently in its relations with foreign investor, so that it may be known beforehand any and all rules and regulations that will govern its investments, as well as the goals of the relevant policies and administrative practices or directives, to be able to plan its investment and comply with such regulation". [61]

On the contrary, defendant States recall narrow arbitral readings of the principle at issue. For instance, in the *Saluka v. Czech Republic* case, the tribunal held that:

> "[t]he expectations of foreign investors certainly include the observation by the host State of such well-established fundamental standard as good faith, due process, and non– discrimination". [62]

Applying this statement, the tribunal ruled that a foreign investor whose interests are protected under the Treaty may expect that the host State:

> "will not act in a way that is manifestly inconsistent, non-transparent, unreasonable (i.e. unrelated to some rational policy) or discriminatory (i.e. based on unjustifiable distinctions)". [63]

In light of the above considerations, the question is whether changes in water services regulations may affect the reasonable expectations of investors to receive financial returns, thus breaching the FET clause.

Another standard often invoked by the parties in order to define the content of the FET clause is compliance with contractual obligations. Indeed, as investors' expectations are often based on contractual arrangements with the host State, the State's inobservance of the obligations arising from contracts may frustrate these expectations. [64]

Tribunals have adopted different approaches as to which contractual breaches may be deemed to be violations of the FET clause. However, it seems to be widely agreed that not all contractual breaches amount to a violation of the FET rule. Ac-

---

[61] *Ibid.*, para. 154.

[62] *Saluka Invs. B.V. v. Czech Republic*, Partial Award (n 51), paras. 301-303.

[63] *Ibid.*, para. 309.

[64] R. Dolzer, C. Schreuer, *Principles of International Investment Law*, Oxford, 2012, p. 152.

cording to some tribunals, for a State to violate the FET clause by means of contractual breaches it has to act in the exercise of its sovereign power.[65] In other words, the public authorities' violation has to be so significant as to raise the international responsibility of the State concerned.

Sub-sections 3.2.2. and 3.3.2. consider the approach that arbitral tribunals have taken in water services disputes with regard to the FET clause.

3.1.3. Full protection and security

The meaning of the full protection and security clause is no less controversial than that of fair and equitable treatment. The main doubt concerns whether this standard refers only to "*physical security*" or if it extends to "*legal security*" as well. According to the latter approach, a State could be held responsible for a violation of the investment treaty even when it adopts regulations likely to undermine the environmental and legal stability of the investment so as to affect investors' rights.

One can question whether the adoption of measures apt to interfere with the private management of water services, in an attempt to guarantee a minimum quality and quantity of water supply, may be deemed to be a breach of the FPS provision.

In addition, this clause is not always expressed with the same wording. For instance, sometimes the adjective *full* is absent. Some scholars have inferred from the analysis of case law that the lack of the word *full* does not entail that "*the standard must be given a narrower meaning which extends to physical security only*".[66]

The standard at issue is occasionally linked to customary international law, suggesting that it should be interpreted narrowly according to the minimum international standard of treatment of aliens.[67] Yet, there is no univocal reading supporting this assumption.

As far as disputes over water services are concerned, the approach taken by arbitral tribunals will be analyzed in the next sub-sections 3.2.3. and 3.3.3.

3.2. Cases lacking clear reference to the human right to water

The majority of the cases analyzed arose in Argentina,[68] which has faced the largest

---

[65] *Impregilo S.p.A. v. Pakistan*, ICSID Case No. ARB/03/3, Decision on jurisdiction, 22 April 2005, para. 260; *Consortium FRCC v. Royaume du Maroc*, ICSID Case. No. ARB/00/6, 22 December 2003, Award, para. 65; *Azurix Corp. v. Argentina*, ICSID Case No. ARB/01/12, Award, 14 July 2006, para. 53.

[66] Dolzer, Schreuer, p. 165 (n 64).

[67] In this sense, NAFTA Free Trade Commission, Notes of Interpretation of Certain Chapter 11 Provisions, 31 July 2001, B.

[68] See P. Mayer, *Les Arbitrages CIRDI en Matière d'eau,* in *Societé francaise pour le droit international* (SFDI) (ed.), Colloques d'Orléans, *L'eau en droit international*, Paris, 2011.

number of claims related to the privatization of water services.[69] In 1989, Argentina enacted the State Reform Law,[70] kicking off a far-reaching process of investment liberalization and privatization. The aim was to address the emergency experienced in the country's public services. In accordance with the State Reform Law, most Provinces – including Tucumán, Buenos Aires and Mendoza – adopted measures aimed at boosting national liberalization efforts.[71] Moreover, Argentina, in an effort to gain international credibility and to attract foreign investments, adopted the Convertibility Law that pegged the Argentine peso to the US dollar.[72]

Problems arose when the government later repealed these laws in response to the severe economic and financial crisis that occurred in 1999. A number of measures were adopted that affected foreign investors. *In primis*, in 2002, the link between the Argentine peso to the US dollar was abolished, resulting in a significant devaluation of the peso. Moreover, the executive branch of the government was authorized to renegotiate all public service contracts. These public measures resulted in significant economic losses for investors that had been awarded contracts for the provision of water services. As a consequence, the affected investors claimed compensation before international investment tribunals, alleging breaches of the BITs concluded between their respective home States and Argentina.

The first investment disputes before ICSID Tribunals concerning failed attempts to privatize and liberalize water services contain some vague references to human rights considerations, but no clear mention of the human right to water was made by the respondent governments. Three cases are addressed in this sub-section: the *Azurix* case,[73] the *Vivendi* case[74] and the *Biwater* case.[75]

As for the *Azurix* case, in the late 1990s, the Province of Buenos Aires (Argentina) awarded a 30-year concession for the distribution of potable water and the treatment and disposal of sewerage to a private company (ABA).[76] Owing to local authorities'

---

[69] O. De Schutter, J. Swinnen, J. Wouters, *Introduction*, in O. De Schutter, J. Swinnen, J. Wouters (eds.), *Foreign Direct Investment and Human Development. The Law and Economics of International Investment Agreements*, London, 2012, p. 6.

[70] Federal Law No. 23.696 of 17 August 1989.

[71] It is worth recalling that Argentina is a federal Republic consisting of twenty-three provinces plus the autonomous city of Buenos Aires.

[72] Federal Law No. 23.928 of 27 March 1991.

[73] *Azurix Corp. v. Argentine Republic*, Award (n 65). See F. Costamagna, *Legitimate Regulation vs Regulatory Expropriation in Public Infrastructure Investments after Azurix: A Case Study*, in *Transnational Dispute Management*, 2007.

[74] *Compañía de Aguas del Aconquija S.A. and Vivendi Universal v. Argentine Republic*, ICSID Case No. ARB/97/3.

[75] *Biwater Gauff (Tanzania) Ltd. v. United Republic of Tanzania*, ICSID Case No. ARB/05/22.

[76] The services, previously provided by a public company, Administratión General de Obras Sanitarias de la Provincia de Buonos Aires ("AGOSBA"), were awarded to two indirect subsidiary companies of the US Azurix group, namely Azurix AGOSBA S.R.L. ("AAS") and Operadora

extensive interference – concerning, *inter alia*, the tariff regime,[77] the billing of customers[78] and the maintenance and operation of the reservoirs[79] – the concessionaire experienced serious difficulties that undermined the concession. After having requested the Province to put an end to its contractual breaches without avail, ABA terminated the concession agreement and filed for bankruptcy. The Province rejected the request and, in March 2002, terminated the concession, alleging abandonment by ABA.

In 2001, by virtue of the BIT in force between the United States of America and the Republic of Argentina,[80] Azurix filed a request for arbitration with the ICSID tribunal against Argentina claiming that it had breached the BIT by expropriating its investment and failing to accord FET and FPS to the company. In order to support its claim, Azurix alleged, in particular, that the terms of the BIT were breached due to: the public authorities' failure to apply the tariff regime of the concession for political reasons; failure of the Province to complete certain essential works that were supposed to be transferred to the concessionaire upon completion; and the Province's denial of the recovery of the canon through tariffs.[81]

Concerning the termination of the concession, Argentina raised the issue of a conflict between the BIT and human rights treaties, which would protect consumers' rights. This reference to human rights was made in general terms, without mentioning the human right to water. It was argued that said conflict should have been resolved in favor of human rights because of the public interest involved, which must prevail over the service provider's private interest.[82]

The tribunal found that no conflict between the BIT and human rights treaties arose in the case, as consumers were provided with the services without interruption, first by ABA (during the months after the termination), and then by the new provincial utility to which the service was transferred.[83]

---

de Buonos Aires S.R.L. ("OBA"). In accordance with domestic law, AAS and OBA incorporated a domestic company in Argentina, Azurix Buonos Aires S.A. ("ABA"), to act as the concessionaire. Upon release of an extremely expensive "canon payment" of 438,555,551 million US dollars, ABA was granted the concession.

[77] *Azurix Corp. v. Argentine Republic*, Award (n 65), para. 90.

[78] *Ibid.*, para. 102.

[79] *Ibid.*, para. 144.

[80] Treaty concerning the Reciprocal Encouragement and Protection of Investment between the Argentina Republic and the United States of America, Washington, 14 November 1991.

[81] Azurix made an aggressive bid thinking that it would recover the canon by means of tariff increases. The Province accepted Azurix' bid and benefited from the price paid by the company, but forbid the tariff increase. The Tribunal denied that the canon was an investment not included in the existing tariff under the concession agreement. The company should have prepared the bid by considering, for purposes of tariff setting and amortization, the value of the earnings stream of the concession at the time of the transfer. *Azurix Corp. v. Argentine Republic*, Award (n 65), para. 240.

[82] *Ibid.*, para. 254.

[83] *Ibid.*, para. 261.

The *Vivendi* case[84] originated from the 1993 decision of the Province of Tucumán (Argentina) to privatize water and sewage services, which had previously been operated by DiPOS, a provincial authority.[85] In 1995, the Province of Tucumán concluded a concession contract with Compañía de Aguas del Aconquija, S.A. ("CCA"), an affiliate of Compagnie Générale des Eaux (CGE) incorporated under the Argentine law.[86]

The provincial government acknowledged the necessity of significant tariff increases in order to make the system financially viable for the investors and allowed the shifting of the cost of services to customers. It is worth mentioning that the "*CAA's first invoices reflected on average, an approximate 110% increase over the rates previously charged by DiPOS*"[87]. Soon after, the newly elected government publicly expressed its opposition to water services privatization and made clear its intention to reverse the process.

As a consequence, several disputes arose between the water company and the Province with regard to, in particular, the amount of the tariff increases and remedies for non-payment. The local authorities put in place a number of measures that resulted in a fall in the recovery rate, which had been foreseen by the concession.[88] Under pressure from the local regulatory agency for water services ("ERAT"), the concessionaire agreed to renegotiate the contract, in particular to redefine tariffs. However, negotiations failed and CGE notified the provincial governor of Tucumán its rescission from the concession contract, alleging multiple breaches by Tucumán. The Province rejected the notice of rescission and instead terminated the contract for breach by CGE. Tucumán authorities required CGE to continue providing water and sewage services for a period of 18 months or until a successor

---

[84] *Compañía de Aguas del Aconquija S.A. and Vivendi Universal v. Argentine Republic* (n 74).

[85] Direccion Provincial de Obras Sanitarias, "DiPOS". DiPOS had encountered several problems in running the services efficiently, which resulted in the Tucumán water and sewer system being deeply undermined and water infrastructure badly deteriorated. One of the major problems related to the subsided tariffs, which did not reflect the cost of the services and were inadequate to finance investments in the sector. DiPOS revenues covered only 30% of its expenses, with the remainder of its operating funds coming from state subsidies. *Compañía de Aguas del Aconquija S.A. and Vivendi Universal v. Argentine Republic*, Second Award (n 74), 20 August 2007, para. 4.2.3.

[86] Upon invitation to submit bids, only one bid was received, presented by the consortium "Aguas del Aconquija", which was subsequently awarded the concession.

[87] *Compañía de Aguas del Aconquija S.A.and Vivendi Universal v. Argentine Republic*, Second Award (n 74, n 85), para. 4.10.3. However, "*[t]his led to higher increases in the middle and higher range, with the lower income population experiencing little or no change*". *Ibid.*

[88] Among others, these measures included: regulations calling for unilateral and retroactive reduction of tariffs; calls to customers not to pay invoices; ombudsman decisions aimed at preventing the cutting off of service to customers in arrears; imposition of an extraordinary number of fines; unilateral changes in the renegotiated agreement and various post-termination conducts.

operator would be found. Despite CGE's protests, the company continued to operate the water and sewage system for ten months until, in 1998, the concession was turned over to an agency of the Argentina Republic. Finally, following the termination of the contract, the company's efforts to collect payment for the services provided were frustrated by the provincial legislature.

On December 1996, the French company, Compagnie Générale des Eaux and its affiliate CCA, requested the institution of proceedings against the Argentine Republic under the ICSID Convention.[89] The companies complained that the Province had expropriated the investment of the concessionaire and had taken actions amounting to a denial of the FET standard. Initially, the tribunal declined to adjudge the case on the merits, but, after a request for partial annulment upheld by the ICSID Annulment Committee, the claimants[90] resubmitted the dispute to ICSID in 2003. During the second proceedings, the arbitral tribunal considered the facts of the case extensively in order to establish whether the Tucumán authorities violated the BIT clauses.

Interestingly, Argentina requested the tribunal to dismiss the claims, alleging that Tucumán's conduct was intended to discharge its responsibilities towards the community, since "*the Province had the responsibility to take steps to ensure the availability of safe drinking water for its population on an affordable and accessible basis*".[91] The respondent referred to the duty to "*provide a reliable supply of quality water, a fundamental human need which the state has a responsibility to safeguard and maintain*".[92] Although no clear reference to the right to water was made by Argentina, the above argument is a first attempt to invoke human rights obligations in opposition to those arising under investment treaties. However, the tribunal did not address human rights issue as such. As will be discussed in sections 3.2.1-3.2.3, the tribunal adopted a wide, pro-investor interpretation of all BIT provisions.

In the *Biwater* case, the dispute arose from a failed attempt to privatize the supply of water and sewerage services in the region of Dar es Salaam (Tanzania),[93] previously provided by a Tanzanian public corporation ("DAWASA"). Due to decades of low tariffs and a lack of capital expenditure to maintain and improve the existing infrastructure, the services were in extremely poor condition. In 2003, the British

[89] The companies based their request on the 1992 Argentina – French BIT: *Accord entre le Gouvernement de la République française et le Gouvernement de la République Argentine sur l'encouragement et la protection réciproques des investissements (ensemble une déclaration)*, Paris, 3 July 1991.

[90] In the meanwhile, Compagnie Générale des Eaux had changed its corporate name to Vivendi.

[91] *Compañía de Aguas del Aconquija S.A. and Vivendi Universal v. Argentine Republic*, Second Award (n 74, n 85), para. 3.3.5.

[92] *Ibid.*, para. 6.5.1.

[93] *Biwater Gauff (Tanzania) Ltd. V. United Republic of Tanzania* (n 75).

joint venture Biwater Gauff (Tanzania) Limited ("BGT") was awarded a ten-year lease for the provision of water and sewerage services. For the purpose of taking over the services, the joint venture incorporated a new company, City Water. One year later, a number of problems emerged, resulting in contractual breaches for non-performance. In May 2005, given the company's poor performance, DAWASA issued a notice to terminate the contract, which was rejected by City Water.

In June 2005, in order to put an end the company's operations, representatives of the Republic and DAWASA entered City Water's offices, took control and seized the company's assets, detained City Water's senior management, held them in custody (without formal arrest) and, the same evening, deported them from Tanzania. A new governmental entity, DAWASCO, was created and its managerial team installed to take over City Water's business.

BGT subsequently lodged a claim with the ICSID tribunal,[94] claiming to have been expropriated without compensation and to have suffered harm from breaches of the FET and FPS standards.

On 27 November 2006, five petitioners filed a request for *amicus curiae status* with the Secretariat of the ICSID tribunal.[95] The arbitrators, recognizing that the proceedings raised a number of issue of public concern and that the petitioners, experts in human rights and environmental issues, would have provided a useful contribution,[96] granted them leave to file a written submission.[97] In their joint *amicus curiae* submission, the *amici* contended that the investor had the responsibility to provide essential water services as access to clean water was characterized as a basic human right by the CESCR in 2002, and "*BGT itself had acknowledged the existence and importance of this right*".[98] The *amici* condemned the company's lack of due dil-

[94] The company grounded its request on the Agreement between the Government of the United Kingdom of Great Britain and Northern Ireland and the Government of the United Republic of Tanzania for the Promotion and Protection of Investments, Dar es Salaam, 7 January 1994.

[95] *Biwater Gauff (Tanzania) Ltd. v. United Republic of Tanzania*, Petition for Amicus Curia Status (n 75), 27 November 2006. The five Petitioners were: Lawyers' Environmental Action Team; Legal and Human Rights Centre; Tanzania Gender Networking Programme; Centre for International Environmental Law; International Institute for Sustainable Development.

[96] *Biwater Gauff (Tanzania) Ltd. v. United Republic of Tanzania*, Award (n 75), 24 July 2008, paras. 358-359. On the contrary, the arbitral tribunal dismissed the Petitioners' requests to attending the hearings and to have access to the documents filed by the parties in the arbitration (under Arbitration Rule 32(2), the arbitral tribunal had no power to permit the petitioners' presence or participation at the hearing). In any case, the tribunal reserved the right to ask the petitioners specific questions in relation to their written submissions, and to request the filing of further written submissions or documents or other evidence.

[97] *Biwater Gauff (Tanzania) Ltd. v. United Republic of Tanzania*, Procedural Order No. 5 (n 75), 2 February 2007. In 2006, Rule 37(2) of the ICSID Arbitration Rules had been amended. The new Rule admitted non-party participation in the proceedings as long as public interest was concerned.

[98] *Ibid.*, para. 379.

igence in the provision of a service "*intimately related to human rights*".[99]

It may be argued that the right to water in the *Biwater* case started to be relevant in resolving investment claims, as the tribunal took into consideration the *amici*'s views in establishing a high threshold for a violation of the FET standard, as will be illustrated in section 3.2.2.

3.2.1. Expropriation

In the *Azurix* case, the claimants complained of a creeping expropriation as a result of a number of measures, including the repudiation of the tariff regime and a public call for customers not to pay their bills. Recalling the *Metalclad* and *Tecmed* case law, Azurix claimed to have been deprived of the "*reasonably-to-be-expected economic benefit*" of the investment.[100]

Argentina contested that the breaches were contractual, and accordingly did not call into question the international responsibility of the State. In any case, the State underlined the importance of examining the *intent* behind regulatory acts, as "*is important to differentiate between legitimate regulation and confiscatory regulation*".[101]

The Tribunal assumed that contractual rights can be expropriated when the contractual breaches are the result of actions taken by a State or its delegates in the exercise of their sovereign authority.[102] In this respect, it found that most of the measures taken by the Province (e.g. the tariff conflict; the invitation to customers to not pay their bills; the public threats against public officials for having allowed ABA to resume billing) exceeded any contractual rights and showed the politicization of the concession.[103]

As to the controversial issue of whether to consider only the effects of measures tantamount to expropriation, or both the effects and the purpose of such measures, the tribunal underlined the existence of an inconsistent case law and, finally, took an intermediate position. It found the criterion of public purpose insufficient to distinguish between legitimate regulation and expropriation, arguing that even expropriation must be justified in the public interest.[104] In order to determine whether the regulatory actions were expropriatory and hence gave rise to a right to compensation, the tribunal referred to the proportionality test developed by the European Court of Human Rights, according to which a measure depriving a person of its

---

[99] *Ibid.*, para. 380.

[100] *Ibid.*, para. 286.

[101] *Ibid.*, para. 297.

[102] *Ibid.*, para. 315.

[103] *Ibid.*, para. 319.

[104] *Ibid.*, para. 310.

property must not only pursue the public interest, but must also have "*a reasonable relationship of proportionality between the means employed and the aim sought to be realized*".[105] Such proportionality is absent when the investor concerned bears "*an individual and excessive burden*" and the measures adopted are not appropriate for achieving the proposed aim.[106]

Finally, the tribunal considered whether the legitimate expectations of the company had been frustrated. Several elements were deemed to contribute to shaping these expectations: not only contractual clauses, but also assurances or representations made by the host State that the investor took into account in making the investment.[107]

Against these premises, the tribunal ruled that the Province's actions did not have an impact on the investment of Azurix to the extent required for it to deem that they amounted to an expropriation,[108] as Azurix had maintained the ownership of the shares in ABA.

In the *Vivendi* case, the parties disagreed as to the scope of the provision on the prohibition of expropriation without compensation. The tribunal's position with respect to the State's regulatory power doctrine is noteworthy. It denied that the bad faith of a State had to be demonstrated in order for the tribunal to find that there has been an illegitimate expropriation:

> "[t]here is extensive authority for the proposition that the state's intent, or its subjective motives are at most a secondary consideration (...) the effect of the measure on the investor, not the state's intent, is the critical factor".[109]

Expropriatory measures that are taken for a public purpose, but without adequate compensation, violate BIT clauses. In other words, invoking a public purpose does not exempt a State from its duty to provide adequate compensation.

Accordingly, the tribunal held that the provincial authorities had not undertaken legitimate regulatory measures, but instead sovereign acts "*designed illegitimately to end the concession or to force its renegotiation*".[110] Such acts, taken together, were found to have radically deprived the claimants of the use and enjoyment of their contractual rights, forcing the concessionaire to terminate the concession agreement. Thus, Argentina had unlawfully expropriated the claimants' investments.

---

[105] *Ibid.*, para. 311 which recalls: European Court of Human Rights, *James and Others v. The United Kingdom*, 21 February 1986, paras. 50, 63; *Técnicas Medioambientales Tecmed S.A. v. The United Mexican State*, Award (n 53), paras. 121-122.

[106] *Ibid.*, para. 311.

[107] *Ibid.*, paras. 318, 320.

[108] *Ibid.*, para. 322.

[109] *Ibid.*, para. 7.5.20.

[110] *Ibid.*, para., 7.5.22.

In the *Biwater* case, the company claimed to have been expropriated without compensation, citing the case law endorsing the doctrine of investors' legitimate expectations.[111] Tanzania attempted to justify the measures undertaken by referring to moral obligations related to the provision of essential services, such as water and sanitation. The respondent held: "*[w]ater and sanitation services are vitally important, and the Republic has more than a right to protect such services in case of crisis: it has a moral and perhaps even a legal obligation to do so*".[112]

In adjudging the claim of expropriation, the tribunal did not take a stand on the public powers doctrine, but instead focused on certain facts (*inter alia*: the public announcement of the termination of the contract; a political rally; the withdrawal of the VAT exception; the seizure of the assets of City Water; the immediate installation of DAWASCO, and the deportation of City Water's management), to hold that, on a cumulative basis, the actions taken by the government amounted to an expropriation of the foreign investment.[113]

3.2.2. Fair and equitable treatment

Turning to the standard of fair and equitable treatment, arbitral tribunals have similarly faced challenges in providing clarity and certainty to this rule.

In the *Azurix* Case, the Argentina-USA BIT did not include a definition of a "*fair and equitable standard.*" Accordingly, the first issue was to establish whether the BIT referred to the minimum standard of treatment of aliens under customary international law, as contended by Argentina,[114] or whether "*the phrase represents an independent, self–contained principle*", as argued by Azurix.[115] In response, the tribunal first analyzed the wording of Article II(2)(*a*) BIT,[116] which tied FET and

---

[111] See, *Metalclad v. United Mexican States*, Award, (n 49) para. 395; and *Técnicas Medioambientales Tecmed S.A. v. The United Mexican* State, Award (n 53), para. 414.

[112] *Biwater Gauff (Tanzania) Ltd. v. United Republic of Tanzania*, Award (n 75, n 96), para. 434.

[113] *Ibid.*, para. 519.

[114] *Azurix Corp. v. Argentine Republic*, Award (n 65), para. 350 makes reference to the NAFTA Waste Management Award, according to which: "*the minimum standard of fair and equitable treatment is infringed by conduct attributable to the State and harmful to the claimant if the conduct is arbitrary, grossly unfair, unjust or idiosyncratic, is discriminatory and exposes claimant to sectional or racial prejudice or involves a lack of due process leading to an outcome which offends judicial propriety – as may be the case with a manifest failure of natural justice in judicial proceedings or a complete lack of transparency and candour in an administrative process. In applying his standard, it is relevant that the treatment is in breach of representations made by the host State which were reasonable relied on by the claimant*".

[115] *Ibid.*, paras. 324-325.

[116] Art. II(2)(*a*) of the BIT provides: "*investments shall at all times be accorded fair and equitable treatment, shall enjoy full protection and security and shall in no case be accorded treatment less than required by international law*".

FPS standards to a treatment no "*less than required by international law*". According to the tribunal, these words were to be understood as putting "*a floor, not a ceiling, in order to avoid a possible interpretation of these standards below what is required by international law*".[117] Moreover, the tribunal held that even the international minimum standard has evolved above the level of 1926, when it was established in the *Neer* case.[118] As a consequence, "*its content is substantially similar whether the terms are interpreted in their ordinary meaning, as required by the Vienna Convention or in accordance with customary international law*".[119]

Additionally, the tribunal analyzed other relevant elements of the FET clause; namely whether bad faith was essential and if the investor's legitimate expectations had been frustrated. Having examined the relevant case law on the matter,[120] it concluded that according to a recent trend, the bad faith of the host State was not necessary for establishing a failure to respect the FET clause. As for the frustration of the investors' legitimate expectations, the tribunal argued that the standards of conduct agreed under the BIT assume a favorable disposition of the host State to encourage and protect foreign investments and are thus not limited to preventing outrageous or egregious actions taken in bad faith.

In brief, Argentina was held to have breached the FET standard because of, *inter alia*: the refusal by the Province to accept the notice of termination and its insistence on terminating the contract on account of abandonment;[121] the politicization of the tariff regime due to the forthcoming elections; the unequal treatment afforded to the new public service provider, which was allowed to raise tariffs;[122] and the calls for non-payment.[123]

In the *Vivendi* case, the tribunal considered whether the FET standard was limited to the so-called minimum standard of treatment under international law. It concluded that "*such an interpretation runs counter to the ordinary meaning of the text of Article 3*" of the BIT,[124] which refers to fair and equitable treatment *in conformity* with the principles of international law, and not to the minimum standard of treatment. Contemporary principles of international law, it is said, are broader than the mere minimum standard of treatment. Accordingly, the tribunal held that Ar-

---

[117] *Azurix Corp. v. Argentine Republic*, Award (n 65), para. 361.

[118] *L.F.H. Neer and Pauline Neer v. United Mexican States*, Award, 15 October 1926.

[119] *Azurix Corp. v. Argentine Republic*, Award (n 65), para. 361.

[120] Including, *inter alia*, *Waste Management v. The United Mexican States*, Award (n 53), para. 98; *Técnicas Medioambientales Tecmed S.A. v. The United Mexican State* Award (n 53), para. 154. See *Azurix Corp. v. Argentine Republic* (n 65), paras. 361, 365.

[121] *Azurix Corp. v. Argentine Republic*, Award (n 65), para. 374.

[122] *Ibid.*, para. 375.

[123] *Ibid.*, para. 376.

[124] *Ibid.*, para. 7.4.5.

gentina had breached the FET clause by failing to grant the investors this standard in conformity with the principles of international law.

In the *Biwater* case, the tribunal found the *amici*'s observations rather convincing [125] and openly referred to their arguments [126] in order to establish the scope of the FET standard against a conflicting case law, [127] holding that the threshold for finding a violation of the FET clause is a high one. [128] In the end, however, the tribunal held that the Tanzanian actions (such as the unilateral withdrawal of the VAT exemption, the seizure of City Water's offices, and deportation of its managers) were so serious as to have reached the level of gravity necessary to find a breach of the FET clause. [129]

3.2.3. Full protection and security

As for the breach of the full protection and security clause, in the *Azurix* case the tribunal interpreted this clause broadly, beyond mere physical security ensured by police forces. FPS was deemed by the tribunal to include the security of the investment environment, a reading which was corroborated by the adjective "*full*" that qualifies and extends the standard of protection. In addition, the tribunal insisted on the relationship between the FET and the FPS standards, considering that a breach of the former clause entails a breach of the latter. [130]

Similarly, in the *Vivendi* case, the tribunal embraced a wide interpretation of the FPS clause. Considering that this clause is not limited to physical security, but includes "*legal security*", that is "*the legally protected terms of operation of the investment*", [131] it found a violation of the standard.

Equally, in the *Biwater* case, the tribunal adhered to the holding in *Azurix* that when the terms "*protection*" and "*security*" are qualified by "*full*", the content of the standard may extend to matters other than physical security. It implies the State's guarantee of stability in a secure environment, both physical, commercial and legal. [132] In light of this reading, the government's acts were abusive and in violation of the FPS standard.

---

[125] *Ibid.*, para. 392.

[126] *Ibid.*, para. 601.

[127] *Ibid.* At para. 589, for instance, the tribunal refers to *Azurix v. Argentina* (para. 361), in which it was held that the FET is different from the international minimum standard, whereas in *Siemens v. Argentina* (para. 291), the two concepts were held to be the same.

[128] *Ibid.* At para. 597 the tribunal recalls *Waste Management v. The United Mexican States*, Award (n 53), para. 98.

[129] *Ibid.*, para. 604.

[130] *Ibid.*, para. 408.

[131] *Ibid.*, para. 7.4.15.

[132] *Ibid.*, para. 729.

3.3. Cases acknowledging the human right to water

Having analyzed a selection of awards that do not address the human right to water in the context of investment disputes over water services liberalization and privatization, this sub-section focuses on a selection of three cases in which the protection of the human right to water received growing attention in the narrative of the tribunals, namely the *Suez* case, [133] the *SAUR* case [134] and the *Urbaser* case. [135]

The human right to water was broadly considered in the *Suez* case, which concerned a thirty-year concession for the supply of water and waste water services in the City of Buenos Aires, at that time, "*the largest privatized water concession in the world*". [136] A new local company, Aguas Argentinas S.A. ("AASA"), [137] was incorporated in Argentina with the task of controlling and managing the concession. As required by the concession contract, investors committed to large amounts of investments, which resulted in "*substantial improvement and expansion of the water distribution and sewage systems*". [138] The companies knew that their investment would have exceeded the amount recoverable from tariffs in the short term, but believed that in the long run they would have recovered the initial investment and made profit.

These expectations were frustrated by the emergency measures that Argentina adopted in the aftermath of the economic crisis, such as the depreciation of the Argentine peso, the freezing of tariff increases and the request to renegotiate services

[133] *Suez, Sociedad General de Aguas de Barcelona, S.A. and Vivendi Universal, S.A. v. Argentine Republic*, ICSID Case No. ARB/03/19. For an in-depth discussion of the case see: A. Olleta, *The World Bank's Influence on Water Privatisation in Argentina: The Experience of the City of Buenos Aires*, in P. Cullet, A. Gowlland-Gualtieri, R. Madhav, U. Ramanathan (eds.), *Water Governance in Motion, towards Socially and Environmentally Sustainable Water Laws*, New Delhi, 2010.

[134] *SAUR International v. Argentine Republic*, ICSID Case no. ARB/04/4, Decision on Jurisdiction and Liability, 6 June 2012.

[135] *Urbaser S.A. and others v. The Argentine Republic*, Award (n 30).

[136] *Suez, Sociedad General de Aguas de Barcelona, S.A. and Vivendi Universal, S.A. v. Argentine Republic*, Decision on Jurisdiction (n 133), 3 August 2006, para. 23. These services, previously provided by a state-owned company, suffered from a severe lack of investments due to the company's deficits, which also undermined the quality and quantity of the water supplied.

[137] In 1992, at the end of an international bidding process, a consortium made up of Suez (incorporated in France), Sociedad General de Aguas de Barcelona S.A. ("AGBAR", incorporated in Spain), Vivendi Universal S.A. ("Vivendi", incorporated in France) and AWG Group Ltd ("AWG", incorporated in the United Kingdom), together with other entities, was awarded the concession and incorporated AASA.

[138] *Suez, Sociedad General de Aguas de Barcelona, S.A. and Vivendi Universal, S.A. v. Argentine Republic*, Decision on Liability (n 133), 30 July 2010, para. 36. In particular, "*access to drinking water increased from 5,559,270 persons to 7,859,000 persons (an increase of 41.37%) and the population with access to sewage services increased from 4,532,856 persons to 5,989,000 persons (an increase of 32.12%)*".

contracts. Claiming that these measures had injured their investments and violated the commitments made by the State, the companies sought to obtain tariff adjustments and modifications of other operating conditions. In particular, the tariff revision was meant to counterbalance the increase in AASA's operational costs due to the devaluation of the Argentine peso. Although the concession contract clearly foresaw the possibility of extraordinary tariff revisions in case of "*legal changes in the currency parity fixed by the Convertibility Law*", the proposed tariff adjustment was rejected. Hence, AASA began to suffer significant losses which, in the end, led to its liquidation. In the meanwhile, Argentina continued to require the full performance of AASA's investment obligations under the concession contract and imposed several fines for failure to meet the agreed targets. Finally, in 2005, AASA requested termination of the concession contract. The government initially rejected this request but, several months later, it terminated the contract for breach. The operation of the water distribution and sewage system was transferred to a new public entity, Agua y Saneamientos Argentinos S.A. ("AySA"), financed and managed by Argentina.

In April 2003, after four years of fruitless negotiations between the concessionaire and the government, AASA (which withdrew from the proceeding), and its shareholders, Suez, AGBAR, Vivendi and AWG Group Ltd ("AWG") lodged a Request for Arbitration with the ICSID against the Argentine Republic. Suez and Vivendi invoked Argentine consent to ICSID arbitration pursuant to the Argentina–France BIT,[139] AGBAR relied on the Argentina-Spain BIT[140] and AWG on the Argentina-UK BIT.[141] The alleged BIT breaches consisted in the failure to protect the concessionaire against direct and indirect expropriation of their investments, and to accord investments full protection and security and fair and equitable treatment. In July 2010, the tribunal issued its decision on liability.

Before proceeding with the analysis of this award, it is worth noting the existence of an *amici curiae* brief that seems to have influenced the tribunal's reasoning in this case. In 2005, five non-governmental organizations filed a petition for participation as *amici curiae*.[142] Even if the ICSID did not allow for the participation of individuals

[139] Accord entre le Gouvernement de la République française et le Gouvernement de la République Argentine sur l'encouragement et la protection réciproques des investissements (ensemble une déclaration), Paris, 3 July 1991.

[140] Acuerdo para la promoción y protección recíprocas de inversiones entre el Reino de España y la República Argentina, Buenos Aires, 3 October 1991.

[141] Agreement between the Government of the United Kingdom of Great Britain and Northern Ireland and the Government of the Republic of Argentina for the Promotion and Protection of Investments, London, 11 December 1990.

[142] Asociación Civil por la Igualidad y la Justicia ("ACIJ"), Centro de Estudios Legales y Sociales (CELS), Center for International Environmental Law ("CIEL"), Consumidores Libres Cooperativa Ltda. de Provisión de Servicios de Acción Comunitaria, and Unión de Usuarios y Consumidores

other than investors,[143] the tribunal, for the first time in the ICSID case law, upheld the NGO's request and set out the conditions under which it would accept *amicus curiae* submissions.[144] According to the tribunal, the *Suez* case raised complex questions of international law, "*including human rights considerations*" so important as to recommend the participation of civil society representative.[145] The joint submission of the five NGOs was entirely focused on the relevance of the right to water for the case at issue and on the related responsibilities of the State.[146] As will be discussed below, it seems to have influenced the arbitral decision in several respects.[147]

The *SAUR* case[148] concerns the privatization of the water and sewage services in the Province of Mendoza (Argentina).[149] In 1997, the Province decided to privatize the public company running water services, Obras Sanitarias de Mendoza S.A ("OSM").[150]

---

[143] The first request for intervention was submitted before the amendment of Rule 37(2) of the ICSID Arbitration Rules, which took place in 2006 in order to expressly foresee the possibility for the tribunal to admit third-parties' briefs.

[144] *Suez, Sociedad General de Aguas de Barcelona, S.A. and Vivendi Universal, S.A. v. Argentine Republic*, Order in Response to a Petition for Transparency and Participation as Amicus Curiae (n 133), 19 May 2005; Order in Response to a Petition by Five Non-Governmental Organizations for Permission to make an Amicus Curiae Submission, 12 February 2007. Arbitrators based the power to accept *amicus curia* briefs on Article 44 of the ICSID Convention, which confers on the tribunal the power to decide upon procedural matters not disciplined by other rules. Soon after, however, the ICSID Arbitration rules were amended to explicitly permit the participation of non-parties. See F. Francioni, *Access to Justice, Denial of Justice and International Investment Law*, in *European Journal of International Law*, 2009, pp. 742-743.

[145] Order in Response to a Petition for Transparency and Participation as Amicus Curiae, 19 May 2005, paras. 19, 20: "*[t]he factor that gives this case particular public interest is that the investment dispute centers around the water distribution and sewage systems of a large metropolitan area, the city of Buenos Aires and surrounding municipalities. Those systems provide basic public services to millions of people and as a result may raise a variety of complex public and international law questions, including human rights considerations. (...) These factors lead the Tribunal to conclude that this case does involve matters of public interest of such a nature that have traditionally led courts and other tribunals to receive amicus submissions from suitable non-parties. This case is not simply a contract dispute between private parties*".

[146] *Suez, Sociedad General de Aguas de Barcelona, S.A. and Vivendi Universal, S.A. v. Argentine Republic, Amicus Curiae* Submission (n 133), 4 April 2007.

[147] *Contra*, Mayer, p. 183 (n 68).

[148] *SAUR International v. Argentine Republic*, ICSID Case no. ARB/04/4, Decision on Objections to Jurisdiction, 27 February 2006; Decision on Jurisdiction and Liability, 6 June 2012; Award, 22 May 2014.

[149] In the early 1990s, in the context of a modernization process of said services, the Province divided the functions of regulation and control from those of exploitation. The former was assigned to the newly created "Ente Provincial del Agua y de Saneamiento" (EPAS), while the latter were granted to a public company, "Obras Sanitarias de Mendoza S.A" (OSM).

[150] To this end, the Province launched an international process of tender for the partial sale of OSM's shares and for the purchase of the concession technical operator's shares.

A concession of ninety five years was awarded to a consortium formed by Sauri, Enron Capital & Trade Resources Argentina SA, Società Italiana per il Gas SpA and two Argentine partners, with the payment of 150 million dollars.[151] Sauri alone paid a total of 72.4 million dollars for its participation in OSM.[152] In addition to the price paid for the concession, OSM was required to pay an annual fee to the Province and to make investments in order to meet a number of qualitative and quantitative objectives established in a plan of exploitation and expansion ("PEE"). Annexed to the PEE there was an indicative list of approved investments. In case of delay in the realization of the quantitative objectives, the regulator was allowed to adopt sanctions. Additionally, the Province could rescind the contract for non-fulfillment of the annual investment requirements or of the quantitative objectives agreed by the parties. Given that the PEE obliged the concessionaire to invest an amount of 336 million dollars by 2020, and that the price paid for the concession was almost entirely assigned to the Province, the concessionaire was supposed to finance the required investments by means of the tariffs collected. Indeed, the concessionaire was granted the right to collect tariffs according to the cost recovery principle. Both the Province regulation and the concession contract established that tariffs should have reflected the cost of operation and maintenance of the services, together with a reasonable return for the operator. Moreover, the contract envisaged the possibility of an extraordinary revision of the tariff regime, for instance, in case the parity dollar-pesos were abandoned (to let the concessionaire recover the additional costs it would have incurred).

The concession lasted eleven years. From 1998 to 2002, when the Emergency laws were enacted, Sauri realized a modest plus-value and met the quantitative objectives indicated in the contract. The regulator, however, claimed that the indicative list of investments was compulsory and had not been duly respected by the company. In 2002, Argentina declared a state of emergency and all public service contracts were renegotiated. The negotiation between the Province and OSM lasted five years. A first Memorandum of Understanding ("MOU") was reached by the parties in 2005, but it included only general principles. During this period, the tariffs approved in 1991 continued to be in force, despite the OSM's requests for an increase, causing OSM severe economic losses, which had an impact on water infrastructure and the quality of the services.

In 2007, in order to give binding effect to the principles included in the first MOU, the parties concluded a second Memorandum, in which the respondent agreed to a tariff increase and the concessionaire committed to respecting a certain

[151] This payment included 132 million dollars to the Province and only 18 million dollars into OSM funds.

[152] In the context of the tendering process, Sauri incorporated an Argentina company, Aguas de Mendoza S.A (AdM), which in turn acquired 32,08 % of OSM's shares. After making the investment, Sauri and OMS concluded a contract for technical assistance, making Sauri the technical operator of the concession.

minimum annual level of investments. The MOU was not respected.[153] The Province delayed the entry into force of an executive Protocol by almost one year and EPAS delayed by another year the approval of the tariff increases requested by OSM. On 3 August 2009, at the same time when the increase of the tariff rate was finally allowed, the Governor intervened with OSM. As a consequence of the administrative intervention, Sauri and the other associated companies were dismissed, and all powers were conferred to an administrator appointed by the Executive. In the end, the Governor decided to terminate the concession contract, claiming that OMS was at fault. In September 2010, the services were transferred to a new public company, Aysam, created by the Province.[154] OSM entered into liquidation.

In 2003, the French company SAUR International S.A.[155] filed a claim with the ICSID against the Argentina Republic alleging the violation of the 1991 Argentina-French BIT. The company contended that Argentina, through its administrative intervention and the termination of the contract, has expropriated Sauri of its investment in OSM, and that the Republic had breached its obligations to provide FET and FPS to the investors. SAUR requested damages for 143.9 million US dollars, including the 72.4 million US dollars invested in 1998 to join the OSM shareholders, and then to become the concession operator. The claimant maintained that since the beginning the Argentine authorities did not comply with the obligations provided by the laws and by the concession agreement. In addition, the Republic refused any increase in tariffs, which OSM was entitled to expect. Finally, on August 2009, having undermined the finances of OSM, the provincial authorities intervened and in 2010 terminated the concession contract.

Argentina asked for the rejection of all claims, alleging several faults of the concessionaire.[156] It contended that the provincial intervention with the concession was due to the risk of collapse of the public service, whereas the termination of the concession contract, which occurred a year later, was meant to avoid serious harm to the public health and to safeguard the right to water of the population. Argentina

[153] The concessionaire respected its investment obligations under the MOU, but failed to pay the fee and the provincial taxes, and did not repay a loan. The company alleged that its lack of funds was due to the non-compliance of the Province with its obligations. Indeed, the Province not only denied the tariff revision, but also did not pay promised subsidies for pensioners and disadvantaged people.

[154] Aysam, despite being allowed to raise tariffs, lamented of the insufficiency of such an increase to cover the expenses of operating the concession. The new public company foresaw a significant deficit for the following year (2011) which should have been covered through public subsidies.

[155] Sauri was a 100% subsidiary of the French company Société d'Aménagement Urbain et Rural, S.A. (SAUR). Sauri was created in 1994 in order to manage all of SAUR's international activities.

[156] Argentina submitted that it had made all efforts to make the concession work, such as signing two Memoranda of Understanding in 2005 and in 2007, which compensated the reciprocal debts and adjusted the contract to the new Argentine situation.

further posited that the human right to water had to guide the interpretation of the BIT, as the BIT did not modify the State's obligations under human rights treaties. It held that the administrative intervention, as well as the termination of the contract, had been undertaken in order to guarantee the right to water. The claimant, on the contrary, maintained that Argentina's intent in adopting the above measures was irrelevant and could not justify the violation of the BIT.

In defining the general principles applicable to the present case,[157] the tribunal devoted significant attention to human rights norms. In general terms, it explained that the applicable law consisted in the French-Argentina BIT, the Argentine domestic law, and the principles of international law applicable to the matter. Given that no hierarchy existed among these sources of law, whose relationship is governed by the principle of specialization, each question had to be solved according to the relevant provisions. For example, international law governs the interpretation of BIT and the international responsibility of States. The tribunal listed the right to water among the applicable sources of law for the settlement of the investment dispute. It took the following view:

> "En réalité, les droits de l'homme en général, et le droit à l'eau en particulier, constituent l'une des diverses sources que le Tribunal devra prendre en compte pour résoudre le différend car ces droits sont élevés au sein du système juridique argentin au rang de droits constitutionnels, et, de plus, ils font partie des principes généraux du droit international. L'accès à l'eau potable constitue, du point de vue de l'État, un service public de première nécessité et, du point de vue du citoyen, un droit fondamental. Pour ce motif, en cette matière, l'ordre juridique peut et doit réserver à l'Autorité publique des fonctions légitimes de planification, de supervision, de police, de sanction, d'intervention et même de résiliation, afin de protéger l'intérêt général".[158]

Moreover, the tribunal endorsed the police powers doctrine,[159] but considered that the State's right to regulate in the public interest was not incompatible with its obligation under investment treaties as: "*[l]e droit fondamental à l'eau et le droit de l'investisseur à bénéficier de la protection offerte par l'APRI opèrent sur des plans différent*".[160] Arbitrators expressly committed themselves to counterbalancing human

---

[157] At the outset, the tribunal excluded its competence to adjudge facts preceding the conclusion of the second Memorandum of Understanding, which, being a transactional agreement, had the effect of *res judicata*. However, given the Province's administrative intervention in the concession and the termination of the contract after the second MOU, the tribunal considered itself competent to adjudge the case for the part not affected by the transactional effects of the MOU.

[158] *SAUR International v. Argentine Republic*, Decision on Jurisdiction and Liability (n 134), para. 330.

[159] *Ibid.*, para. 330.

[160] *Ibid.*, para. 331.

rights and investment obligations.[161] In their view, even though public authorities enjoy special powers in order to guarantee the right to water, such powers are not absolute. The measures adopted must also be consistent with their obligations to foreign investors in the investment treaty. Therefore, when States violate investors' rights, compensation is due when the BIT so provides.

In conclusion, the decision gave attention to human rights issues, devoting several paragraphs to the relation between the obligations arising from human rights law, namely the human right to water, and investment treaties.

Finally, the human right to water was at the heart of an ICSID award in the *Urbaser* case.[162] The dispute concerned a concession for the provision of water and sewage services in the Province of Greater Buenos Aires. In 2000, the concession was granted to a company – Aguas Del Gran Buenos Aires S.A. ("AGBA") – established by foreign investors and shareholders, including Urbaser S.A. and Consorcio de Aguas Bilbao Bizkaia, Bilbao Biskaia Ur Partzuergoa (the "claimants"). They held that the provincial authorities had obstructed their work to such an extent as to render the concession unprofitable. The Argentine economic crises further worsened the relationship between the Province and AGBA. Due to the depreciation of the peso, AGBA requested a revision of the contract in order to be allowed to raise its tariffs. The Province engaged in the renegotiation process, but failed to meet the company's requests and, ultimately, in July 2006, terminated the concession contract.

The claimants lodged a request for arbitration with the ICSID complaining of the violation by Argentina of Articles III, IV and V of the Argentina-Spain BIT concerning, respectively: the obligation to protect foreign investments and the prohibition of adopting unjustified or discriminatory measures; the obligation to afford fair and equitable treatment to foreign investments; and the prohibition of any illegal and discriminatory expropriation of foreign investments, as well as the obligation to compensate the investor in the event of expropriation.

As for the alleged breach of Article III(1) of the Spain-Argentina BIT, unlike in other cases, this time claimants did not claim a violation of the FPS but referred to discriminatory and unjustified measures, as the relevant provisions did not mention the FPS standard. This claim has greater prospects for success, given that investment tribunals had already interpreted such a standard as restrictively encompassing only material injuries,[163] a situation clearly excluded in the instant case.

---

[161] *Ibid.*, para. 332.

[162] *Urbaser S.A. and others v. The Argentine Republic*, Award (n 30). The case has been commented by various authors, *inter alia*: M. Feria-Tinta, *Like Oil and Water? Human Rights in investment Arbitration in the Wake of* Philip Morris v. Uruguay, in *Journal of International Arbitration*, 2017; Guntrip (n 31); Crow, Lorenzoni Escobar, (n 31).

[163] *Suez, Sociedad General de Aguas de Barcelona S.A., and InterAguas Servicios Integrales del Agua S.A. v. The Argentine Republic*, ICSID Case No. ARB/03/17, para. 173.

Argentina rejected all the claims and contended that the difficulties alleged by the claimants were not due to measures adopted by the Republic, but to manifest inefficiencies on the part of the concessionaire due, *in primis*, to the failure to collect on the users' bills.

As will be illustrated in the following sub-sections, the award is particularly interesting if considered in terms of harmonization of international investment law and human rights law. In it, the tribunal rejected the claim of expropriation and upheld only in part the violation of the FET clause. However, in interpreting the notion of investors' expectations, it said that the investors' expectations must include the awareness of the State's duty to provide water. This ruling may lower the protection given to investors by the FET standard.

3.3.1. Expropriation

The tribunals' views on the role of the police powers doctrine and the duty to compensate in cases of legitimate expropriation is rather divergent in the cases at issue.

In *Suez*, the tribunal dismissed all the investors' claims to have been victims of direct and indirect expropriation on several grounds. It distinguished the general measures enacted by Argentina to cope with the crisis (i.e. the abolition of the tie between the Argentine peso to the US dollar) from the individual measures directed against the claimants, that is, the refusal to revise the tariffs of the water services and the termination of the concession following the concessionaire's attempts to abandon it.

Addressing the question of whether Argentina's general measures amounted to an indirect expropriation, the arbitrators stated that:

> "in evaluating a claim of expropriation it is important to recognize a State's legitimate right to regulate and to exercise its police power in the interests of public welfare and not to confuse measures of that nature with expropriation".[164]

In the case at issue, since the Argentine measures sought to address a severe crisis, they were "*within the general police powers of the Argentine State, and they did not constitute a permanent and substantial deprivation of the Claimants' investments*".[165]

Next, the tribunal continued by analyzing the specific measures undertaken *vis à vis* the claimants. The claim that Argentina's refusal to revise the tariffs constituted an expropriation was dismissed (unlike in the *Vivendi* case) on the grounds that the measures adopted did not substantially deprive the concessionaire of its investment.[166] As for the termination of the concession, no expropriation was found to

---

[164] *Suez, Sociedad General de Aguas de Barcelona, S.A. and Vivendi Universal, S.A. v. Argentine Republic*, Decision on Liability (n. 138), para. 139.

[165] *Ibid.*, para. 140.

[166] *Ibid.*, para. 145.

have occurred, given that this measure was taken by the Republic in the exercise of its contractual rights.[167]

In the *SAUR* case, the tribunal found that the measures adopted by the Province of Mendoza after the second MOU, namely the administrative intervention, the termination of the contract and the transfer of the concession to a public owned company, amounted to an illegitimate expropriation of Sauri's investment and also to the nationalization of the Province water and sewage sector, which warranted Sauri the right to be compensated.

To reach this conclusion, the tribunal rejected all the objections raised by the Republic, including those referring to the police powers doctrine. While sharing the view expressed by the Republic that a State has special powers to regulate and to interfere with the management and ownership of private companies when they provide essential services and the well-being of the public is at risk,[168] the tribunal admitted that the exercise of police powers can amount to measures tantamount to expropriation, the so-called regulatory expropriation. The *legitimate* exercise of police powers excludes the State's responsibility for wrongful acts and may even exempt the State from paying adequate compensation to the persons affected. The tribunal held:

> "[l]e fait que l'exercice légitime de pouvoirs de police ne constitue pas un délit international est un principe général du droit international coutumier, communément accepté, et dans certains cas, il est même justifié que la personne lésée ne soit pas indemnisée".[169]

However, in the case at issue, the tribunal maintained that the Province had not exercised its police powers legitimately, instead committing serious breaches of its obligations under the second MOU.[170]

In any event, the tribunal underlined that even assuming that the Republic had acted legitimately in the exercise of it police powers, it would still be obliged to compensate the claimant because the BIT in force so required. In brief, although in theory the exercise of legitimate police power may not give rise to compensation, when BITs require its payment, the State is obliged to reimburse investors even for legitimate expropriatory measures. This is the case of Article 5 of the Argentina-French BIT, which established the conditions under which the adoption of expropriation, nationalization and all equivalent measures are not forbidden (namely when they are taken for public interest, are not discriminatory, and are not contrary to a specific commit-

---

167 *Ibid.*, para. 146.

168 *SAUR International v. Argentine Republic*, Decision on Jurisdiction and Liability (n 134), para. 396.

169 *Ibid.*, para. 398.

170 *Ibid.*, paras. 400-405.

ment made by the State), together with the duty to compensate.[171]

Commenting on the nature and scope of the regulatory power doctrine, it has been argued that for a tribunal to be allowed to derogate the obligation to pay compensation, undertaken under a BIT, there "*must be another rule of international law (either conventional or customary) providing otherwise*".[172] Given that the existence of a customary rule on the State's right to regulate in the public interest, which would allow States to expropriate investments without compensation, is far from settled, the conclusion of the arbitrators would seem reasonable. The theory of systemic integration, indeed, cannot go so far as to provide an interpretation of a BIT clause that runs counter to the literal meaning of its words.[173]

In the *Urbaser* case, the claimants contended that they had been the victims of both an indirect expropriation, due to the unilateral modification of the concession contract by the Province of Buenos Aires under the Emergency Laws, and of a direct expropriation consequent to the termination of the concession contract by the Province. According to the claimants, the tribunal should not have considered the intention behind the expropriatory measures adopted by the State, but only the resulting effects. While expropriation must always be in the public interest, the intention of the State does not exempt it from the duty to compensate. On the contrary, when there is no just cause for expropriation, the State must comply with the duty to provide reparation.[174] Likewise, proportionality is also a condition that renders expropriation lawful, but it does not exclude compensation.[175]

The respondent argued that for an indirect expropriation to exist, several requirements must be met, including that the government's measures must go beyond the State's police power.[176] In such a case, the investor has a right to be compensated for its losses. Quite the opposite, when a State exercises its sovereign powers and acts for legitimate public reasons, it has no duty to compensate investors.[177] Given that the emergency measures adopted by Argentina did not have an expropriatory aim but were only intended to protect legitimate public policy interests

---

[171] *Ibid.*, paras. 406-412, para. 413: "*il est indiscutable qu'un État souverain, pour cause d'utilité publique et agissant en défense de ce qu'il estime être l'intérêt général, peut décider à tout moment de nationaliser un service public essentiel comme l'est l'approvisionnement en eau potable et l'assainissement. Mais, une fois l'investissement appartenant à un investisseur étranger protégé par l'APRI exproprié, l'État ne peut passer outre à son obligation internationale, énoncée dans l'APRI lui-même, d'indemniser à leur valeur réelle les actifs dont elle a été privée*".

[172] G. Zarra, *Right to Regulate, Margin of Appreciation and Proportionality: Current Status in Investment Arbitration in Light of Philip Morris v. Uruguay*, in *Brazilian Journal of International Law*, 2017, p. 104.

[173] Simma, Kill, p. 694 (n 26).

[174] *Urbaser S.A. and others v. The Argentine Republic*, Award (n 30), paras. 965-966.

[175] *Ibid.*, para. 969.

[176] *Ibid.*, para. 980.

[177] *Ibid.*, paras. 981, 987.

during the economic crisis, they were part of the Argentine police power and did not entail any expropriation.[178]

The tribunal dismissed both the claims of direct and indirect expropriation without taking a clear stand as to the role played by State's intent and its exercise of legitimate regulatory powers. It limited itself to citing the relevant provision of the BIT establishing the conditions to be met for there to be a lawful taking of an investment without triggering a duty to provide reparation. Under Article V of the BIT, nationalization and expropriation are lawful provided that the measures adopted are: *i*) in the public interest; *ii*) in accordance with the law; *iii*) not discriminatory. When these conditions are met, the State is under an obligation to pay compensation. Otherwise, unlawful expropriation triggers the investor's right to reparation.[179] It seems that this approach does not distance itself from the findings in *SAUR*, according to which compensation is due every time the BIT so requires.

The tribunal did not apply these conditions in the instant case, as it held that the measures taken by Argentina did not amount to an expropriation, having only temporarily reduce the concessionaire's income. AGBA was not deprived of its rights under the concession in a way tantamount to an expropriation and the termination of the concession contract was mainly based on the faults of concessionaire, which had not complied with the Expansion Program agreed upon.[180] Thus, the tribunal dismissed the claim based on expropriation under Article V of the BIT.

3.3.2. Fair and equitable treatment

In the *Suez* case, Argentina argued that its BIT obligations should have been interpreted in the light of other rules of international law binding Argentina, including the human right to water.[181]

The tribunal noted preliminarily that it would interpret the FET clause in accordance with all relevant sources of international law (not only against the international minimum standard), and that it would take into account the purpose of the BIT, consisting in fostering the economic cooperation between the States parties.[182]

---

[178] *Ibid.*, para. 993.

[179] *Ibid.*, para. 1000.

[180] *Ibid.*, paras. 1001-1009.

[181] See L. E. Peterson, *Human Rights and Bilateral Investment Treaties. Mapping the Role of Human Rights Law Within Investor-State Arbitration*, Montreal, 2009, p. 28, referring to Counter-Memorial of Argentine Republic in ICSID Case No. ARB/03/19, para. 864.

[182] A. Tanzi, *Recent Trends in International Investment Arbitration and the Protection of Human Rights in the Public Services Sector*, in N. Boschiero, T. Scovazzi, C. Pitea, C. Ragni (eds.), *International Courts and the Development of International Law. Essays in Honour of Tullio Treves*, The Hague, 2013, p. 593; A. Tanzi, *On balancing Foreign Investment Interests with Public Interests in Recent Arbitration Case Law in the Public Utilities Sector*, in *The Law and Practice of International Courts and Tribunals*, 2012, p. 58.

In order to find whether a violation of the standard had occurred, arbitrators attached importance to the legitimate expectations of the claimants as to the profitability of the investment. The tribunal explained that there is a violation of the FET clause owing to the frustration of investors' expectations when several conditions are met, namely: *i)* such expectations were based on the legal framework of the concession that had been set forth by the State; *ii)* investments were made relying on this legal framework; *iii)* States must have failed to apply said legal framework or have significantly changed it. Applying these criteria to the case at issue, the tribunal concluded that Argentina had violated the FET clause for having refused to adjust the tariffs in accordance with the legal framework of the concession and for having forced the concessionaire into the renegotiation process. [183]

In addition, reviewing Argentina's conduct, the tribunal condemned its lack of cooperation with the claimants, which were contrary to the purpose of the treaty. In particular, once the peak of the crisis had passed and the economy recovered, the State should have, at least temporarily, relieved the concessionaire of its investment commitments. By showing no intention to cooperate, it was stated, the Republic had abused its regulatory power. [184]

On the contrary, the government's termination of the concession contract was considered to be legitimate. The tribunal upheld the respondent's argument that the abrupt termination of the contract was due to the risk of abandonment of the services by the concessionaire. Having the responsibility to provide the essential water services to its population, Argentina correctly prepared to take over the services.

In the *SAUR* case, the analysis of the alleged breaches of the FPS and FET clauses were limited to the facts that occurred subsequent to the second MOU. The tribunal first established whether the fair and equitable treatment standard, which the Argentina-French BIT tied to principles of international law, was an autonomous principle or whether it coincided with the minimum standard of treatment of foreigners under general international law. In this regard, it stated that:

> "[e]n réalité, la question de savoir si le 'traitement juste et équitable conformément aux principes du droit international défini dans l'APRI coïncide ou non avec le niveau dit 'minimal de traitement dû aux étrangers selon le droit international coutumier' constitue une discussion plutôt dogmatique et conceptualiste. Dans le fond, ce dont les parties discutent est l'exigence ou non d'un élément volitif renforcé dans la conduite de l'État". [185]

---

[183] *Suez, Sociedad General de Aguas de Barcelona, S.A. and Vivendi Universal, S.A. v. Argentine Republic*, Decision on Liability (n 138), paras. 222-231, in particular para. 226.

[184] *Ibid.*, para. 235.

[185] *SAUR International v. Argentine Republic*, Decision on Jurisdiction and Liability (n 134), para. 491.

The tribunal held that, contrary to the findings in the *Neer* case,[186] the volitional element, that is the bad faith of a State, was no longer necessary in order to find a violation of the FET standard, which has evolved over time so as to exclude this element.[187]

The tribunal did not take a stand on whether the legitimate expectations of the investors should be taken into account in establishing a violation of the FET because the only measures capable of modifying the legal framework and affecting the investors' expectation were covered by the second MOU.[188]

Nonetheless, the tribunal concluded that there had been an evident breach of the FET standard due to fact that the provincial authorities' denial of tariff increases seemed intended to worsen the concessionaire's financial situation to such an extent as to justify the intervention of the authorities, the termination of the contract and, finally, the re-nationalization of the water service.[189]

In the *Urbaser* case, the claimants held that they had been the victim of a violation of the FET clause as Argentina had failed to guarantee the protection accorded to the investors by the Regulatory Framework – which was very attractive as it provided, *inter alia*, that even in case of monetary crisis, tariffs would have been maintained at adequate levels to cover costs and a rate of returns.[190] Instead, when the emergency was declared, the Province eliminated the tariffs adjustment method, denying AGBA any possibility to restore the economic-financial equilibrium of the concession.[191] Subsequently, AGBA was forced into a renegotiation process until the concession contract was finally terminated.[192]

According to the claimants, the standard to be applied for ascertaining a violation of the FET not only exceeds the scope of the minimum treatment standard under customary international law, as it is no longer necessary to prove the bad faith of the State (*contra Neer* case),[193] but is also much broader. This standard "*protects the reasonable expectations of the investor at the time it made the investment*" when these expectations "*were based on representations, commitments or specific conditions offered by the State concerned*".[194] Recalling previous awards in which arbitral

[186] *Neer* case, General Commission for Claims, *Mexico v. United States of America*, 1926.

[187] *SAUR International v. Argentine Republic*, Decision on Jurisdiction and Liability (n 134), para. 494: "*actuellement, l'interprétation selon laquelle le principe n'exige pas d'élément volitif renforcé dans la conduite de l'État offenseur est pratiquement unanime*".

[188] *Ibid.*, para. 498.

[189] *Ibid.*, para. 506.

[190] *Urbaser S.A. and others v. The Argentine Republic*, Award (n 30), paras. 560-561.

[191] *Ibid.*, para. 562.

[192] *Ibid.*, para. 563.

[193] *Ibid.*, para. 565.

[194] *Ibid.*, para. 567.

tribunals considered the FET standard as unrelated to the bad or good faith of the State,[195] the claimants sought to link the notion of legitimate expectations to only those based on regulations and assurances favorable to the investors.

Argentina, relying *inter alia* on Section 1105 of the NAFTA, argued on the contrary that the FET standard reflects the minimum standard of customary international law, which requires a high threshold (such as a grossly unfair and arbitrary conduct) for finding a breach.[196] According to the respondent, it is to be excluded that the FET standard incorporates the expectations of the investors for the stability of the regulatory framework.[197] In addition, the bidder was well aware of the high risks that the concession entailed since, on the one hand, it required significant investments and, on the other hand, the collectability rate was very low due to the low coverage of the service and the extremely limited financial resources of the population living in the Region to be supplied.[198] Briefly, the expectations of the investors should also encompass the acknowledgment that States may take measures justified by public policies, which have to be considered part of the environment in which they operate.[199] According to Argentina, the request made by the concessionaire aimed at linking the evolution of tariffs to the exchange rate between Argentine peso and the US dollar was unacceptable given the collapse of the convertibility regime and the devaluation of the peso. It would have led to unreasonable tariffs, causing harm to users.[200] Faced with this scenario:

> "[t]he Province had to guarantee the continuation of the basic water supply to millions of Argentines. The protection of this universal basic human right constitutes the framework within the Claimants had to frame their expectations and should still do so".[201]

The tribunal purportedly attempted to find a middle ground between the opposite positions of the parties. On the one hand, it found that the FET standard has evolved since the first half of the 20th century.[202] It also posited that an investment necessarily includes a certain amount of risk and the legitimate expectations of investors do not result in the immutability of legal commitments made with the contract.[203]

---

[195] It referred to the cases analyzed in the previous sections, the *Azurix* case, the Suez/Agbar/Interagua case and the Suez/Agbar/Vivendi, see paras. 568, 569, 575.

[196] *Ibid.*, paras. 580-582.

[197] *Ibid.*, para. 585, 588-591.

[198] *Ibid.*, paras. 593, 596.

[199] *Ibid.*, para. 594.

[200] *Ibid.*, para. 599.

[201] *Ibid.*, para. 602.

[202] *Ibid.*, paras. 604-605.

[203] *Ibid.*, paras. 606-607.

The investor's rights related to the contract must be considered in the wider context of the State's legal framework, which includes its obligations under international law and constitutional law.[204] Measures taken to implement fundamental rights protected under the Constitution (i.e., in the instant case, access to water to the population):

> "cannot hurt the fair and equitable treatment standard because their occurrence must have been deemed to be accepted by the investor when entering into the investment and the Concession Contact. In short they were expected to be part of the investment's legal framework".[205]

What is more, the investors cannot expect their interests to take precedence over other interests "*protected by sources of law prevailing over the Contract, based on international or on constitutional law*".[206]

Moreover, the expectations of the investors cannot only be linked to the investment's legal framework, but also to the social and economic environment of the host State, which the investor has to be aware of when making its business decisions.[207]

Finally, the tribunal held that the rights and expectations of the investors must be significantly affected before there is a finding of violation of the FET standard. Only acts or omissions, more than mere contractual breaches, that go beyond a certain threshold of gravity can be considered unfair and inequitable.[208] The intensity or gravity of unfair acts and omissions varies in relation to the duration of their impact in the case.[209] Indeed, while some measures may *prima facie* appear unfair and inequitable, they may no longer be considered as such if negotiations are conducted having the effects of removing or compensating their consequences.[210]

Against these premises, the tribunal turned to analyze the events which had occurred during the course of the concession, dividing them in three periods. The first part concerned the emergency measures taken in the aftermath of the deepest economic crisis ever experienced by Argentina. The tribunal did not consider that these emergency measures entailed a breach of the FET standard. It acknowledged the negative consequences of the tariff freeze and tying rates to the peso, which caused the tariff value to decrease by approximately two-thirds. However, accord-

[204] *Ibid.*, paras. 619-621.

[205] *Ibid.*, para. 622

[206] *Ibid.*, para. 622.

[207] *Ibid.*, para. 623.

[208] *Ibid.*, para. 626.

[209] *Ibid.*, para. 629

[210] *Ibid.*, para. 632.

ing to the tribunal, the concessionaire could have continued to operate by providing its own funding or by resorting to shareholder resources. Moreover, the emergency measures were not the main cause of the concessionaire's difficulties, which had begun well before the implementation of the emergency measures.[211]

A different conclusion was reached by the tribunal with regard to the obligation to carry out the renegotiation of the concession contract in good faith. Despite the fact that a number of proposals were submitted by the concessionaire and discussed, the renegotiation failed due to the government's decision to reverse the privatization process and to return the operation of water and sanitation services to state-owned companies. This political shift brought the renegotiation to a deadlock, without the investors being informed of the true reasons behind the breakdown of the negotiations in February 2005.[212] The tribunal therefore concluded that during the renegotiation of the concession contract (2003-2005) the respondent had breached the FET standard for having failed to negotiate in a transparent manner.[213]

As for the third period taken into consideration, the tribunal found no breach of the FET standard for the events culminating in the termination of the concession contract, given the serious contractual breaches committed by the concessionaire.[214]

3.3.3. Full protection and security

Turning to the alleged breaches of the "protection and security" clause, in the *Suez* case, the tribunal departed from the holdings in *Azurix* and *Biwater* and endorsed the traditional interpretation of this clause, which aims to protect investors and investments against physical injury. There was no reason for extending this legal concept to "*encompass the maintenance of a stable legal and commercial environment*".[215] What is more, in the tribunal's view, this conclusion was in no way different when the words "*protection*" and "*security*" are qualified by the adjective "*full*", as the above case law has suggested. The tribunal argued that the "*legal security*" of the investment environment is protected under the fair and equitable treatment clause; hence, an extension of the meaning of the protection and security standard would have resulted in an undesirable overlap. Thus, it rejected the claim of violation of the FPS standard.

In the *SAUR* case, the decision did not address the question of whether the content of the FPS clause also embraces "*legal security*", since the claimant had alleged

---

[211] *Ibid.*, paras. 672-675, 678, 682.

[212] *Ibid.*, para. 843.

[213] *Ibid.*, para. 845.

[214] *Ibid.*, para. 950.

[215] *Suez, Sociedad General de Aguas de Barcelona, S.A. and Vivendi Universal, S.A. v. Argentine Republic*, Decision on Liability (n 138), para. 179.

only material harm.[216] Sauri's assertion of having been victim of a violent administrative intervention was rejected, as such intervention occurred according to domestic rules and the mere presence of the police was not *per se* sufficient to infer a breach of the FPS standard.[217]

Finally, in the *Urbaser* case, the tribunal and the parties did not address this issue, as the relevant BIT did not include this treaty clause.

3.3.4. The defence of necessity

In cases in which the human right to water has been invoked, States have also submitted that should a violation be found, this violation was justified on the ground of necessity,[218] as the contested measures sought to safeguard the right to water of users.

In the *Suez* case, to determine whether the defence of necessity absolved Argentina from responsibility, the tribunal applied the conditions set forth in Article 25 of the 2001 Draft Articles on the Responsibility of States for Internationally Wrongful Acts and found that two of them were not satisfied, namely: *i)* that the violations of the BITs were not the only means to protect Argentina's essential interests; *ii)* and the Republic had contributed to the situations of emergency.

In the *SAUR* case, the defense of necessity was also rejected, without being analyzed in detail. Indeed, the tribunal considered such a defense completely groundless owing to the lack of any cause-effect relation between the emergency measures taken by Argentina in 2002 to cope with the economic crisis and the expropriation, which occurred in 2009, when the situation of the country had normalized.[219]

In the *Urbaser* case, the tribunal instead provided an in-depth analysis of the state of necessity defence raised by Argentina, reaching a different conclusion. It ruled that, were it to find that the adoption of the emergency measures constituted a wrongful act, the State would have no responsibility under international law.

Faced with the claimants' argument that the State had contributed to causing the state of necessity, a circumstance that would have precluded the applicability of the defence, the tribunal observed that the Argentine contribution in terms of wrong economic policies was not of such a magnitude to have caused the economic crisis.

---

[216] *Ibid.*, paras. 500-501.

[217] *Ibid.*, paras. 508-509.

[218] ILC, Articles on the Responsibility of States for Internationally Wrongful Acts, ILC Ybk 2001/II(2), 26; Commentary to the ILC Articles on the Responsibility of States for Internationally Wrongful Acts, ILC Ybk 2001/II(2) 31, reprinted in J. Crawford (ed.), *The International Law Commission's Articles on State Responsibility: Introduction, Text and Commentaries*, Cambridge, 2002; J. Crawford, *State Responsibility. The General Part*, Cambridge, 2013, pp. 305-3015.

[219] *SAUR International v. Argentine Republic*, Decision on Jurisdiction and Liability (n 134), para. 460.

There was no clear causal link between the conduct of Argentina and the outbreak of the crisis.[220]

The claim that Argentina had other means available to avoid a violation of the FET standards was also dismissed. According to the tribunal, Argentina had proved that the emergency measures were the only ones available at that time, taking into consideration the extreme situation experienced by its population.[221] On the contrary, the alternative measures suggested by the claimants, such as a tariff increase or the provision of subsidies to users, were impractical for the State at that time.[222] The only practicable solution was the renegotiation of the concession contract, as was requested by the State.[223]

3.4. *Interim* conclusion

The case law described in the previous sub-sections 3.2-3.3 has shown an emerging trend under which the right to water has been playing a role in the tribunals' reasoning, contributing to mitigating States' responsibilities for breaches of BIT provisions due to human rights considerations.

In *Azurix*, while there was no clear reference to the right to water, the tribunal gave a wide interpretation of the notion of an "*investor's legitimate expectation*" in adjudicating the claims of expropriation and of unfair and inequitable treatment. It held that such expectations included not only those based on the legal background (the law, the contract, etc), but also expectations based on further unspecified assurances and representations made by the State. Additionally, it affirmed that for a State to frustrate investors' legitimate expectations, the volitional element, bad faith, is not required and that the standard of protection required by the FET clause is higher than the minimum standard of treatment of aliens. The claim of violation of the FPT standard was also upheld on the ground that this standard includes physical security but also legal security. The adjective "*full*" was posited to confirm such a reading.

The *Vivendi* case, registered at the ICSID in 1997, is the oldest among the investment disputes on water services analyzed. In this case, no reference was made to the human right to water, perhaps due to the lack of its full recognition at the relevant time. Indeed, the ICESCR had not yet issued General Comment No. 15 and neither the General Assembly nor the Human Right Council had yet proclaimed the existence of a right to water. Here, the tribunal upheld all the claims raised by the investor

---

[220] *Urbaser S.A. and others v. The Argentine Republic*, Award (n 30), paras. 710, 713-714.

[221] *Ibid.*, paras. 716-717.

[222] *Ibid.*, paras. 724-729

[223] *Ibid.*, paras. 732-738.

companies. In particular, with regard to expropriation, the doctrine of the regulatory power for public purpose was rejected and it was held that a public purpose does not exempt the State from compensation. Moreover, the tribunal added that only the effects of the State's measures matter in finding a violation of a BIT rule. As in *Azurix*, broad interpretation was also given to the FET and FPS standards.

In *Biwater*, human rights considerations began to be timidly asserted. Although the tribunal upheld all of the company's claims, it seems that it adhered to the interpretation of the FET clause suggested by the *amici curiae*, who argued that a high threshold must be met in order to find a violation of the clause.

In *Suez*, the right to water received greater attention. The tribunal held that a State is not responsible for internationally wrongful acts if measures affecting investors' rights are adopted in the exercise of police powers. In this situation, States should not even be called to compensate investors. The *amicus curiae* brief, which dealt extensively with States' obligations arising from the right at issue, seems to have influenced the holdings of the tribunal in relation to the police powers doctrine.[224] The FPS claim was rejected as well. The purpose of such a clause, it was ruled, is only that of protecting the *physical* security of the investment and of the investors, and *Suez* suffered no physical harm. Departing from the *Azurix*, *Vivendi* and *Biwater* holdings, the tribunal maintained that the adjective "*full*", qualifying the protection to be accorded to investors, does not change the conclusion that FPT refers to physical security alone. As such, only a breach of the FET clause was found. Interestingly, the tribunal did not call into question the legitimacy of the measures adopted during the crisis despite the fact that they impaired investors' rights, but instead blamed Argentina for its lack of cooperation with the concessionaires in the aftermath of the economic crisis.

The *SAUR* decision also devoted several paragraphs to the right to water and to the obligations arising therefrom. This right was considered a general principle of international law and, thus, a source of law applicable to the dispute. The importance of counterbalancing different obligations arising for States from human rights and investment law was also stressed. Unlike the *Suez* case,[225] the tribunal did not simply require the simultaneous fulfillment of the conflicting obligations but sought to find a balance between them. On the one hand, it acknowledged that public authorities possess the regulatory and police powers necessary to guarantee essential services, such as water services. On the other hand, even the legitimate exercise of authoritative prerogatives does not exempt the State from the duty to compensate foreign investors so far this is required by the BIT.[226] In this respect,

[224] De Schutter, p. 172 (n 19).

[225] *Suez, Sociedad General de Aguas de Barcelona, S.A. and Vivendi Universal, S.A. v. Argentine Republic* (n 133).

[226] In this respect, it cannot be overlooked that if States are faced with the threat of having to

the tribunal departed from the *Suez* decision, which had stated that measures taken within the State's police powers are not expropriatory in nature, and, for this reason, gave no right to compensation, regardless of what may be set forth in the BIT. On the contrary, it was affirmed that States may be exempted from paying compensation in case of legitimate expropriations undertaken in the exercise of their police powers, provided that it is not otherwise established by BIT provisions.

In *Urbaser*, the tribunal considered the right to water in order to shape the notion of investors' legitimate expectation, establishing that the duty of the State to guarantee water to its citizens must be taken into account by a company investing in the provision of water services when its expectations are formed. In addition, reference to the right to water was made in addressing the state of necessity defence. The tribunal held that the State's duty to guarantee the provision of water to its population trumps investors' interest in the profitability of their investment. It held that, given the exceptionally serious economic crisis faced by Argentina, the only way for the State to safeguard access to water was by failing to perform international investment obligations, which therefore, in the light of Article 25 of the Draft Articles on Responsibility of States for Internationally Wrongful Acts, are deemed to be of lesser weight or urgency. Finally, the right to water was the object of an autonomous counterclaim.

The progressive recognition of the human right to water is thus reflected in the growing reference to this right made by States in their defences before investment arbitral tribunals, and, in turn, by the influence it has progressively exercised on the tribunals' interpretation of key BIT provisions. It is noteworthy that in these cases the existence of the right to water was taken for granted. Aside from the respondent States, neither the claimants, nor the investment tribunals, cast doubt on its existence. Thus, not only has the emergence of such a right started to shape investment tribunal's rulings, but also investment arbitral tribunals' decisions are contributing to its recognition "*as evidence of a general practice accepted as law*".[227]

4. The impact of the human right to water on compensation in investor-State arbitration

This section considers whether the human rights defence has played any role in terms of the valuation of claims and, in particular, in limiting the amount of compensation due to claimants for breaches of BIT provisions. If the impact of this de-

pay compensation, they may be deterred from undertaking measures otherwise perceived as necessary from a human rights point of view. W. Schreiber, *Realizing the Right to Water in International Investment Law: An Interdisciplinary Approach to BIT Obligations*, in *Natural Resources Journal*, 2008, p. 451.

[227] Statute of the International Court of Justice, Art. 38(1)(*b*).

fence on the merits of the cases at hand is not mirrored in the decisions on compensation, the result achieved in terms of harmonization and systemic integration of investment law and human rights law would be significantly weakened.

Arbitrators exercise discretion in assessing damages, and considerations of "*reasonableness*" are not infrequent in investment arbitral decisions.[228] This section seeks to analyze whether these considerations have emerged in the case law under examination.

Another issue to be taken into account is whether compensation is a requisite of lawful expropriation.[229] If it is sufficient to prove a number of conditions for an expropriation to be deemed lawful – notably, that it occurs in a non discriminatory manner, in the public interest and in accordance with due process of law – when these are met, the failure to provide compensation would not give rise to the State's international responsibility. On the contrary, if compensation is a condition predicated for a lawful expropriation, noncomplying States would be required to abide by the duty to full reparation of damages,[230] which might result in monetary commitments much higher than the value of the property expropriated.[231] This section comments on the stand taken by arbitrators in the cases at hand.

The choice of the valuation method to be used by arbitrators is also relevant in determining the possible amount of compensation due to claimants.[232] While the fair market value of the investment expropriated is likely to be used to determine the amount due in case of lawful expropriation, the differential method – notably the difference between the current situation and that in which the claimant would have found itself in all probability had the unlawful act not been committed – seems better suited for providing full reparation in case of unlawful expropriation. However, it has been underlined in the literature that in practice this difference has not been duly considered[233] so a risk exists that the consequences of lawful and unlawful expropriation are put at the same level.

---

[228] *Impregilo S.p.A. v. Argentine Republic*, ICSID Case No. ARB/07/17, Award, 21 June 2011, para. 371; *Marion Unglaube v. Republic of Costa Rica*, ICSID Case No. ARB/08/1, Award, 16 May 2012, para. 318, nt. 240; *Técnicas Medioambientales SA. Mexico*, ICSID Case No. ARB (AF)/00/2, Award, 29 May 2003, para. 190.

[229] Among those favorable to the conclusion that customary international law requires compensation to be paid upon expropriation as a condition of lawfulness of the latter see: UNCTAD, *Expropriation*, UNCTAD Series on Issues in International Investments Agreements II, 2012, p. 27; OECD, *'Indirect Expropriation' and the 'Right to Regulate' in International Investment Law*, OECD Working Papers on International Investment, No. 2004/4, OECD Publishing, p. 3, available at: https://www.oecd.org/daf/inv/investment-policy/WP-2004_4.pdf.

[230] PCIJ, *Factory of Chorzów, Germany v. Poland*, of 13 September 1928, p. 47.

[231] For a clear discussion of the difference between compensation for lawful expropriation and reparation for unlawful expropriation see Marboe, pp. 9-36 (n 46).

[232] *Ibid.*, pp. 36-41 (n 46).

[233] *Ibid.*, p. 49 (n 46).

4.1. Cases lacking clear reference to the human right to water

In *Azurix*, although the tribunal held Argentina responsible for the violations of the FET and FPS clauses, it awarded compensation far lower than that which was claimed by the company (around 165 million US dollars against an initial investment of more than 550 million US dollars).[234] Despite the broad interpretation of the BIT provisions – namely, the indirect expropriation, the FET and the FPS standards – the tribunal awarded to the claimant only a small portion of its initial investment. However, the tribunal's reasoning[235] does not suggest that its decision was influenced by human rights considerations; after all, the human right to water was neither invoked by Argentina nor mentioned by the tribunal.

In the *Vivendi* case, the tribunal resorted to the principle of full compensation equal to fair market value. Interestingly, Argentina challenged the application of this principle, relying, *inter alia*, on the fact that it had acted in the public interest.[236] The tribunal rejected this objection.[237] However, against a claim of over 317 million US dollars for damages, only 105 million US dollars was awarded, given that the claimants had failed to establish with certainty the profitability of the concession.

In *Biwater*, the arbitrators denied claims for damages and issued a declaratory decision on the grounds that the causal link between the breaches of the BIT and the alleged losses suffered by the claimant had not been proved.[238] However, one may wonder whether human rights considerations influenced the refusal to award compensation, a decision that seems at odds with the violations of the most relevant BIT provisions, namely those concerning indirect expropriation, the FET clause and the FPS standard.

4.2. Cases acknowledging the human right to water

The final award on compensation in the *Suez* case seems to disregard the human rights considerations granted in the decision on liability.[239] In establishing the

---

[234] *Azurix Corp. v. Argentine Republic*, Award (n 65), para. 442.

[235] The low amount of money granted in compensation was motivated by the fact that the company had failed to make the right estimate when it paid the Canon of 438,555,551 million US dollars. Under the concession agreement, this Canon (which covered almost all the initial investment) was not recoverable, at least not completely, through periodic tariff increases. Accordingly, it could not be claimed in compensation.

[236] *Ibid.*, para. 8.4.1.

[237] *Ibid.*, para. 9.4.3.

[238] *Ibid.*, paras. 781, 807.

[239] *Contra*, L. Liberti, *The Relevance of Non-Investment Treaty Obligations in Assessing Compensation*, in P.-M. Dupuy, F. Francioni, E.-U. Petersmann (eds.), *Human Rights in International Investment Law and Arbitration*, Oxford, 2009, p. 564.

standard to be applied in order to determine the amount of compensation for non-expropriatory breaches, the tribunal remained anchored to the customary law approach to compensation for expropriation, ordering full compensation based on the fair market value of the investment made.[240]

It argued that customary international law requires full compensation for losses incurred by investors as a result of the internationally wrongful acts committed by the State in order to place the claimants in the situation which would, in all probability, have existed had State not committed its illegal acts (in other words, had not breached the fair and equitable standard clause).[241]

Against Argentina's claim that the tribunal had accepted to undertake an expropriation valuation despite determining that no expropriation had taken place,[242] the arbitrators objected that the financial expert had constructed a framework for the valuation process specific to the case of denial of equitable treatment and that the high compensation requested was due to the fact that the Republic had taken measures which resulted "*in a complete loss of the Claimants' investments*".[243]

Some doubts may be cast on the effective weight attached to human rights arguments in terms of compensation. While the tribunal granted consideration to human rights in its decision on liability – establishing that no expropriation had taken place – it applied a valuation standard that lead to the same result as if it had found a violation of the expropriation clause.

In the *SAUR* case, arbitrators adhered to the principle of full reparation of damages caused to the investor by the Republic,[244] as the State was held responsible for the direct expropriation of the claimant's investment and for unjust and unfair treatment. Compensation was awarded in the amount requested by the claimant, calculated to pay for actual losses and lost profits.[245] However, the tribunal wished to underline the reasonableness of its decision grounded on the fact that the claimant received in compensation slightly more than half of what it invested in the concession fifteen years earlier, and only one-quarter of what it originally claimed (before the second MOA).[246]

---

[240] *Suez, Sociedad General de Aguas de Barcelona, S.A. and Vivendi Universal, S.A. v. Argentine Republic*, Award (n 133), 9 April 2015, paras. 23-24.

[241] *Ibid.*, para. 27.

[242] *Ibid.*, para. 50.

[243] *Ibid.*, para. 56.

[244] *SAUR v. Argentine Republic*, Award (n 148), para. 160, making reference to art. 36(2) of the Draft Articles on Responsibility of States for Internationally Wrongful Acts, 2001, and to the judgment of the PCIJ, *Factory of Chorzów, Germany v. Poland*, of 13 September 1928.

[245] Except as per the conversion to USD, since the claimant applied a slightly higher exchange rate. *Ibid.*, paras. 318, 385.

[246] *Ibid.*, para. 395.

In the *Urbaser* case, the claim of compensation was dismissed on different grounds. The tribunal found only a breach of the FET standard with respect to the renegotiation of the concession contract between 2003-2005 due to the failure of the respondent State to carry out the renegotiation process in good faith. However, it did not award compensation for this breach as it had caused no economic losses to the investors and the concession had no future in any event.[247]

4.3. *Interim* conclusion

The analysis above shows that human rights considerations have not had a consistent impact on investment arbitral decisions on compensation. However, some "*seeds*" may be found in cases where the human right to water has clearly been invoked as a defence for the measures adopted in detriment to the investor. In *Suez*, the Tribunal took a stand on the debated issue of compensation as a condition for the lawfulness of an expropriation, excluding this to be the case. In *SAUR*, the tribunal justified its conclusion in terms of compensation by citing grounds of "*reasonableness*" due to the significant losses incurred by the investor and compensated only minimally. Finally, the tribunal in the *Urbaser* case took the most coherent approach. Having rejected the claims raised by the investors almost entirely, it found that no compensation was due.

5. Harmonizing investment protection with the human right to water

The analysis above has discussed a number of cases in which a conflict between obligations stemming from international investment law and human rights law emerged.[248] In almost all of these cases, governments had prevented private investors from increasing water tariffs, breaching not only domestic contracts but also BIT provisions as a result. Some measures were justified by the States' duty to protect the human right to water. While occasionally the human rights defence has been used to justify public authorities' misconduct, more often it has resulted from the existence of a genuine conflict between international investment rules and human rights duties under the right to water. These conflicts and their possible solutions are the object of this section.

As anticipated in chapter one, the issue can be framed within the debate on the so-called "*fragmentation of international law*". Searching for a possible balance between investor's rights and consumers' rights in the water services sec-

---

[247] *Urbaser S.A. and others v. The Argentine Republic*, Award (n 30), para. 846.

[248] The ILC has adopted a wide notion of conflict, namely "*a situation where two possible rules or principles suggest different ways of dealing with a problem*". ILC Report, para. 25 (n 22).

tor,[249] sub-section 5.1. considers possible means to prevent conflicts between obligations stemming from international investment law and obligations grounded in the human right to water. Section 5.2. reflects on the possibility of a human rights-oriented interpretation of the relevant BIT provisions once a dispute has arisen and has been brought before arbitral tribunals. Finally, section 5.3. addresses cases of "*genuine*" conflicts of law, when interpretation has proven to be insufficient, in order to assess whether a relationship of priority between investment rules and human rights obligations can be put forward.

5.1. Harmonization by means of conflict prevention

As anticipated in chapter two, from a human rights' perspective, States parties to the ICESCR bear the responsibility to respect, protect and fulfill the human right to water in all contexts, including in the case of privatization of water services and liberalization of investments in the water sector. The duty to respect requires States to take into consideration the right to water when entering into investment agreements with a view to identify potential conflicts and, where present, to refrain from entering such treaties.[250] Given that foreign investments are usually based on domestic contracts concluded between the host State's authorities and investors, and on investment treaties concluded between host and home States, the duty to regulate in the public interest has to be equally fulfilled when a State sets the legal framework of privatization, as well as when it enters into IIAs. In both cases, human rights infringements may also be prevented by resorting to a human rights impact assessment before entering investment agreements. All these possibilities are dealt with in the following sub-sections, starting from the last.

5.1.1. Human rights impact assessment

It has been argued that before delegating the provision of water services, public authorities should consider its potential impact on the rights to water and sanitation. In this connection, the Human Rights Commissioner has recommended, as a possible field for future study, "*the development of methodologies for human rights impact*

[249] P.-M. Dupuy, *Unification rather than Fragmentation of International Law? The Case of International Investment Law and Human Rights Law*, in P.M. Dupuy, F. Francioni, E.-U. Petersmann (eds.), *Human Rights in International Investment Law and Arbitration*, Oxford, 2009; G. Puma, *Human Rights Law and Investment Law: Attempts at Harmonization Through a Difficult Dialogue between Arbitrators and Human Rights Tribunals*, in M. Arcari, L. Balmond (eds.), *Judicial Dialogue in the International Legal Order. Between Pluralism and Legal Certainty*, Naples, 2014, pp. 193-243; Kriebaum, pp. 16-36 (n 31).

[250] General Comment No. 15, para. 35 (n 2); CESCR, *General Comment No. 24 (2017) on State obligations under the International Covenant on Economic, Social and Cultural Rights in the context of business activities*, UN Doc. E/C.12/GC/24, 10 August 2017, paras. 13, 29.

assessments of trade and investment rules and policies and the appropriate assistance needed to undertake them".[251]

A human rights impact assessment ("HRIA") for trade and investments agreements is an *ex ante* assessment, a "*systematic process to investigate and measure the impact of policies, programs, projects, and interventions on human rights*".[252]

This assessment should be made by States before undertaking commitments to foreign investors at a domestic or international level. From the perspective of international law, it would contribute to ensuring the coherence between States' investment treaty obligations and those resulting from the human rights conventions to which they are a party, thus mitigating problems resulting from fragmentation of international law.[253] An *ex ante* HRIA should be complemented by an *ex post* assessment following the conclusion of investment agreements once their impact becomes measurable in order to provide a response in case of incompatibilities not previously noted.[254]

Like the environmental impact assessment, the HRIA should involve the participation of the public, in particular of persons and groups directly affected by the investment agreements.[255]

Scholars expressed their approval of this option for preventing and mitigating normative conflicts. De Schutter has endorsed the human rights impact assessment in the course of negotiations for the conclusion of BITs or IIAs treaties,[256] while Krajewski has recommended inserting a clause on HRIA in a future treaty on business and human rights.[257] In this connection, it cannot be overlooked that the cur-

---

[251] Commission on Human Rights, *Human rights, trade and investment*, p. 5 (n 5).

[252] *Ibid.*, paras. 36, 43.

[253] Human Rights Council, *Guiding Principles on Human Rights Impact Assessments of Trade and Investment Agreements, Report of the Special Rapporteur on the rights to food*, Oliver De Schutter: Addendum, UN Doc. A/HCR/19/59/Add. 5, 19 December 2011, Principle No. 1. See also Human Rights Council, *Guiding Principles on Human Rights Impact Assessments of Economic Reforms, Report of the Independent Expert on the effects of foreign debt and other related international financial obligations of States on the full enjoyment of human rights, particularly economic, social and cultural rights*, UN Doc. A/HCR/40/57, 19 December 2018.

[254] Human Rights Council, *Guiding Principles on Human Rights Impact Assessments of Trade and Investment Agreement,* Principle No. 3 (n 253).

[255] *Ibid.*, Principle No. 4. The High Commissioner suggests the promotion of "*popular participation, transparency, legality, equality and accountability – in relation to essential services sectors, including in the process of decision-making concerning privatization as well as the implementation and monitoring of private sector concession agreements*". See Commission on Human Rights, *Human rights, trade and investment,* p. 5 (n 5).

[256] De Schutter, p. 163 (n 19).

[257] M. Krajewski, *Ensuring the Primacy of Human Rights in Trade and Investment Policies – Model Clauses for a UN Treaty on Transnational Corporations, Other Businesses and Human Rights*, CIDSE, 2017, p. 28, available at SSRN: https://ssrn.com/abstract=2939354.

rent revised draft on a *Legally Binding Instrument to Regulate, in International Human Rights Law, the Activities of Transnational Corporations and Other Business Enterprises* ("Legally Binding Instrument") does include a provision requiring States to ensure that transnational companies undertake, within their territories or under their jurisdiction, due diligence obligations throughout their business activities (on the *Legally Binding Instrument* see below sub-section 5.1.4.). This should include a HRIA covering not only their activities but also those of their subsidiaries or entities under their control in order to take appropriate action.[258]

On a different note, Simma has proposed a "*human right audit*" consisting in "*a joint undertaking of foreign investors and host States, to survey the host State's human rights treaty commitments (especially in the field of economic and social rights) and methods for implementing such commitments*".[259] The eminent scholar reasons as follows. Investors often allege breaches of the FET clause for having had their legitimate expectation frustrated by host State's regulatory measures. Investors' legitimate expectations are based on the information available at the time of the conclusion of the investment contract, including the legal framework of the host State. Hence, it is suggested that making foreign investors aware of the host State's actual and prospective international human rights obligations (which are a part of that State's applicable law) would prevent them from claiming frustration of their legitimate expectations. In other words, the human rights audit aims at recasting the investor's legitimate expectations under the foreign investment contract and at avoiding compensation for FET breaches.

5.1.2. Revising domestic rules and stabilization clauses

Once the decision to privatize essential services has been taken, public authorities ought to consider revising the domestic legal system in order to evaluate whether domestic rules adopted to attract investment could raise false expectations in foreign investors, which would somehow impair the fulfillment of their human rights obligations.

As for the legal framework, public authorities must refrain from providing investors with overly broad guarantees that would form grounds for a claim of infringe-

---

[258] OEIGWG Chairmanship revised draft, *Legally Binding Instrument to Regulate, in International Human Rights Law, the Activities of Transnational Corporations and Other business Enterprises*, 16 July 2019, (hereinafter "Revised Draft" or "Legally Binding Instrument), art. 5(3)(*a*); Zero Draft, *Legally Binding Instrument to Regulate, in International Human Rights Law, the Activities of Transnational Corporations and Other business Enterprises*, 16 July 2018 (hereinafter "Zero Draft"), art. 9(2)(*e*). See also the *Draft Optional Protocol to the Legally Binding Instrument to Regulate, in International Human Rights Law, the Activities of Transnational Corporations and Other Business Enterprises*, annexed to the Zero Draft (hereinafter "annexed Protocol").

[259] B. Simma, *Foreign Investment Arbitration: A Place for Human Rights?*, in *International & Comparative Law Quarterly*, 2011, p. 594.

ment of "*legitimate expectations*" amounting to a violation of the FET standard. Assuming obligations that are too broad may be detrimental for the host State's power to regulate in the public interest and undermine not only the human rights of its population, but also their public finances. While empirical studies have not yet proved the favorable impact of overt pro-investors BIT provisions in terms of increased foreign investments, the side effect of these provisions has been felt by States that have been called to pay high amounts of compensation in the context of investment disputes.[260]

According to some authors, recent case law seems to favor the State's right to adapt its legislation to changing circumstances even to the detriment of the legal stability of the investment.[261] However, arbitral tribunals have taken divergent positions on the role of investors' expectations. As a matter of fact, in the cases analyzed in the previous sections, the FET claims have always been upheld (albeit only in part in *Urbaser*). Argentina had indeed established a legal framework that was too favorable to investors and once the Republic failed to meet its obligations, investors had an easy way of successfully claiming the frustration of their legitimate expectations, requiring compensation for their lost investments.

As far as domestic agreements between host public authorities and foreign investors are concerned, water services are often outsourced through concessions or leasing contracts. These contracts establish the terms under which the service has to be supplied, as well as the respective rights and duties of both investors and host States.[262] In this context, guarantees to secure investments have to be balanced with the investors' duty to meet quality standards and territorial coverage targets. In fact, unless explicitly mandated to do so, private providers may attempt to selectively serve attractive areas where they expect higher rates of return.[263]

Further, States should refrain from including stabilization clauses in State-investors contracts.[264] Through such clauses, the domestic law in force at the time the contract is signed is incorporated into the agreement with the aim of freezing the applicable law over the years, usually for the duration of the contract. These clauses raise public concern because they prevent the application to the contract of any modifications to the legal framework, without regard for whatever factual changes may occur.[265]

---

260 Hallward-Driemeier (n 18).

261 Dolzer, Schreuer, p. 148 (n 64).

262 L. Boisson De Chazournes, *Fresh Water in International Law*, Oxford, 2013, p. 96.

263 Commission on Human Rights, *Human rights, trade and investment,* paras. 39-40, (n 5).

264 Dolzer, Schreuer, pp. 82-85 (n 64).

265 Recently some authors have made forward-looking suggestions concerning the drafting of stabilization clauses in line with sustainable development objectives. J. Gjuzi, *Stabilization Clauses in International Investment Law. A sustainable Development Approach*, Cham, 2018; A. Crockett,

5.1.3. Incorporating human rights considerations in IIAs

Turning to the level of international law, the right to water requires States (parties to the ICESCR) to regulate in the public interest. This duty to protect must be taken into account when entering into international investment agreements by avoiding clauses that might affect their power to use regulation to respect, protect and fulfill the right to water and, possibly, by incorporating human rights provisions in these agreements.

As for the former, the duty to protect requires States to consider the consequences of undertaking commitments that, by linking contractual violations to treaty violations, may eventually give rise to international responsibility for minor contractual breaches. Investment treaties may indeed include a so-called "*umbrella clause*", under which States commit themselves to comply with obligations arising from the contract *vis à vis* foreign investors. The more the contractual commitments towards investors are detailed, the stricter the international obligations will be. Contractual obligations are 'internationalised' to the effect that a breach of a contractual clause may amount to a violation of the treaty that can be raised before international investment tribunals.[266]

Some tribunals have sought to narrow the scope of the umbrella clause by referring to the distinction between sovereign acts and contractual acts. They have considered that only acts binding upon State in its sovereignty capacity can raise international responsibility.[267] However, such arbitral outcomes cannot be taken for granted, as investment tribunals are not bound by their precedent.

To the extent that the right to water is concerned, umbrella clauses may limit the ability of a State to modify concession contracts of water services, for instance, in order to require higher quality of water in line with new scientific findings or to low tariffs in case of a national financial crisis. To prevent small contractual breaches from giving rise to an international claim for the violation of investors' rights under the investment treaty, such a clause ought to be avoided.

In the respect of the second, several proposals have been offered to include human rights consideration within IIAs in order to prevent normative conflicts between investment treaty rules and human rights norms. The High Commissioner for Human Rights refers to the possibility of "*[i]ncluding the promotion and protection*

Stabilisation clauses and sustainable development: Drafting for the future, in C. Brown, K. Miles, *Evolution in Investment Treaty Law and Arbitration*, Cambridge, 2011, p. 516 ff.

[266] K. Yannaca-Small, *Interpretation of the Umbrella Clause in Investment Agreements*, OECD Working Papers on International Investment, 2006, available at: http://dx.doi.org/10.1787/415453814578; R. Pereira de Souza Fleury, *Treaty-Protected Investment Agreements: of Umbrella Clauses and Privity of Contract*, in *Willamette University College of Law*, 2016, pp. 319-334.

[267] *El Paso Energy v. Argentina*, ICSID Case No. ARB/03/15, Decision on Jurisdiction, 27 April 2006, paras. 70, 72-74; *Pan America/ BP v. Argentina*, ICSID Case No. ARB/03/13, Decision on Preliminary Objections, 27 July 2006, paras. 101-103, 108.

of human rights among the objectives of investment agreements".[268] Some scholars have proposed including "*explicit provisions regulating the possible conflict with other treaties*" in IIAs.[269] BITs could then include clauses of compatibility or subordination, which specify that they should not be considered inconsistent with existing or future human rights treaty provisions. The CESCR, as well as some scholars, have suggested incorporating a human rights clause in investment agreements[270] or a specific clause on public interest exceptions.[271] Others have argued that international financial institutions should include human right clauses in their financial instruments.[272]

The possibility of incorporation of an explicit reference to human rights law or to single human rights provision in IIAs is not so farfetched. It is noteworthy that the imbalance between investors' rights and States' obligations has started to be acknowledged even by capital exporting countries. A "new generation" of IIAs is emerging,[273] especially on the African Continent,[274] together with a trend toward the revision of previous models of investment agreements and the renegotiation of BITs.[275] A common feature of these new investment treaties is that they seek to re-balance investment protections with the host State's power to regulate in the public interest.

An influential example is the 2012 US Model BIT.[276] Its preamble explains its objectives and the aim of achieving them "*in a manner consistent with the protection of health, safety, and the environment, and the promotion of internationally recognized labour rights*". This model also provides a far-reaching protection of the State's regulatory power. Article 5 expressly links the FET standard and the FPS standard to the "*Minimum Standard of Treatment*". In order to avoid misunderstanding, it adds that:

---

[268] Commission on Human Rights, *Human rights, trade and investment,* p. 5 (n 5).

[269] G. Hafner, *Pros and Cons Ensuing from Fragmentation of International Law*, in *Michigan Journal of International Law*, 2004, p. 861.

[270] General Comment No. 24, para. 13 (n 250); Schreiber, pp. 473-474 (n 226).

[271] A. van Aaken, *Fragmentation of International Law: The Case of International Investment Protection*, University of St. Gallen Law School, Law and Economics Research Paper Series, Working Paper No. 2008/1, p. 20.

[272] F. Marrella, *On the Changing Structure of International Investment Law: The Human Right to Water and ICSID Arbitration*, in *International Community Law Review*, 2010, p. 358.

[273] UNCTAD, *Towards a New Generation of Investment Policies*, in *Investment Policy Framework for Sustainable Development* (n 7).

[274] M. M. Mbengue, S. Schacherer, *The 'Africanization' of International Investment Law: The Pan-African Investment Code and the Reform of the International Investment Regime*, in *The Journal of World Investment & Trade*, 2017, pp. 414-448.

[275] Wouters and others, pp. 49-66 (n 13); Simma, p. 581 (n 259).

[276] Treaty between the Government of the United States of America and the Government of [Country] Concerning the Encouragement and Reciprocal Protection of Investment.

"'fair and equitable treatment' includes the obligation not to deny justice in criminal, civil, or administrative adjudicatory proceedings in accordance with the principle of due process embodied in the principal legal systems of the worlds; and 'full protection and security' requires each Party to provide the level of police protection required under customary international law legal systems".

Finally, with regard to indirect expropriation, Annex B of the US Model provides that:

"Except in rare circumstances, non-discriminatory regulatory actions by a Party that are designed and applied to protect legitimate public welfare objectives, such as public health, safety, and the environment, do not constitute indirect expropriations".

One may infer that such measures should not entail compensation given that they do not amount to expropriation, as was held in the *Suez* decision, in which the tribunal found that the measures adopted by Argentina to cope with the severe economic and social crisis of the country were within the State's regulatory power and did not amount to expropriation.[277] Should future investment agreements be drafted in accordance with this model, the interpretive leeway of arbitral bodies to award compensation in case of regulatory measures aimed to protect public purposes would be significantly limited.

The recently adopted Comprehensive and Progressive Agreement for Trans-Pacific Partnership ("CPTPP"),[278] which incorporates the provisions of the proposed Trans-Pacific Partnership Agreement ("TPP"),[279] is a case in point. Annex 9-B(3)(*b*) TPP expressly provides that: "*[n]on-discriminatory regulatory actions by a Party that are designed and applied to protect legitimate public welfare objectives, such as public health, safety and the environment, do not constitute indirect expropriations, except in rare circumstances*".

Likewise, the amendment of Annex I of the Southern African Development Community ("SADC") Finance and Investment Protocol is notable.[280] It was prompted by the acknowledgment that some provisions of the Annex had failed to

[277] *Suez, Sociedad General de Aguas de Barcelona, S.A. and Vivendi Universal, S.A. v. Argentine Republic*, Decision on Liability (n 138), paras. 139-140. See above section 3.3.1.

[278] Comprehensive and Progressive Agreement for Trans-Pacific Partnership, Santiago, 8 March 2018. On 30 December 2018, it entered into force for Australia, Canada, Japan, Mexico, New Zealand and Singapore. On 14 January 2019, it entered into force also for Vietnam.

[279] Trans-Pacific Partnership Agreement, Wellington, 4 February 2016, not in force. Available at: https://ustr.gov/sites/default/files/TPP-Final-Text-Investment.pdf. C. McLachlan QC, L. Shore, M. Weiniger, *International Investment Arbitration. Substantive Principle*, Oxford, 2017, pp. 367-369.

[280] SADC, Agreement Amending Annex 1 – Cooperation on investment – on the Protocol on Finance & Investment, Kingdom of Swaziland, 31 August 2016.

"adequately balance investor protection and development policy space for host States".[281] Interestingly, while the Annex confirms the duty to compensate the investor in case of a legitimate expropriation – namely an expropriation carried out *"for public purpose, under due process of law, on a non-discriminatory basis"* [282] –, it also allows the assessment of fair and equitable compensation to be based *"on equitable balance between the public interests and the interest of those affected"*.[283] The public interest may thus enter as an element to be taken into consideration in quantifying compensation. A provision of this kind, if inserted in BITs, might preclude awarding high compensation in situations where countries are facing a serious financial crisis.[284]

The amended protocol also includes clauses that establish the right of host countries to regulate investments consistently with the public interest and the principles and goals of sustainable development.[285] Finally, this protocol does not include an Investor-State Dispute Settlement ("ISDS") clause for solving investment disputes. The investor is only granted the possibility to avail himself of the remedies provided for by the domestic courts of the host State.[286] This choice seems to reflect the concerns expressed by many States about the lack of transparency of international investment tribunals and the excessive compensation awarded compared to the financial capacity of developing countries.

An interesting compatibility clause has been inserted in the ECOWAS Supplementary Act on Investment[287] and in the Morocco-Nigeria BIT[288] as well, which sets forth that State parties *"shall ensure that their laws, policies and actions are consistent with the international human rights agreements to which they are Party"*. This should allow the adoption of regulatory measures that, while affecting investors' rights, would be justified by the duty to respect human rights agreements. However, the consequences in terms of compensation are not clear as the duty to respect human rights agreements does not *per se* trump States' obligations under the investment treaty. The outcome of this and similar provisions needs to be monitored in the years to come.

---

[281] See the third alinea of the Preamble of the Agreement.

[282] Art. 5(1).

[283] Art. 5(2).

[284] Marboe, pp. 158-162 (n 46).

[285] Arts. 11-12.

[286] Art. 5(8), art. 25.

[287] ECOWAS, Supplementary Act A/SA.3/12/08 Adopting Community Rules on Investment and the Modalities for their Implementation with ECOWAS, Abuja, 19 December 2008, entered into force on 19 December 2009, art. 21(5).

[288] Reciprocal Investment Promotion and Protection Agreement between the Government of the Kingdom of Morocco and the Government of the Federal Republic of Nigeria, 3 December 2016, not yet into force, art. 15(6). T. Gazzini, *Nigeria and Morocco Move Towards a 'New Generation' of Bilateral Investment Treaties*, in *EJIL:* Talk!, 2017.

5.1.4. Drafting a business and human rights treaty

In a 2017 study, Krajewski pointed out that non-binding obligations, such as the Guiding Principles on Business and Human Rights,[289] have not led States to change their practices in respect of trade and investment agreements. In order to ensure the primacy of human rights obligations *vis-à-vis* obligations stemming from these agreements, the author endorsed efforts to draft a treaty on business and human rights which would bind States to ensure primacy to human rights when developing new trade and investment agreements. In order to do so, the scholar suggested three possible ways to regulate the relationship between human rights and trade and investment agreements in favor of the primacy of human rights, notably: inserting a supremacy clause; ensuring the observance of human rights in trade and investment settlement proceedings; and incorporating human rights obligations in future investment and trade agreements.[290]

In 2014, the Human Rights Council appointed an open-ended intergovernmental working group on transnational corporations and other business enterprises ("IGWG") with respect to human rights with the mandate to draft a legally binding international instrument to regulate the activities of transnational corporations and other business enterprises.[291] In 2019, the IGWG has discussed a revised draft of a *Legally Binding Instrument to Regulate, in International Human Rights Law, the Activities of Transnational Corporations and Other Business Enterprises*,[292] which warrants attention, despite being a mere draft (with unsure prospects of becoming a treaty).

---

[289] Human Rights Council, *Report of the Special Representative of the Secretary General on the issue of human rights and transnational corporations and other business enterprises,* John Ruggie *Guiding Principles on Business and Human Rights: Implementing the United Nations 'Protect, Respect and Remedy' Framework*, UN Doc. A/HRC/17/31, 21 March 2011 (hereinafter "Guiding Principles on Business and Human Rights").

[290] M. Krajewski, pp. 24-27 (n 259).

[291] Human Rights Council, Res. 26/9, 26 June 2014, UN Doc. A/HCR/RES/26/9, 14 July 2014. Since 2015, the IGWG takes annual sessions to negotiate this treaty. F. Marrella, *Protection internationale des droits de l'homme et activités des sociétés transnationales*, *Collected Courses of the Hague Academy of International Law*, Leiden-Boston, 2017, pp. 80-82.

[292] Revised Draft (n 258). The Revised Draft considerably amends the Zero Draft. For early comments on the revised binding treaty see: by C. Lopez, *The Revised Draft of a Treaty on Business and Human Rights: A Big Leap Forward*, in *OpinioJuris*, 2019, available at http://opiniojuris.org/2019/08/15/the-revised-draft-of-a-treaty-on-business-and-human-rights-a-big-leap-forward/. See also posts in the symposium of the *BHRJ blog*, 2019, available at: https://www.cambridge.org/core/blog/tag/bhrj-treaty/, in particular: N. Carrillo Santarelli, *A Step in The Right Direction: Corporate Responsibility Under the 2019 Revised Draft. Part I: Beyond Transnational Conduct and Corporations by Means of Non-Reductionist Approaches*; N. Carrillo Santarelli, *A Step in the Right Direction: Corporate Responsibility Under the 2019 Revised Draft. Part II: The Recognition of Corporate Violations And its Implications*; C. Lopez, *Legal Liability for Business Human Rights Abuses Under the Revised Draft of a Treaty on Business and Human Rights*; D. Cassel, *Ecuador's Revised Draft Treaty: Getting Down to Business*; J. Letnar Černič, *The 2019 Draft of the Business and Human Rights Treaty: Nothing Left to Improve?*

The revised draft falls short of expectations for the options set forth by Krajewski, above all if compared with the former "Zero draft". Under the heading of "*Consistency with International Law*", the current version includes a compatibility clause of the following kind:

> "States Parties agree that any bilateral or multilateral agreements, including regional or sub-regional agreements, on issues relevant to this (Legally Binding Instrument) and its protocols, shall be compatible and shall be interpreted in accordance with their obligations under this (Legally Binding Instrument) and its protocols".[293]

On the contrary, the relevant part of the "Zero draft" included both a supremacy clause, which attached prevalence to the provisions of the *Legally Binding Instrument vis-à-vis* obligations stemming from future trade and investment agreements, and a requirement to incorporate human rights obligations in future trade and investment agreements.[294]

Moreover, with respect to the interpretation of other treaty provisions under the *Legally Binding Instrument*, the revised version is more generic than the Zero draft. The latter established the State parties' duty to interpret investments agreements in conformity with their obligations under the Legally Binding Instrument, notwithstanding dispute settlement proceedings established under the rules of trade and investment agreements.[295]

As a first comment on the revised draft, the watering down of the provision concerning the relations between human rights and investment and trade agreements is open to criticism. While the Zero draft puts forward a number of options to provide for preeminence of human rights treaty obligations over trade and investment treaty obligations, the current version merely seeks compatibility between the provisions enshrined in the *Legally Binding Instrument* and those of any other agreements.

Both the supremacy clause and the interpretative clause enshrined in the "Zero Draft" had a limited scope in that they provided conflict solutions only in respect of the obligations ensuing from the same *Legally Binding Instrument* and trade and investment treaties. However, they addressed the foremost source of concern in the field in a more accurate way.

---

[293] Revised Draft, art. 12(6) (n 260).

[294] Zero Draft, art. 13(6) (n 260). It provided: "*States Parties agree that any future trade and investment agreements they negotiate, whether amongst themselves or with third parties, shall not contain any provisions that conflict with the implementation of this Convention and shall ensure upholding human rights in the context of business activities by parties benefiting from such agreements*".

[295] *Ibid.*, art. 11(7) (n 260): "*States Parties agree that all existing and future trade and investment agreements shall be interpreted in a way that is least restrictive on their ability to respect and ensure their obligations under this Convention, notwithstanding other conflicting rules of conflict resolution arising from customary international law or from existing trade and investment agreements*".

In addition, as Krajewski points out, the provision under discussion, both in its current and former version, provides conflict solution clauses only for normative conflicts touching on the human rights obligations ensuing from the Legally Binding Instrument, while it does not endeavor to deal with conflicts arising from trade and investment treaties, on the one hand, and any other human rights treaty, on the other hand.

5.2. Harmonization by means of interpretation of relevant BITs provisions

This section considers systemic integration of international law as a principle to solve normative conflicts between investment treaty provisions and human rights law, by looking at the work of the International Law Commission on fragmentation of international law[296] as well as at the writings of authoritative scholars.[297]

Before considering the possibility of resorting to the systemic interpretation of investment treaty provisions in the light of human rights law, a number of preliminary issues must be addressed.

The first question is whether arbitral tribunals adjudging investment disputes are allowed to apply customary international law and rules belonging to other subsystems, such as human rights law. I would argue they do have this competence. According to the above-mentioned ILC Report on fragmentation, the fact that the "*jurisdiction of most international tribunals is limited to particular types of disputes arising under particular treaties*" does not imply a limitation of the scope of the law applicable in the interpretation and application of such treaties.[298] BITs limit arbitral tribunals' jurisdiction over claims that arise under investments treaties, but they usually do not limit the applicable law[299] to investment law alone. Neither the ICSID Convention, nor the UNCITRAL Arbitration Rules, require investment tribu-

---

[296] ILC Report (n 22).

[297] Among others: C. McLachlan, *The Principle of Systemic Integration and Article 31(3) of the Vienna Convention*, in *International & Comparative Law Quarterly*, 2005, pp. 279-320; Reiner, Schreuer, pp. 88-94 (n 26); Simma, Kill, pp. 678-707 (n 26); J. E., Viñuales, *Access to Water in Foreign Investment Disputes*, in *Georgetown International Environmental Law Review*, 2009, pp. 752-757; Simma, pp. 573-596 (n 259); A. Rachovitsa, *The Principle of Systemic Integration in Human Rights Law*, in *International & Comparative Law Quarterly*, 2017, pp. 557-588; G. Bücheler, *Proportionality in Investor-State Arbitration*, Oxford, 2015; D. Kalderimis, *Systemic Integration and International Investment Law – Some Practical Reflections*, Siel Working Paper No. 2012/46, 2012; O. Dörr, *Interpretation of Treaties*, in O. Dörr, K. Schmalenbach (eds.), *Vienna Convention on the Law of Treaties. A Commentary*, Berlin, 2018, pp. 603-613.

[298] ILC Report, para. 45 (n 22).

[299] *Mutatis mutandis*, the applicable law indicates the law governing "*the interpretation and the validity of the contract, the right and the obligation of the parties, the mode of performance, and the consequences of breaches of the contract*". See A. Redfern, J. M. Hunter, N. Blackaby, C. Partasides, *Redfern and Hunter on International Arbitration*, Oxford, 2009, para. 3.90.

nals to apply investment law exclusively.[300] The law applicable to international investment disputes may be chosen by the parties. This choice usually includes the national law of the parties to an investment agreement and public international law.[301] Given that the latter includes human rights law, nothing seems to prevent an investment tribunal from considering human rights in an investment dispute. The same conclusion was reached by the arbitral tribunal in the *SAUR* case.

The second issue refers to the three cumulative conditions set forth by Article 34(3)(*c*) VCLT for resorting to systemic interpretation.[302] According this Article, in interpreting treaty provisions, there shall be taken into account "*any relevant rules of international law applicable in the relations between the parties*". Thus, for the human right to water to be applied in investment disputes, it must be determined that it is an international (customary or a treaty) rule, "*relevant*" to resolve the dispute, and "*applicable in the relations between the parties*".

As regards the application of the human right to water in investment disputes, a problem was raised by some authors in relation to the asserted uncertain *status* of such a right in international law.[303] In the second chapter, I contend that the *status*

---

[300] Art. 42(1) of the ICSID Convention rules that: "*[t]he Tribunal shall decide a dispute in accordance with such rules of law as may be agreed by the parties. In the absence of such agreement, the Tribunal shall apply the law of the contracting State party to the dispute (including its rules on the conflict of laws) and such rules of international law as may be applicable*". In the case *Phonix Action v. Czech Republic*, the tribunal states that "*the ICSID Convention's jurisdictional requirement cannot be read in isolation from public international law, and its general principle*", *Phoenix Action v. Czech Republic*, ICSID Case No. ARB/06/5, Award, 15 April 2009, para. 78. Likewise, art. 35(1) of the UNCITRAL Arbitration Rules establishes that: "the *Tribunal shall apply the rules of law designated by the parties as applicable to the substance of the dispute. Failing such designation by the parties, the arbitral tribunal shall apply the law which it determines to be appropriate*". See UNCITRAL Arbitration Rules as revised in 2010 (n 10).

[301] Redfern and others, paras. 8.48-8.49 (n 300).

[302] Balcerzak, pp.156-159 (n 27); H. Ascensio, *Article 31 of the Vienna Convention on the Law of Treaties and International Investment Law*, in *ICSID Review*, 2016, pp. 366-387; V. S. Tzevelekos, *The Use of Article 31(3)(c) of the VCLT in the Case Law of the ECtHR: An Effective Anti-fragmentation Tool or a Selective Loophole for the Reinforcement of Human Rights Teleology?*, in *Michigan Journal of International law*, 2010; E. de Wet, J. Vidmar, *Conflicts between International Paradigms: Hierarchy versus Systemic Integration*, in *Global Constitutionalism*, 2013; J. Udich, *Human Rights and Interpretation: Limits and Demands of Harmonizing Interpretation of International Law*, in N. Weiß, J.-M. Thouvenin (eds.), *The Influence of Human Rights on International Law*, Cham, 2015; van Aaken, paras. 37-43 (n 273).

[303] Thielbörger referred to the "*double dilemma*" of the right to water in international investment law: the first problem is its uncertain *status* in international law, the second is whether arbitrators would regard human rights as applicable in international arbitration. P. Thielbörger, *The Human Right to Water versus Investors Rights: Double Dilemma or Pseudo-conflict?*, in P.-M. Dupuy, F. Francioni, E.-U. Petersmann (eds.), *Human Rights in International Investment Law and Arbitration*, Oxford, 2009, pp. 487-510. However, in the most recent publications, the author acknowledges the customary status of the right to water. See P. Thielbörger, *Re-Conceptualizing the Human Right to Water: A Pledge for a Hybrid Approach*, in *Human Rights Law Review*, 2015.

of the right to water in international law is no longer uncertain. In the first place, it is a derivative right, embedded in other human rights treaty provisions, such as the right to life, the right to an adequate standard of living and the right to health. All these rights are established, *inter alia*, by the two 1966 International Covenants binding on a large number of States: for these States, the right to water entails binding obligations. Moreover, I provide evidence that supports the customary *status* of the right to water. This is not prejudiced by the fact that its content has yet to be fully established. In this connection, it is noteworthy that the tribunal in *SAUR* considered the human right to water as a general principle of law to be included among the rules applicable to the case.[304] However, given that for an external rule to assist in the interpretation of BIT provisions the content of this rule must be clear, for the time being, I suggest considering the sole derivative right to water for the purpose of systemic interpretation.

Second, the possibility for investment arbitral tribunals to apply rules belonging to other self-contained regimes, such as human rights law, is controversial because of the need for the external treaty norm to be *relevant* to international investment arbitrations. According to the preferable opinion, the term *relevant* is to be understood in a broad sense, so that a rule external to the subject matter of the treaty under interpretation would be pertinent when capable of providing *operational guidance* for the determination of the meaning of the treaty provision.[305] Thus, the right to water, as embedded in other human rights treaty provisions, would be *relevant* in an investment dispute to the extent that it assists in the determination of potential BIT breaches.

An example can be useful to clarify this issue. Investors often claim a breach of the FET clause due to the fact that their legitimate expectations were frustrated by the host State. As happened in several disputes related to the failed privatization and liberalization of water services in Argentina, investors have argued that the freezing of water tariffs frustrated their expectation to operate in financial equilibrium. On their part, States have argued that such a policy was needed to avoid the negative effects that an increase in water tariffs would have had on the affordability of water services, and ultimately, on the health of their population.[306] In such cases, the right to water, embedded, in Articles 11(1) and 12(1) ICESCR, respectively concerning the right to an adequate standard of living and the right to the highest attainable standard of health, may provide "*operational guidance*". It would contribute to determining whether the investors' expectations should have also includ-

---

[304] *SAUR International S.A. v. Republic of Argentina*, Decision on Jurisdiction and Liability (n 134), para. 330.

[305] Simma, Kill, pp. 695-696 (n 26).

[306] See, for instance *Urbaser S.A. and others v. The Argentine Republic*, Award (n 30), para. 622.

ed the awareness that in exceptional circumstance States have to adopt measures necessary to prevent water tariff increases that would render the service unaffordable and led to outbreaks of illness and disease, as under human rights treaty law they must guarantee the right to water of their population. From this point of view, the right to water appears to be *relevant* in order to inform the way the FET clause is interpreted.

Finally, the external human rights rule must also be *applicable* in the relations between the parties to both the BIT and the human rights treaty under consideration. Therefore, for the right to water to be *applicable*, it would be necessary to establish that all parties to the BIT under dispute are also parties to the human rights treaties under consideration.[307] Given the widespread participation in the human rights treaties encompassing the right to water,[308] it is likely that a precise coincidence in the identity of the parties to the two treaties would occur.

If the applicability of the derivative right to water in investment disputes is admitted, this right would inform the interpretation of a number of notions relevant in investment disputes. The right to water requires States to protect access to water from third party interference, including by private suppliers. State are required to regulate and control water services effectively in order to protect water availability, affordability and quality from any abuse. It has been held that such a duty can shape the interpretation of notions such as creeping or indirect expropriation, public purpose, non-discrimination, just compensation in lawful regulatory takings, by attaching importance to the host State's police powers to regulate for social objectives.[309]

In short, the right to water could influence the way arbitrators interpret investment treaty provisions when adjudging disputes related to water services, as was contended by the *amici curiae* in the *Suez* case[310] and as occurred in the *Urbaser* case.

---

[307] McLachlan, p. 314 (n 298).

[308] Notably, States parties to the ICCPR and to the ICESCR are, respectively, 173 and 170. Data available at (last accessed on December 2019): https://treaties.un.org/Pages/ViewDetails.aspx?src=TREATY&mtdsg_no=IV-4&chapter=4&clang=_en and https://treaties.un.org/Pages/ViewDetails.aspx?src=TREATY&mtdsg_no=IV-3&chapter=4&clang=_en.

[309] B. Simma, p. 589 (n 259).

[310] *Suez, Sociedad General de Aguas de Barcelona, S.A. and Vivendi Universal, S.A. v. Republic of Argentina*, Amicus Curiae Submission (n 146). In brief, *amici* contended that the measures adopted by Argentina in the context of the severe economic crisis, in particular the freezing of the water tariffs, were in compliance with human rights law and that human rights law should have been considered relevant and applicable in the case for several reasons. First, they submitted, such law is applicable to the dispute since the tribunal has to apply not only the BIT provisions and the laws of the contracting parties, but also the rules of international law relevant to the dispute. International law includes human rights and the human right to water, which requires the State to take measures in order to ensure access to drinking water. Recalling the principle of systemic interpretation enshrined in art. 31(3)(*c*) VCLT, the petitioners held that human rights law is rele-

However, from the above premises on the *status* of the human right to water as a treaty rule and on the conditions set forth by Article 31(3)(*c*) VCLT, I am compelled to conclude that when BIT and international human rights treaty memberships do not overlap, the human right to water may not be invoked in order to influence BITs interpretation.

In relation to this conclusion, one consideration deserves attention. Simma and Kill posit that "*rules relating to a State's obligations to meet the basic material needs of its own citizens can indeed also become a matter of community concern*".[311] As a consequence, according to the authors, such rules might be considered applicable in the relations of all States, even though there is no treaty obligation between the States in question, and even if such rules are not formally owed *erga* omnes.[312] It seems that behind this argument there is an attempt to claim a sort of primacy of core human rights norms over investment rules. As is well known, this issue is controversial.

In this connection, it must be acknowledged that while investors' rights and human rights usually operate on different levels, in exceptional circumstances they may give rise to genuinely conflicting obligations that cannot be resolved by way of interpretation, but only by attaching priority to one or the other. This argument will be developed in the next sub-section.

5.3. Establishing systemic relationships of priority

A conflict of norms among competing international legal regimes may be irreconcilable by means of systemic interpretation, which cannot go so far as to modify treaty provisions or to displace the normative environment of the rule being interpreted.[313] This section acknowledges that establishing the meaning of investment treaty

---

vant to interpreting BIT standards, such as the FET clause and the provision about expropriation. As regards the FET standard, *amici* contended, *inter alia*, that the tribunal has to take into account the purpose of the measures undertaken by Argentina, that is to avoid an excessive increase in water and sanitation tariffs during a severe economic crisis. Analyzing the measures adopted by Argentina through the lens of human rights, they did not amount to an indirect expropriation, as they were taken in the legitimate exercise of the State's regulatory powers and in accordance with the police powers doctrine.

[311] Simma, Kill, p. 701 (n 26).

[312] *Ibid.*, pp. 701-702 (n. 26). The authors maintain that severe breaches of economic and social rights have become a matter of community interest and that economic, social and cultural rights "*have taken the first steps away from bilateralism*". Thus, such rights could be applied in the relations among States despite the fact that there is no corresponding treaty obligation between them.

[313] J. d'Aspremont, *The Systemic Integration of International Law by Domestic Courts: Domestic Judges as Architects of the Consistency of the International Legal Order*, in A. Nollkaemper, O. K. Fauchald (eds.), *The Practice of International and National Courts and the (De-)Fragmentation of International Law*, Oxford-Portland, 2012, p. 149.

norms by reference to external sources, such as human rights law, is not always a viable solution. It aims to consider whether, in case of a genuine conflict between obligations stemming from investment law and human rights law, the latter ought to prevail.

It has been claimed that human rights obligations enjoy priority over other obligations stemming from conditional and synallagmatic rights and duties. The High Commissioner for Human rights has defined investors' rights as merely instrumental "*to meet certain economic and developmental objectives*", whereas human rights law is "*fundamental to a life of human dignity*".[314] The *amici curiae* in the *Suez* case claimed that were the tribunal to deem it impossible to reconcile the conflicting obligations arising from human rights law and investment law through systemic interpretation, human rights law should prevail.[315]

Some scholars contend that priority can be claimed only for Article 103 of the UN Charter and norms of an imperative nature.[316] Given that the peremptory nature of the right to water is excluded, this right cannot be considered hierarchically superior to other international norms, including investment rules.

Other authors argue that a "*normative superiority*" may also be claimed for human rights norms *not* belonging to the category of *jus cogens*, as they incorporate substantial values of the international community that should enjoy precedence over merely instrumental norms, such as bilateral investment treaty rules.[317] This prevalence would be different from that of imperative rules, as the conflicting norms would not be invalid, but only set aside. The disapplication of the conflicting norms would not be an automatic result of their incompatibility with human rights rules, but rather the result of an assessment of proportionality between the human rights affected and the other interests involved.[318]

As this line of reasoning has been partially shared by human rights treaty bodies,[319] I have attempted to evaluate whether the same theory of the prioritization of human rights obligations over other bilateral or "bilateralizable" obligations has been followed by investment arbitral tribunals faced with conflicts between the right to water and investment treaty rules.

---

[314] Commission on Human Rights, *Human rights, trade and investment*, para. 24 (n 5).

[315] *Suez, Sociedad General de Aguas de Barcelona, S.A. and Vivendi Universal, S.A. v. Argentine Republic*, *Amicus Curiae* Submission (n 146), p. 26. *Amici* contended: "*[h]uman rights law could displace investment law in a conflict of norms situation, i.e., where the host State is unable to comply simultaneously with its obligations under human rights law and investment law*".

[316] Hafner, p. 861 (n 269).

[317] Tzevelekos, pp. 641-643 (n 303).

[318] *Ibid.*, pp. 643-644.

[319] ECtHR, *Ireland v. United Kingdom*, 18 January 1978, § 239; ECtHR, *Al-Saadoon v. The United Kingdom*, 2 March 2010, para. 140; Inter-American Court of Human Rights, *Sawhoyamaxa Indigenous Community v. Paraguay*, 29 March 2006, para. 140.

The decisions and awards analyzed above have shown that the investment tribunals have expressed rather inconsistent views in this regard. In the *Suez* case, the tribunal assumed the compatibility between obligations stemming from investment law and human rights law and requested the fulfillment of both legal obligations simultaneously. It affirmed:

> "Argentina and the amicus curiae submissions received by the Tribunal suggest that Argentina's human rights obligations to assure its population the right to water somehow trumps its obligations under the BITs and that the existence of the human right to water also implicitly gives Argentina the authority to take actions in disregard of its BIT obligations. The Tribunal does not find a basis for such a conclusion either in the BITs or international law. Argentina is subject to both international obligations, i.e. human rights and treaty obligation, and must respect both of them equally. Under the circumstances of these cases, Argentina's human rights obligations and its investment treaty obligations are not inconsistent, contradictory, or mutually exclusive. Thus, as discussed above, Argentina could have respected both types of obligations".[320]

This conclusion is based on a fragile assumption: the normative compatibility between rules belonging to different special systems adopted without any coordination. The tribunal preferred to avoid the recognition of a normative conflict and took a stand against the argument suggested by the petitioners in the *amici* brief. Rejecting the preeminence of human rights over investors' rights, it ruled that Argentina should have respected both human rights and investment treaty obligations, which in the case at hand were not mutually exclusive.[321]

In the *SAUR* decision, the compatibility of said different obligations was contended on account of the possibility to counterbalance human rights law and investment law by awarding compensation to investors. To the extent that a BIT requires it, a legitimate expropriation must be compensated so that, on the one hand, the State may exercise its regulatory power, and, on the one hand, the investor does not suffer excessive harm from the expropriation of its investment. This line of reasoning shows a more balanced approach, although it cannot be overlooked that the possibility of owing compensation risks preventing States from adopting measures in the public interest.

Finally, in the *Urbaser* award, without expressly quoting the argument followed in the *Suez* decision, the tribunal took a clear stand against the assumption that the two sets of obligations, those deriving from human rights law and those ensuing from investment law, are by definition compatible and must be complied with simultaneously.[322]

---

[320] *Suez, Sociedad General de Aguas de Barcelona, S.A. and Vivendi Universal, S.A. v. Argentine Republic*, Decision on Liability (n. 138), para. 262.

[321] *Ibid.*, para. 262.

[322] *Ibid.*, para. 720

It stated that:

> "Claimants accept that Argentina had two kinds of obligations. There are its obligations regarding the population's right to water, and its obligations towards international investors. The Argentine Republic can and should fulfil both kinds of obligations simultaneously. In so doing, the obligations resulting from the human right to water do not operate as an obstacle to the fulfilment of its obligations towards the Claimants. Nonetheless, Claimants' argument is too short. It does not resolve the conflict between the obligation to guarantee the Concessionaire's right under the concession and the access of the poor and vulnerable population to water when this cannot be ensured otherwise than by failing to comply with the host state's obligations towards the Concessionaire".[323]

Given that the possibility exists for a State to be confronted with irreconcilable obligations, the tribunal resolved the issue of the conflict between the investors' rights and the right of the population to water by giving priority to the latter. By framing the State's human rights obligations within the legal framework of the concessions that had shaped the investors' expectations, the tribunal admitted that precedence should be given to human rights. It contended that, even without entering into the complex issue of the investors' duty to respect the right to water:

> "[i]t is entirely sufficient to note that AGBA and its Concessionaire must have been aware that they were indirectly bound by the fundamental right to water of the population of Region B due to the provision ordering ORAB to take account in its decisions of the 'protection of the community's interests'(Sec. 13-II of Law No. 11820), including the 'protection of the users' interests', which are a concern based on Section 4.3 of the Concession Contract and in light of Article 42 of the Constitution".[324]

and that:

> "the Government of Argentina and the Executive of the Province were under an obligation, based on Constitutional Law as well as on elementary policy of protecting the population's health, to preserve their access to drinking water".[325]

The claimants should have expected that the government was bound by the "elementary" duty to preserve its population's access to drinking water, a duty that deserves priority over investors' interests.

However, although the tribunal did not cast into doubt the existence of the international human right to water, it grounded the investors' expectations on the

---

[323] *Ibid.*, para. 720

[324] *Ibid.*, para. 721.

[325] *Ibid.*, para. 723.

concession contract, on Argentine constitutional law, and, vaguely, on the fundamental policy goal of protecting the population's health, rather than on this right.

In this way, the tribunal did not put the problem in terms of priority to be attached to human rights obligations stemming from international rules over obligations owed towards investors in force of international investment provisions, but rather remained at the level of interpretation so as to attach priority to human rights considerations. While the result would probably have been the same in terms of effective human right protection, a clearer stand would have added theoretical precision to this area.

This case law shows that the hypothesis of the present analysis – notably whether treaty bodies belonging to branches of international law other than human rights assign priority to human rights obligations *vis-à-vis* bilateral or "bilateralizable" obligations – has not been confirmed. While a trend has emerged, under which growing importance is attached to human right considerations in the context on international investment disputes,[326] there is neither a consistent practice nor a well-settled theoretical underpinning supporting the primacy of human rights law over other branches of international law.

6. The attempts to ground corporate human rights obligations

BITs may give rise to gross disparities between the rights guaranteed to investors and the obligations they bear.[327] It has been held that no IIAs "*set out any obligations on the part of investors in return for the protection rights they are granted*".[328] Therefore, "*[n]egotiators could consider including obligations for investors to comply with national laws of the host country*".[329] The High Commissioner for Human Rights insisted on the necessity of "*[b]alancing investors' rights with investors' obligations*" towards individual and communities within investment agreements. Com-

---

[326] See Feria-Tinta (n 162); G. Zarra (n 172). Both commenting *Philip Morris Brands Sàrl, Philip Morris Products S.A. and Abal Hermanos S.A. v. Oriental Republic of Uruguay*, ICSID Case No. ARB/10/7, Award, 8 July 2016.

[327] In general terms, the issue is that multinational corporations do not bear international human rights obligations. See, *inter alia*: Marrella, pp. 227-253 (n 292); E. De Brabandere, *Non-State Actors and Human Rights: Corporate Responsibility and the Attempts to Formalize the Role of Corporations as Participants in the International Legal System*, in J. d'Aspremont (ed.), *Participants in the International Legal System. Multiple Perspectives on Non-State Actors in International Law*, Abingdon, 2011, pp. 268-283; Human Rights Committee, General Comment No. 31, *Nature of the General Legal Obligation Imposed on States Parties to the Covenant*, UN Doc. CCPR/C/21/Rev.1/Add.13, 26 May 2004, which excludes international corporate human rights obligations.

[328] UNCTAD, *Towards a New Generation of Investment Policies*, in *Investment Policy Framework for Sustainable Development*, p. 7 (n 7).

[329] *Ibid.*

plementary measures are required to protect human rights in the context of investment liberalization. In this connection, investment agreements should *"promote corporate social responsibility – both on a voluntary basis and through the recognition of investors' direct accountability for their actions with regard to human rights"*.[330]

So far, corporate human rights obligations have been promoted only by non-binding instruments, as a standard of conduct.[331] The so-called II pillar of the well-known *Guiding Principles on Business and Human Rights* calls upon business enterprises to avoid infringing human rights and to address the adverse impact of human rights abuses that they cause or to which they contribute.[332] In order to do so, business enterprises are requested to put in place due diligence measures to prevent and mitigate human rights abuses, together with processes enabling remediation.

The revised draft of the *Legally Binding Instrument*, previously discussed, requires States parties to ensure that business enterprises within their jurisdiction undertake due diligence in order to evaluate and possibly prevent negative impact of their business activities on human rights.[333] However, the Revised Draft follows the traditional approach by imposing on States the obligations to require due diligence commitments by corporations. On the contrary, it does not establish direct human rights obligations on business enterprises and transnational corporations; a choice that reflects the current uncertainty on the matter[334] and that has received some criticism.[335]

---

[330] Commission on Human Rights, *Human rights, trade and investment*, p. 4 (n 5). See G. Aguilar Cavallo, *The Human Right to Water and Sanitation: Going Beyond Corporate Social Responsibility*, in *Utrecht Journal of International and European Law*, 2013.

[331] Only guiding principles address the human rights obligations of multinational corporations and other business enterprises. See Human Rights Council, *Guiding Principles on Business and Human Rights* (n 290); OECD, *OECD Guidelines for Multinational Enterprises*, 2011; Human Rights Council, *Protect, Respect and Remedy: a Framework for Business and Human Rights. Report of the Special Representative of the Secretary-General on the issue of human rights and transnational corporations and other business enterprises*, John Ruggie, UN Doc. A/HRC/8/5, 7 April 2008; *Human Rights and Transnational Corporations and other Business Enterprises*, UN Doc. A/HRC/RES/17/4, 6 July 2011. See P. M. Protopsaltis, *La mise en œuvre des Principes directeurs de l'OCDE à l'intention des entreprises multinationales: Réflexions sur le nouveau mandat des Points de contact nationaux*, in L. Liberti (ed.), *La Responsabilité des Entreprises en Droit International: Chimère ou Réalité*, in *International Law Forum du Droit International*, 2005, pp. 261-272.

[332] Human Rights Council, *Guiding Principles on Business and Human Rights* (n 290), paras. 11-24. Under the first and the third pillars States are requested respectively to: fulfill their traditional duty to protect, namely, to prevent and redress human rights abuse within their territories/jurisdiction committed by business enterprises (paras. 1-10); and to ensure that those affected by business-related human rights abuse have access to effective remedies (paras. 25-31). See chapter II, section 4.2.

[333] Revised Draft, art. 5 (n 258). Zero Draft, art. 9 (n 258); Annexed Protocol (n 258).

[334] A. Peters, *Beyond Human Rights. The Legal Status of the Individual in International Law*, Cambridge, 2016, pp. 92-110; J. E. Alvarez, *Are Corporations 'Subjects' of International Law?*, in *Santa Clara Journal of International Law*, 2011; De Brabandere, pp. 268-283 (n 328).

[335] Letnar Černič (n 293).

In this context, the award in the *Urbaser* case warrants attention.[336] While it might be argued that the counterclaim in the *Urbaser* case has opened the door to human rights counterclaims in the context of international investment disputes, the tribunal paid attention to linking possible positive human rights obligations of investors to the existence of these obligations at the international and national level.

In detail, the core issue addressed by the tribunal was whether private companies bear any human rights obligations. The tribunal did not deny such a possibility but restricted its scope. Given that investors are entitled to invoke rights granted under the BIT (not only the procedural right to seek redress for impairment of its investment, but also the rights deriving from the most favorable treatment clause), they must be equally subject to duties stemming from international law.[337]

As far as human rights are concerned, the tribunal posited that private parties have an obligation to abstain from engaging in activities capable of impairing their enjoyment.[338] The legal basis for a private party's obligation to abstain from infringing human rights is found by the tribunal in Article 30 of the Universal Declaration of Human Rights ("UDHR"), in Article 5(1) ICESCR and in the ILO Tripartite Declaration of Principles concerning Multilateral Enterprises and Social Policy.[339]

Against this background, the tribunal wondered whether the investors bore obligations stemming from the human right to water. It concluded that, while private parties must abstain from interfering in the enjoyment of the right to water, there is no corresponding positive duty to provide the host State's population with drinking water, as the human right to water creates positive obligations only for States.[340]

According to the tribunal, a private company may be bound to perform activities to comply with the human right to water solely in two circumstances; first, if these obligations are established under the BIT, are part of another treaty or are a general principle of international law;[341] second, if the legal and regulatory environment of the host State so prescribes.[342] The foreign investor should be made aware that it is operating within a State where private companies bear some obligations related to the human right to water, which are requested under the host State's laws or the concession contract, or under the BIT concluded between its home State and the host State. Other than in these two cases, only an obligation to abstain from committing acts that violate human rights would be of immediate application upon private parties.[343]

---

336 Crow, Lorenzoni Escobar (n 31); Guntrip (n 31); Krajewski (n 31).

337 *Urbaser S.A. and others v. The Argentine Republic*, Award (n 30), para. 1194.

338 *Ibid.*, paras. 1199, 1210.

339 *Ibid.*, paras. 1196-1198.

340 *Ibid.*, para. 1208.

341 *Ibid.*, para. 1207.

342 *Ibid.*, paras. 1209, 1212.

343 *Ibid.*, para. 1210.

Applying these premises, the tribunal dismissed the counterclaim, finding, on the one hand, that the human right to water imposes positive obligations only upon States[344] and, on the other hand, that the regulatory environment did not clearly establish duties upon the claimant companies in respect to the right to water, especially considering that it was the Republic that had failed to prevent human rights infringements caused by third parties in the first place.[345] In addition, the tribunal posited that under international law individuals lack both entitlement to claim the supply of water service against private companies and to receive compensation from private companies for their non-performance of obligations related to the right to water.[346]

The tribunal's ruling marks an important step in the reflection on the subjectivity and responsibilities of transnational companies, by confirming the first and positing the existence of corporate human rights obligations. Regarding this ruling, it is my contention that, while the legal basis for the negative corporate duty to abstain from interfering with the enjoyment of human rights might be considered fragile – as they are found in soft law instruments and in a provision on the interpretation of the ICESCR (notably Article 5.1 ICESCR) –,[347] the tribunal's holding that the legal basis for positive corporate human rights obligations might be found in international law sources might be promising.

In this connection, recent trends cannot be overlooked. The ECOWAS Supplementary Act on Investment[348] and the Morocco-Nigeria BIT[349] are examples in point. The former dedicates an entire chapter to the investors' obligations, including the duty to "*uphold human rights in the workplace and the community in which they are located*", and to refrain from undertaking "*acts that breach such human rights*" or operating "*their investment in a manner that circumvents human rights obligations*" to which the host and/or the home State are parties.[350] In similar terms, the Morocco Nigeria BIT requires investors and investments to "*uphold human rights in the host state*".[351]

Following the line of reasoning of the *Urbaser* tribunal, one might be ready to advance the conclusion that should corporate human rights obligations be estab-

---

[344] *Ibid.*, para. 1210.

[345] *Ibid.*, para. 1219.

[346] *Ibid.*, para. 1220.

[347] Guntrip, p. 3 (n 31).

[348] ECOWAS, Supplementary Act A/SA.3/12/08 Adopting Community Rules on Investment and the Modalities for their Implementation with ECOWAS (n 288).

[349] Reciprocal Investment Promotion and Protection Agreement between the Government of the Kingdom of Morocco and the Government of the Federal Republic of Nigeria (n 289).

[350] ECOWAS, Supplementary Act A/SA.3/12/08 Adopting Community Rules on Investment and the Modalities for their Implementation with ECOWAS (n 288), art. 14(2).

[351] Reciprocal Investment Promotion and Protection Agreement between the Government of the Kingdom of Morocco and the Government of the Federal Republic of Nigeria (n 289), p. 2.

lished in investment treaties, investors would be called to respond for possible abuses committed in connection with their activities in the host States.

7. Conclusion

In the 1990s, attempts to privatize water services generated substantial public opposition, in part because privatization has generally been accompanied by tariff increases and more efficient collection of water bills. Against a background of below cost and subsidized services, users have not welcomed the move towards full-cost pricing of water. In all of the cases analyzed in this chapter, public authorities have ultimately reversed their initial decision to privatize the municipal water supply. However, consent to increase tariffs was usually accompanied by the request that concessionaires undertake plans of investment aimed at expanding and improving water services infrastructure and, thus, the standard and quality of water services.

The case law discussed has shown that both the respondent States and international investment tribunals have paid increasing attention to the human right to water. While it was only implicitly referred to in the earlier proceedings, *Azurix*, *Vivendi* and *Biwater*, it has been explicitly invoked in the more recent cases, *Suez*, *SAUR* and *Urbaser*. This growing interest goes hand in hand with a stricter reading of BIT rules. However, in both sets of cases, decisions on compensation have not always mirrored those on liability. The *Urbaser* case alone runs against this overall trend, offering greater coherence between the findings on liability and the decision on compensation.

The cases analyzed in this chapter have provided a unique field to evaluate theoretical underpinnings *vis-à-vis* concrete experiences. In my view, one shortcoming in the line of reasoning followed by some arbitral tribunals consists in not having duly considered the emergency experienced by Argentina. If a Government adopts emergency measures aimed at safeguarding the human rights of the population within its territory or jurisdiction, which consequently trump investors' rights, it is my contention that a reasonable solution could be suggested.

On the one hand, the conduct of the State should be justified to some extent. In the end, the State has violated bilateral investment rules in order to respect a human rights norm.

This conclusion does not imply a hierarchy between human rights norms and investment treaties, but only that in an emergency situation, the State is justified if it grants priority to human rights obligations and postpones compliance with other obligations to the *post*-emergency stage. In this connection, the conclusion of the tribunal in the *Suez* case, notably that a State should comply with both set of obligations at once, may simply be out of the range of possibilities that a State is confronted with in an emergency situation. To be sure, once the state of emergency has ended, the international obligations of the State towards investors would resurface, as human rights cannot trump investors' rights, which is what the tribunal in *Urbaser* seems to suggest.

On the other hand, the view cannot be shared that when the taking of an investment is justified by the legitimate aim of pursuing public interests in a non-discriminatory manner, no expropriation takes place, as suggested in the *Suez* decision on liability. Investors cannot be required to be the prime bearers of the consequences of a State's economic crisis. The problem of balancing competing interests should be shifted to the *post*-emergency stage. Briefly, once the emergency has come to an end, the State should be required to provide adequate compensation to the investors.

However, *adequate compensation* cannot be equated to *full reparation*. It should be meant to replace the value of the property taken from the investors, not to repair all the damages suffered by the latter. It seems that requiring the host State to wipe out all the consequences of the measures taken to respect human rights obligations, as if the State has no justification for the action taken, would be out of all proportionality. In practical terms, the amount of compensation should be equal to the fair market value of the investment, while the payment of damages should be excluded.

To justify this conclusion, the sole legal reasoning this author can envisage is to frame emergency situations under the umbrella of the defence of necessity and, if the case may be, provide a human rights-oriented interpretation of the latter. If the wrongful act, notably the violation of the investors' rights, is justified by the need "*to safeguard an essential interest against a grave an imminent peril*", such as the deprivation of access to drinking water service for a large part of the population, the consequences cannot be equated to those of unjustified wrongful acts, even though compensation is still due.[352] In this connection, the decision of the tribunal in the *Urbaser* case can provide some guidance. Following the tribunal's line of reasoning, the absence of hierarchy among different branches of international law and the apparent incoherent request to comply at once with conflicting obligations arising from these branches would be brought back into coherence through the secondary rules on State responsibility.

In the light of the case law analyzed in sections 2-4, section 5 dealt with the issue of harmonisation of investor's rights and human rights, scrutinizing its possible legal basis. First, ways to prevent the rise of normative conflicts between the right to water and investment rules was considered. The suggested path is to require *ex-ante* human rights impact assessments and to insert into BITs clauses of compatibility and subordination, as well as human rights clauses.

Second, the issue of systemic integration of apparently conflicting norms in order to counterbalance opposite interests was addressed. As far as the human right

---

[352] See art. 27(*b*) of the Draft Articles on Responsibility of States for Internationally Wrongful Acts, 2001, according to which: "*The invocation of a circumstance precluding wrongfulness in accordance with this chapter is without prejudice to (…) b) the question of compensation for any material loss caused by the act in question*".

to water is concerned, it has been held that the possibility of systemic integration of the customary human right to water and investment law suffers from the currently uncertain content of this right in customary international law, beyond a very limited core. Nonetheless, I argued that given that the right to water is also embedded in other treaty rights – such as the right to life, to an adequate standard of living and to health – reference could be made to the latter for the purpose of harmonization. In line with Article 31(3)(*c*) VCLT, a derivative right to water ought to be considered in interpreting BIT provisions when all the parties to the BIT under dispute are also parties to the human rights treaty called into question. This situation is likely to occur, given the wide participation of States in the human rights treaties enshrining the right to water.

Finally, the case of a genuine normative conflict, which cannot be avoided or reconciled by means of systemic interpretation, was discussed. It was concluded that conflict rules do not allow the interpreter to grant human rights law, including the right to water, any definite hierarchical superiority over investment norms (except for *jus cogens* human rights). Neither has the so-called theory of the prioritization of human right obligations over obligations stemming from bilateral or "bilateralizable" international rules found a clear foundation and a theoretical underpinning in the practice of investment tribunals, despite being in part acknowledged by human rights treaty bodies. However, the precedence of human rights obligations has started to be predicated in the most recent award analyzed, that of *Urbaser*.

Chapter IV

THE LIBERALIZATION OF TRADE IN WATER SERVICES UNDER THE GATS AND THE HUMAN RIGHT TO WATER

SUMMARY: 1. Introduction. – 2. The applicability of the GATS to water services. – 2.1. An overview of the GATS. – 2.2. The lack of specific commitments in the water sector. – 3. The compatibility between the GATS and the State's regulatory autonomy in the water services sector. – 3.1. The general GATS provisions likely to raise concern from a human right perspective. – 3.1.1. Domestic regulations. – 3.1.2. Subsidies. – 3.1.3. Monopolies and exclusive service suppliers. – 3.2. The GATS provisions on specific commitments. – 3.2.1. Market access. – 3.2.2. National treatment. – 4. Harmonizing trade in services with the human right to water. – 4.1. Harmonization by means of conflict prevention. – 4.1.1. Scheduling commitments for water services. – 4.1.2. The subordination clause in favor of measures necessary to protect human life and health. – 4.2. Harmonization by means of interpretation of GATS provisions applicable to water services. – 4.2.1. The right to regulate in the public interest and the interpretation of the GATS provisions concerning market access and national treatment. – 4.2.1.1. The interpretation of the market access clause. – 4.2.1.2. The interpretation of the national treatment clause. – 4.2.2. The right to regulate in the public interest and the interpretation of the GATS provisions related to public services. – 4.2.2.1. The interpretation of the notion of services supplied in the exercise of governmental authority. – 4.2.2.2. The interpretation of the notion of government procurement for the supply of public services. – 4.2.3. *Interim* conclusion. – 4.3. Establishing systemic relationships of priority. – 5. Conclusion.

1. Introduction

For a long time, services were considered to be non-tradable, while nowadays most of them are traded across borders. [1] However, the desirability of developing trade in essential services, such as water services, whose management involves human rights and environmental considerations, is still disputed. Critics have focused primarily on the possible constraints that the liberalization of public sectors may place on the governments' ability to pursue public policy objectives and to protect consumers against abuses by private providers.

Water services, like other public services, have been reached by the wave of liberalization and privatization, but to a lesser extent. Indeed, most public authorities have chosen to maintain this sector in public hands. Considerations for the essential character of water resources, as well as for the unique features of water services, [2]

[1] For a detailed description of the volume of international trade in services by partner countries of the OECD, see: *OECD Statistics on International Trade in Services*, 14 March 2020, Paris.

[2] As mentioned in chapter I, the water service industry has monopolistic features that suggest

may have influenced this choice. As was seen in the previous chapter, poor countries, when confronted with large multinational companies,[3] may fear losing control over water resources and witnessing the increase of water tariffs to an unaffordable level. These fears have been fuelled by the fact that some foreign investments in water services have limited home States' regulatory autonomy and have resulted in international disputes submitted before investment tribunals.

With these considerations in mind, we turn to analyzing the situation in which investments in water services are made under the umbrella of a multilateral treaty, namely the General Agreement on Trade in Services ("GATS").[4]

The GATS is the first and, for the time being, the only multilateral agreement governing international trade in services. Negotiated during the Uruguay Round, the Agreement is included in Annex 1 B of the Agreement establishing the World Trade Organization ("WTO").[5] In part, the GATS is an investment agreement that regulates international trade in services according to different modes of supply.[6] One of these modes (mode 3) refers to the commercial presence of WTO States' foreign suppliers within the territory of other Member States in order to supply services.

International trade in water services mainly occurs by means of this mode. Foreign firms need to establish subsidiaries or to incorporate local companies within the territory of other WTO Member States where they plan to operate. Tuerk et al argue that *"[b]y covering 'mode 3' supply, the GATS effectively prescribes disciplines respecting how a country may regulate foreign companies operating inside its borders"*.[7]

Liberalization of water services in favor of foreign private firms may occur under

---

that maintaining strong regulatory powers may be opportune. Supplying water services presupposes building and maintaining expensive infrastructure such as, *inter alia*, aqueducts, mains and pipelines. Since large-scale investments have to be made for this infrastructure, any duplication is highly inefficient. Since one network is more economical than two or more, the scope for introducing competition is limited. For this reason, water services have generally been considered a "*natural monopoly*", which arises as a consequence of the high cost of their infrastructure, instead of being established by law.

[3] Among the largest multinational corporations providing water services there are: Veolia Environnement, Suez Environnement and United Utilities.

[4] General Agreement on Trade in Services, Marrakesh Agreement Establishing the World Trade Organization, Annex 1B, Legal Instrument – Results of the Uruguay Round vol. 31, 33 ILM 81 (1994), 15 April 1994.

[5] For the GATS history see, J. A. Marchetti, P. C. Mavroidis, *The Genesis of the GATS (General Agreement on Trade in Services)*, in *European Journal of International Law*, 2011; N. Munin, *Legal Guide to GATS*, Alphen aan den Rijn, 2010, pp. 14-17.

[6] A.R. Ziegler, *Water-Related Investment: A European Perspective*, in L. Boisson de Chazournes, N. Bernasconi-Osterwalder (eds.), *Fresh Water and International Economic Law*, Oxford, 2005, p. 250.

[7] A. Ostrovsky, R. Speed, E. Türk, *GATS, Water and the Environment – Implications of the General Agreement on Trade in Services for Water Resources*, CIEL, WWF, Geneva, 2003, p. 23.

the umbrella of the GATS. Unlike bilateral investment agreements, commitments to market liberalization assumed under the GATS are undertaken towards all WTO Member States. This broader liberalization entails valuable benefits as well as higher risks than those ensuing from bilateral investment agreements. Accordingly, opening the water sector to all WTO States has both the potential to bolster the right to water as well as to affect its realization. [8]

On the one hand, the GATS system may be a valuable *forum* for negotiation on where to promote foreign investments. Domestic private firms may lack the high expenditure capacity to meet the growing demands of low income households and to increase water quality standards. [9] On the contrary, large financial inflows are needed in the water sector [10] in order to expand existing water infrastructure and to guarantee wider territorial coverage. [11] Moreover, there has been a dramatic decline in the engagement of multinational companies in developing countries' water sectors. [12] The GATS, by providing guarantees to foreign investors, may encourage investments in the water sector.

On the other hand, a strong presumption against liberalization of water services under the GATS umbrella has been expressed by some. [13] In addition to the general

---

[8] C. Kirkpatrick, D. Parker, *Domestic Regulation and the WTO: The Case of Water Services in Developing Countries*, in *The World Economy*, 2005, pp. 1491-1508. In general terms, as for the potential of liberalization of social services under the GATS, see R. Chanda, *Social Services and the GATS: Key Issues and Concerns*, in *World Development*, 2003, pp. 1997-2011; R. Adlung, *Public Services and the GATS*, in *Journal of International Economic Law*, 2006, pp. 455-485; P. Kulkarni, *Impact of the GATS on Basic Social Services Redux*, in *Journal of World Trade*, 2009, pp. 245-284.

[9] On the contrary, some multinational companies have been shown to meet these goals. For instance, since Suez's takeover of water services in the City of Buenos Aires, the proportion of population with access to drinking water increased 41.37 per cent and the population with access to sewage services 32.12 per cent. *Suez, Sociedad General de Aguas de Barcelona, S.A. and Vivendi Universal, S.A. v. Argentine Republic*, ICSID Case No. ARB/03/19, Decision on Liability, 30 July 2010, para. 36.

[10] Private investments in the water sector in poor countries are extremely limited compared to those in other sectors. UNCTAD, *Promotion of investment into infrastructure. A survey of investment promotion agencies*, Geneva, 2008, available at: https://unctad.org/en/docs/webdiaeia20082_en.pdf.

[11] In the early 2000s, it was found that only 10 per cent of investments made in the water sector came from private funds and that a significant part were invested in three countries, namely Chile, China and Mexico. D. Morley, *The Right to Water – A Step in the Right Direction*, in E. H. Riedel, P. Rothen (eds.), *The Human Right to Water*, Berlin, 2006, p. 185.

[12] T. Slaymaker, P. Newborne, S. Grimm, D. W. te Velde, *Water and GATS: Lots of smoke but where exactly is the fire?*, in *ODI blog*, 2005, available at: https://www.odi.org/sites/odi.org.uk/files/odi-assets/publications-opinion-files/740.pdf.

[13] T. Concannon, H. Griffiths, *Stealing our water: Implications of GATS for Global Water Resources*, London, 2001, available at: https://www.ircwash.org/sites/default/files/Concannon-2001-Stealing.pdf; *Call to Cancún: Halt the GATS negotiations. Take essential services, such as water,*

criticism of the liberalization for this sector, the GATS raises special concerns. In short, it is feared that it could lead to an irreversible liberalization process likely to excessively restrict the State's power to regulate the water sector in the public interest.[14] The High Commissioner for Human Rights has highlighted that, to be compatible with human rights, liberalization agreements should ensure that States have the flexibility to withdraw liberalization commitments in the light of experiences.[15] Flexibility should be retained also to introduce new regulations and other regulatory measures. There is concern that regulations to protect water consumers or water quality would be regarded as trade restrictions, and thus prohibited under the Agreement. What is more, the Agreement provides for the periodic renegotiation of specific commitments with the aim of increasing the level of liberalization of service markets.[16]

These concerns have been contested by other authors on account of the flexibility of the Agreement, which some have defined *à la carte*,[17] as it provides numerous exceptions and safeguard clauses.[18] By referring to the wide decision-making autonomy left to public authorities, the WTO Secretariat denies that there is any sort of risk inherent in the liberalization of essential services within the GATS framework.[19]

Against this scenario, it remains to be seen whether concerns about water service liberalization at an international level under the GATS umbrella are merely ideological or, rather, if they have some legal grounds.

---

out of the WTO. Civil Society Submission to the World Trade Organisation's 5th Ministerial Conference in Cancun, 10-14 September 2003.

[14] E. Türk, A. Ostrovsky, R. Speed, *GATS and Its Impact on Private Sector Participation in Water Services*, in E. Brown Weiss, L. Boisson de Chazournes, N. Bernasconi-Osterwalder (eds.), *Fresh Water and International Economic Law*, Oxford, 2005, p. 149; A. Lang, *The GATS and Regulatory Autonomy: A Case Study of Social Regulation of the Water Industry*, in *Journal of International Economic Law*, 2004, p. 810.

[15] Commission on Human Rights, *Human Rights, Trade and Investment*, *Report of the High Commissioner for Human Rights*, UN Doc. E/CN.4/Sub.2/2003/9, 2 July 2003, p. 3.

[16] GATS, art. XIX.

[17] R. Mastroianni, A. Arena, *I Servizi pubblici nel GATS e nel TFUE: una radicale divergenza di impostazione?*, in *Diritto del Commercio Internazionale*, 2010, pp. 34-36. On the GATS flexibility see R. Adlung, *Services Negotiations in the Doha Round: Lost in Flexibility?*, in *Journal of International Economic Law*, 2006.

[18] F. Munari, *L'Applicazione del GATS ai Servizi di Interesse Generale*, in *Diritto del Commercio Internazionale*, 2004.

[19] The WTO Secretariat, being conscious of the great debate around the possible application of the GATS to essential public services, replied to the queries on liberalization of water services. Due to the flexible structure of the Agreement, it is said, the GATS "*does not require the privatization or deregulation of any service*" and would not affect the right of governments to set such levels of quality, safety, price or any other policy objectives as they deem appropriate. WTO Secretariat, *GATS – Fact and Fiction*, The World Trade Organization. Source: https://www.wto.org/english/tratop_e/serv_e/gatsfacts1004_e.pdf.

This chapter considers, from a human rights-oriented point of view, whether it may be deemed advisable to undertake commitments to the liberalization of water services under the GATS. In particular, it assesses whether and to what extent this Agreement may impair the fulfillment of the right to water by limiting States' regulatory autonomy and whether, in such a case, it would be possible to strike a balance between the opportunities offered by opening up the water service market and the risk of jeopardizing governmental regulatory powers.[20]

In order to evaluate the possible impact that the liberalization of trade in water services under the GATS may have on the State's power to pursue public policy objectives, such as the fulfillment of the human right to water, the chapter proceeds as follows. Section 2 provides an overview of the GATS rules relevant for the present study and considers the applicability of the Agreement to water services. Section 3 focuses on the constraints that are likely to limit the States' regulatory autonomy in the water sector. In this sense, the section will first address the GATS general provisions – such as domestic regulations, subsidies and monopolies – and then the GATS specific commitments concerning market access and national treatment. Section 4 applies the model of analysis set out in chapter one to test the potential for harmonizing rules on trade in services with the human right to water. In particular, the first sub-section considers ways to prevent normative conflicts by scheduling well-framed commitments allowing States to maintain their regulatory powers. Next, the second sub-section evaluates the scope of some relevant GATS exceptions, whose interpretation may accommodate the different interests at stake. Finally, the third sub-section attempts to address the issue of the prioritization of human rights in exceptional circumstances. Section 5 draws some conclusions on the possible impact that water services liberalization under the GATS umbrella may have on the right to water.

2. The applicability of the GATS to water services

The scope of the GATS *ratione materiae* is rather wide, covering "any service in any

---

[20] The High Commissioner for Human Rights expresses doubts on the opportunity of liberalizing essential services. He emphasized the importance of making accurate preliminary assessments on whether and through what means essential public services may be opened to the market in reference to the impact of the liberalization of trade in services on human rights. Commission on Human Rights, *Liberalization of Trade in Services and Human Rights, Report of the High Commissioner for Human Rights*, UN Doc. E/CN.4/Sub.2/2002/9, 25 June 2002, para. 44. See also G. Aguilar Cavallo, *The Human Right to Water and Sanitation: Going Beyond Corporate Social Responsibility*, in *Utrecht Journal of International and European Law*, 2013, p. 49. The author maintains that: "*liberalization should be carefully handled. The human right to water does not preclude water provision privatisation as far as minimum water standards vis-à-vis the whole population are guaranteed, as clarified by the CESCR*".

sector".[21] Therefore, in principle, water services may come under the purview of the Agreement. However, for the GATS to be applied to water services, Member States are required to undertake specific commitments to the liberalization of this sector.

The notion of water services may be broadly defined as: "*the supply of water for consumption and the treatment of wastewater*".[22] In more specific terms, water service may refer only to the supply of drinking water that includes the collection, purification, transportation through aqueducts or mains and delivery of water to users through pipelines and taps.[23] For the purpose of the present study, water services are understood according to the latter meaning.

2.1. An overview of the GATS

In order to assess the impact that the GATS may have on the enjoyment of the human right to water, this section provides a brief description of the treaty provisions relevant for the purpose of the present study.[24]

In a nutshell, the Agreement aims at progressively liberalizing and expanding trade in services.[25] The term liberalization in the field of trade is not defined by the

---

[21] GATS, art. I:3(*b*). According to art. XXVIII(*b*), the "*supply of a service" is understood as including "production, distribution, marketing, sale and delivery of a service*".

[22] WTO, Council for Trade in Services, *Background Note on Environmental Services, Note by the Secretariat*, S/C/W/320, 20 August 2010, p. 6.

[23] Treatment of wastewater includes: "*removal of sewage through pipes and drains and treatment with various techniques*" in order to release water into the environment. *Ibid.*

[24] For more information about the Agreement, see: WTO, *Guide to the GATS: An Overview of Issue for Further Liberalization*, The Hague, 2001; A. Mattoo, *Shaping Future GATS Rules for Trade in Services*, World Bank Policy Research Working Paper No. 2596, Washington, 2001, available at http://elibrary.worldbank.org/doi/pdf/10.1596/1813-9450-2596; OECD, *GATS: The Case for Open Services Markets*, Paris, 2002; P. Picone, A. Ligustro, *Diritto dell'Organizzazione Mondiale del Commercio*, Padova, 2002, pp. 360-395; WTO, *A Handbook of the GATS Agreement: a WTO Secretariat Publication*, Cambridge, 2005; P.-T. Stoll, F. Schorkopf, *WTO – World Economic Order, World Trade Law*, Leiden, 2006, pp. 181-205; Munin (n 5).

[25] See, GATS, Preamble, second recital: "*[w]ishing to establish a multilateral framework of principles and rules for trade in services with a view to the expansion of such trade under conditions of transparency and progressive liberalization*"; and, art. XIX:1: "*[i]n pursuance of objectives of this Agreement, Members shall enter into successive rounds of negotiations, beginning not later than five years from the date of entry into force of the WTO Agreement and periodically thereafter, with a view to achieving a progressively higher level of liberalization*". WTO, Report of the Panel, *United States – Measures Affecting the Cross-Border Supply of Gambling and Betting Services*, WT/DS285/R, 10 November 2004, adopted on 20 April 2005, para. 6.313: "*Progressive liberalization entails including more sectors in Members' schedules and reduction or elimination of limitations, terms, conditions and qualifications on market access and national treatment through successive rounds of negotiations*".

Agreement. However, it may be understood as: "*[t]he removal of or reduction in the trade practices that thwart free flow of goods and services from one nation to another. It includes dismantling of tariff (such as duties, surcharges, and export subsidies) as well as nontariff barriers (such as licensing regulations, quotas, and arbitrary standards)*".[26] With specific regard to trade in services, liberalization entails the opening of the domestic service market to foreign providers and investors.[27]

When domestic services are publicly owned, the liberalization of trade in services goes hand in hand with the privatization of the sector. Although the two terms, liberalization and privatization, are often taken as synonyms, they have different meanings.[28] Strictly speaking, privatization refers to the "*sale or return of publicly owned enterprises to private ownership and control*".[29] If understood more broadly, it indicates any kind of private involvement in the supply of public services.[30]

Privatization of public utilities is chiefly driven by the need for financial inflows into public accounts, as the liberalization of privatized services is likely to increase the flow of direct investments.[31]

However, the privatization of public services does not automatically imply the removal of barriers to trade in services. For political reasons, governments may choose to limit private involvement to domestic operators. On the contrary, liberalization of public services needs to be preceded by the privatization of public utilities. It is hard to see the reason for liberalizing the domestic services market to foreign providers if said markets are entirely in public hands. Therefore, while privatization of public utilities can occur without liberalizing the domestic market, liberalization needs to be accompanied by privatization.

Translating these considerations into the terms of the GATS, privatization is

---

[26] Source: http://www.businessdictionary.com/definition/trade-liberalization.html, last accessed on 21 February 2020.

[27] R. Bates, *The Trade in Water Services: How Does GATS Apply to the Water and Sanitation Services Sector?*, in *Sydney Law Review*, 2009, p. 128. The entry of foreign private investors in the domestic market does not necessarily imply the direct involvement of foreign providers in services operations. Whereas this occurs in case of green field investment, merger or acquisition of existing industries, in other cases the foreign involvement may be limited to investment in shares and bonds.

[28] M. Krajewski, *National Regulation and Trade Liberalization in Services: The Legal Impact of the General Agreement on Trade in Services (GATS) on National Regulatory Autonomy*, The Hague, 2003, pp. 1, 4-9.

[29] Source: http://www.businessdictionary.com/definition/privatization.html. Last accessed on 16 March 2020.

[30] Some authors highlight that privatization may be understood both as contracting out public services or as increasing private equity participation. See, Türk and others, pp. 155-158 (n 14).

[31] UNCTAD, *World Investment Report 1999, Foreign Direct Investment and the challenge of Development*, New York-Geneva, 1999, p. 33.

necessary for the Agreement's main provision to be operational, namely the market access clause. Formally, the GATS does not oblige Member States either to liberalize or to privatize service sectors. It leaves Members free to decide whether and which sectors to liberalize and which services to keep under public management, instead requiring States to engage in successive rounds of negotiations to progressively liberalize trade in services.[32]

As far as public services are concerned, each State is faced with a choice between maintaining public service ownership, and thus avoiding market access commitments, or undertaking these commitments at the expense of holding service ownership in the public hand. Although the Agreement promotes the liberalization of services without requiring Member States to privatize their public utilities, this neutrality on the issue of ownership is merely apparent, as noted by some commentators.[33] In relation to the water sector, it has been held that "*requests to liberalize trade in water services through GATS are only relevant to those countries who have already decided to allow PSP [private sector participations]*".[34]

Having made these preliminary observations, we turn to analyzing the framework of the Treaty and its relevant provisions. In general terms, it is a nascent system that grants Member States a high degree of flexibility.[35] It is the result of a compromise between the States' need to liberalize trade in services and their need to maintain their regulatory autonomy.[36] The preamble, indeed, refers to "*the right of Members to regulate, and to introduce new regulations, on the supply of services within their territories in order to meet national policy objectives*".[37]

Two kinds of obligations are foreseen, namely general obligations and specific obligations. While general obligations are binding on all Member States, specific obligations are conditioned on freely assumed commitments. Among the few general obligations, there are the so-called "*most favored nation*" treatment clause (MFN)[38] and the transparency obligation.[39] They give meaning to the principle of non discrimination.

---

[32] Türk and others, p. 149 (n 14); E. Türk, M. Krajewski, *The Right to Water and Trade in Services: Assessing the Impact of GATS Negotiations on Water Regulation,* Draft Paper presented at the CAT+E Conference *"Moving Forward from Cancún"*, 2003, p. 8.

[33] Türk and others, pp. 150-151 (n 14); M. Fitzmaurice, *The Human Right to Water*, in *Fordham Environmental Law Review*, 2007, pp. 570-571.

[34] Slaymaker and others (n 12).

[35] Munari (n 18).

[36] Lang (n 14).

[37] GATS, fourth recital of the Preamble.

[38] GATS, art. II. On the MFN clause in the GATS, see R. Adlung, A. Carzaniga, *MFN Exemptions under the General Agreement on Trade in Services: Grandfathers Striving for Immortality?*, in *Journal of International Economic Law*, 2009.

[39] GATS, art. III.

The MFN clause enshrined in Article II GATS provides that "*the best access conditions that have been conceded to one country must automatically be extended to all other participants in the system*".[40] In the GATS system, this means guaranteeing Member States "*treatment no less favourable*" than that accorded to "*like services and service suppliers of any other country*".[41]

This clause applies to all measures that affect trade in services regardless of whether specific commitments have been made, but it is fully operational when a domestic market has been opened to foreign investors.[42] Once a State has committed to open a service sector, it cannot discriminate among foreign stakeholders.

Pursuant to Article II GATS, a Member may maintain measures inconsistent with the MFN clause upon condition of listing such measures into a specific list of exceptions.[43] MFN exceptions can be listed only once, and only at the time of joining the Agreement, and cannot be applied where Member States have undertaken specific commitments.[44] In principle, no new MFN exceptions can be applied later, unless they consist in a waiver of obligations under the WTO agreements.[45]

---

[40] WTO, p. 8 (n 24).

[41] As for the likeness of services and service suppliers, the Appellate Body has pointed out that this requirement involves an examination of their "*degrees of 'competitiveness' or 'substitutability'*". WTO, Appellate Body Report, *Argentina – Measures Relating to Trade in Goods and Services*, WT/DS453/AB/R, 14 April 2016, adopted on 9 May 2016, para. 6.26. Accordingly, among the circumstances to be taken into account there are: "*(a) the nature and characteristics of the services and service suppliers; (b) the end-uses of the services; (c) consumers' preferences in respect of the services and service suppliers; and (d) the classification and description of the services under, for instance, the CPC*". WTO, Report of the Panel, *European Union and its Member States – Certain Measures Relating to the Energy Sector*, WT/DS476/R, 10 August 2018, para. 7.419, quoting WTO, Report of the Appellate Body, *Argentina – Measures Relating to Trade in Goods and Services*, WT/DS453/AB/R, 14 April 2016, para. 6.32.

[42] In the absence of specific commitments on Market access and National treatment, the MFN Principle only implies that advantages accorded to services and service supplier of other States have to be accorded to all other Members.

[43] GATS, art. II:2 rules: "*[a] Member may maintain a measure inconsistent with paragraph 1 provided that such a measure is listed in, and meets the conditions of, the Annex on Article II Exemptions*". According to this Annex, exemptions to art. II should be revised each five years and should last no longer than ten years. However, the rule is not expressed in peremptory terms, thus some Members have listed indefinite exception. Munin, p. 112 (n 5).

[44] WTO, p. 8 (n 24); Munin, p. 111 (n 5).

[45] Pursuant to Annex on art. II: "*[a]ny new exemptions applied for after the date of entry into force of the WTO Agreement shall be dealt with under paragraph 3 of Article IX of that Agreement*". Art. IX:3 of the WTO Agreement provides that: "*[i]n exceptional circumstances, the Ministerial Conference may decide to waive an obligation imposed on a Member by this Agreement or any of the Multilateral Trade Agreements, provided that any such decision shall be taken by three fourths of the Members unless otherwise provided for in this paragraph*". The paragraph follows by specifying the procedure and conditions governing the application of the waiver, which in any event is time limited. See Adlung, Carzaniga, pp. 365-366 (n 38).

In addition to general obligations, there are also "*specific commitments*" [46] of liberalization that each Member State is free to assume in any given sector of services and according to any chosen mode of supply.

Indeed, the Agreement differentiates between trade in services according to four modes of supply: Mode 1 – "*Cross-border supply*" refers to the supply of a service across a border where both the service provider and the consumer do not leave their respective countries; Mode 2 – "*Consumption abroad*" refers to the supply of a service where the consumer physically travels from one country to another to obtain a service; Mode 3 – "*Commercial presence*" refers to a service supplier offering a service in another country through an agency, branch, subsidiary or joint venture; Mode 4 – "*Presence of natural persons*" refers to people temporarily entering another country in order to provide services. [47]

Specific commitments are scheduled into States' individual lists. Without listing specific commitments, Member States do not open service markets to foreign suppliers. The most significant provisions of the GATS, namely market access and national treatment, apply only to those service sectors included in the States' Schedule of commitments, and according to the mode of supply specified thereto. [48]

Market access commitments refer to Member States' obligations to accord treatment to service and service suppliers of any other Member that is no less favorable than specified in their Schedule. [49] The national treatment clause requires Members to accord services and service suppliers of any other Member treatment no less favorable than that accorded to their own like services and service suppliers. [50]

The above legal framework is further complicated by the fact that each Member

---

[46] M. Cossy, *Water Services at the WTO*, in L. Boisson de Chazournes, N. Bernasconi-Osterwalder (eds.), *Fresh Water and International Economic Law*, Oxford, 2005, p. 120 defines specific commitments "*as legal guarantees enjoyed by foreign services suppliers; they govern access to market and conditions of competition vis-à-vis domestic suppliers*". See also M. Cossy, *Le Statut de l'Eau en Droit International Économique. Principaux Aspects au Regard des Règles de l'Organisation Mondiale du Commerce*, in L. Boisson de Chazournes, S. M. A. Salman (eds.), *Les Ressources en Eau et Le Droit International, Water Resources and International Law*, Leiden, 2005.

[47] GATS, art. I:2.

[48] Commitments are recorded in Schedules by using a uniform terminology, notably: NONE means that there are no limitations on market access and national treatment in a given sector and mode of supply; UNBOUND indicates that a Member remains free to introduce or maintain measures inconsistent with market access or national treatment in a given sector and mode of supply. In addition to this uniform terminology, States can describe limitations on market access and national treatment attached to bound commitments. On the need to schedule clear commitments see R. Adlung, P. Morrison, M. Roy, W., Zhang, *Fog in GATS commitments – Why WTO Members should care*, in *World Trade Review*, 2013.

[49] GATS, art. XVI.

[50] GATS, art. XVII.

State can attach conditions and limitations upon the scope of its own specific commitments.[51]

Furthermore, once specific commitments have been assumed, it is rather difficult, if not impossible, to modify or withdraw them. In fact, according to Article XXI GATS, other Member States fearing that said modifications or withdrawals would affect their interests can ask for "*compensatory adjustments*". These adjustments do not entail pecuniary compensation, but consist in commitments to open other service markets or modes of supply in order to maintain a general level of mutually advantageous commitments no less favorable than that provided by the previous list of commitments. If no agreement is reached for compensatory adjustments, the alleged injured State may refer the matter to arbitration. At this point, all States that consider themselves to be injured by the amendment and/or withdrawal at issue must join the arbitration if they also want to obtain compensatory adjustments.[52]

Given the high burden ensuing from compensatory adjustments, once a given public sector has been liberalized (after having been privatized), it is rather difficult to withdraw commitments to market access (and return the sector to public hands). This is the reason why scholars refer to the effect of Article XXI GATS as the "*lock-in effect*".[53]

Applying these rules to the water sector, if a Member State privatizes and then liberalizes the water service sector under the GATS without stipulating limitations, reversing the privatization process after a period of disappointing private management may prove difficult as the state might be called to compensate the losses caused to other States.

Finally, in the event that Members adopt legislation or maintain laws inconsistent with their GATS commitments, the affected States may resort to the WTO adjudication bodies. Disputes raised under the GATS are adjudicated according to the WTO State-to-State dispute settlement mechanism. The latter allows Member States to bring a complaint before a specially appointed panel composed of trade experts who interpret and apply the GATS. The panel decision (report) may be appealed to the Appellate Body. The panel and Appellate Body reports need to be adopted by the Dispute Settlement Body. If a State fails to abide by the WTO bodies' decisions, the other State may retaliate against the State in breach upon authorization of the Dispute Settlement Body.[54]

Against this scenario, it should be understood whether, and to what extent, the Agreement may limit governmental leeway to regulate essential services, such as wa-

---

[51] GATS, art. XX:1(*a*)(*b*).

[52] GATS, art. XXI.

[53] Cossy, pp. 138-140 (n 46); Türk and others, pp. 148-149 (n 14).

[54] See, Commission on Human Rights, *Human Rights, Trade and Investment*, (n 15).

ter services, once they have been liberalized and, as a consequence, whether it has the potential to affect the enjoyment of the right to water.

2.2. The lack of specific commitments in the water sector

Water services are provided under Mode 3, that is, through the establishment of a commercial presence.[55] The commercial presence of foreign investors may foster foreign direct investments and may entail the transfer of expertise and technology. However, according to the High Commissioner for human rights, Mode 3 is "*possibly the most problematic for the protection of human rights, raising both opportunities and challenges*".[56]

So far, Member States have been reluctant to offer foreign suppliers legal guarantees of market access and national treatment under Mode 3. In the water sector, no such commitment has been undertaken for the management and distribution of water services.[57] As a consequence, Member States are obliged to respect very few obligations, such as transparency and non discrimination among foreign providers (MFN). Only with regard to wastewater treatment services have some WTO Members made specific commitments.[58]

Among the reasons for the lack of commitments in the water services sector, one may include, in addition to the considerations mentioned in the introductory section, the exclusion of drinking water treatment and distribution services from the WTO Services Sectoral Classification List (so-called W/120).[59]

---

[55] For a better understanding of the meaning of 'commercial presence' see WTO, Council for Trade in Services, *Mode 3 – Commercial Presence, Background note by the Secretariat*, S/C/W/314, 7 April 2010, para. 10: "*[a] commercial presence may be set up as a* new *establishment or so-called 'greenfield investment', e.g. a foreign bank establishing a new, wholly-owned branch or subsidiary that competes with domestic firms. Alternatively, a commercial presence may result from the acquisition, in whole or in part, of an* already existing *domestic firm, in which the foreign natural or juridical person acquires a controlling interest or majority ownership. The GATS, however, makes no formal distinction between these two situations*".

[56] Commission on Human Rights, *Liberalization of Trade in Services and Human Rights,* para. 46 (n 20).

[57] L. D. Choukroune, *Water and Sanitation Services in International Trade and Investment Law: For a Holistic Human Rights-Based Approach*, in J. Chaisse (ed.), *The Regulation of the Global Water Services Market*, Cambridge, 2017, p. 198.

[58] Currently, 59 Members (including the European Union) have undertaken commitments in sanitation services and 59 Members (including the European Union) in sewage services (both included into the category "*Environmental Services*"). See data on the website: http://i-tip.wto.org/services/ReportResults.aspx (last accessed 10 April 2020).

[59] Services Sectoral Classification List, MTN.GNS/W/120, 10 July 1991, available at: http://i-tip.wto.org/services/. It "*consists of eleven broad sectors as well as a residual category 'Other Services Not Included Elsewhere', further divided into over 150 subsectors. As the List is intended to be*

This List is an illustrative catalogue of services on which Member States rely in order to define their commitments and to draw up their Schedules. This classification system for services was created by the WTO to assist Members and provide greater certainty on the scope of specific commitments. The W/120 List is, in turn, based on the classification provided for by the United Nations known as the Central Product Classification (CPC).[60]

While the first CPC version, which dates back to 1989, did not include water services, the UN classification has been revised several times and the last version does so.[61] Despite the progress in the CPC on water service classification, the W/120 still does not include the services of water treatment and distribution.

In general terms, the WTO classification system is regarded as being obsolete and suggestions have been made for updating it. Worth mentioning is the former European Community's proposal to modify the Environmental services[62] classification according to the environmental media; air, water, solid and hazardous waste, noise, etc.[63] More specifically, according to the EC proposal, the new Environmental services classification would have included "*[w]ater for human use & wastewater management*".[64] The EC proposal received support from some WTO Member

comprehensive, each sector and various sub-categories include a residual range of 'other' services". See WTO, Committee on Specific Commitments, *Service Classification in the WTO Jurisprudence – Note by the Secretariat*, S/CSC/W/61, 12 March 2013, para. 1.1. On the general subject, see R. Adlung, *Services Liberalization From a WTO GATS Perspective: In search of Volunteers*, WTO Staff Working Paper, ERSD-2009-05, 2009.

[60] Since the W/120 was prepared on the basis of the 1991 Provisional CPC, subsectors in the List W/120 are annotated with CPC numbers when there is congruence between the two lists.

[61] The current Central Product Classification ("CPC") Ver. 2.1 has been released in 2015. According to the last version, section 6 "*electricity, gas and water distribution services*" includes "*water distribution through mains, except steam and hot water (on own account)*" (CPC 2.1, Group 692, Class 6921, Subclass 69210) and "*water distribution, except through mains (on own account)*" (CPC 2.1, Group 692, Class 6923, Subclass 69230).

[62] About environmental services see: A. Mattoo, *Environmental Services*, in WTO (ed.), *A Handbook of the GATS Agreement: a WTO Secretariat Publication*, Cambridge, 2005, pp. 295-314; WTO, Council for Trade in Services, *Background note on Environmental Services* (n 22).

[63] Water services are commonly regarded as belonging to the environmental services sector. See WTO, Council for Trade in Services, *Background Note on Environmental* Services (n 22). For a deeper understanding of trade in environmental services see, C. Kirkpatrick, *Trade in Environmental Services: Assessing the Implications for Developing Countries in the GATS*, Geneva, 2006, available at: http://www.ictsd.org/downloads/2010/02/env-services_kirkpatrick.pdf.

[64] WTO, *Communication from the European Communities and their Member States, GATS 2000: Environmental Services*, S/CSS/W/38, 22 December 2000; EU's 28 September 1999 submission to the Committee on Specific Commitments, *Classification Issues in the Environmental Sector* (S/CSC/W/25). The first proposal dated 1999 has been amended in 2000. It is specified that the new proposed sub-sector include "*6A. Water for human use & wastewater management*" and water services are defined as "*Water collection, purification and distribution services through mains, except steam & hot water*".

States, such as Switzerland[65] and Australia,[66] and opposition from others. In the end, no modification has taken place due to the general failure to amend the W/120.

While the absence of water services from the WTO List does not preclude Member States from undertaking commitments in the water sector, it does not facilitate this task. Although reference to the W/120 or the CPC classification system is encouraged when scheduling commitments "*in order to ensure the accuracy and clarity in the description of each sector or sub-sector scheduled*",[67] Member States are not bound to use these systems. Member States are instead free to refer to their own sub-sectoral classification, provided that their own sector and sub-sector descriptions are clear and accurate. Cossy underlines that the GATS covers "*any services in any sector*" regardless of whether they are included or not in the WTO Classification List.[68]

The lack of an entry (voice) for water services makes taking commitments on drinking water treatment and distribution services more difficult.[69] At the same time, it prevents WTO adjudicating bodies from assuming the existence of com-

---

[65] WTO, Council for Trade in Services, *Communication from Switzerland, GATS 2000: Environmental Services*, S/CSS/W/76, 4 May 2001. Switzerland maintained that the classification currently in use is no longer suitable to present circumstances and proposed to adapt items under subsector 6 (environmental services).

[66] WTO, Communication from Australia, Negotiating Proposal for Environmental Services, S/CSS/W/112, 1 October 2001. Australia's Negotiating Proposal for Environmental Services endorsed the EC communication on classification of environmental services. It is argued that this would "*broaden the sectoral classification of environmental services to bring the WTO classification of environmental services into line with current practice in trade in services, and to use this new sectoral classification for negotiations in environmental services*".

[67] WTO, Committee on Specific Commitments, *Service Classification in the WTO Jurisprudence*, para. 1.7 (n 59). See WTO, *Guidelines for the Scheduling of Specific Commitments under the General Agreement on Trade in Services (GATS), Adopted by the Council for Trade in Services on 23 March 2001*, S/L/92, 28 March 2001, Part I, para. 23: "*[t]he legal nature of a schedule as well as the need to evaluate commitments, require the greatest possible degree of clarity in the description of each sector or sub-sector scheduled. In general the classification of sectors and sub-sectors should be based on the Secretariat's Services Sectoral Classification List. Each sector contained in the Secretariat list is identified by the corresponding Central Product Classification (CPC) number. Where it is necessary to refine further a sectoral classification, this should be done on the basis of the CPC or other internationally recognised classification*".

[68] M. Cossy, *Environmental Services and the General Agreement on Trade in Services (GATS): Legal Issues and Negotiating Stakes at the WTO*, in *European Yearbook of International Economic Law*, 2011, p. 154.

[69] For instance, Japan has rearranged its commitments on Environmental Services according to the EC classification proposal, but it did not offer commitments on "*Water for Human Use, as a consensus among Members on classification in this sector is yet to be seen*". See, Ministry of Foreign Affairs of Japan, available at: http://www.mofa.go.jp/policy/economy/wto/submit0304.html (last accessed on 20 March 2020).

mitments in water services by analogy with other sectoral commitments, as in the *US-Gambling* case.[70]

This case concerned various measures taken by the United States at a federal level, which prohibited the remote supply of betting and gambling services.[71] As a result of the US ban, operators of Antigua and Barbuda were prevented from providing said services by telematic means to consumers within the territory of the United States.

Antigua contested the legitimacy of the US measures under the GATS on the grounds that the United States had scheduled specific commitments on market access and national treatment in the sector named "*other recreational services (except sporting)*" including services supplied under "*mode 1*" or "*cross-border*" supply, as defined in Article I.2(*a*) GATS.[72]

The dispute between Antigua and the United States concerned whether or not gambling and betting services were included within the scope of "*other recreational services (except sporting)*". According to the US, they were not. The US argued that they had never made any reference to "*gambling and betting services*" in their Schedule of commitments. Moreover, since the US had not tied their commitments in recreational services to the WTO Sectoral List of Classification, nor to the UN CPC classification, their commitments were not to be read in the light of these instruments. Such commitments were to be interpreted according to the common means of interpretation established under Articles 31-33 VCLT. Referring to the ordinary meaning of "*gambling and betting*", the US maintained that the related services were outside the scope of "*recreational*" services.

Following a different line of reasoning, the US defence was rejected both by the panel and by the Appellate Body. The WTO bodies agreed that the US had not clearly and transparently defined the scope of their "*recreational services*" commitments under their Schedule. Therefore, both adjudicating bodies sought to clarify its meaning by means of the VCLT rules on interpretation.[73] Resorting to the

---

[70] WTO, Report of the Panel, *United States – Measures Affecting the Cross-Border Supply of Gambling and Betting Services* (n 25).

[71] WTO, Report of the Appellate Body, *United States – Measures Affecting Cross-Border Gambling and Betting Services*, WT/DS285/AB/R, 7 April 2005. The federal laws at issue were: the Wire Act; the Travel Act; the Illegal Gambling Business Act. In addition to federal laws, the Panel took into consideration eight State laws. With respect to these States laws, the Appellate Body considered that Antigua had failed to make a *prima facie* case of inconsistency with GATS, art. XVI.

[72] WTO, Report of the Panel, *United States – Measures Affecting the Cross-Border Supply of Gambling and Betting Services*, para. 3.29 (n 25).

[73] Both bodies resorted to the interpretative tools of the VCLT. Whereas the Panel assumed that the WTO Sectoral List of Classification W/120 and the 1993 Scheduling Guidelines were the GATS "*context*" under art. 31(2) VCLT, the Appellate Body considered the Secretariat's document "*supplementary means of interpretation*", according to art. 32 VCLT. Since the meaning of

W/120 and to the 1993 Scheduling Guidelines as supplementary means of interpretation, the Appellate Body ruled that the US was "*assumed to have relied on W/120 and the corresponding UN CPC references*".[74] Given that the UN CPC includes gambling and betting service within recreational services,[75] the adjudicating bodies concluded that the US had undertaken specific commitments in this area.

In relation to the sector "*recreational services*", the US had also made no limitation on market access under the cross-border supply mode. Thus, their ban on the remote supply of gambling services was held to be inconsistent with the obligations assumed under Article XVI GATS. Aware of the effects of its decision, the panel highlighted that:

> "the United States may well have inadvertently undertaken specific commitments on gambling and betting services. However, it is not for the Panel to second-guess the intentions of the United States at the time the commitment was scheduled. Rather, our role is to interpret and apply the GATS in light of the facts and evidence before us. We also wish to emphasize what we have not decided in this case. We have not decided that WTO Members do not have a right to regulate".[76]

The panel and Appellate Body's holdings have been sharply criticized as they resulted in a Member being "*bound to a commitment that it did not intend to make when its negotiators drafted the relevant Schedule*".[77] By using the ordinary means of interpretation, these bodies gave to schedule terms "*a meaning different from that ascribed to them in the national legal system of the Member concerned*".[78]

In the *Gambling* case, the possibility for the adjudicating bodies to infer US commitments in gambling and betting services was given by the correspondence between the W/120 and the CPC instruments of Classification.[79] In the water sector, given the absence of an entry on water services in W/120 Classification List sectors,

---

the US Schedule was still not clear, the Appellate Body resorted to the above instruments in order to assess if gambling and betting services were included in the US Schedule.

[74] WTO, Report of the Appellate Body, *United States – Measures Affecting Cross-Border Gambling and Betting Services*, para. 204 (n 71).

[75] CPC Class 9649 "*Other recreational services*" included the sub-class gambling and betting services (96492).

[76] WTO, Report of the Panel, *United States – Measures Affecting the Cross-Border Supply of Gambling and Betting Services*, paras. 7.3-7.4 (n 25).

[77] D. Prévost, *Services and Public Policy Regulation in WTO Law: The Example of the US-Gambling Case*, in J. van de Gronden (ed.), *EU and WTO Law on Services. Limits to the Realization of General Interest Policies within the Services Markets?*, Alphen aan den Rijn, 2009, p. 227.

[78] *Ibid.*

[79] As affirmed by Leroux, Members' GATS specific commitments are interpreted according to the W/120 and the corresponding CPC codes. E. H. Leroux, *Eleven Years of Gats Case Law: What Have We Learned?*, in *Journal of International Economic Law*, 2007, pp. 765-766.

the risk of unintentional assumption of obligations is less likely to be incurred by Members.[80]

Despite the lack of specific commitments in water services, the GATS still exercises some influence on these. Indeed, some services that are preparatory or auxiliary to drinking water service are included in the List of Classification and have been the object of specific commitments.[81]

The current lack of specific commitments for the liberalization of water services might ultimately change. The GATS explicitly promotes the progressive achievement of higher levels of liberalization of the service market and, to this end, it calls on Member States to take part in successive rounds of negotiation.[82] As mandated by Article XIX, the first round started in 2000. In the following year, services negotiations were incorporated in the now-stalled "Doha Round".[83]

Negotiations on specific commitments were carried out on a bilateral and a plurilateral basis following a request offer-method approach.[84] The EU has encouraged negotiations in water services,[85] both on a bilateral basis[86] and on a plurilateral ba-

---

[80] Although a detailed analysis is beyond the reach of this study, with respect to potential risks ensuing from the GATS, one may also refer to the *EU Banana case* (*European Communities – Regime for the Importation, Distribution and Sale of Bananas*, WT/DS27), where the AB ruled that even a measure that regulates trade in goods may fall within the GATS scope as long as it affects the supply of a service or a service supplier. In light of this holding, one may contend that if a measure regulating the output of water affects the supply of water services, it would fall within the scope of the GATS. In this respect, see G. Hufbauer, S. Stephenson, *Services Trade: Past Liberalization and Future Challenges*, in *Journal of International Economic Law*, 2007, p. 615.

[81] Among others, groundwater resources assessment; engineering services for the construction of water supply and sanitation work and water well drilling.

[82] GATS, art. XIX.

[83] WTO Members did not overcome the stalemate at the Ministerial Conference held in Buenos Aires in December 2017. As a consequence of the deadlock at the Doha Round, some Members have started to negotiate Plurilateral Trade Agreements, such as the Trade in Services Agreement ("TiSA"), which is based on the GATS. See T. Bertelsmann-Scott, S. J. van Rensburg, W. Viviers, A. Parshotam, A. Parry, R. Rossouw, A. Langalanga, D. Nkhata, *The impact of plurilateral trade agreemetns on developing countries – to participate or not to participate?*, in *South African Journal of International Affairs*, 2018, pp. 177-198; E. Kessie, *The Doha Development Agenda at a Crossroads: What Are the Remaining Obstacles to the Conclusion of the Round – Part III?*, in *European Yearbook of International Economic Law*, 2012, pp. 558-560.

[84] WTO, Council for Trade in Services in Special Session, *Guidelines and Procedures for the Negotiations on Trade in Services*, 28 March 2001, S/L/93, 29 March 2001, para. 11. Plurilateral negotiations were mandated by the 2005 Hong Kong Ministerial Declaration, para. 27, and its Annex C, para. 7.

[85] WTO, Council for Trade in Services, *Background Note on Environmental Services*, p. 8 (n 22).

[86] Requests are confidential, but those of the former EC have been made public. In the framework of the round of negotiations GATS 2000, the EC has made 109 requests to WTO Members. The EC requested seventy countries to undertake specific commitments on "*water for human use & wastewater management*" according to its classification proposals. No request on water services

sis,[87] suggesting scheduling commitments according to its revised classification list, which notably includes water and sanitation. However, negotiations on water services have not been successful to date, suffering from the overall impasse of the Doha Round. Nonetheless, it cannot be excluded that future negotiations on specific commitments may bring water services under the purview of the GATS.[88]

In addition, Member States can add new commitments to the existing ones outside the GATS negotiations at any time and without following the burdensome procedure set forth in Article XXI GATS for modifying or withdrawing commitments.[89]

For these reasons, it is worth assessing the possible implications of the Agreement on the regulatory powers of States in the water sector and, in particular, the ways to prevent or accommodate incompatible obligations that may arise from the Agreement and the human right to water.

3. The compatibility between the GATS and the State's regulatory autonomy in the water services sector

The interest of trade liberalization and domestic regulatory autonomy have to be balanced in order to both promote economic growth and development and pursue non trade objectives, such as human rights and environmental protection.[90]

From a human rights perspective, governmental regulation of essential public services is crucial. In the case of the right to water, States need regulatory leeway to protect and fulfill this right. The obligation to protect requires public authorities to establish effective regulatory systems, above all where water services are operated or

according to its proposed classification of environmental services has been made to: Angola, Benin, Burkina Faso, Burundi, Central African Republic, Cameroon, Chad, Congo, Democratic Republic of the Congo, Djibouti, Gabon, Gambia, Ghana, Guinea, Guinea Bissau, Ivory Coast, Malawi, Mali, Mauritania, Niger, Rwanda, Sierra Leone, Swaziland, Togo, Uganda, Zambia. Source: http://www.esf.be/003/003.html. Noteworthy, the EC exempted water services from its initial offer.

[87] On 28 February 2006, the European Commission submitted a plurilateral request on environmental services on behalf of: Australia, Canada, the European Communities, Japan, Korea, Norway, Switzerland, The Separate Customs Territory of Taiwan, Penghu, Kinmen and Matsu, and the United States. This request is available at: http://www.esf.be/003/009.html. See also WTO, Council for Trade in Services, *Background Note on Environmental Services,* p. 18 (n 22).

[88] Thus far, however, no Member has tabled a proposal to undertake commitments on water services.

[89] See WTO, Council for Trade in Services, *Procedures for the certification of rectifications or improvements to schedules of specific commitments*, 14 April 2000, S/L/84, 18 April 2000; WTO, Council for Trade in Services in Special Session, *Modalities for the treatment of autonomous liberalization*, 6 March 2003, TN/S/6, 10 March 2003.

[90] Krajewsky (n 28); Kirkpatrick, Parker, pp. 1491-1508 (n 8).

controlled by third parties.[91] As water services are still considered natural monopolies,[92] privatization entails replacing "*a state-owned monopoly with a private one*"[93] and in a monopolistic context the risk of abuse by a sole private provider is high. Thus, liberalization of privatized natural monopolies raises complex issues for States lacking the necessary regulatory framework "*particularly when a reversal of the liberalization is hard to achieve*".[94]

Pursuant to the human right to water, when States contract out the supply of drinking water they keep the duty of guaranteeing that private providers meet water availability, quality and accessibility standards. In order to comply with the availability requirement, a private company has to supply sufficient and continuous amount of water for personal and domestic uses. States then have to regulate the output pressure as well as the flow rate of the water supplied. As for the quality standard, States have to require that water supplied from a distribution network and intended for human consumption is free from any substances which may constitute a potential danger to human health. Technical requirements prescribe the properties of drinking water to be ensured, subject to periodic monitoring. With respect to the accessibility requirements, States have to ensure that even poor households enjoy a minimum amount of water for personal and domestic uses, despite their inability to pay. Therefore, disconnection from the mains may be forbidden under certain conditions. Moreover, States have to ensure that drinking water is distributed also to suburban or rural areas, despite the fact that this may be highly uneconomical.

To attain the above universal service goals, States may grant subsidies to the water industry and/or establish domestic regulations and monopolies. These factors are essential for pursuing public policy objectives, but risk affecting competition. The question arises whether these standards may be construed as illegitimate barriers to trade in services, thus forbidden under the GATS.

Under some conditions, the GATS admits domestic regulations, subsidies and monopolies even when the service at stake has been liberalized. However, much of the current discipline is under review as the GATS mandates negotiations in four areas, namely: domestic regulations (Article VI:4); emergency safeguard measures (Article X:1); government procurement (Article XIII:2); and subsidies (Article

[91] United Nations, Economic and Social Council, Committee on Economic, Social and Cultural Rights, *General Comment No. 15 (2002), The right to water (arts. 11 and 12 of the International Covenant on Economic, Social and Cultural Rights)*, UN Doc. E/C. 12/2002/11 (2002), 20 January 2003, (hereinafter, "General Comment No. 15") paras. 23-24.

[92] As will be shown below, although the network segment of the water industry is likely to be a natural monopoly, there could be competition in other segments of the industry.

[93] F. Marrella, *On the Changing Structure of International Investment Law: The Human Right to Water and ICSID Arbitration*, in *International Community Law Review*, 2010, p. 343.

[94] UNCTAD, *International Investment Agreements in Services*, Geneva, 2005, p. 10.

XV:1).[95] Thus far, a careful analysis of the relevant GATS provisions shows that they are not clearly framed for guaranteeing States' regulatory autonomy. The following sections give reasons for this contention.

3.1. The general GATS provisions likely to raise concern from a human right perspective

This section provides an overview of the GATS provisions concerning domestic regulations, subsidies, and monopolies and exclusive service suppliers that raise human rights concerns in as much as they have the potential to constrain Member States' regulatory power.

3.1.1. Domestic regulations

The right to water requires States parties to the ICESCR to regulate the water industry in the public interest. To abide by this obligation, States may have to set forth domestic legal frameworks concerning, *inter alia*: water quality and quantity; territorial coverage in remote areas even at non-market prices; price caps; the supply of a minimum amount of water to non paying-users; and the prohibition of disconnecting poor households.

Regulations on public services are in principle allowed under the GATS on condition that their distortive effects on trade in services are not *unnecessary* barriers to the service market.[96] More specifically, the GATS requires that domestic regulations comply with the requirements established under Article VI.

Pursuant to Article VI:1, when specific commitments have been undertaken in a given sector, each Member State must ensure that all *measures of general application* which may affect trade in services are administered in a reasonable, objective and impartial manner. Measures of general application may be defined as those measures which are indistinctly applicable to all operators, both national and foreign, and are not discriminatory. In particular, the GATS refers to domestic regulations concerning licensing requirements, technical standards, and qualification requirements and procedures.[97]

---

[95] These sectors of negotiations are known as the GATS "*built-in agenda*".

[96] On the tension between trade liberalization and domestic regulatory autonomy see, among others: J. P. Trachtman, *Lesson for GATS Article VI from the SPS, TBT and GATT Treatment of Domestic Regulation*, in *Social Science Research Network*, 29 January 2002, source: http://papers.ssrn.com/sol3/papers.cfm?abstract_id=298760; Lang (n 14); Munari (n 18).

[97] For a definition of each category of domestic regulation, see: WTO, Working Party on Professional Services, *The relevance of the Disciplines of the Agreements on Technical Barriers to Trade (TBT) and on Import Licensing Procedures to Article VI.4 on the General Agreement on Trade in Services, Note by the Secretariat*, S/WPPS/W/9, 11 September 1996, para. 4; WTO, Council for

As far as water services are concerned, licensing requirements and procedural and technical standards may constitute barriers to trade. Licensing requirements consist of "*substantive requirements, other than qualification requirements, with which a natural or a juridical person is required to comply in order to obtain, amend or renew authorization to supply a service*".[98] Technical standards "*are measures [that prescribe] the characteristics of a service or the manner in which it is supplied*".[99] For instance, water quality standards and price caps on water service tariffs may be regarded as domestic regulations.[100]

As noted by scholars, Article VI complements the rules on market access.[101] Whereas market access restrictions refer to quantitative limitations on the number of services or service suppliers admitted into a country's domestic market, domestic regulations refer to the quality of the service supplied or to the ability of the service supplier. However, as will be explained in section 4.2.1.1, in practice, the distinction between market access restrictions and domestic regulations is not so obvious.[102]

Measures which fall within Article VI are permitted upon the conditions that they are neither discriminatory nor unnecessary. As for the condition of non-discrimination, the fact that domestic regulations have to be applied in a reasonable, objective and impartial manner has been understood as referring to both national and foreign services and service suppliers. Even when applied on equal grounds, domestic regulations should not be more burdensome for foreign operators than for domestic ones. Domestic regulations must not constitute disguised restrictions on trade in services, for instance, by means of complex or opaque licensing procedures.

Trade in Service, *Article VI:4: Disciplines on Domestic Regulation applicable to all Services, Note by the Secretariat*, S/C/W/96, 1 March 1999, para. 4; WTO, Working Party on Domestic Regulation, *Disciplines on Domestic Regulation pursuant to GATS Article VI:4, Chairman's Progress Report*, S/WPDR/W/45, 14 April 2011, pp. 10-14.

[98] WTO, Working Party on Domestic Regulation, *Disciplines on Domestic Regulation pursuant to GATS Article VI:4, Chairman's Progress Report* (n 97), pp. 10-11: "'*Licensing procedures' are administrative or procedural rules that a natural or a juridical person, seeking authorization to supply a service, including the amendment or renewal of a licence, must adhere to in order to demonstrate compliance with licensing requirements*".

[99] *Ibid.*, p. 14. Technical standards also include the procedures relating to the enforcement of such standards.

[100] The Working Party on Domestic Regulation has listed "*Examples of Measures to be Addressed by Disciplines under GATS Article VI: 4 [Domestic Regulation]*". Among the examples of measures that would be prohibited under the GATS the Working Party included "*restrictions on fee setting*". See WPDR– Job (02)20/Rev.2.

[101] F. Costamagna, *L'impatto del GATS sull'autonomia regolamentare degli Stati membri nei servizi idrici ed energetici*, in *Diritto del commercio internazionale*, 2005, p. 524.

[102] G. Muller, *Troubled Relationships under the GATS: Tensions between Market Access (Article XVI), National Treatment (Article XVII), and Domestic Regulation (Article VI)*, in *World Trade Review*, 2017, pp. 457-463.

To prevent domestic measures from constituting unnecessary barriers to trade in services, Article VI:4 lists terms of reference for future negotiations on domestic regulations. The Council for Trade in Service has the mandate of developing a discipline on domestic requirements in accordance with a set of criteria. Among these, domestic regulations should be "*based on objective and transparent criteria, such as competence and the ability to supply the service*" and should not be "*more burdensome that necessary to ensure the quality of the service*".[103]

A specific Working Party on Domestic Regulation was established with the task of forwarding recommendations to the Council for Trade in Service "*no later than the conclusion of the forthcoming round of services negotiations*".[104] No new set of disciplines has been issued yet[105] and negotiations on domestic regulations are still ongoing.[106]

Pending the adoption of a specific discipline by the Council for Trade in Services, Members wishing to apply new domestic regulations likely to nullify or impair previous specific commitments are allowed to do so provided that such regulations: *i*) are "*based on objective and transparent criteria, such as competence and the ability to supply the service*" and are "*not more burdensome that necessary to ensure the quality of the service*"; *ii*) and could "*reasonably have been expected of that Member at the time the specific commitments in those sectors were made*".[107]

It has been underlined that those States endowed with regulations that were al-

---

[103] GATS, art. VI:4.

[104] Council for Trade in Service, *Decision on Domestic Regulation*, adopted on 26 April 1999, S/L/70, 28 April 1999.

[105] On 14 April 2011, the Chairman of the Working Party on Domestic Regulation produced a Progress Report, *Disciplines on Domestic Regulation Pursuant to Gats Article VI:4* (n 97) reflecting the progress achieved in the negotiations as well as divergences between the Members interested in protecting governmental regulatory autonomy and those focused on eliminating barriers to trade in services. Delimatsis made a strong case for the inclusion of a necessity test applicable across all services sectors in the Disciplines on Domestic Regulations, positing that it was necessary to draw a line between legitimate regulatory measures and disguised protectionism. See P. Delimatsis, *Concluding the WTO services negotiations on domestic regulation – hopes and fears*, in *World Trade Review*, 2010, pp. 663-667.

[106] The last available Report by the Chairperson of the Working Party on Domestic Regulation describes a deadlock in the work of the Working Party for the development of domestic regulation disciplines according to GATS art. VI:4 (S/WPDR/22, 27 November 2018, which refers to the previous report S/WPDR/21, 21 November 2017). Lately, India submitted a communication dated 22 November 2018 on GATS Article VI:4 – Disciplines for supply of a service through the presence of a natural person of a Member in the territory of another Member (S/WPDR/W/61, 26 November 2018), which was discussed by the WGDR in a meeting held on 5 December 2018, together with the "*APEC Non-binding Principles for Domestic Regulation of the Services Sector*" adopted by APEC States on 13 November 2018 in Papua New Guinea (S/WPDR/M/74, 13 February 2019).

[107] GATS, art. VI:5.

ready into force at the time the commitments on liberalization were undertaken are exempted from complying with the above criteria.[108] Hence, developing countries will be more affected by Article VI GATS than developed countries, as the former may suffer some delays in the adoption of domestic regulations. In the water sector, such a potential discrimination must not be overestimated. Indeed, new findings and technologies for facing worsening water conditions may require the enactment of new regulations both in developed and developing countries.

Among the above-mentioned set of criteria, the definition of "*necessity*" in domestic regulations has raised concern. In fact, if interpreted broadly, it might mean that no alternative measure less restrictive to trade should exist for the domestic rule to be applied. This interpretation would excessively restrict the regulatory leeway of Members.

Thus far, the WTO adjudicating bodies have not yet interpreted the term "*necessity*" within the meaning of Article VI,[109] but have done so in the different context of the general exceptions clause provided for by Article XIV (see section 4.3.). In the absence of a "*necessity test*" specifically construed in Disciplines on domestic regulations,[110] it is likely that WTO adjudicating bodies will resort to, or take inspiration from, a test developed in other contexts, which leaves an overly broad discretion in the hand of the WTO adjudicating bodies. It is thus questionable how "*necessity*" can be assessed with respect to rules dictated for the fulfillment of public service obligations without interfering with the Member States' discretion to regulate services of general interest.

It may be concluded that if a State undertakes specific commitments in order to liberalize services of general interest and does not place restrictive conditions on its commitments, its leeway to adopt norms aimed at safeguarding universal services goals risks being weakened by a possible "*test of necessity*". According to some commentators, not only do the criteria put by Article VI seem to pursue liberalization goals, but the WTO Dispute Settlement Body is also entitled to evaluate the necessity of national measures even when such measures lack protectionist intent or effects.[111] In this respect, the GATS seems to fail in responding to the unique characteristics of public services.

---

[108] Costamagna, p. 529 (n 101).

[109] WTO, Report of the Panel, *European Union and its Member States – Certain Measures Relating to the Energy Sector* (n 41). The Russian Federation claimed, *inter alia*, a violation of art. VI GATS, but the Panel, having found a violation of art. XVII GATS not justified under art. XIV(*a*) GATS, exercised judicial economy with respect to Russia's claims under arts. VI:1 and VI:5 GATS.

[110] P. Delimatsis, *Determining the Necessity of Domestic Regulations in Services. The Best Yet to Come*, in *European Journal of International Law*, 2008.

[111] Mastroianni, Arena, p. 50 (n 17).

3.1.2. Subsidies

The affordability of water services is one of the core elements of the human right to water.[112] Affordability targets have often been achieved by public authorities through subsidies given directly to consumers or indirectly to water providers.[113] In the past years, thanks to subsidies, connection charges and water tariffs have been kept artificially low.

Artificially depressed tariffs have caused negative effects, such as the depletion of financial resources to be invested in water infrastructure and the poor quality of the service. According to the Special Rapporteur on the right to water *"[w]hen utilities are not adequately and sustainably resourced, they cannot ensure operation and maintenance, let alone invest in the network"*.[114]

To improve the poor state of public water utilities, States have resorted to the privatization and liberalization of the water sector as well as to the implementation of the cost-recovery principle, which has caused an increase in water tariffs. A strict application of this principle, however, may disproportionately affect households unable to afford the cost of water service or the connection to the mains. It should be kept in mind that in some countries, water tariffs are disproportionately high compared with poor households' income.[115] For people unable to pay, access to water services may be precluded.

The right to water requires that the provision of water is also guaranteed to low income households, even if it is uneconomical. To abide by human rights obligations, States need to depart from a strict application of the cost recovery principle and ensure compensation to service operators for the costs they are required to bear in order to meet social policy objectives.

In order to fulfill essential service obligations, States have to put in place social policies, such as safety nets and subsidies.[116] In the water sector, subsidies may be provided to reimburse losses incurred in providing services to disadvantaged peo-

---

[112] General Comment No. 15, para. 12(*c*)(*ii*) (n 91).

[113] Several forms of financial assistance to service sectors exist including, *inter alia*: direct grants; preferential credit and guarantees; equity injections, tax incentives, concessions and allowances; duty-free inputs, free zones and offshore.

[114] Human Rights Council, *Report of the independent expert on the issue of human rights obligations related to access to safe drinking water and sanitation*, *Catarina de Albuquerque*, UN Doc. A/HRC/15/31, 29 June 2010, para. 55.

[115] According to the World Bank, the average water service connection fee is 33% of the average monthly household income in Cambodia; 27% in Bangladesh and 116% in Benin. See J. Sy, R. Warner, J. Jamieson, *Tapping the Markets: Opportunities for Domestic Investments in Water and Sanitation for the Poor. Directions in Development--Private Sector Development*, Washington, DC, 2014. World Bank. http://www.worldbank.org/content/dam/Worldbank/Feature%20 Story/SDN/Water/Water-TTM-Infographic-WATER-English-FINAL-900px.jpg.

[116] Human Rights Council, *Report of the independent expert on the issue of human rights obligations related to access to safe drinking water and sanitation*, para. 63(*l*) (n 114).

ples or to scarcely populated areas. As some scholars put it, essential services, such as water services, should be regarded as a sort of exception to liberalization goals because guaranteeing the enjoyment of these services may require the provider to bear extra costs.[117]

For the time being, the GATS puts no direct restriction on the States' rights to grant subsidies. Article XV sets out that if a State deems its rights to have been impaired by subsidies granted by another State, the former may request consultations with the latter. The State that has provided subsidies has to give due consideration to such a request,[118] but there is no duty to enter into consultation, or to achieve a result.

This *laissez faire* discipline is due to the fact that "*negotiators of the GATS were unable to reach an agreement on disciplines governing the provision of subsidies to service suppliers*".[119] Although during the Uruguay Round WTO Members acknowledged the potential for subsidies to have distortive effects on trade in services, they did not reach an agreement on how to deal with them. Therefore, Members decided to continue discussing the problem in future negotiations. As is the case for domestic regulations and other provisions, the GATS mandates further negotiations in order to develop a multilateral discipline on subsidies aimed at limiting their trade-distortive effects and assessing the appropriateness of countervailing measures.[120]

Negotiations on subsidies, which are carried out within the Working Party on GATS Rules ("WPGR"),[121] have ended in a stalemate.[122]

To sum up, for the time being, the GATS discipline does not explicitly constrain States' rights to grant subsidies, but does so only indirectly. As will be discussed in greater detail below, subsidies are not exempted from GATS obligations.[123] In particular, when States grant subsidies, they have to respect non discrimination rules, namely the MFN clause and the national treatment provision (provided that com-

---

[117] Mastroianni, Arena, p. 32 (n 17).

[118] GATS, art. XV:2.

[119] WTO, Report of the Panel, *United States – Measures Affecting Trade in Large Civil Aircraft (2nd Complaint)*, WT/DS353/R, 31 March 2011, para. 7.968.

[120] GATS, art. XV:1. The GATS also requires negotiators to "*take into account the needs of Members, particularly developing country Members, for flexibility in this area*".

[121] The Working Party on GATS Rules (WPGR) is the body charged to carry out negotiations in three thematic areas: emergency safeguard measures (GATS, art. X); government procurement in services (GATS, art. XIII) and; subsidies (GATS, art. XV).

[122] WTO, *Report by the Chairperson of the Working Party on GATS Rules*, S/WPGR/21, 14 April 2011, p. 1; WTO, Council for Trade in Services Special Session, *Negotiation on Trade in Services, Report by the Chairman,* Ambassador Fernando de Mateo*, to the Trade Negotiations Committee,* TN/S/36, 21 April 2011, para. 80.

[123] See, in this respect, Krajewski, pp. 44-45 (n 28).

mitments have been undertaken). Through these requirements, the State power to provide subsidies to meet essential services targets, including in the water sector, may suffer restrictions.

3.1.3. Monopolies and exclusive service suppliers

Article VIII GATS deals with monopolies and exclusive service suppliers. "Monopoly supplier of a service" is defined as "any person, public or private, which in the relevant market of the territory of a Member is authorized or established formally or in effect by that Member as the sole supplier of that service" (Article XXVIII (h)).

Cossy argued that Article VIII does not apply to natural monopolies, and thus to water services, since the definition of monopoly provided by Article XXVIII refers to legal monopolies "*authorized or established formally or in effect*" within a Member State, whereas natural monopolies do not need any governmental actions to come into effect.[124] It could be answered that a natural monopoly may also be established *in effect* by a State, which holds that building and maintaining more than one network infrastructure is uneconomic.[125]

In any case, the nature of natural monopoly of the water sector has begun to be challenged, as there seems to be the possibility of introducing competition into this service sector. Although the water and sewerage sectors are usually vertically integrated, resulting in a monopoly, they may be also disaggregated into various operations, notably that of the extraction, collection, purification and distribution of water, and wastewater treatment. These activities may then be assigned to different operators.[126] The possibility of separating these network operations from the management aspects of the service has started to be discussed.[127]

In light of the foregoing, Article VIII may apply to water services.

The provision does not prohibit monopolies and exclusive services, either publicly or privately managed,[128] provided that they are not inconsistent with obligations established under Article II GATS concerning the MFN treatment or with

---

[124] Cossy, p. 128 (n 46).

[125] This line of reasoning differs from that of other scholars. For instance, Munin argues that the provision refers only "*to de jure or de facto monopolies created through active government involvement*". Munin, p. 255 (n 5).

[126] Toolkits for Private Participation in Water and Sanitation, the World Bank, 1997, available online at: www.worldbank.org.

[127] For instance, England and Wales are making attempts to reverse the policy of vertical integration by separating existing activities in the water and sewerage supply chain. A. Maziotis, *Breaking Up Water Monopolies: Costs and Benefits*, in *Review of Environment, Energy and Economics*, 6 June 2013, available at: http://papers.ssrn.com; F. Cintioli, *Concorrenza, Istituzioni e Servizio Pubblico*, Milan, 2010, p. 155.

[128] Munin (n 5). Pursuant to art. VIII:5, each reference to monopoly applies also to cases of exclusive services suppliers.

other specific commitments. At present, given that water services are not subject to specific commitments, Member States have only to ensure that the monopoly supplier does not discriminate among foreign suppliers (MFN).

Should Member States undertake market access commitments, Article XVI:2(*a*) GATS prohibits the maintenance of monopolies or exclusive service suppliers, unless otherwise specified in Schedules. I contend that this rule cannot be read as imposing a Member the burden to duplicate water infrastructure in order to allow competition, as it does not require Members to take measures to end the monopoly, but only to refrain from maintaining or creating monopolies. As regards the compatibility of domestic monopolies with obligations under Article II and national treatment commitments, Article VIII would require that all domestic and foreign suppliers be allowed to compete for the water monopolist market on equal footing.

In brief, when it comes to natural monopolies, the GATS would not affect the choice to establish or maintain monopolies in public hands as long as no commitment is undertaken. However, once market access and national treatment commitments are made, the "natural" monopoly can no longer be entrusted to a sole domestic public supplier, as foreign providers should have at least the right to compete "*for*" the monopoly[129].

Turning to the second paragraph of Article VIII, it seeks to prevent monopoly suppliers from abusing their position in order to restrict access to adjacent markets that operate under competition. Pursuant to Article VIII:2, where a Member's monopoly supplier competes either directly or through subsidiaries in the supply of a service that is outside the scope of its monopoly and subject to specific commitments, such a Member must guarantee that the monopoly supplier will not abuse its position. In other words, the monopoly supplier is forbidden from abusing its dominant position in areas adjacent to the market in which it operates. It has been noted that Article VIII:2 only requires Members to ensure that monopoly suppliers do not abuse their monopoly position in a manner inconsistent with the specific commitments undertaken in other sectors. No reference is made to MFN obligations.[130]

Applying Article VIII:2 to water services in those States that have undertaken specific commitments in the provision of wastewater services – a market very close to that of water services –, monopoly suppliers of water services would be required to avoid abusing their position in the wastewater sector.

Finally, pursuant to Article VIII:3, the State's obligations under paragraphs 1 and 2 are not enforceable. If a State fails to abide by such obligations, it will pay no penalty, but will be only subject to the opening of a formal request for information

---

[129] G. Juen, *Trading Rights: A Human Rights Perspective to Water Service Liberalization in the Framework of the General Agreement on Trade in Services (GATS)*, in *Brussels Journal of International Studies*, 2005, p. 62.

[130] Munin, p. 259 (n 5).

by the Council for Trade in Services. Hence, as long as no specific commitment is undertaken, not only does the GATS admit monopolies and exclusive service suppliers, but there is also no system of sanctions to curb its abuse.

On the contrary, the legal discipline is much stricter when a State decides to grant monopolistic rights in a sector where it has already undertaken specific commitments. In such a case, pursuant to Article VIII:4, the State must notify its intention to the Council for Trade in Services in order to commence negotiation for compensatory adjustments under Article XXI. Similarly to the modification of a Schedule, States are exposed to the risk of having to provide compensation in other sectors or modes of supply.[131] Therefore, if a government becomes disappointed with foreign private management and decides to restore a public monopoly, it would be called to provide compensatory adjustments. Clearly, such compensation may have chilling effects on poor countries.

This latter provision adds further weight to the argument that monopolies, either public or private, are exempted from liberalization and privatization as long as no commitment is undertaken. Once a Member gives up such an exemption, the competition "*for*" the monopolist market has to be opened to foreign suppliers under conditions of parity, and States might be *de facto* prevented from reversing a privatization process.

3.2. The GATS provisions on specific commitments

In addition to the general obligations on and disciplines of domestic regulations and subsidies, specific commitments to market access and national treatment may also constrain the State's power to tailor domestic rules to its social and economic needs. Below, I consider how specific commitments may limit a State's leeway in this area.

3.2.1. Market access

Article XVI:1 provides that Member States must "*accord services and service suppliers of any other Member treatment no less favourable than that provided for under the terms, limitations and conditions agreed and specified in its Schedule*".

The second paragraph lists an exhaustive[132] number of measures that Members shall not maintain or adopt in the sectors in which they have undertaken market-access commitments, unless otherwise specified in their Schedules. It is noteworthy

[131] GATS, art. VIII:4.

[132] WTO, Report of the Panel, *United States – Measures Affecting Cross-Border Supply of Gambling and Betting Services, Recourse to Article 21.5 of the DSU by Antigua and Barbuda*, WT/DS285/RW, 30 March 2007, para. 3.318; WTO, Report of the Panel, *China – Measures Affecting Trading Rights and Distribution Services for Certain Publications and Audiovisual Entertainment Products,* WT/DS363/R, 12 August 2009, para. 7.1353.

that not all measures affecting the supply of services fall under the scope of this provision, but only those included in the six categories listed therein.[133] Recently, a panel has stressed that the test to be applied in order to establish whether measures fall under these categories is a strict one. It should be construed taking into account the object and purpose of the GATS as reflected in its preamble, which underlines the right to regulate of Member States in order to meet their national policy objectives.[134]

Among the limitations prohibited are those established under Article XVI:2(*a*) concerning "*limitations on the number of service suppliers whether in the form of numerical quotas, monopolies, exclusive service suppliers or the requirements of an economic needs test*".

Noteworthy, according to WTO dispute settlement bodies, the reference to "*limitations on the number of service suppliers 'in the form of monopolies and exclusive suppliers' should be read to include limitations that are in the form* or in effect, *monopolies or exclusive service* suppliers".[135] Article XVI:2(*a*) indeed does not "*require that quantitative limitations be explicitly expressed in numerical terms*";[136] what matters is not the form of limitations, notably if a monopoly or an exclusive service supplier has been formally established, but their numerical, or quantitative, nature, i.e. whether they seek to limit the service suppliers to one or to a small number.[137] Accordingly, a full commitment to market access would prohibit the adoption or maintenance of measures consisting in, *inter alia*, limitations on the number of service suppliers in the form of monopolies, or exclusive service suppliers.[138]

Given that the water services sector is still considered a natural monopoly where competition "*in*" the market is beyond the reach of private suppliers, undertaking market access commitments would seem unfeasible.

---

[133] WTO, Report of the Panel, *China – Certain Measures Affecting Electronic Payment Services*, WT/DS413/R, 16 July 2012, para. 7.652.

[134] WTO, Report of the Panel, *European Union and its Member States – Certain Measures Relating to the Energy Sector*, para. 7.650, and nt. 1134 (n 41), recalling: WTO, Report of the Panel, *Argentina – Measures Relating to Trade in Goods and Services*, WT/DS453/R, 30 September 2015, para. 7.423; WTO, Report of the Panel, *United States – Measures Affecting the Cross-Border Supply of Gambling and Betting Services*, paras. 6.314-6.317 (n 25). See fourth recital of the GATS preamble.

[135] WTO, Report of the Appellate Body, *United States – Measures Affecting Cross-Border Gambling and Betting Services*, para. 230 (n 71).

[136] WTO, Report of the Panel, *European Union and its Member States – Certain Measures Relating to the Energy Sector*, para. 7.598 (n 41); WTO, Report of the Appellate Body, *United States – Measures Affecting Cross-Border Gambling and Betting Services*, para. 236 (n 71).

[137] WTO, Report of the Appellate Body, *United States – Measures Affecting Cross-Border Gambling and Betting Services*, para. 232 (n 71); WTO, Report of the Panel, *China – Certain Measures Affecting Electronic* Services, paras. 7.592-7.593 (n 133); WTO, Report of the Panel, *European Union and its Member States – Certain Measures Relating to the Energy Sector*, paras. 7.598-7.599 (n 41).

[138] Türk, Krajewski, p. 8 (n 32).

As mentioned in section 3.1.3, it has been argued that the provision does not concern *natural* monopolies which exist as a result of excessive costs of network duplication and which are neither created nor maintained by public authorities. Assuming this conclusion, one may question the point of undertaking market access commitments in natural monopolies such as the water services sector.

There might be two answers to this question. First, commitments may be honoured by introducing competition "*for*" the market, thus opening the bidding process for the concession of the right to operate the sector to foreign providers. Recently, a panel has posited that, while being uncommon, "*nothing would prevent a monopoly and/or exclusive service suppliers from being of foreign origin*".[139]

Secondly, competition may be introduced by eliminating vertical integration across the water services chain in order to open the market to different suppliers. In this case, monopolies or exclusive service suppliers might be regarded as regulatory instruments chosen by States and prohibited as such under Article XVI:2(*a*) GATS. In this scenario, if a State decided to keep the water sector under monopoly (i.e. in order to compensate the provider for losses incurred to comply with universal services obligations), it would be required to specify this intention in its Schedule of commitments.

3.2.2. National treatment

The national treatment provision establishes that each Member has to accord to foreign services and service suppliers treatment no less favorable than that it grants to its own like services and service suppliers, unless otherwise specified in its Schedule. Article XVII:2 clarifies that this requirement is met when a Member grants "*to services and service suppliers of any other Member, either formally identical treatment or formally different treatment to that it accords to its own like services and service suppliers*". Article XVII:3 GATS provides that "*[f]ormally identical or formally different treatment shall be considered to be* less favourable *if it modifies the conditions of competition in favour of services or service suppliers of the Member compared to like services or service suppliers of any other Member*".

In the *China – Publications and Audiovisual Products*, the panel found that the prohibition of the offering of certain services by a foreign supplier – services which a like domestic operator was allowed to provide – "*cannot constitute treatment 'no less favourable', since it deprives the foreign service supplier of any opportunity to compete with like domestic suppliers*".[140] This treatment modified the conditions of competition and was inconsistent with China's national treatment commitments

---

[139] WTO, Report of the Panel, *European Union and its Member States – Certain Measures Relating to the Energy Sector*, para. 7.715 (n 41).

[140] WTO, Report of the Panel, *China – Measures Affecting Trading Rights and Distribution Services for Certain Publications and Audiovisual Entertainment Products,* para. 7.979 (n 132).

under the terms of Article XVII:3 GATS.[141] Likewise, in *EU – Energy Sector*, the panel held that the third-country certification measures, namely certifications requested only for transmission system operators controlled by third-country or by persons from third countries,[142] adopted by some EU States in order to implement Article 11 of the EU Directive 2009/73/EC, were inconsistent with Article XVII GATS as they failed to accord to services and service suppliers of other Members treatment not less favorable than that accorded to their own like services and suppliers.[143]

The test for assessing a violation of Article XVII follows a number of steps: *i*) ascertaining whether the Member State has assumed national treatment commitments in the relevant sector(s) and mode(s) of supply in its GATS Schedule; *ii*) establishing whether the measure contested does affect the supply in the relevant sector(s) and mode(s) of supply; *iii*) assessing if the relevant services and services suppliers are like; *iv*) and, finally, finding whether by way of the measures contested the Member accords to third country services or services suppliers treatment less favorable than that accorded to its own services or services suppliers.[144] Scholars highlight that the formula "*formally identical or formally different treatment*" suggests that this provision prohibits not only *de jure* discrimination between foreign and domestic suppliers, but also forms of *de facto* discriminations.[145]

The criteria for identifying discriminatory treatment towards foreign services and service suppliers are objective: they do not take into account the government's intent in the determination of a violation of national treatment commitments, but only the effect of the differentiated treatment in terms of worst conditions of competition for foreign services and service suppliers.

The Appellate Body, following the precedents developed under the GATT,[146] has refused to apply the so-called "*aim and effects*" test, which attaches weight to regulatory considerations. It has instead stated that: "*[w]e see no specific authority either in Article II or in Article XVII of the GATS for the proposition that the 'aim and effects' of a measure are in any way relevant in determining whether that measure is inconsistent with those provisions*".[147]

Cossy argues that recent jurisprudence seems more prone to consider the pur-

---

[141] *Ibid.*, para. 7.981

[142] WTO, Report of the Panel, *European Union and its Member States – Certain Measures Relating to the Energy Sector*, para. 2.2.7.2 (n 41).

[143] *Ibid.*, para. 7.10.2 (n 41).

[144] *Ibid.*, para. 7.1119.

[145] Türk, Krajewski, p. 9 (n 32).

[146] WTO, Reports of the Appellate Body, *Japan – Taxes on Alcoholic Beverages*, WT/DS8/AB/R, WT/SS10/AB/R, WT/DS11/AB/R, 4 October 1996, pp. 27-28.

[147] WTO, Report of the Appellate Body, *European Communities – Regime for the Importation, Sale and Distribution of Bananas*, WT/DS27/AB/R, 9 September 1997, para. 241.

pose of the contested measures in deciding on GATS violations,[148] but she refers only to "*hints*" to be read between the lines of the panels and the Appellate Body reports. The author recommends that the Appellate Body revisit its previous holding on the "*aim and effect*" doctrine and underlines the importance of determining violations of national treatment by taking into account regulatory distinctions that go beyond the list of exception enshrined in Article XIV GATS.[149]

In the water sector, this situation of differentiated treatment between national and foreign service suppliers is likely to occur, in particular because water services are often decentralized and different local authorities may give different treatment to providers established in various areas of the country.[150] Some sub-regions may prefer holding the water sector in public hands, whereas others may opt for private involvement. Public domestic water companies may be given more favorable treatment than private foreign water companies in terms of subsidies, possibilities of raising tariffs or be made subject to more limited requests for improving and expanding the water network.

To give a practical example, we can refer to the *Impregilo v. Argentina* case.[151] The Argentine Republic is subdivided in 23 Provinces and one autonomous city, Buenos Aires. Within the Province of Buenos Aires, concessions of the water service have been granted to different providers in distinct areas and under different conditions. This has raised claims of discrimination before an investment tribunal. The case is worth recalling in order to show how claims of discrimination are likely to receive greater consideration in a trade dispute than in an investment one.

In the *Impregilo* case, the investor claimed to have been affected by discriminatory treatments amounting to a breach of the fair and equitable treatment clause. The international investment tribunal acknowledged that, in the light of the Argentina-Italy BIT, the claim of discrimination was a "*specification of the general requirement of fair and equitable treatment*", but having already found a breach of the fair and equitable treatment obligation on other grounds, it did not examine allegations of discrimination.[152] In general terms, it is difficult for a discriminatory measure to amount, *per se*, to a breach of the fair and equitable treatment clause, if not accompanied by other non transparent or unreasonable acts.

---

[148] M. Cossy, *Determining 'Likeness' Under the GATS: Squaring the Circle?*, WTO Staff Working Paper No. ERSD-2006-08, 2006, p. 27, available at: http://papers.ssrn.com. The author quotes: WTO, Reports of the Appellate Body, *Japan – Taxes on Alcoholic Beverages*, p. 18 (n 146); WTO, Report of the Panel, *US – Taxes on Automobiles*, DS31/R, 11 October 1994, para. 5.12; WTO, Report of the Appellate Body, *European Communities – Measures affecting Asbestos and Asbestos-Containing Products*, WT/DS135/AB/R, 12 March 2001 para. 100.

[149] Cossy, pp. 39-40, 45, 47 (n 148).

[150] For a range of examples, see Lang, pp. 811-812 (n 14).

[151] *Impregilio S.p.A. v. Argentina Republic*, ICSID Case No. ARB/07/17, Award, 21 June 2011.

[152] *Ibid.*, para. 333.

On the contrary, the role of non-discrimination within the GATS is greater, both under the *most favored clause* and the *national treatment clause*. A full commitment on national treatment prevents a State from adopting measures in favor of national public operators. Therefore, a similar commitment may affect the possibility of granting more favorable conditions to domestic public service suppliers.[153]

Furthermore, commitments on national treatment may have repercussions on the most favored nation obligations. Indeed, if a Member makes specific commitments in a given sector, it can no longer enjoy potential MFN exceptions in the sector concerned.[154] Thus, this Member will be obligated to provide at least the minimum standard of treatment specified in its schedule to all WTO Members.[155] This implies that any other Member State may raise objections of discrimination if it deems to have received less favorable treatment than that provided to other suppliers in other areas of the country.

In light of the foregoing, the GATS national treatment clause may raise issues of incompatibility with national regulatory measures in the water sector. It remains to be seen whether the Agreement provides some leeway in case Members decide to adopt measures aimed at regulating services in the public interest.

4. Harmonizing trade in services with the human right to water

This section follows the model of analysis set out in chapter one by starting with assessing possible ways to prevent the rise of normative conflict between GATS commitments in the water sector and the obligations stemming from the derivative right to water. It then proceeds by considering the role that may be played by systemic interpretation of relevant GATS provisions to avoid the rise of these conflicts and, finally, establishes whether priority can be attached to the right to water in the context of trade disputes before the WTO dispute settlement bodies.

4.1. Harmonization by means of conflict prevention

According to the CESCR, "*[a]greements concerning trade liberalization should not curtail or inhibit a country's capacity to ensure the full realization of the right to water*".[156] The GATS, thanks to its flexibility, offers opportunities to prevent normative conflicts between the obligations assumed under the treaty and those stemming from human rights norms. How to handle this flexibility when undertaking specific

[153] See, for an example on Health Services, Krajewski, p. 188 (n 28).

[154] Munin, p. 113 (n 5).

[155] *Ibid.*, pp. 121-122, para. 6.6.1.4.

[156] General Comment No. 15, para. 35 (n 91).

commitments of trade liberalization is the topic of the following sub-section. In addition, the GATS includes a clause of subordination, which can be read as exempting States from responsibility for treaty violations in exceptional circumstances. The scope of this provision, however tight, warrants attention and will be addressed in sub-section 4.1.2.

4.1.1. Scheduling commitments for water services

The GATS allows States to tailor their commitments to trade liberalization according to their own needs by inserting terms, limitations, conditions, and qualifications to individual Schedules of specific commitments.[157] The relevant question for the present work is how to benefit the most from such flexibility when scheduling specific commitments in the water sector in order to take into account the States' duty to protect under the human right to water.

The core features of water services to be kept in mind may be summarized as follows. In the first place, the supply of water services is often decentralized. This means that services are not provided by central governmental authorities, but locally over a determined geographical area. Secondly, the service may be provided alternatively by local public authorities themselves through public entities, or else by private providers who have been granted exclusive rights to operate the service or have acquired the ownership of the water utilities. In the third place, water services are still considered natural monopolies. Given this monopolistic nature, the sector cannot be opened to competition "*in*" the market, but only "*for*" the market.

Limitations aimed at specifying the extent to which a State consents to open its water market sector should be scheduled so to take into account each country's specific needs and expectations. In general terms, it seems to me that in the water sector the most important limitations are those intended to bind the role of private entities in the supply of public services. In this connection, restrictions and conditions may take different forms.

In the first instance, pursuant to Article XVI:2 GATS, conditions for market access may be scheduled on the basis of regional subdivisions. Given that water services are mainly decentralized, Members may exclude public services from the scope of the GATS only in respect of those regions that have not privatized the water sector. Thus, market access for foreign suppliers would not be granted over the entire territory, but only within the area where commitments to market access are undertaken.[158]

---

[157] Art. XX:1 GATS refers to: "*(a) terms, limitations and conditions on market access; (b) conditions and qualifications on national treatment*". In this chapter, for the sake of simplicity, we will refer generically to "*limitations*" and "*conditions*". For further details on the distinctions among these terms, see Munin, p. 128 and pp. 186-187 (n 5).

[158] Cossy, p. 138 (n 46).

As a consequence, there could be differences among sub-national divisions with respect to liberalization commitments. For instance, water services may be public and closed to foreign suppliers in some regions and liberalized and open in others.

Moreover, conditions may be based on sub-regional divisions. Indeed, although Article XVI on market access refers only to "*regional subdivision*", "*[t]he concept of 'region' may refer to states, provinces, or cantons, but also to municipalities*".[159] Member States may resort to this possibility, as the management of water services may be organized locally.[160] For instance, in Italy the water supply is organized according to infra-regional territorial organizations named optimal territorial basins.[161] However, where the provision of water services is organized within small local contexts and according to different ownership models, it cannot be easy to list all public utilities present in the national territory.[162]

Aside from these conditions on a regional basis, commitments may be limited on a sectoral basis. For instance, thus far, commitments on environmental services have been constrained by means of sectoral headnotes or footnotes included in Members' Schedules that have exempted environmental services supplied by public authorities from the scope of the specific commitments undertaken.[163]

In addition, restrictions on market access commitments may be scheduled in re-

---

[159] *Ibid.* Although art. XVI does not define the meaning of the term "*regional subdivision*", a combined reading of art. I:3(*a*) and the Scheduling Guidelines suggests that Members can set the geographical scope of their limitations on a sub-regional level. See WTO, *Guidelines for the Scheduling of Specific Commitments under the General Agreement on Trade in Services (GATS)*, para. 4 (n 67).

[160] For instance: Argentina, Chile, France, Italy, Malaysia, Sri Lanka, Ukraine, and Zambia. On the issue of water services decentralization see the World Bank website: http://www1.worldbank.org/publicsector/decentralization/service.htm#5.

[161] On this matter see, L. Arnaudo, *Holes in the Water. The Reforme of Water Services and Competition in Italy,* in *Competition and Regulation in Network Industries*, 2011, pp. 173-187; V. Parisio, *La gestione dei servizi pubblici a rete: il servizio idrico integrato tra monopoli e concorrenza*, in *Giustizia civile*, 2007, pp. 435-444; V. Parisio, *Demanio idrico e gestione del servizio idrico in una prospettiva comparata. Una riflessione a più voci*, Brescia, 2011; S. Urbinati, *L'état de la reconnaissance du droit de l'homme à l'eau potable et à l'assainissement en Italie*, in Smets H. (ed.), *Le droit à l'eau potable et à l'assainissement en Europe. Implementing the right to drinking water and sanitation in 17 European countries*, Paris, 2012, pp. 355-372. However, Italy enjoys of the EU horizontal limitation which will be discussed below in this section.

[162] Cossy, p. 138 (n 46).

[163] WTO, Council for Trade in Services, *Background Note on Environmental Services*, pp. 23-24 (n 22). For instance, the Swedish Schedule specifies that in respect of environmental services: "*[t]he offer does not include public works functions whether owned and operated by municipalities, state or federal governments or contracted out by these governments*". Sweden, *Schedule of Specific Commitments*, GATS/SC/82, 15 April 1994. Similarly, the Norwegian Schedule provides: "*[t]hese commitments do not include public service functions whether owned and operated or contracted out by local, regional or central government*". Norway, *Schedule of Specific Commitments*, GATS/SC/66, 15 April 1994.

lation to specific mode of supply. Given that water services are supplied through "*commercial presence*", limitations may be inscribed under mode 3 with respect to the role of public authorities.[164] For example, as regards wastewater services, one Member has confirmed that "*services supplied in the exercise of governmental authority as defined in Article 1:3(c) may be subject to public monopolies or exclusive rights granted to private operators*".[165]

Furthermore, horizontal limitations – which apply in relation to all GATS provisions and to all services sectors – may carve out all public services from the scope of the GATS. Interestingly, the former European Community has listed a public services limitation in the horizontal part of its Schedule.[166] It reads as follows:

> "in all EC Member States services considered as public utilities at a national or local level may be subject to public monopolies or to exclusive rights granted to private operator".[167]

Moreover, a footnote clarifies that:

> "Public utilities exist in sectors as related scientific and technical consulting services, R&D services on social science and humanities, technical test and analysis services, environmental services, health services, transport services and services auxiliary to all modes of transport. Exclusive rights on such services are often granted to private operators, for instance operators with concessions from public authorities, subject to specific service obligations. Given that public utilities often also exist at the sub-central level, detailed and exhaustive sector-specific scheduling is not practical".[168]

This limitation not only concerns specific sectors but, being horizontal, can also be applied to all GATS provisions, including the MFN clause and the national treatment clause. As far as public utilities are concerned, European Union States can hence discriminate between national and foreign providers, as well as among foreign providers.

With respect to wastewater treatment services, a sector where the European Union has undertaken specific commitments of liberalization, the horizontal limitation implies that as long as such a service is considered a *public utility* in the territory of

---

[164] This possibility has been envisaged by the Council for Trade in Services with regard to "*the role of local authorities with respect to the provision of infrastructure services*". WTO, Council for Trade in Services, *Background Note on Environmental Services*, p. 25 (n 22).

[165] WTO, *Vietnam, Schedule of Specific Commitments*, GATS/SC/142, 19 March 2007.

[166] WTO, *European Communities and their Member States, Schedule of Specific Commitments*, GATS/SC/31, 15 April 1994.

[167] *Ibid.*

[168] *Ibid.*

a Member State, it is exempted from the scope of the GATS. Thanks to this limitation, the European Union leaves Member States broad discretion to determine which services are to be "*considered as public utilities*". [169]

Finally, the European Union has made an explicit reference to private operators subject to specific service obligations. The meaning of such a notion has not been specified, but it may be understood as referring to any universal service obligation. [170] Therefore, should specific commitments be adopted in the water sector within the European Union, public authorities will retain the power to confer exclusive rights on domestic private operators.

Against this scenario, scholars have taken different positions as to the extent to which the State's regulatory power is preserved under the GATS. Given the possibility for Members to put individual limitations on their own commitments, some scholars have concluded that the Agreement provides governments with sufficient freedom to choose their level of commitment and does not risk affect the enjoyment of essential services as a result. [171]

Others have argued that the possibility of setting individual limitations does not provide sufficient safeguards, as it leaves this choice to the discretion and capacities of the State. Quite the opposite, the GATS should envisage a specific discipline for public services applicable in all Member States. [172]

There are also authors who have contended that, to serve their scope, conditions have to be framed in such a way as to remain effective in any circumstance, even when a change occurs in the private equity participation of the service provider. [173] It has been noted that if a limitation simply refers to public services *owned* by governmental authorities, an increase in equity participation is likely to affect the scope of the limitation. [174] Since Article XXVIII defines ownership as the participation in a juridical person with "*more than 50 per cent of the equity interest*", [175] an increase of private equity over 50 per cent would make the limitation inapplicable.

Ultimately, it seems that the possibility of carving out regulatory autonomy for public authorities rests on the State's ability to frame effective limitations. [176] States

---

[169] Türk and others, pp. 153-154 (n 14).

[170] *Ibid.*, p. 167.

[171] Munari, pp. 844-845 (n 18); Costamagna, p. 521 (n 101).

[172] Mastroianni, Arena, p. 33 (n 17).

[173] According to some authors, privatization may be understood as increasing private equity participation in public services. See, Türk and others, pp. 155-158 (n 14).

[174] *Ibid.* The authors took as example the Swedish Schedule of Specific Commitments (n 163).

[175] GATS, art. XVIII(*n*)(*i*).

[176] In this connection, see M. Krajewski, *Model Clauses for the Exclusion of Public Services From Trade and Investment Agreements*, Vienna, 2016.

lacking technical skills and expertise would thus run the highest risk in undertaking commitments in the water services sector.[177]

Furthermore, if an error is made in framing limitations within a Schedule of specific commitments, or if commitments are mistakenly taken without limitations, there is little opportunity to modify them in order to maintain a general level of mutually advantageous commitments, owing to the compensatory adjustments requested under Article XXI GATS.[178]

4.1.2. The subordination clause in favor of measures necessary to protect human life and health

The exceptional clause enshrined in Article XIV of the Agreement allows States to adopt measures otherwise prohibited when they are necessary to protect interests considered to be of particular importance. This clause carves out the applicability of the GATS rules in specific circumstances, including when the conflicting measures are "*necessary to protect human, animal or plant life or health*". Confronted with the necessity of protecting these supreme values – life and health – the Agreement takes a step back and recognises that trade interests may be trumped.

However, a number of conditions are listed in the exception clause that have to be met for a conflicting measure to be adopted or enforced without breaching the Agreement. In addition, these conditions have been interpreted by WTO adjudicating bodies in a trade-friendly perspective, adding complexity to its reading and contributing to the *de facto* deprivation of much of the scope of this clause. In sum, doubts may be cast as to the effective subordination of trade objectives to the safeguarding of human life and health. Having the right to water as our term of reference, we will address this matter in sub-section 4.3.

4.2. Harmonization by means of interpretation of GATS provisions applicable to water services

In addition to the possibility of inserting limitations into the Schedules of specific commitments so as to avoid possible conflicts between liberalization commitments and human rights obligations, the GATS provides some leeway for States to regu-

---

[177] Kurkarni discourages WTO Members from scheduling commitments related to basic social services, such as water services, due to the lack of regulatory capacity. Kulkarni, pp. 262, 267 (n 8).

[178] A case in point is that of the privatization of water services in Great Britain, which brought a substantial rise in water fees and, consequently, an increased rate of disconnection for non-payment. In order to protect weaker consumers, the British government adopted legislation which prevented private providers from disconnecting poor households in a number of cases. Had the government taken commitments of service liberations under the GATS, these measures would likely be in breach of the GATS rules. Kulkarni, pp. 261-262 (n 8).

late the supply of services in order to pursue their public interest objectives. As far as the human right to water is concerned, it is contended that the exercise of this right to regulate can be the meeting point of conflicting obligations stemming from the right to water and the GATS commitments.[179]

In this connection, the interpretation of GATS provisions[180] should be shaped by the preamble of the Agreement,[181] which explicitly recognises "*the right for Members to regulate, and to introduce new regulations, on the supply of services within their territories in order to meet national policy objectives*" (fourth recital). In the first place, this recital provides context for interpreting the GATS,[182] and, secondly, it offers indications for establishing the purpose of the Agreement.[183] Contextual interpretation and teleological interpretation could provide tools for harmonizing different obligations that may arise from human rights law and trade law.

Krawjeski proposes considering the right to regulate as a term of reference for interpreting the GATS. The author acknowledges the possibility of conflict between trade liberalization and domestic regulations and, in this respect, refers to a human rights approach to GATS. In his view, the Agreement should be interpreted consistently with the national regulatory autonomy aimed to fulfill human rights obligations and, thus, to guarantee equal access to all essential services.[184]

In general terms, authors have taken different positions about the role effectively played by the States' right to regulate in the public interest in the WTO case law. According to some, the WTO adjudicating bodies have started to take regulatory concerns into consideration in interpreting relevant provisions of WTO Agreements other than the GATS.[185] Although the precedents have not been openly overruled,

---

[179] C.-H. Wu, H. Hai-Ning Huang, *Right to Water in the Shadow of Trade Liberalization*, in J. Chaisse (ed.) *The Regulation of the Global Water Service Market*, Cambridge, 2017, pp. 139-166.

[180] As for the possibility to interpret WTO provisions so as to respect human rights, see G. Marceau, *WTO Dispute Settlement and Human Rights*, in *European Journal of International Law*, 2002, pp. 753-814.

[181] M. H. Hulme, *Preambles in Treaty Interpretation*, in *University of Pennsylvania Law Review*, 2016, pp. 1281-1346; I. Van Damme, *Treaty Interpretation by the WTO Appellate Body*, in *European Journal of International Law*, 2010, pp. 605-648; L. R. Popa, *Patterns of Treaty Interpretation as Anti-Fragmentation Tools: A Comparative Analysis with a Special Focus on the ECtHR, WTO and ICJ*, Cham, 2018.

[182] Vienna Convention on the Law of Treaties, Vienna, 23 May 1969, art. 31(1)(2). See Cossy, p. 40 (n 148).

[183] O. Dörr, *Article 31. General Rule of Interpretation*, in O. Dörr, K. Schmalenbach (eds.), *Vienna Convention on the Law of Treaties. A Commentary*, Berlin, 2018, p. 584, para. 52.

[184] Krajewski, pp. 60-62 (n 28).

[185] Recently the regulatory purpose of measures has been taken into account in shaping the meaning of the concept of "*likeness*" in art. 2(1) of the TBT Agreement and of art. III:4 of the GATT 1994. See WTO, Report of the Appellate Body, *United States – Measures Affecting the Production and Sale of Clove Cigarettes*, WT/DS406/AB/R, 4 April 2012, paras. 117-120; A. D.

it is argued that this new trend may support and shape the interpretation of relevant GATS provisions in the years to come.[186]

Other commentators maintain that the WTO jurisprudence has proved to be reluctant to take into account interests other than trade liberalization in interpreting the covered Agreements. In this connection, Connolly refers to the *EC-Biotech* case, where the panel was asked to interpret the covered Agreements systematically, pursuant to Article 31(3)(*c*) VCLT. It held itself to be prevented from interpreting these Agreements in light of other international instruments [notably, the Convention on Biological Diversity and the Biosafety Protocol], as the latter were not binding between all WTO Members.[187] Moreover, the WTO Appellate Body has recently applied a "*test of rationality*" to evaluate the consistency of States' regulations in sensitive fields, such as public health and morals, in order to assess whether or not regulations were discriminatory.[188] It is argued that such a test would negatively impact States' regulatory power, as it puts an excessive burden on States. On the one hand, Members have to prove the non-discriminatory purpose of the measure undertaken.[189] On the other hand, dispute settlement bodies are put in a position to "*critically review Member State's regulation*",[190] hence affecting the regulatory leeway left to Members.

Against this background, sub-sections 4.2.1 and 4.2.2 assess the role played by the right to regulate in the public interest, first in the modest GATS case law concerning violations of market access and national treatment commitments and, then, in the GATS rules directed to public services with specific regard to the applicability to water services.

Mitchell, D. Heaton, C. Henckels, *Non-Discrimination and the Role of Regulatory Purpose in International Trade and Investment Law*, Cheltenham, 2016, p. 61.

[186] Cossy, p. 47 (n 148).

[187] K. Connolly, *Finding Space for Regulatory Autonomy in GATS Article XVII after EC-Seals: Public Services and the 'Likeness' of Public and Private Service Providers*, in *Legal Issues of Economic Integration*, 2015, p. 60; WTO, Report of the Panel Report, *European Communities – Measures Affecting the Approval and Marketing of Biotech Products*, WT/DS291/R, 29 September 2006, paras. 7.73-7.75.

[188] WTO, Report of the Appellate Body, *Brazil – Measures Affecting Imports of Retreaded Tyres*, WT/DS332/AB/R, 3 December 2007; WTO, Report of the Appellate Body, *United States – Measures Concerning the Importation, Marketing and Sale of Tuna and Tuna Products*, WT/DS381/AB/R, 16 May 2012; WTO, Reports of the Appellate Body, *European Communities – Measures Prohibiting the Importation and Marketing of Seal Products*, WT/DS400/AB/R, WT/DS401/AB/R, 22 May 2014.

[189] E. Lydgate, *Is it Rational and Consistent? The WTO's Surprising Role in Shaping Domestic Public Policy*, in *Journal of International Economic Law*, 2017, p. 562.

[190] *Ibid.*

4.2.1. The right to regulate in the public interest and the interpretation of the GATS provisions concerning market access and national treatment

This sub-section evaluates the jurisprudence of WTO adjudicating bodies concerning disputes involving GATS rules so to consider the role played by the States' regulatory autonomy *vis-à-vis* commitments of liberalization of trade in services.

4.2.1.1. The interpretation of the market access clause

Unless otherwise scheduled, market access limitations are prohibited under Article XVI GATS. The bordering line between these limitations and domestic regulations, which are in principle permitted pursuant to Article VI GATS, is of the utmost importance in order to grant a certain regulatory space to Members. In this connection, it is useful to recall that Article VI GATS admits domestic regulations that may affect commitments of liberalization to the extent that they do not discriminate against foreign services and service providers and are not unnecessary barriers to trade (no "*more burdensome than necessary*" to ensure the quality of the service).

An erroneous qualification is not without consequences. Not only are market access restrictions prohibited, while domestic regulations are in principle permitted, but qualitative restrictions also enjoy broader justifications than market access restrictions, which are limited to those listed in Article XIV GATS.

Moreover, the burden of proof rests on the Member who complains against domestic restrictions, while it is for the defendant to prove that its measures do not restrict access to markets or that such measures are otherwise justified. [191]

Criticisms have been made concerning the criteria followed by WTO dispute settlement bodies to distinguish between domestic regulations and market access limitations prohibited under Article XVI GATS. In the *US-Gambling* case, the panel qualified a remote gambling and betting prohibition, which had the effect of quantitative restrictions, as a market access limitation [192] rather than as a technical standard. [193] It held that since the prohibition had the effect of limiting the number of service suppliers and the number of service operations and/or the service output, it amounted to a quantitative limitation, forbidden under Article XVI:(*a*)(*c*). [194]

Quantitative limitations are restrictions on the *number* of service suppliers or service operations expressed *in the form* of numerical quota. Relying on the wording of Article XVI, the United States posited that interpreting the meaning of the terms

---

[191] J. Pauwelyn, *Rien ne Va Plus? Distinguishing Domestic Regulation From Market Access in GATT and GATS*, in *World Trade Review*, 2005, p. 138.

[192] WTO, Report of the Panel, *United States – Measures Affecting the Cross-Border Supply of Gambling and Betting Services*, para. 6.437 (n 25).

[193] Pauwelyn, p. 132 (n 191). See also Prévost (n 77).

[194] WTO, Report of the Panel, *United States – Measures Affecting the Cross-Border Supply of Gambling and Betting Services*, paras. 6.338, 6.355 (n 25).

"*in the form of numerical quotas*" as equivalent to "*having the* effect *of*" quantitative restrictions "*would be inconsistent with the balance between liberalization and the right to regulate that is reflected in the GATS*",[195] tilting such balance in favor of the former.[196]

Since the Appellate Body dismissed the US's argument and upheld the panel's finding,[197] some authors considered the WTO dispute settlement bodies' interpretation as being incompatible with the direction given in the GATS preamble to narrowly interpret restrictions on the State's regulatory power.[198] It is argued that in the light of the GATS preamble (which recognizes the right of Members to regulate) the US ban on remote gambling should have been qualified as a technical standard as it prescribed how gambling services were to be performed.[199] On the contrary, the panel and the Appellate Body's interpretations suggest that where domestic regulations have effects equivalent to quantitative restrictions, Article VI fails to apply. Scholars have contested this conclusion, observing that if all domestic regulations having the effect of quantitative restrictions were subject to Article XVI, most domestic regulations would be prohibited.[200]

However, in the aftermath of the *US-Gambling* case, another panel felt bound to clarify that the scope of Article XVI does not encompass indirect quantitative restrictions. In the *Argentina-Financial Services* case, Argentina had imposed a number of measures on services and service suppliers from jurisdictions that refused to exchange information for the purpose of fiscal transparency (so-called non-cooperative jurisdictions). The panel held that while "*[u]ltimately, each measure could be reduced to a limitation on the number of suppliers*", this interpretation "*would run counter to an effective interpretation of the GATS*".[201] In brief, *"[a]ny measure which only has the indirect effect of limiting any of the elements covered by subparagraphs (a) to (d) would not therefore be covered by that subparagraph*".[202]

In reaching this conclusion, the panel underlined that this approach was consistent with the GATS preamble that granted Members the right to regulate in order to meet national policy objectives. It pointed out that also in those sectors where Members have made specific commitments under Article XVI GATS, they

---

195 WTO, Report of the Appellate Body, *United States – Measures Affecting Cross-Border Gambling and Betting Services*, para. 224 (n 71).

196 *Ibid.*, para. 224.

197 *Ibid.*, paras. 224-252.

198 Pauwelyn, p. 160-161 (n 191). Prévost, p. 232 (n 77). See also Türk, Krajewski, p. 6 (n 32).

199 Pauwelyn, p. 132 (n 191). See also Prévost (n 77). *Contra*, Muller, pp. 60-462 (n 102).

200 Pauwelyn, p. 160-161 (n 191). Prévost, p. 232 (n 77). See also Türk, Krajewski, p. 6 (n 32).

201 WTO, Report of the Panel, *Argentina –Measures relating to Trade in Goods and Services*, para. 7.420 (n 134).

202 *Ibid.*, para. 7.421.

"*retain the right to regulate in order to meet their national policy objectives, subject to the relevant GATS disciplines, Article VI in particular*".[203] Accordingly, the panel dismissed the market access claim under Article XVI:2(*a*) GATS as the measure contested (requirements relating to reinsurance services) was not covered by that provision.[204]

This ruling, which overtly rejects the line of reasoning followed in the *US-Gambling* case, is more consistent with the objective set out in the GATS preamble to balance the right to regulate in the public interest with trade liberation commitments.[205] The case law concerning the boundary between domestic regulations and market access limitations is still under development to draw clear conclusions. However, it seems that the latest findings are inclined to follow a more balanced approach.

Having discussed the relationship between market access commitments and domestic regulations, we move to assessing the scope of Members' regulatory power under Article XVII.

4.2.1.2. The interpretation of the national treatment clause

Article XVII GATS prohibits Members from granting to foreign like services and service suppliers treatment less favorable than that accorded to domestic service and services suppliers. This provision is likely to constrain Members' regulatory power when it comes to according different treatment to domestic public providers of essential services.[206]

In an early report that followed the jurisprudence developed under the GATT, the Appellate Body rejected the so-called "*aim and effect*" doctrine[207] invoked by the former EC for interpreting national treatment commitments under Article XVII GATS in line with the States' right to regulate.[208] In the *EC-Banana III* case, the complainants challenged the European Communities' regime for the importation, distribution and sale of bananas established by EEC Council Reg. 404/93 under a number of counts, including Articles II and XVII GATS. The Appellate Body clarified that the aims and effects of the contested measures were irrelevant for establishing whether the conditions of competition had been modified so to be less fa-

---

203 *Ibid.*, para. 7.423.

204 *Ibid.*, para. 7.429.

205 Muller, pp. 462-463 (n 102).

206 Connolly, pp. 57-84 (n 187).

207 Under the aims and effects doctrine, the regulatory objective pursued by a certain measure is to be taken into account in order to distinguish between otherwise like services or service providers. Cossy disagrees with the Appellate Body's decision to rule out the aims and effects doctrine in the context of art. XVII GATS. Cossy, p. 23, fn. 56 (n 148).

208 WTO, Report of the Appellate Body, *European Communities – Regime for the Importation, Sale and Distribution of Bananas*, para. 241 (n 147).

vorable to service suppliers of third country origin *vis-à-vis* service suppliers of EC origin. Upholding the panel's ruling, the Appellate Body found that the measures complained of were discriminatory as they created less favorable conditions of competition for like service suppliers of complainants' origin and were thus inconsistent with Article XVII GATS.[209]

By the same token, more recently, the Appellate Body took the condition of competition as the sole criteria to establish a violation of Article XVII, excluding the relevance of the regulatory purpose in the less favorable treatment analysis.[210] In *Argentina-Financial Service*, the Appellate Body reversed the panel's finding that an analysis of the "*treatment no less favourable*" had to take into account "*regulatory aspects*",[211] such as those relating to the ability of Argentina to have access to tax information on foreign service suppliers.[212] According to the panel, the interpretation of the no less favorable requirement should have been directed by the recognition in the preamble of the Agreement of the Members' right to regulate in the public interests.[213]

In the Appellate Body's view, the panel analysis was mistaken as, by taking into consideration the "*regulatory aspects*" of the contested measures when interpreting the no less favorable requirement, it held a measure to be consistent with Article XVII even though it modified the conditions of competition to the detriment of foreign like services or service suppliers.[214] On the contrary, the legal standard enshrined in Article XVII:

> "does not contemplate a separate step of analysis regarding whether the 'regulatory aspects' relating to services suppliers could 'convert[]' the measure's detrimental impact on the conditions of competition into 'treatment no less favourable'".[215]

Regulatory aspects or concerns could not enter the less favorable treatment analysis but only justify a measure otherwise inconsistent with the non-discriminatory provisions of the GATS in the context of the relevant exceptions.[216]

---

[209] *Ibid.*, paras. 244, 246, 248.

[210] Muller, p. 368 (n 102).

[211] WTO, Report of the Panel, *Argentina – Measures Relating to Trade in Goods and Services*, para. 7.232 (n 134). The panel's reasoning on the no less favorable conditions of competition is applicable to both art. II GATS and art. XVII GATS, see para. 7.220. The same is posited by the Appellate Body. WTO, Appellate Body Report, *Argentina – Measures Relating to Trade in Goods and Services*, para. 6.105 (n 41).

[212] *Ibid.*, para. 7.235.

[213] *Ibid.*, paras. 7.233, 7.217.

[214] Appellate Body Report, *Argentina – Measures Relating to Trade in Goods and Services*, para. 6.2.4 (n 41).

[215] *Ibid.*, para 6.111.

[216] *Ibid.*, paras. 6.113-6.117.

I do not contest the conclusion reached by the Appellate Body that the legal standard set by Article XVII does not contemplate any additional step concerning the consistency of the contested measure with its regulatory purpose, but I am bound to note that regulatory aspects or concerns are likely to fail to justify a measure inconsistent with Article XVII also under the general exceptions clause, leaving little, if any, space for regulatory concerns. Indeed, as it will be shown in the next section, the *chapeau* of Article XIV also enshrined non-discriminatory concerns, which tilts the balance in favor of liberalization commitments rather than Members' regulatory autonomy.

Connolly suggests focusing on the notion of "*likeness*" in order to differentiate between domestic public providers and foreign private providers so as to rule out the applicability of Article XVII GATS in case of discriminatory measures taken in favor of the former.[217] Moving from the premises that so far WTO adjudicating bodies have been reluctant to interpret the WTO covered Agreements in light of other rules of international law, let alone international human rights rules, the author posits that a possible strategy to attract human rights considerations within the reasoning of the WTO Dispute Settlement Body rests on regarding the public and private providers of public services as different.

However attractive this proposal may be, it has not been followed by WTO DSB. Recently, a panel found that domestic and foreign suppliers of pipeline transport services were *like* service suppliers within the meaning of Article XVII GATS, specifying that in reaching this conclusion it was not influenced by the fact that certain transmission system operators (TSOs), notably the domestic ones, were controlled by public bodies.[218] This case deserves attention as, on a different ground, the panel considered a public body measure that set out a legal regime for service suppliers controlled by public bodies different from that applicable to all other service suppliers, consistent with Article XVII GATS. In the *EU-Energy Package* case, Russia challenged in several respects the EU regulatory framework in the energy market sector, the so-called "*Third Energy Package*", in particular Directive 2009/73/EC concerning the natural gas sector and the implementing legislation of Croatia, Hungary and Lithuania. Among the measures challenged there was the "*unbundling measure*" aimed to separate the functions of natural gas production and supply from the activities of natural gas transmission, against vertically integrated undertakings that performed both types of activities. In this context, Croatia,

---

[217] Connolly, pp. 69-77 (n 187).

[218] WTO, Report of the Panel, *European Union and its Member States – Certain Measures Relating to the Energy Sector*, para. 7.743 (n 41). The Panel Report is under appeal by both parties, the EU notified the DSB of its decision to appeal on 21 September 2018 (WT/DS476/6) and Russia notified the DSB of its decision to cross-appeal on 26 September 2018 (WT/DS476/7). For an early comment of the Panel report see V. Pogoretskyy, K. Talus, *The WTO Panel Report in EU-Energy Package and Its Implications for the EU's Gas Market and Energy Security*, in *World Trade Review*, 2019, pp. 1-19.

Hungary and Lithuania had taken advantage of the possibility left by Directive 2009/73/EC to apply the ownership unbundling requirement differently if the person concerned was a public body. Notably, if two separate public bodies of the same Member exercised control over a transmission system operator, on the one hand, and over an undertaking performing any function of production or supply, on the other hand, they were not considered to be the same person to the effect of the unbundling requirement. Russia considered this measure in breach of Article XVII GATS because it was regarded as an exception to the unbundling requirement available only to domestic service suppliers.

The panel posited that the sole fact that a different legal regime for public body was established did not *per se* demonstrate that the condition of competition had been modified to the detriment of like service suppliers of other Members.[219] Indeed, in that case, although the unbundling rules were different for services suppliers controlled by public bodies *vis-à-vis* those applicable to all other energy service suppliers, these rules were equivalent "*in ensuring a separation of function of natural gas transmission from the function of natural gas production and/or supply*"[220] and, in addition, the public body measure could in principle be applied also to service suppliers controlled by foreign public bodies.[221] Remaining within the limits traced by previous case law, and without referring to regulatory purposes, the panel reached the conclusion that service suppliers controlled by public bodies may be subject to different measures, but only to the extent that they do not modify the conditions of competition in detriment of service suppliers of other Members.[222]

4.2.2. The right to regulate in the public interest and the interpretation of the GATS provisions related to public services

Aside from the above case law concerning the regulatory space left to Member States in case of measures regarding services controlled by public bodies, the Agreement enshrines several provisions that seem to offer wider regulatory leeway when public services are at stake. Notably, these are the rules concerning "*governmental services*" (Article I:3(*b*)) and "*government procurement*" (Article XIII) that allow, under certain conditions, public services to be excluded from the scope of the GATS. Given that water services are public services, the following sub-sections focus on the interpretation of these rules.

---

[219] WTO, Report of the Panel, *European Union and its Member States – Certain Measures Relating to the Energy Sector*, para. 7.6 (n 41).

[220] *Ibid.*, para. 7.786.

[221] *Ibid.*, para. 7.822.

[222] This reasoning is in line with that suggested by J. Pauwelyn, *The Unbearable Lightness of Likeness*, 2006, pp. 5-6, available at SSRN: https://papers.ssrn.com/sol3/papers.cfm?abstract_id=2030940.

Preliminarily, it must be pointed out that the GATS does not give a definition of the notion of public services, instead showing a certain indifference to their unique features.[223] For the purpose of the present research, this notion is meant to indicate essential services for the attainment of general interest objectives.[224]

Apparently, the GATS does not impose a particular policy regime for public services, but leaves Member States free to decide whether the ownership of essential service, such as water services, is to be public or private.[225] Given the flexibility that characterizes the Agreement, some commentators have posited that the GATS does not risk affecting Members' choices concerning the organization of public services.[226]

I contend that the issue is less clear-cut than it may appear.[227] In the first place, as will be shown below, the scope of Articles I:3(*b*) and XIII GATS is vague.[228] Moreover, rarely are essential services, such as water services, provided entirely by public companies. Usually, public authorities involve private companies to various extents in the provision of the service.[229]

---

[223] The very notion of public services is ambiguous. It may be understood both as the provision of essential services, or as the public ownership or control of services. Adlung, pp. 456-457 (n 8); Mastroianni, Arena, p. 27 (n 17); Costamagna, pp. 113-145 (n 101); Connolly, p. 62 (n 187).

[224] For studies on other public services: S. J. Tania, S. Alam, *Liberalisation of sewerage and waste management services and the GATS: Implications and challenges for developing countries*, in *Journal of World Investment Trade*, 2011, pp. 519-550; D. Bakhouya, *The General Agreement on Trade in Services (GATS) and international trade in health services. Impact and regulations*, in *Juridical Tribune*, 2017, pp. 54-68.

[225] Cossy, p. 125 (n 46).

[226] Munari, p. 844 (n 18).

[227] M. Zettel, *The GATS, Privatization and Water Services – An overview of Legal Services*, in *Maastricht Working Papers, Faculty of Law*, 2006, pp. 23-24.

[228] M. Krajewski, *Public Services and Trade Liberalization – Mapping the Legal Framework*, in *Journal of International Economic Law*, 2003, p. 348.

[229] Water services may be provided through different "*ownership models*" notably public, private or mixed models. Services are publicly owned when a public authority is the sole provider and there is no involvement of the private sector. Public owned companies are fully or predominantly directed or controlled by national or regional authorities. Secondly, States may choose to involve private stakeholders in the water sector in several ways. Finally, States may opt for the full privatization of water service, water infrastructure included. When a public authority completely divests itself of the assets, its role is transformed into that of a mere regulator. This full-scale privatization is rather rare: see Human Rights Council, *Report of the independent expert on the issue of human rights obligations related to access to safe drinking water and sanitation*, para. 9 (114). So far, full privatization has occurred only in England and Wales, and in Chile. S. Hendry, *Ownership Models for Water Services: Implications for Regulation*, in A. McHarg, B. Barton, A. Bradbrook, L. Godden (eds.), *Property and the Law in Energy and Natural Resources*, Oxford, 2010. According to Krajewski, public ownership can be divided in three forms, consisting in: direct provision of services by the government without an intermediate body; creation of a publicly owned company under public law on the basis of special statutory provisions; incorporation of a

The previous section (section 4.1.1.) concluded that, given the flexibility of the GATS, the possibility exists to carve out a discipline of public services within the framework of the Agreement.[230] However, where no specific limitations or conditions have been inserted into the individual Schedule of specific commitments in this connection, the following sub-sections deal with the GATS rules generally applicable to public services, respectively concerning "*services supplied in the exercise of governmental authority*" (section 4.2.2.1.) and "*procurement of services purchased for governmental purposes*" (section 4.2.2.2.). The issue is to establish whether and to what extent these provisions do exempt public services from the scope of the Agreement.

4.2.2.1. The interpretation of the notion of services supplied in the exercise of governmental authority

Article I:3(*b*) GATS defines the term "*services*" as including any service in any sector with the exclusion of those "*supplied in the exercise of governmental authority*". According to some authors, this is a total, permanent and transversal exception,[231] which exempts any type of service supplied in the exercise of governmental powers from any provision of the Agreement, without time limits. Negotiations on trade liberalization cannot be conducted in the public sector which, as a governmental prerogative, must be free from trade liberalization commitments.

The terms services provided "*in the exercise of governmental authority*" are defined as "*any service which is supplied neither on a commercial basis, nor in competition with one or more service suppliers*" (Article I:3(*c*)).[232] This definition is rather vague and does not clearly sets forth the scope of the exception at issue. Much depends on the interpretation of the two cumulative requirements, namely the absence of "*commercial basis*" and of "*competition*".

---

company, under company law, where a government or a public authority holds all or the majority of its equity. See Krajewski, p. 32 (n 38). Some refer to a fourth mode of supply through social enterprises, such as cooperative and collective interest companies. See, S. Varghese, *Water Services under the World Trade Organization*, in Institute for Agriculture and Trade Policy (ed.), *WTO Cancun Series Paper No. 6*, 2003, available at https://www.files.ethz.ch/isn/115083/2003-08-18_Water_Services.pdf; OECD, *Private Sector Participation in Water Infrastructure. OECD Checklist for Public Action*, London, 2009, p. 20. Other modes of provision have been implemented, for instance, in Zambia, where commercial utilities have created "Water Kiosks". See, A. Kuck, *Human Right to Water – Millennium Development Goals: How Do They Go Together in Practice*, in E. H. Riedel, P. Rothen (eds.), *The Human Right to Water*, Berlin, 2006, p. 178.

[230] Türk and others, pp. 152-158 (n 14). On the contrary, other authors argue that the GATS does not foresee any specific discipline for public services. See, in this sense, Mastroianni, Arena, pp. 57-58 (n 17); Munari, p. 825 (n 18).

[231] Mastroianni, Arena, p. 36 (n 17).

[232] GATS, art. I:3(*c*).

Scholars have sought to shed some light on both notions.[233] As for the "*commercial basis*", services supplied free of charge fall within the exception. On the contrary, services supplied for profit are excluded from the scope of the exception and thus subjected to trade liberalization rules.

Aside from these cases, there is a gray area in which it is unclear whether or not public services fall within the scope of the exception. The main question is whether the expression "*commercial basis*" encompasses only services supplied for profit or also services provided upon payment of tariffs. If the absence of "*commercial basis*" is equated to services totally free of charge, the scope of the exception would be extremely limited, given that public providers usually require the payment of tariffs. In particular, if tariffs are below or equal to the cost of the service, would it be considered supplied on a "*commercial basis*"?

Some authors argue that "*commercial basis*" is equivalent to "*for profit*".[234] Thus, even though tariffs are paid to cover the cost of services, as long as the public company does not aim to turn a profit, its activity falls under the scope of the exception. Other commentators maintain that this conclusion is not supported by a literal reading of the GATS provisions and that the two concepts of "*commercial basis*" and "*profit*" cannot be taken as synonymous.[235]

The WTO Secretariat admits that "*it is not completely clear what the term 'commercial basis' means*" and "*if services were deemed to be supplied on a commercial basis, then, regardless of whether ownership was in public or private hands, the sector would be subject to the main GATS disciplines and to the negotiation of commitments under Articles XVI and XVII*".[236]

In short, uncertainties remain on the exact scope of the notion "*commercial basis*".[237]

Turning to the condition of the absence of competition under Article I:3(*c*), according to Leroux, the notion of competition implies that different service suppliers are "*contending one with another in the same services market*", that is a defined geo-

---

[233] E. H. Leroux, *What is a 'Service Supplied in the Exercise of Governmental Authority' Under Article I:3(*b*) and (*c*) of the General Agreement on Trade in Services?*, in *Journal of World Trade*, 2006; M. Krajewski, *Public Services and the Scope of the General Agreement on Trade in Services (GATS)*, Centre for International Environmental Law (CIEL), 2001; Krajewski (n 228); Cossy (n 46).

[234] Krajewski, p. 351 (n 228); Leroux, pp. 349-360 (n 233).

[235] Mastroianni, Arena, pp. 37-38 (n 17); A. Arena, *The GATS notion of public services as an instance of intergovernmental agnosticism: comparative insights from the EU supranational dialectic*, in *Journal of World Trade*, 2011, p. 501. According to Arena: "*the meaning of 'commercial basis' cannot be restricted to 'profit-seeking', as commercial presence' also refers to non-profit-seeking juridical persons*".

[236] Cossy, p. 126 (n 46).

[237] *Ibid.*, p. 126.

graphical market where services "*can be considered substitutes*".[238] This definition does not consider forms of upstream competition for running monopolies.

Applying the above considerations to water services, it is necessary to clarify when they are provided in the exercise of governmental authority, thus are exempted from the scope of the GATS.

With regard to the absence of "*commercial basis*", if these terms are understood as equivalent to the lack of any profit, the management of water service would unlikely meet the first condition to be exempted.

As for the absence of competition, Cossy doubts that the notion of competition can be applied to water services provided by public authorities in a position of monopoly. The author argues that since water services are still natural monopolies, the condition of lack of competition required by Article I:3(*c*) is respected. Moreover, she contends that even when competition "*for*" accessing the market exists among private providers (for instance in the bidding process for the concession), there is no competition between a public authority and a private provider because, in such a case, governmental authorities are only seeking to contract out the provision of the service.[239]

Some criticisms may be made of the above arguments. In the first place, Article I:3(*c*) does not confine the exception to the lack of competition between a public entity and private providers. Moreover, if the exception also covers cases in which a service is provided by means of private companies chosen through public procedures, a certain degree of competition may be achieved by resorting to the so-called competition "*for*" the market, that is, competition among operators, including private providers, in order to be granted exclusive rights to serve a given market.[240] Finally, the water industry may be reorganized in order to encourage competition, for instance by abolishing vertical integration.

To sum up, the total lack of competition necessary to meet the second requirement and to apply the exception under Article I:3(*b*) would only occur when the service is directly provided by public authorities through their own agencies or bodies or through public companies across all segments of the water service chain. On the contrary, the exception would not apply when exclusive rights to provide the service are granted to private operators by means of a call for tender. In fact, in such a case, there is a sort of upstream competition among private companies in order to be awarded the contract, although after the takeover, the provider will manage the service under monopolistic conditions.

These considerations lead us to admit the narrow scope of the exemption at issue, which does not exclude public services as such from the GATS purview.[241] It is

---

[238] Leroux, pp. 362, 384 (n 233).

[239] Cossy, p. 127 (n 46).

[240] Hendry, 2010 (n 229).

[241] Arena, p. 505 (n 235); Krajewski, p. 3 (n 176); M. Krajewski, *National Regulation and Trade*

noteworthy that the concession of water service (notably, of the principal mode of supply of this service) would not be exempted as such in the presence of a commercial interest for the provision of the service (indeed, concessionaires provide services on a commercial basis). Ultimately, Article I:3(*b*) has lost relevance as a result of the privatization of water services.[242]

4.2.2.2. The interpretation of the notion of government procurement for the supply of public services

Article XIII GATS exempts public procurement from the key GATS obligations. It provides that the MFN clause and commitments on market access and national treatment do not apply to "*laws, regulations or requirements governing the procurement by governmental agencies of services purchased for governmental purposes and not with a view to commercial resale or with a view to use in the supply of service for commercial sale*".[243]

The norm lacks clarity in many respects.[244] As explained by a WTO panel, this Article "*reflects the fact that negotiators of the GATS were unable to reach agreement on disciplines regarding governmental purchases of service*".[245] Due to lack of agreement on the issue, Article XIII:2 mandates further negotiations.

In the first place, the relationship between GATS Article XIII and Article I:3(*b*) is uncertain.[246] The WTO Secretariat has, indeed, highlighted the "*need to clarify the scope of government procurement (as referred to in GATS Article XIII) in relation to services supplied in the exercise of governmental authority (covered by GATS Article I:3)*".[247] For instance, the Secretariat makes the case of "*situations in which the government has privatized certain services as local monopolies and the private firms receive payment from the government rather than from individual users*".[248] It is not clear whether these situations have to be considered services supplied in the exercise of governmental authority or as public procurement.[249]

Liberalisation in Services: The Legal Impact of the General Agreement on Trade in Services (GATS) on National Regulatory Autonomy, The Hague, 2003, p. 73; Krajewski, p. 354 (n 228); Lang, pp. 817-818 (n 14).

[242] Costamagna, p. 533 (n 101); Munin, pp. 81-82 (n 5); Bates, pp. 138-139 (n 27).

[243] GATS, art. XIII:1

[244] Arena, p. 509 (n 235).

[245] WTO, Report of the Panel, *United States – Measures Affecting Trade in Large Civil Aircraft* (2nd Complaint), para. 7.968 (n 119).

[246] Mastroianni, Arena, p. 40 (n 17).

[247] WTO, Council for Trade in Services, *Environmental Services, Background Note by the Secretariat*, S/C/W/46, 6 July 1998, para. 53. See, in the same sense, Mattoo, p. 313 (n 24, n 62).

[248] WTO, Council for Trade in Services, *Environmental Services, Background Note by the Secretariat*, para. 53 (n 247).

[249] *Ibid.*, para. 53: "*One view could be that these are still services supplied in the exercise of gov-*

Examining the results of the ongoing negotiations on public procurements does not provide much help as, so far, these have been inconclusive.[250]

Attempts to clarify the scope of the provision should start by establishing the meaning of the terms "*government procurement*",[251] which are not defined in the GATS. It is agreed that government procurement does not include full divestiture to private providers of service facilities and operations. Therefore, when water infrastructure is dismissed and sold to private operators, the applicability of the GATS is beyond doubt.[252] However, with regard to water services, full divestiture is unlikely to occur. Governments, in fact, are reluctant to fully withdraw from the water sector as water is a politically sensitive issue.

Instead of divesting from the water sector, public authorities prefer to involve private partners in the management of water utilities.[253] There are several forms of private sector participation in public services[254] and the relevant disciplines can vary considerably from country to country. For instance, public authorities, while maintaining the public property over the assets, may outsource activities ranging from minor tasks, such as billing, to major undertakings, such as building and maintaining water infrastructure or supplying drinking water.[255] Contractual arrangements between governments and private providers may vary in several respects, including: the degree of control that the private provider has over the water system,

---

ernment authority, as defined by GATS Article I:3 – since they are not supplied on a commercial basis to individual users and they continue to be (local) monopolies – and, therefore, do not fall within the scope of GATS disciplines. Another view could be that these services are being procured by the government and, therefore, the manner of purchase per se would fall within the scope of GATS Article XIII and any future disciplines on procurement".

[250] WTO, *Report by the Chairperson of the Working Party on GATS Rules*, p. 1 (n 122). The European Union has proposed an Annex to the GATS on government procurement in services, which has not been adopted. WTO, Working Party on GATS Rules, *Communication from the European Communities, Government Procurement in Services*, S/WPGR/W/54, 20 June 2006. This Communication has been followed by the EU proposals on future work, Communication by the European Union, *Proposal for Future Work on Government Procurement*, JOB/SERV/215, 25 September 2015. So far, no progress has been made due to the general deadlock of the negotiations.

[251] The business dictionary defines government procurement as: "*[t]he act of obtaining goods or services for a public agency*". Source: http://www.businessdictionary.com/definition/Government-procurement.html.

[252] Cossy, p. 129 (n 46).

[253] Human Rights Council, *Report of the independent expert on the issue of human rights obligations related to access to safe drinking water and sanitation*, para. 9 (n 114).

[254] There are several models of public-private partnerships (PPPs). OECD, *Private Sector Participation in Water Infrastructure*, p. 18 (n 229).

[255] I intend the terms "*privatization of water services*" as referring to the transfer of control of the assets, including management contracts, leases, concessions, and Build-Operate-Transfer ("BOT").

the allocation of risks and responsibilities between the public and the private stakeholders, the duration of the contract.

The problem arises about how to single out a model of public-private partnership (PPPs) in the water sector that should be regarded as public procurement under the meaning of Article XIII and, thus, exempted from the MFN obligations and commitments on market access and national treatment. Indeed, WTO Member States wonder which types of "*PPPs are to be considered as governmental procurement under GATS Article XIII*".[256]

The notion of PPPs may be used with a generic meaning as including any involvement of private enterprises in public authorities' projects,[257] or in a restricted manner referring to specific contractual forms. As for the latter, there is no agreed categorization. The OECD lists the main forms of PPP contracts as follows: service contract; management contract; lease contract; concession; build, operate, transfer (BOT) and build, own, operate and transfer (BOOT); joint ownership; build own operate (BOO).[258]

For a schematic presentation of this spectrum of PPP contracts, we rely on OECD studies. Under a management contract, a private provider offers managerial services to operate the assets, often against a fixed fee (duration three-five years). The ownership of assets and the financial risks of investments are vested in the public sector.

The lease contract entails that the assets remain public, while the service is operated by the private provider (duration eight-fifteen years). Investment risks are shared between private and public stakeholders; the private provider is remunerated by customers, while public authorities are responsible for financing investment in infrastructure.

The concession model confers the management, risk and responsibilities for investments on the private sector (duration twenty-thirty years). Only the assets remain public.

Finally, BOT[259] contracts are the closest to a full divestiture, as all aspects are

---

[256] WTO, *Communication from Australia, the European Communities, Japan, New Zealand, the Separate Customs Territory of Taiwan, Penghu, Kinmen and Matsu and the United States. Joint report on informal discussion on environmental services in the context of the DDA*, TN/S/W/28, 11 February 2005, p. 3.

[257] The business dictionary defines public private partnership as: "*[i]nvolvement of private enterprise (in the form of management expertise and/or monetary contributions) in the Government projects aimed at public benefit*". Source: http://www.businessdictionary.com/definition/public-private-partnership.html.

[258] OECD, *Private Sector Participation and Regulatory Reform in Water Supply: The Southern Mediterranean Experience*, Working Paper No. 265, 2008; OECD, *Private Sector Participation in Water Infrastructure,* p. 19 (n 229).

[259] BOT are defined as a form of concession in which the ownership of an operating asset remains with the operator for a fixed term and is transferred to the public upon payment of an agreed sum.

privatized, and the ownership of the asset is shared between private and public operators (duration twenty-thirty years).[260]

The main differences among these contracts lie in the allocation of risks and responsibilities between the public and the private operators.

Distinguishing between concessions and BOT contracts is controversial. One of the main differences may be that only BOTs require the private partner to completely build a new facility upon payment of a fee by public authorities. Instead, the concessionaire is remunerated by user charges and may "*pay a rent or a certain percentage of the sales or earnings to the grantor*".[261] Hence, concessions imply higher economic risks than BOT.

Moreover, in the BOO model the facility remains in the private operator's possession for a pre-determined time, while the concession contract excludes the transfer of ownership of the public assets to the concessionaire. The concessionaire is only entitled to manage the network for a long period, usually around twenty-thirty years, in exchange for investment in the utility infrastructure.

Keeping in mind that these distinctions are approximate, as domestic definition of PPPs contracts vary, we turn to evaluating the applicability of the GATS public procurement exception to each of the above models in order to assess what contractual model meets the requirements set forth in Article XIII, namely that services are: *i*) purchased by governmental agencies; *ii*) for governmental purposes; *iii*) not with a view to commercial resale; *iv*) or, with a view to use the service purchased in the supply of services for commercial sale.

Management contracts may be regarded as public procurement contracts under the meaning of GATS Article XIII, as they entail the private execution of mere managerial tasks under the supervision and control of the public operator. One scholar, however, warns about the possibility that managerial tasks, such as "*fixing leaks, billing and meter reading*" may be utilized by governmental authorities in order to provide water services "*for commercial sale*". This being the case, management contracts would fall within the scope of the GATS.[262]

BOT contracts for drinking water supply may be considered public procurement, as a prominent part of the contract consists in the construction of the utility. Moreover, the private firm operates the water utility upon payment of a fee by public authorities. Thus, the service is purchased by governmental authorities for the public purpose of providing water and without a view to resale or to use in the supply of commercial services.

---

[260] R. Simpson, *Universal Access in the Water and Sanitation Sector*, in OECD/The World Bank, Trade Policy Studies, *Liberalisation and Universal Access to Basic Services, Telecommunications, Water and Sanitation, Financial Services, and Electricity*, Paris, 2006, p. 100, available at: http://dx.doi.org/10.1787/9789264028685-en.

[261] Source: http://www.businessdictionary.com/definition/concession.html#ixzz2xcnvDlKt.

[262] Cossy, p. 131 (n 46).

I submit that concession contracts in water services are not public procurement. The service is directly delivered to consumers who pay tariffs in return. Tariffs usually cover the costs plus a margin of profit. Thus, under a concession, the water service is purchased by consumers from a private concessionaire who risks their own financial capital and sets tariffs on a commercial basis.[263] Some Member States have denied that concessions constitute public procurement on the grounds that when the government grants the right to operate a public service to a private operator through this contract, there is neither a purchase of goods nor acquisition of services.[264]

The current rule does not leave much margin of interpretation for reaching a different conclusion. Therefore, once specific commitments are undertaken, if the PPP contract is one of concession, the service is subject to the GATS rules unless otherwise scheduled. Given that the concession model is widely used by public authorities in the water sector, one may infer that as far as water services are concerned, restraints to the scope of the GATS are limited.[265]

4.2.3. *Interim* conclusion

This section has revealed the limits of interpretation in harmonizing opposing obligations in the context of GATS disputes. On the one hand, the Agreement leaves little room to consider interests other than trade liberalization and, on the other hand, the WTO adjudicating bodies have not availed themselves of the opportunities left in this connection by the GATS.

Once commitments of market access are taken without limitations, regulatory measures are likely to be considered inconsistent with trade obligations since the dividing line between legitimate regulations under Article VI GATS and illegitimate quantitative restrictions under Article XVI GATS is unclear and subject to inconsistent interpretation by the Appellate Body. Likewise, regulatory measures may be found in breach of full commitments of national treatment as their purpose is considered irrelevant in the less favorable treatment analysis.

While in a few cases the WTO adjudicating bodies have resorted to the contextual interpretation of the Agreement in order to take into consideration Members' right to regulate in the public interest, no mention has been made about systemic interpretation of GATS obligations and human rights commitments.

---

[263] The same applies to lease contracts.

[264] This view has been expressed by Argentina and Venezuela. See Working Party on GATS Rules, Report of the Meeting of 6 October 1998, Note by the Secretariat, S/WPGR/M/18, 13 November 1998, para. 17-18. However, it has been argued that granting concessions falls within the meaning of service supplied in the exercise of governmental authority, and is thus excluded from the purview of the GATS.

[265] For instance, "*Concession was the predominant contractual arrangements adopted in Latin America in the 1990's*". OECD, *Private Sector Participation in Water Infrastructure*, p. 19 (n 229).

Finally, as far as public services are concerned, the scope of the exceptions concerning "*services supplied in the exercise of governmental authority*" enshrined in Article I:3(*b*) and "*government procurement*" under Article XIII is ambiguous and interpretative techniques do not allow to reach a clear-cut solution.

4.3. Establishing systemic relationships of priority

When confronted with conflicting obligations stemming from different subsystems of international law, a State is obliged to decide which obligation deserves priority. In light of the considerations expressed in chapter two, access to safe drinking water is a human right implied, among others, in the right to an adequate standard of living and in the right to the highest attainable standard of health. It entitles everyone "*to a system of water supply and management that provides equality of opportunity for people to enjoy this right*".[266] Water services must be affordable for all,[267]and States have to "*provide those who do not have sufficient means with the necessary water and water facilities*".[268] In addition, States have to comply with the mandatory core obligation of immediate effect to "*ensure access to the minimum essential amount of water, that is sufficient and safe for personal and domestic uses to prevent disease*".[269] In this connection, States have to undertake measures aimed at providing water even in remote or unprofitable areas and prohibiting disconnection from the mains in case of non-payment for lack of financial resources. In order to reach these objectives, States may adopt domestic regulations affecting trade in services, measures limiting competition or decisions aimed at reverting the private market into one supplied by governmental authorities after having undertaken specific commitments of market access. Some of these measures may restrict trade in water services and jeopardize other WTO Members' rights.

The question arises as to whether and to what extent the possible violation of basic trade rules to protect human life and health may be justified under the Agreement. In case of a normative conflict between duties ensuing from the right to water and those deriving from commitments undertaken in the GATS, the exception clause enshrined in Article XIV of the Agreement might prove useful in order to protect the former.[270]

---

[266] General Comment No. 15, para. 10 (n 91).

[267] *Ibid.*, para. 12(*c*)(*ii*).

[268] *Ibid.*, para. 15.

[269] General Comment No. 15, paras. 37, 40 (n 91).

[270] Commission on Human Rights, *Human Rights, Trade and Investment*, para. 25 (n 15). To draw a parallel, art. 36 of the Treaty on the Functioning of the European Union ("TFEU") (Official Journal of the European Union, C 115/47, 9 May 2008) allows the adoption of restrictive measures on imports and exports of goods and measures having equivalent effect on grounds that

As mentioned in section 4.1.2, GATS Article XIV establishes the right of Members to adopt measures incompatible with the Agreement provided that they pursue one among the objectives identified in an exhaustive list of general exceptions. It seeks to strike a balance between the need to adopt regulatory measures designed to achieve non-trade objectives and basic trade rights of other WTO Members.

The Article reads as follows:

> "Subject to the requirement that such measures are not applied in a manner which would constitute a means of arbitrary or unjustifiable discrimination between countries where like conditions prevail, or a disguised restriction on trade in services, nothing in this Agreement shall be construed to prevent the adoption or enforcement by any Member of measures: (a) necessary to protect public morals or to maintain public order;[271] (b) necessary to protect human, animal or plant life or health; (c) necessary to secure compliance with laws or regulations which are not inconsistent with the provisions of this Agreement (…)".

The exception under Article XIV(*b*) concerning measures "*necessary to protect human, animal or plant life or health*" could be invoked to justify measures taken to prevent serious risks to life and health deriving from the lack of access to water.

So far, Article XIV(*b*) has not been invoked by Member States in dispute settlement procedures. Hence, we cannot rely on jurisprudence on the point. However, in some previous cases, the WTO panels and the Appellate Body have been called upon to address the general exception under Article XIV(*a*), which concerns "*public morals*". The respective reports provide useful guidance on the meaning of the common preliminary introductory clause (the so-called "*chapeau*") and the meaning of the term "*necessary*" enshrined in Article XIV.

Moreover, Article XIV GATS is worded in terms similar to Article XX GATT,[272] especially Article XIV (*b*) and Article XX (*b*). Since both Agreements are

---

such measures are necessary to safeguard: "*public morality, public policy or public security; the protection of health and life of humans, animals or plants; the protection of national treasures possessing artistic, historic or archaeological value; or the protection of industrial and commercial property*". Moreover, like the *chapeau* of GATS art. XIV, art. 36 of the TFEU requires that: "*[s]uch prohibitions or restrictions shall not, however, constitute a means of arbitrary discrimination or a disguised restriction on trade between Member States*". With specific regard to the right of establishment and the freedom to provide services within the European Union, restrictions are allowed respectively under art. 52(1) and art. 62 combined with the former, provided that such restrictions are taken "*on ground of public policy, public security or public health*". See L. Daniele, *Diritto del Mercato Unico Europeo, Cittadinanza – Libertà di circolazione – Concorrenza – Aiuti di Stato*, Milan, 2012, pp. 82-94, p. 152, pp. 141-147.

[271] The footnote of Article XIV (*a*) reads: "*[t]he public order exception may be invoked only where a genuine and sufficiently serious threat is posed to one of the fundamental interests of society*".

[272] General Agreement on Tariffs and Trade. The original Agreement of 1947 is incorporated into GATT 1994, which is in turn included into Annex 1A – Multilateral Agreements on Trade in Goods – to the Agreement Establishing the World Trade Organization. A commentator under-

framed within the umbrella of the WTO Agreement, they are interpreted consistently with each other.[273] In particular, the interpretation of Article XX GATT has been restrictive[274] and has provided guidance on that of Article XIV GATS.[275]

In general terms, for the exception to be applied, the dispute settlements bodies have established a two-tier test: first, measures have to be justified under one of the sub-paragraphs; and, then, they have to satisfy the conditions set out in the *chapeau.*[276] Thus, the WTO adjudicating bodies have to first be satisfied that the measures concerned were adopted to protect human life and health and were "*necessary*" in the instant case to that purpose and, then, that the same measures were not discriminatory or aimed at restricting trade in services.

While the classification of a measure within those aimed at protecting human life and health must be made on a case by case basis, and seems to not raise particular concern, the interpretation of the term "*necessary*" risks affecting the effectiveness of the provision.

The interpretation of the "*necessity test*" by WTO panels and the Appellate

---

lines that art. XIV GATS diverges form art. XX GATT as it does not include a specific subparagraph concerning natural resources. She suggests adding a new exception to art. XIV GATS, such as that of art. XX (*g*) GATT, that may be useful in respect to water services to the extent that the "*necessity test*" will be omitted. Cossy, pp. 205-207 (n 46).

[273] On the use of GATT as auxiliary interpretative instrument see: Munin, pp. 48-49 (n 5).

[274] See: WTO, Report of the Appellate Body, *United States – Standards for Reformulated and Conventional Gasoline*, WT/DS2/AB/R, 29 April 1996; WTO, Report of the Panel, *United States – Import Prohibition of Certain Shrimp and Shrimp Products*, WT/DS58/R, 15 May 1998; WTO, Report of the Appellate Body, *United States – Import Prohibition of Certain Shrimp and Shrimp Products*, WT/DS58/AB/R, 12 October 1998; WTO, Report of the Panel, *Brazil – Measures Affecting Imports of Retreaded Tyres*, WT/DS332/R, 12 June 2007; WTO, Report of the Appellate Body, *Brazil – Measures Affecting Imports of Retreaded Tyres* (n 188); WTO, Report of the Appellate Body, *European Communities – Regime for the Importation, Sale and Distribution of Bananas* (n 147). The WTO website, on the contrary, contends that: "*[i]n light of the jurisprudence to date, it is fair to say that WTO rules provide ample space for environmental concerns to be accommodated. Even if a measure is found to be inconsistent with basic WTO disciplines, it may be justifiable under one of the exceptions, for example, if it pursues an environmental or human health objective and if its application does not reveal a protectionist intent*". Source: http://www.wto.org/english/tratop_e/envir_e/envt_rules_intro_e.htm. S. Gaines, *The WTO's Reading of the GATT Article XX Chapeau: A Disguised Restriction on Environmental Measures*, in *University of Pennsylvania Journal of International Economic Law*, 2001.

[275] WTO, Report of the Appellate Body, *European Communities – Regime for the Importation, Sale and Distribution of Bananas*, para. 231 (n 147); WTO, Report of the Appellate Body, *United States – Measures Affecting Cross-Border Gambling and Betting Services*, para. 291 (n 71); WTO, Report of the Panel, *European Union and its Member States – Certain Measures Relating to the Energy Sector*, para. 7.1.244 (n 41).

[276] WTO, Report of the Appellate Body, *United States – Standards for Reformulated and Conventional Gasoline*, p. 22 (n 274); WTO, Report of the Panel, *European Union and its Member States – Certain Measures Relating to the Energy Sector*, para. 7.10.2.3.2 (n 41).

Body has evolved over time. At its origin, the term "*necessary*" has been interpreted as the choice of least restrictive measure available.[277] Since the "*least trade means*" test was too strict, it was later replaced with a softer "*weighing and balancing*" test. First enunciated in the *Korea-Beef* case,[278] the balancing test has been applied by WTO adjudicating bodies in subsequent disputes.[279] In the *Korea-Beef* case, the Appellate Body underlined that there is a range of degrees of necessity; hence a measure may be necessary even when it is not "*indispensable*" or "*inevitable*".[280]

In detail, the WTO bodies listed the main factors to be ascertained in order to determine if a measure is "*necessary*", namely: the importance of the interest or values that the measure intends to protect; the contribution of such measure to the realization of the end pursued; the restrictive impact of the measure on trade.[281] In addition, the availability of an alternative, less trade restrictive measure, must be considered.[282]

The "*necessity test*", as construed by the WTO dispute settlement bodies, has been sharply criticized as an illegitimate intrusion into Members' autonomy. A commentator argues that the meaning attributed to the word "*necessary*" by WTO adjudicating bodies has, to date, diverged from the language of the treaty,[283] and excessively curtailed domestic regulatory freedom.[284] By requiring the adjudicating

---

[277] WTO, Report of the Panel, *United States – Section 337 of the Tariff Act of 1930*, L/6439, 7 November 1989, para. 5.26; WTO, Report of the Panel, *Thailand – Restrictions on Importation of and Internal Taxes on Cigarettes*, DS10/R, 7 November 1990, para. 23.

[278] WTO, Report of the Appellate Body, *Korea – Measures Affecting Imports of Fresh, Chilled and Frozen Beef*, WT/DS161.169/AB/R, 11 December 2000.

[279] Such a test has been followed by, *inter alia*, the Appellate Body in the case *European Communities-Measures Affecting Asbestos-Containing Products*, para. 172 (n 148); *Dominican Republic Measures Affecting the Importation and Internal Sale of Cigarettes*, WT/DS302/AB/R, 25 April 2005.

[280] WTO, Report of the Appellate Body, *Korea – Measures Affecting Imports of Fresh, Chilled and Frozen Beef*, para. 161 (n 278).

[281] WTO, Report of the Appellate Body, *Korea – Measures Affecting Imports of Fresh, Chilled and Frozen Beef*, para. 164 (n 278): "*a process of weighing and balancing a series of factors which prominently include the contribution made by the compliance measure to the enforcement of the law or regulation at issue, the importance of the common interest or values protected by that law or regulation, and the accompanying impact of the law or regulation on imports or exports*"; WTO, Report of the Appellate Body, *United States – Measures Affecting Cross-Border Gambling and Betting Services*, para. 306 (n 71); WTO, Report of the Panel, *European Union and its Member States – Certain Measures Relating to the Energy Sector*, para. 7.1209 (n 41).

[282] WTO, Report of the Appellate Body, *Korea – Measures Affecting Imports of Fresh, Chilled and Frozen Beef*, para. 166 (n 278); WTO, Report of the Appellate Body, *United States – Measures Affecting Cross-Border Gambling and Betting Services*, paras. 307-308 (n 71); WTO, Report of the Panel, *European Union and its Member States – Certain Measures Relating to the Energy Sector*, para. 7.1209 (n 41).

[283] G. Kapterian, *A Critique of the WTO Jurisprudence on 'Necessity'*, in *International & Comparative Law Quarterly*, 2010, p. 127.

[284] *Ibid.*, p. 91, the author states that "*the balancing test expands the jurisdiction of the adjudicat-*

bodies to weigh the "*values protected*" by the inconsistent measures, it is submitted, this test grants them an overly broad margin of discretion, one which may interfere greatly with the State's decisional autonomy.[285] Following this line of reasoning, Kapterian disputes that the WTO bodies have the competence to balance the values underlying regulatory goals against their negative trade effects. The author maintains that *"at no point is the Panel mandated to enquire into the relative value of the goal being pursued"*,[286] and that *"the balancing test implies a hierarchy of values (with trade liberalization at the top) simply not provided for in the treaty"*.[287]

In addition, if a measure succeeds under the Article's subparagraphs, then it has to meet the requirements set out in the *chapeau*. The opening clause of GATT Article XX is identical to that of GATS Article XIV. It establishes that, for the adoption of inconsistent measures to be allowed, such measures should not "*constitute a means of arbitrary and unjustifiable discrimination between countries where like conditions prevail, or a disguised restriction on trade in services*". These conditions should allow the distinction between measures adopted to pursue legitimate governmental policies and non-trade goals, and illegitimate protectionist measures taken to give an advantage to domestic industries.

Turning to the analysis of the modest GATS jurisprudence on Article XIV as far as the "*necessity*" test is concerned, contrary to the expectation,[288] to my mind it does not raise *per se* any particular concern.

In the *US-Gambling* dispute,[289] the WTO adjudicating bodies, after having ruled that the US measures[290] were inconsistent with the GATS undertakings, verified

---

ing bodies, demonstrating a disconcerting dependence on their discretion for the survival of domestic regulatory choices. The jurisprudence reveals a strong tendency to judge the value of the policy goal using the adjudicating bodies' own value system and opaque reasoning". See also J. C. Marwell, *Trade and Morality: The WTO Public Morals Exception after Gambling*, in *New York University Law Review*, 2006, pp. 816-819.

[285] Regan, on the contrary, held that the Appellate Body's finding in the *Korea-Beef case* has been misunderstood due to a logical contradiction made by the same WTO organ. In addition to the above-mentioned test, the Appellate Body had also stated that a Member is free to choose its own level of protection. This statement contradicts the balancing test, which requires weighing the domestic benefits resulting from State's policy measures against the cost in terms of trade restrictive effects. The author contends that the Appellate Body considered valid alternatives only those that would have allowed the State to achieve the "*same amount of underlying goal*". D. H. Regan, The *Meaning of 'Necessary' in GATT Article XX and GATS Article XIV: The Myth of Cost-Benefit Balancing*, in *World Trade Review*, 2007, pp. 347-349.

[286] Kapterian, p. 119 (n 283).

[287] *Ibid.*, p.121.

[288] Prévost, p. 244 (n 77).

[289] WTO, Report of the Panel, *United States – Measures Affecting the Cross-Border Supply of Gambling and Betting Services* (n 25); WTO, Report of the Appellate Body, *United States – Measures Affecting Cross-Border Gambling and Betting Services* (n 71).

[290] The panel and the Appellate Body found that the US GATS Schedule was to be interpreted

whether they fell within the general exceptions clause, notably whether they were designed to "*protect public morals or to maintain public order*" within the meaning of Article XIV(*a*).

The panel ruled that the United States had failed to show that their measures were "*necessary*" to protect public morals on the ground that the US did not avail themselves of a reasonable available alternative.[291] Indeed, Antigua had requested the US to begin consultations in order to find an agreement. According to the panel, consultations would have constituted a "*reasonable available*" alternative measure which the US had denied to Antigua. Therefore, the measures adopted by the US failed the "*necessity test*".[292]

The Appellate Body, applying the necessity test established in the *Korea-Beef* case,[293] dismissed this holding and considered erroneous the analysis carried out by the panel. Interestingly, the Appellate Body underlined that "*a 'reasonable available' alternative measure must be a measure which preserves the responding Member's right to achieve its desired level of protection with respect to the objective pursued under paragraph (a) of Article XIV*".[294] The Appellate Body deemed that Antigua's proposal of entering into consultations with the US should not have been regarded as a "*reasonable available*" alternative measure, as consultations do not entail a duty to reach an agreement and do not constitute an alternative to federal laws.[295] Therefore, the US made a *prima face* case that their measures were "*necessary*". As a consequence, according to the Appellate Body, the burden of proof was to be shifted to the complaining party, which had to indicate a WTO-consistent alternative measure.[296] Since Antigua had failed to identify any other alternative, the measures were to be deemed as "*necessary*" under the meaning of Article XIV.[297]

Unlike the panel, it seems that the Appellate Body gave consideration to the regulatory autonomy of Member States. In fact, it required alternative measures to be appropriate for the pursuit of the government's objectives. Moreover, in the end, the Appellate Body shifted the burden of demonstrating the availability of less restrictive measures onto the claimant.

---

as including specific commitments on gambling and betting services. Therefore, the US federal laws, which prohibited the cross-border supply of gambling and betting services, were inconsistent with GATS art. XVI:1, 2(*a*) and (*c*).

[291] WTO, Report of the Panel, *United States – Measures Affecting Cross-Border Gambling and Betting Services*, para. 6.535 (n 25).

[292] *Ibid.*, para. 6.531.

[293] WTO, Report of the Appellate Body, *United States – Measures Affecting Cross-Border Gambling and Betting Services*, paras. 305-306 (n 71).

[294] *Ibid.*, para. 308.

[295] *Ibid.*, para. 317.

[296] *Ibid.*, para. 311.

[297] *Ibid.*, para. 326.

In the *Argentina-Financial Service* case, the panel concluded that the contested measures adopted to allow Argentina to obtain tax information on foreign service suppliers were provisionally justified under Article XIV(*c*) GATS as necessary to secure compliance with GATS-consistent Argentine laws or regulations.[298] The panel found that the protection of the tax collection system and the fight against dangerous tax practices were "*interest or values of the utmost importance for Argentina*" and that the measures contested contributed to achieving these objectives, while having a limited restrictive effect on trade.[299] In addition, the complainant had not identified any reasonably available and less trade-restrictive measure that Argentina could have taken to achieve the same objectives.[300]

In the *EU-Energy Package* case, the panel, having found that the third-country certification measure implemented by Croatia, Hungary and Lithuania breached Article XVII GATS,[301] assessed whether the measure was justified by the need to guarantee the EU's security of energy supply and, thus, to maintain public order under Article XIV(*a*) GATS. The panel weighed the importance of the interests or values at stake by granting consideration to those that the EU deemed fundamental.[302] It found that the objective of ensuring security of energy supply was indeed fundamental and that, although the third-country certification measure did not address *all* potential threats, it was sufficient that it was shown to be at least apt to address the threats posed by third-country transmission system operators. The panel also held that the way the measure was implemented was not shown to be excessively trade restrictive. Moreover, it found that Russia had not proposed reasonable alternative measures or had proposed only alternative measures unable to achieve the same level of protection as those adopted by the EU Member States.[303]

In this case, the respondent State was similarly successful under the "*necessity*" test. The relative importance of the interests or values furthered by the challenged measure was not questioned. Besides, the burden to indicate a less trade restrictive measure capable of achieving the same level of protection was once again shifted onto the claimant; given the difficulties in providing reasonably available alternative measures, the claimant government is almost always bound to fail in this respect.

Moving to the analysis of the *chapeau*, in the *US-Gambling* dispute the Appellate Body upheld only in part the panel's finding that the US did not meet its condi-

---

[298] WTO, Report of the Panel, *Argentina – Measures relating to Trade in Goods and Services*, para. 7.740 (n 134).

[299] *Ibid.*, 7.738.

[300] *Ibid.*, para. 7.739.

[301] Under these measures only third-country transmission system operators were obliged to undergo a security of energy supply assessment prior to certification.

[302] WTO, Report of the Panel, *European Union and its Member States – Certain Measures Relating to the Energy Sector*, para. 7.1212 (n 41).

[303] *Ibid.*, para. 7.1239.

tions. On the one hand, the Appellate Body reversed the panel's decision that the US federal laws were discriminatory, since these measures were applied and implemented without discrimination towards both domestic and foreign operators. On the other hand, solely in respect of a specific regulation (the Interstate Horseracing Act (IHA)), the Appellate Body found grounds of discrimination as domestic operators were authorized to engage in the remote supply of betting services related to horseracing. As the United States' IHA did not apply to both foreign and domestic service suppliers, the prohibitions on remote gambling constituted "*arbitrary and unjustifiable discrimination*" within the meaning of the *chapeau.*[304] Since the measure failed to meet the general exception solely with respect to the IHA, the United States were only recommended to modify the inconsistent regulation.[305]

In the *Argentina-Financial Service* case, the exception could also not be applied as the measure constitutes arbitrary and unjustifiable discrimination within the meaning of the *chapeau* of Article XIV GATS.[306]

Likewise, in the *EU-Energy Package* case, the panel found that the challenged measure constituted "*an arbitrary and unjustifiable discrimination*" due to the fact that no measure had been adopted in order to address potential threats posed by interference from third countries acting through domestic transmission system operators.[307]

The litmus test has hence become the possible discriminatory effects of the measure inconsistent with the provisions of the GATS. Thus, assuming that a measure will be taken in order to secure the right to water in a liberalized water market

---

[304] WTO, Report of the Appellate Body, *United States – Measures Affecting Cross-Border Gambling and Betting Services*, paras. 369, 372 (n 71).

[305] The Dispute Settlement Body adopted the Appellate Report on 20 April 2005. It recommended that the US bring their measures into compliance with the GATS provisions. As the US did not comply with these recommendations, Antigua resorted to the Compliance Panel under art. 21.5 of the DSU. The latter found that the US had failed to comply with the recommendations and ruling of the DSB. WTO, Report of the Panel, *United States – Measures Affecting Cross-Border Supply of Gambling and Betting Services, Recourse to Article 21.5 of the DSU by Antigua and Barbuda*, para. 7.1 (n 132). Antigua requested authorization from the DSB to suspend the application to the United States of concession and related obligations under the GATS and the TRIPS. The United States rejected the level of suspension and made recourse to Arbitration under art. 22.6 of the DSU. WTO, *United States – Measures Affecting the Cross-Border Supply of Gambling and Betting Services, Recourse to Arbitration by The United States under Article 22.6 of the DSU, Decision by the Arbitrator*, WT/DS285/ARB, 21 December 2007. Authorization to retaliate was granted on 28 January 2013.

[306] WTO, Report of the Panel, *Argentina – Measures relating to Trade in Goods and Services*, paras. 7.764, 8.2.d (n 134). Panama challenged the finding that the measures contested were "*necessary to secure compliance with*" certain GATS-consistent Argentine laws and regulations under art. XIV(*c*) GATS, but the Appellate Body upheld the panel's interpretation and application of the necessity test. WTO, Appellate Body Report, *Argentina – Measures Relating to Trade in Goods and Services*, paras. 6.3.4, 7.1.c (n 41).

[307] WTO, Report of the Panel, *European Union and its Member States – Certain Measures Relating to the Energy Sector*, paras. 7.10.2.3.2.2, 7.10.2.3.3 (n 41).

under the GATS umbrella, and that this measure will be considered *necessary* to this purpose, nevertheless no exception to the GATS would be accepted to the extent that it also causes arbitrary or unjustifiable discrimination between countries or a trade disguised restriction.

In the light of the foregoing, it cannot be concluded that the general exceptions clause gives grounds for a systemic relationship of priority between human rights and trade interests, as under the *chapeau* the main concern is always trade liberalization.[308] Conclusively, a possible defence based upon Article XIV(*b*) for exempting water service regulations from the scope of the GATS may fail even if this exception is deemed *necessary* to safeguard human health and life.

5. Conclusion

From the analysis of the GATS framework, it may be reasonably inferred that unlimited commitments to market access and national treatment have the potential to interfere with the public authorities' discretion to regulate the water sector.[309]

In addition, the negotiations mandated by the Agreement – the so called "*built-in agenda*" – have so far failed to produce significant outcomes, leaving much uncertainty on the scope of important rules, such as those concerning domestic regulations, subsidies and government procurement.

With regard to domestic regulations, the scope of the term "*necessity*" is not clear, and negotiations have not reached an agreement on the question of whether a normative standard in the form of a "*necessity test*" should be incorporated into the new discipline.[310] For the time being, domestic regulations affecting trade in services would be admitted, but under unclear terms. In particular, they should not constitute "*unnecessary barriers to trade*". As for the other relevant rules under construction, negotiations concerning subsidies and government procurement are at a deadlock.[311]

---

[308] In this connection, see S. Alam, P. Mukhopadhaya, D. Randle, *The General Agreement on Trade in Services (GATS), Water and Human Rights from the Perspective of Developing Countries*, in *Netherlands International Law Review*, 2011, p. 56. Scholars have illustrated that courts also avoid acknowledging a hierarchy of norms between international trade rules and human rights norms. See A. R. Ziegler, B. Boie, *The Relationship between International Trade Law and International Human Rights Law*, in E. De Wet, J. Vidmar (eds.) *Hierarchy in International Law: The Place of Human Rights*, Oxford, 2012, pp. 272-299.

[309] Arena submits that: "*the GATS is generally indifferent to the policy goals pursued by national regulatory schemes*". Arena, p. 516 (n 235).

[310] WTO, Council for Trade in Services Special Session, *Negotiation on Trade in Services, Report by the Chairman,* Ambassador Fernando de Mateo*, to the Trade Negotiations Committee*, para. 75 (n 122).

[311] WTO, *Annual Report of the Working Party on GATS Rules to the Council for Trade in Services (2017)*, S/WPGR/28, 16 November 2017.

The vagueness of the terms applied by the GATS, coupled with the ongoing negotiations on public procurements, subsidies and domestic regulations, does not allow us to exclude that normative conflicts may arise from liberalization of water services under the GATS and the human right to water.

Additionally, the uncertainty left by the GATS notion of service is not satisfactory. The exception concerning "*services supplied in the exercise of governmental authority*" enshrined in Article I:3(*b*) is ambiguous due to the unsettled meaning of the terms "*commercial basis*" and "*competition*". Likewise, Article XIII GATS on government procurement lacks clarity in many respects.

Violations of the GATS rules and commitments are enforceable through the WTO dispute settlement bodies, whose limited jurisprudence on the scope of market access commitments has been criticized. It has been contended that, following the *Gambling* case, the line between measures belonging to domestic regulations, in principle allowed by the GATS, and measures resulting in illegitimate restrictions to market access commitments, has been tilted towards trade liberalization, to the detriment of States' regulatory autonomy.[312] In this connection, it has been noted that the WTO adjudicating bodies appear more prone to give precedence to trade liberalization commitments over public interest objectives.[313]

In this context, the possibility that conflicting obligations stemming from the human right to water and the Agreement could be harmonized by means of interpretation of the GATS rules is rather dubious.

A fortiori, the chance to establish relationships of priority in favor of human rights obligations over trade commitments by successfully resorting to the general exceptions clause might be excluded. The criteria to be met are strict. Pursuant to the so-called "*two tier approach*", the exception needs to be demonstrated as "*necessary*", and to respect the non-discriminatory conditions established under the introductory clause (the *chapeau*). As far as the "*necessity*" test is concerned, although it confers wide discretion to trade dispute settlement bodies to weigh the importance of the values pursued by public authorities with trade objectives, the WTO adjudicating bodies have so far shown (limited) deference to the States' regulatory autonomy.[314] However, the requirements under the *chapeau* is likely to exclude from the scope of the exception measures necessary to protect human life and health to the extent that they are discriminatory or cause disguised restriction to trade in services.

---

[312] M. Krajewski, *Services Trade Liberalisation and Regulation: New Developments and Old Problems*, in *European Yearbook of International Economic Law*, 2010, p. 173.

[313] Munin, p. 40 (n 5).

[314] For instance, this could be done by taking into account the "*Member's right to achieve its desired level of protection*" with respect to public morals. WTO, Report of the Appellate Body, *United States – Measures Affecting Cross-Border Gambling and Betting Services*, para. 308 (n 71).

Given the concerns raised by the GATS framework, coupled with the propensity of the WTO dispute settlements bodies to attach priority to trade liberalization commitments over States' right to regulate in the public interest, I contend that the sole way for harmonizing different obligations lies in carefully drafting specific commitments. States wishing to liberalize their water services market ought to insert limitations and conditions within their commitments on market access and national treatment. These limitations need to be drafted with a high degree of accuracy in order to preserve States' regulatory power. Notably, the conditions upon which the water sector might be opened have to contemplate the possibility of changes in the ownership of utilities, including that a privatized service may be replaced by a publically owned one. Otherwise, in case of disappointing results of market liberalization, States will be *de facto* prevented from reverting on their commitments to market access and national treatment in the water services sector due to the so-called "*lock-in effect*" envisaged by Article XXI GATS.

CONCLUSIONS

SUMMARY: 1. Outline of the main findings and responses to the research questions. – 2. Appraisal.

1. Outline of the main findings and responses to the research questions

The issue of the privatization and liberalization of water services has been, and still is, at the heart of a rather heated debate. Human rights activists strongly oppose private involvement in the water sector, while private stakeholders stress their contribution to the supply of better managed and financed services. Most governments deal with the issue with a certain unease. On the one hand, they are pushed towards privatization and liberalization by financial constraints, while, on the other hand, such a choice risks hurting their electorate. Against this scenario, the right to water has often been invoked instrumentally, in order to back ideological arguments.

This book considers the problem of the compatibility of the liberalization of water services with the human right to water from an international law perspective and suggests paths of coordination with conflicting norms in trade and investment law, where possible.

In chapter one, the discussion moves from the consideration that the scarcity of freshwater resources, which has begun to be perceived in the last decades, has contributed to increasing the economic value of water. The commoditization of water has taken several forms, not least the privatization of water services. Against a pure economic standpoint, a human rights-based approach to water has arisen. The right to water, absent (from a technical point of view) from the International Bill of Rights, has recently been recognized by a growing number of declarations, resolutions, international and regional treaties as well as States' statements and domestic laws, to mention but a few.

The second chapter analyzed the legal basis, *status*, content and the obligations arising from the international human right water. In this connection, General Comment No. 15 of the Committee on Economic, Social and Cultural Rights has strongly contributed to shedding light on the matter. It is the contention of the second chapter that the *status* of the right to water under international law is no longer uncertain. It is firstly a derivative right encompassed in other treaty rights such as, *in primis*, the right to an adequate standard of living and the right to the highest attainable standard of health enshrined, respectively, in Articles 11 and 12 of the International Covenant on Economic, Social and Cultural Rights. In addition, while many scholars agree on the right at issue as an emergent customary right, a right in *statu nascendi*, or *in fieri*, I argue that it is a customary rule, even if its content is still unclear. However its *status* may be qualified, the right to water has already played an important role in several *fora*, including not only regional human right courts, but also national courts and investment arbitral tribunals.

The privatization of water services and the opening of the relevant market to foreign stakeholders have led to the possibility that conflicting obligations may arise between the human right to water, on the one hand, and investment and trade rules, on the other hand. Chapters three and four dealt with the possible normative conflicts that in the context of the liberalization of water services may occur between the right to water and, respectively, international investment rules and international trade rules.

The book has evaluated several techniques to harmonize these divergent obligations. The model of analysis employed in chapters three and four starts by assessing whether there is room to prevent the rise of normative conflicts. Then, it continues by resorting to interpretive techniques to settle the dispute where there is no genuine normative conflict. Finally, it ends by establishing whether, in contexts other than human rights *fora*, the right to water may prevail over trade and investment rules in case of irreconcilable normative conflicts.

With respect to the possibility to prevent the rise of normative conflicts, it has been noted that while subordination clauses in BITs have the potential to serve this purpose, the general exception enshrined in Article XIV GATS is bound to fail in this regard due to the overly restrictive requirements included in the *chapeaux* of the Article.

As for interpretive techniques, systemic interpretation and teleological interpretation have been addressed to consider if and to what extent they can be employed for solving apparent normative conflicts involving the right to water or its main features when disputes are brought before investment arbitral tribunals and WTO adjudicating bodies.

The case law analyzed in chapter three has shown that, in the context of international investment disputes concerning the management of water services, the progressive recognition of the human right to water has influenced the arbitral tribunals' interpretation of key BIT provisions. *In primis*, arbitral tribunals have considered the right to water as an existing right, thus contributing to its recognition as a customary international norm. Moreover, the chronological analysis of investment disputes awards and decisions has revealed a growing consideration for the human right to water as far as the merits of the disputes is concerned. While this right was referred to only implicitly in the first proceedings, *Azurix*, *Vivendi*, and *Biwater*, it was clearly invoked in the latest cases, *Suez*, *SAUR* and *Urbaser*. Remarkably, this growing interest has gone hand in hand with a stricter reading of BIT rules. In the first three cases, where the Respondent States did not clearly invoke the right to water as a human right to justify their contested measures, the tribunal interpreted the notion of investors' expectations in a broad way (*Azurix* case), took a stand against the doctrine of the regulatory powers for public purpose (*Vivendi* case) and extended the scope of the full protection and security clause to matters other than physical security (*Azurix* and *Biwater* cases). On the contrary, when wider reference to the human right to water has been made, as in the latest cases, arbitrators have sought a better balance between competing interests.

In the *Suez* case, they disregarded previous holdings, and resorted, *inter alia*, to the police power doctrine in order to reject a claim of expropriation. It was maintained that measures taken within the State's police powers are not expropriatory in nature and give no right to compensation.

Interestingly, in the *SAUR* decision, which devotes a few paragraphs to the right to water, this right was openly considered to be a general principle of international law and an applicable source of law in investment arbitral disputes. The tribunal, attempting to accommodate the different obligations arising from human rights and investment law, affirmed that the exercise of police powers can amount to regulatory expropriation but States may nonetheless be exempted from paying compensation, unless otherwise established by BIT provisions (a situation that rarely occurs).

In *Urbaser*, the tribunal granted priority to human rights considerations over investor's interests by interpreting the investors' expectations as also including the consideration that States bear the duty to protect access to water for their population, and by considering that this obligation may trump conflicting investors' rights.

In general terms, it seems that the human right to water has contributed to mitigating the arbitral tribunals' reading of core BIT provisions. The same conclusion cannot be drawn in respect of awards concerning compensation, where the principle of full recovery of the fair market value of the investment has been followed even for breaches of the fair and equitable treatment clause.

An assessment of the compatibility of possible commitments for the liberalization of water services under the GATS Agreement with obligations arising from the human right to water was made in chapter four. For the time being, there is no such a commitment in the water services sector: although some requests in this direction have been tabled by the former European Community, no offer has followed to date. Among the reasons why water services are still exempted from GATS liberalization commitments, one may mention the fact that the Agreement is still under construction, and much uncertainty remains as to the scope of some of its important provisions, such as those concerning domestic regulations, subsidies and government procurement, which have been under negotiation during the stalled Doha Round.

The approach followed by WTO dispute settlement bodies in interpreting GATS rules against the parties' right to regulate in the public interest has clearly favored fostering liberalization commitments. In general terms, it is fair to say that the WTO adjudicating bodies are less permeable to human rights considerations compared to investment tribunals, even when they have been called to interpret the general exceptions clause (Article XIV GATS). In the end, it seems that the sole way to preserve the right to water in the case of liberalization of the trade in water services lies in accurately framing limitations and exceptions in the individual schedule of commitments.

The responses to the research questions addressed by this book may be summarized as follows. In the first place, the answer to the core issue concerning the compatibility between the liberalization of water services and the human right to water differs according to the legal framework taken into consideration, as described in chapters three and four.

International investment law leaves States with sufficient leeway to regulate in the public interest, and, accordingly, allows them to strike a fair balance between the involvement of private foreign investments in the water sector and the guarantees of availability and affordability of water services.

On the contrary, the current international legal framework for trade in services is not sufficiently developed to provide guarantees in the case of liberalization of sensitive markets, such as that of water services. In particular, the possible liberalization of trade in water services risks being at odds with obligations stemming from the human right to water due to the uncertain scope of some core provisions still under development, and the restrictive interpretative approach taken by the WTO adjudicating bodies, anchored to a trade-friendly line of reasoning.

2. Appraisal

The present work raises the following considerations. In the first place, international human rights and investment law share the special feature of conferring upon individuals the right to appeal to tribunals against States' breaches of, respectively, human rights law and investment law. However, the strength of human rights compliance mechanisms is much lower than that of investment dispute settlement mechanisms. Until the recent entry into force of the Optional Protocol to the International Covenant on Economic, Social and Cultural Rights, international human rights law even lacked a system of accountability for violations of economic and social rights directly accessible to the victims of the violation. Thanks to this Protocol, individuals and groups are now allowed to submit individual communications to the Committee on Economic, Social and Cultural Rights for infringements of Covenant rights committed by States parties to the Covenant and to the Protocol. Following General Comment No. 15, it cannot be doubted that the human right to water falls within the purview of the International Covenant on Economic, Social and Cultural Right and, accordingly, that breaches of this right can be complained of under the new Protocol. However, the Protocol has so far been ratified by only a few States and, in any event, it does not grant the Committee the power to sanction States' infringements: compliance with the Committee's recommendations is indeed not enforceable.

Comparing the Committee's powers with those of investment tribunals is illuminating. Investment arbitrators are vested with the right to require States to pay compensation, which might be extremely costly for a developing country. Moreover, ICSID awards must be recognized and enforced as if they were domestic judgments and are not subject to domestic appeals.

As such, investors' rights are granted far more effective mechanisms of redress compared with human rights under international law. This imbalance between the protection of investors' rights and human rights, such as the right to water, has not been remedied by granting – through written submissions – *amicus curiae* participation in investment proceedings. Such participation does not compensate for the lack of individual access to justice for affected populations within an investor-State arbitration. Only the State is allowed to represent and defend the human rights of its population before arbitral tribunals.

Given this disparity between the protection of human rights and investors' rights, the legal framework which governs the liberalization of water services should grant States the leeway to regulate in the public interest.

In this regard, it may be appropriate to compare the regulatory freedom left by BIT treaties and by the GATS Agreement. From the analysis in chapters three and four, it could be inferred that States enjoy broader regulatory autonomy under BITs than under the GATS.

As for BITs, especially in the light of the recent judicial trends, regulations issued in order to ensure the quality, availability and affordability of water services are unlikely to reach the high threshold needed to find that a regulatory expropriation has taken place. On the contrary, such regulations may frustrate investors' legitimate expectations and raise objections of unfair and inequitable treatment. In this respect, much depends on the terms of the BIT at issue, as well as the legal framework of the host country. New BIT models suggest joining the fair and equitable standard to the "*minimum standard of treatment*" of aliens under customary international law. Moreover, an effort towards systemic integration of human rights law and investment law is evident in the arbitral tribunals case law examined in chapter three. Lastly, in case of failure of a given privatization and liberalization experience, States may terminate the contract with the foreign investor upon payment of compensation.

In contrast, the case for liberalizing trade in water services under the GATS umbrella seems rather problematic. Indeed, the GATS disciplines as well as the general and specific obligations, risk interfering with the public authorities' leeway to regulate the water sector in the public interest. Domestic regulations aimed at safeguarding universal services goals in sectors subject to specific commitments may fail to comply with the criteria outlined in Article VI:4. Thus, undertaking market access commitments for water services might imply restrictions to the range of applicable regulatory instruments, such as licensing requirements and technical standards. In addition, the draft disciplines on domestic regulations are likely to further jeopardize the leeway to regulate essential services, such as water services. Further, non-discriminatory rules, notably the "*national treatment*" and the "*most favored nation*" clause, would be difficult to comply with, in part due to the delocalized feature of water services. Uncertainty also governs the scope of important GATS exceptions relevant to public water services, such as those concerning "*services supplied in the exercise of governmental authority*" (Article I:3(*b*)), or services procured by governmental agencies (Article XIII). It appears that most of the public private partnership contracts fall outside both exceptions.

Violations of the GATS rules and commitments are enforceable through the WTO dispute settlement system and the WTO jurisprudence has raised concern for having tilted the balance towards trade liberalization in detriment of States' regulatory autonomy. Additionally, the possibility to successfully resort to the general exception for the protection of "*human life and health*" is doubtful, due to the restrictive test applied to Article XIV. More than the "*necessity*" test, the requirements of the *chapeaux*, as so far interpreted, appear to be excessively strict.

Finally, once commitments of market access and national treatment are undertaken, the lock-in effect stemming from the high compensatory adjustment due under Article XXI *de facto* prevents public authorities from reverting disappointing privatization measures. The market must remain open to WTO Members unless the State that intends to modify or withdraw commitments makes compensatory adjustments on a most-favored-nation basis.

The above comparison of the different sets of rules foreseen by BITs and the GATS leans in favor of bilateral liberalization. However, possible consequences stemming from breaches of the GATS should not be overestimated. One should not overlook that contrary to investor-to-State disputes, State-to-State disputes are rather infrequent. While the former aims to compensate private stakeholders for the losses incurred, the latter grants no compensation to affected investors, but focuses on an overall balance of interests. The ultimate end of the GATS is to lower barriers to trade in services in a mutually profitable way. Therefore, States' involvement must not to be taken for granted, as States' interests may diverge from private interests.

From a State's point of view, *extra-trade* considerations, such as the maintenance of good relations between States, may prevail. Trade disputes, for instance, might frustrate negotiations on market access commitments in other appealing sectors. As pointed out by scholars, a GATS analysis based only on "*technical questions of legal interpretation*" suffers some shortcomings[1] as it does not take into consideration political modes of influence, although political considerations may be privileged within the WTO system. This is proven by the small number of disputes which have

[1] A. Lang, *The GATS and Regulatory Autonomy: A Case Study of Social Regulation of the Water Industry*, *in Journal of International Economic Law*, 2004, p. 806.

so far been adjudged by WTO panels related to the GATS. Indeed, while the number of investor-State disputes grows annually, at the time of writing, only twenty-nine WTO disputes have involved GATS claims. Most of these disputes are still under consultation or have been withdrawn for mutually agreed solutions, and only a few have been settled by WTO adjudicatory bodies. From such data one can reasonably infer that, as far as services are concerned, the WTO dispute settlement mechanism does not play a major role compared with diplomatic approaches to dispute resolution.

In the end, although the GATS may technically affect the State's right to regulate in the public interest, the high political *momentum* that surrounds the Agreement may influence the possible consequences of GATS violations. Potential constraints to the State's regulatory autonomy have to be seen in the light of inter-State relations, whose logic pursues several interests, not limited to trade liberalization.

SELECTED BIBLIOGRAPHY

Books & courses

Balcerzak F., *Investor-State Arbitration and Human Rights*, Leiden-Boston, 2017.

Berti Suman A., *The Human Right to Water in Latin America. Challenges to Implementation and Contribution to Concept*, Leiden, 2018.

Binder, C., Kriebaum, U., Reinisch, August, Wittich, S. (eds.), *International Investment Law for the 21st Century. Essay in Honour of Christoph Schreuer*, Oxford, 2009.

Boisson de Chazournes L., Salman S.M.A. (eds.), *Les Ressources en Eau et le Droit International, Water Resources and International Law*, Leiden-Boston, 2005.

Boisson de Chazournes L., *Fresh Water in International Law*, Oxford, 2013.

Boisson de Chazournes L., Leb C., Tignino M. (eds.), *International Law and Freshwater. The Multiple Challenges*, Cheltenham-Northampton, 2013.

Boisson De Chazournes L., Mbengue M. M., Tignino M., Sangbana K. (eds.), *The UN Convention on the Law of the Non-Navigational Uses of International Watercourses, a Commentary*, Oxford, 2018.

Bourquain K., *Freshwater Access from a Human Rights Perspective. A Challenge to International Water and Human Rights Law*, Boston, 2008.

Bronwen M., *Water on Tap: Rights and Regulation in the Transnational Governance of Urban Water Services*, Cambridge, 2011.

Brown Weiss E., Boisson de Chazournes L., Bernasconi-Osterwalder N. (eds.), *Fresh Water and International Economic Law*, Oxford, 2005.

Brown Weiss E., *The Evolution of International Water Law*, in *Recueil des Cours de l'Académie de droit international de La Haye*, 2007.

Brown Weiss E., *International Law for a Water-Scarce World*, Leiden-Boston, 2013.

Bulto T. S., *The Extraterritorial Application of the Human Right to Water in Africa*, Cambridge, 2014.

Cahill-Ripley A., *The Human Right to Water and Its Application in the Occupied Palestinian Territories*, Oxford-New York, 2011.

Cannizzaro E. (ed.), *The Law of Treaties. Beyond the Vienna Convention*, Oxford, 2011..

Chaisse J. (ed.), *The Regulation of the Global Water Services Market*, Cambridge, 2017.

Choudhury B., *Public Services and International Trade Liberalization: Human Rights and Gender Implication*, Cambridge, 2012.

Cotula L., *Human Rights, Natural Resource and Investment law in a Globalised World. Shades of Grey in the Shadow of the Law*, Abingdon, 2011.

Cox J. M., *Expropriation in Investment Treaty Arbitration*, Oxford, 2019.

Cullet P., Gowlland-Gualtieri A., Madhav R., Ramanathan U. (eds.), *Water Governance in Motion, towards Socially and Environmentally Sustainable Water Laws*, New Delhi, 2010.

Dellapenna J. W., Gupta J. (eds.), *The Evolution of the Law and Politics of Water*, Dordrecht, 2009.
De Schutter O., Swinnen J., Wouters J. (eds.), *Foreign Direct Investment and Human Development. The Law and Economics of International Investment Agreements*, London, 2012.
De Wet E., Vidmar J. (eds.), *Hierarchy in International Law: The Place for Human Rights*, Oxford, 2012.
Dörr O., Schmalenbach K. (eds.), *Vienna Convention on the Law of Treaties. A Commentary*, Berlin, 2018.
Dumberry P., *The Formation and Identification of Rules of Customary International law in International Investment Law*, Cambridge, 2016.
Dupuy P.-M., Francioni F., Petersmann E.-U. (eds.), *Human Rights in International Investment Law and Arbitration*, Oxford, 2009.
Finger M., Allouche J., *Water Privatisation, Trans-National Corporations and the Re-Regulation of the Water Industry*, London-New York, 2002.
Focarelli C., *Trattato di Diritto Internazionale*, Turin, 2015.
Iannello, C., *Il Diritto all'acqua. L'appartenenza collettiva della risorsa idrica*, Naples, 2012.
Kaul I., Conceição P., Le Goulven K., Mendoza R. U., *Providing Global Public Goods: Managing Globalization*, Oxford, 2003.
Klabbers, J., *Treaty Conflict and the European Union*, Cambridge, 2009.
Krajewski M., *National Regulation and Trade Liberalization in Services: The Legal Impact of the General Agreement on Trade in Services (GATS) on National Regulatory Autonomy*, The Hague, 2003.
Kridis N. (ed.), *Maintien de la Paix et de la Sécurité Internationales et la Gestion des Ressources en Eau*, Tunis, 2018.
Langford M., Russell A. F. S. (eds.), *The Human Right to Water. Theory, Practice and Prospects*, Cambridge, 2017.
Lepard B. D. (ed.), *Reexamining Customary International Law*, Cambridge, 2017.
Maestu J., *Water Trading and Global Water Scarcity. International experiences*, Abingdon, 2013.
Marboe I., *Calculation of Compensation and Damages in International Investment Law*, Oxford, 2017.
Marrella F., *Protection internationale des droits de l'homme et activités des sociétés transnationales*, *Collected Courses of The Hague Academy of International Law*, Leiden-Boston, 2017.
McCaffrey S.C., *The Law of International Watercourses: Non-Navigational Uses*, Oxford, 2007.
McLachlan C., Shore L., Weiniger M., *International Investment Arbitration. Substantive Principles*, Oxford, 2017.
Misiedjan D., *Towards a Sustainable Human Right to Water. Supporting Vulnerable People and Protecting Water Resources*, Cambridge, 2019.
Mitchell A. D., Heaton D., Henckels C., *Non-Discrimination and the Role of Regulatory Purpose in International Trade and Investment Law*, Cheltenham, 2016.
Munin N., *Legal Guide to GATS*, Alphen aan den Rijn, 2010.
Murillo Chávarro, J., *The Human Right to Water. A Legal Comparative Perspective at the International, Regional and Domestic Level*, Cambridge, 2015.

Oriolo A., Vigorito A. (eds.), *"L'EAU", questions juridiques et économiques concernant la gestion, l'utilisation et la protection des "ressources hydriques": perspectives compares et internationals*, Rome, 2012.

Palombino F. M., *Il Trattamento 'Giusto e Equo' degli Investimenti Stranieri*, Bologna, 2012.

Palombino F. M., *Il diritto all'acqua. Una prospettiva internazionalistica*, Florence, 2017.

Paparinskis M., *The International Minimum Standard and Fair and Equitable Treatment*, Oxford, 2013.

Parisio V. (ed.), *Demanio idrico e gestione del servizio idrico in una prospettiva comparata. Una riflessione a più voci*, Brescia, 2011.

Picone P., *Comunità internazionale e obblighi 'erga omnes'. Studi critici di diritto internazionale*, Naples, 2013.

Popa L. R., *Patterns of Treaty Interpretation as Anti-Fragmentation Tools: A Comparative Analysis with a Special Focus on the ECtHR, WTO and ICJ*, Cham, 2018.

Riedel E. H., Rothen P. (eds.), *The Human Right to Water*, Berlin, 2006.

Rieu-Clarke A., Moynihan R., Magsig B.-O., *UN Watercourses Convention. User's Guide*, Dundee, 2012.

Sacerdoti G. (ed.), *General Interests of States in International Investment Law*, Cambridge, 2014.

Sadat-Akhavi, S. A., *Methods of Resolving Conflicts between Treaties*, Leiden, 2003.

Salman S. M. A., McInerney-Lankford S., *The Human Right to Water: Legal and Policy Dimensions*, Washington, 2004.

Singh N. (ed.), *The Human Right to Water. From Concept to Reality*, Cham, 2016.

Smets H. (ed.), *Le droit à l'eau potable et à l'assainissement en Europe. Implementing the right to drinking water and sanitation in 17 European countries*, Paris, 2012.

Societé francaise pour le droit international (SFDI) (ed.), Colloques d'Orléans, *L'eau en droit international*, Paris, 2011.

Stoll P.-T., Schortkopf, F. *WTO - World Economic Order, World Trade Law*, Leiden, 2006.

Tanzi A., Arcari M., *The United Nations Convention on the Law of International Watercourses: A Framework for Sharing*, The Hague, 2001.

Thielbörger, P., *The Right(s) to Water. The Multi-Level Governance of a Unique Human Right*, Berlin-Heidelberg, 2014.

Tignino, M., *L'eau et la guerre: éléments pour un régime juridique*, Bruxelles, 2011.

Tignino M., Sangbana K., (eds.), *Public Participation and Water Resources Management: Where Do We Stand in International Law*, Paris, 2015.

van de Gronden J.(ed.), *EU and WTO Law on Services. Limits to the Realization of General Interest Policies within the Services Markets?*, Alphen aan der Rijn, 2009.

van Rijswick H. F. M. W., Havekes H. J. M., *European and Dutch Water Law*, Groningen, 2012.

Viñuales J. E., *Foreign Investment and Environment in International Law*, Cambridge, 2012.

Weiß N., Thouvenin J. M. (eds.), *The Influence of Human Rights on International Law*, Cham, 2015.

Winkler, I. T., *The Human Right to Water. Significance, Legal Status and Implication for Water Allocation*, Oxford-Portland, 2012.

INDEX

A

African Charter on the Rights and Welfare of the Child: right to water 63
African Commission on Human and Peoples' Rights: right to water 119-120
Aguilar Cavallo, G. 34, 50, 54-55, 191, 201
American Convention on Human Rights: right to water 117
amicus curiae 142-143, 149-150, 166, 188, 267
Arab Charter of Human Rights: right to water 64
Arcari, M. 108-109

B

Balcerzak, F. 120, 129, 131, 183
Berti Suman, A. 64
bilateral investment agreements (BITs) provisions *see* international investment law
Boisson de Chazournes, L. 5, 93, 104, 112, 175
Bourquain, K. 2-3, 14, 49
Bronwen, M. 8-10
Brown Weiss, E. 4, 6-7, 15, 38, 48-50, 54, 90, 92
bulk water transfers *see* international trade law
Bulto, T. S. 38, 90, 106, 109, 112, 119

C

Cahill-Ripley, A. 55, 68, 106
Choudhury, B. 8, 17-18
Choukroune, L. D. 208
clauses of compatibility or of subordination: human rights and IIAs 177
Committee on Economic, Social and Cultural Rights (CESCR) 18, 44, 48, 52, 68, 84, 89, 92, 93, 94, 95, 97, 100-101, 107, 110, 111, 113-114, 121, 229, 266
commoditization of water 4-7, 38, 263
compensation for investment expropriation 18, 20, 39, 132-134, 143-145, 154, 156-157, 158, 166-171
Convention for the Protection of Human Rights and Fundamental Freedoms *see* European Convention of Human Rights
Convention on the Law of the Non-navigational Uses of International Watercourses (UN Watercourses Convention) 62-63, 108-109
Convention on the Protection and Use of Transboundary Watercourses and International Lakes ("UNECE Water Convention") 109
Cossy, M. 206-207, 210, 222, 227-228, 230-231, 235-236, 239, 243, 245-246, 248, 250, 254
Cotula, L. 7
Cox, J. M. 132
Cullet, P. 79, 108

D

de Albuquerque, 2, 44
defence of necessity 164-165, 167, 195
Dellapenna, J. W. 6
De Schutter, O. 17, 126, 138, 166, 173
De Wet, E., 183
domestic regulations 40, 201 215, 216-219, 237-239, 260-261, 265, 267-268

Dörr, O. 24-26, 61, 94, 182, 235
Dublin Statement on Water and Sustainable Development 42
Dumberry, P. 56, 61, 83, 132
Dupuy, P.-M. 24, 108, 172

E

European Convention of Human Rights (ECHR): right to water 34, 66, 114-116
expropriation provisions *see* international investment law

F

fair and equitable treatment (FET) provisions *see* international investment law
Focarelli, C. 24, 56, 60-61, 89
fragmentation of international law 19-20, 25, 30, 35, 171, 173, 182
Francioni, F. 150
full protection and security (FPS) provisions *see* international investment law

G

General Agreement on Trade in Services (GATS) 202-208 *see also* international trade law; GATS applied to water services; general exceptions (Article XIV GATS); lock-in clause (Article XXI GATS)
general exceptions (Article XIV GATS) 234, 253-260, 264-265, 268
General Comment No. 15 44, 47-49, 51, 77, 78, 84, 89-93, 94-95, 97-98, 104, 106, 110, 114, 117, 120, 121

H

Harmonization 22-28: investment protection with the human right to water; by means of conflict prevention 172-182; by means of interpretation *see* interpretation; trade in services and right to water 229; by means of conflict prevention 229-234; by means of interpretation *see* interpretation
Heaton, D. 235-236
Henckels, C. 235-236
human rights impact assessment ("HRIA") 172-173, 195,
human right to water: derivative right 51-53 *see also* right to an adequate standard of living (Article 11 ICESCR) and right to health (Article 12 ICCPR); customary right 53-60, 85-88

I

Iannello, C. 72
Inter-American Court of Human Rights: right to water 33, 117-118
International Centre for Settlement of Investment Disputes (ICSID) 18, 36, 124, 127, 131, 182-183, 267 *see also* investor-state arbitration
International Law Commission (ILC): Fragmentation of International Law: Difficulties Arising from the Diversification and Expansion of International Law, Report of the Study Group of the International Law Commission (ILC Report) 20, 182; Identification of Customary International Law, Text of the draft conclusions as adopted by the Drafting Committee on second reading 56; Subsequent Agreements and Subsequent Practice in Relation to Interpretation of Treaties, 93-94
international investment law: expropriations provisions 132-134, 143-145, 155-158, 165-167, 168, 170, 171, 178-179; fair and equitable treatment provisions 132, 134-137, 145-147, 158-163, 165-167; full protection and security provisions 132, 137, 147, 163-164, 165-167

international trade law: bulk water transfers 6; GATS applied to water services 16, 19, 25-26, 39-40, 198, 200-202, 208; virtual water transfer 7
interpretation *see* systemic interpretation, teleological interpretation
investor-state arbitration 120, 137-143, 148-155

K

Klabbers, J. 23, 28-31
Krajewski, M. 129, 173, 180-182, 192, 203-204, 221, 225, 227, 229, 233, 235, 238, 243-247, 261

L

Langford, M. 75
Leb, C. 14, 65
Legally Binding Instrument to Regulate, in International Human Rights Law, the Activities of Transnational Corporations and Other Business Enterprises (*Legally Binding Instrument*) 105-106, 174, 180-182, 191
Lepard, B. D. 57-58
liberalization of water services 10-12, 15, 16-19, 20-21, 36-40, 121, 124, 127, 148, 172, 191, 197-201, 202-204, 206, 213, 214-215, 219, 220-221, 229-232, 234-236, 237-238, 241, 244-245, 251, 260-262, 263-266, 267-269
lock-in clause (Article XXI GATS) 40, 207, 234, 262, 268

M

Magsig, B.-O. 1, 108
Marboe, I. 132, 168, 179
market access 201, 204, 206, 208, 217, 224-226, 230-231, 236, 237-239, 251, 260-262, 267-268
Marrella, F. 120, 177, 180, 190, 215
Mayer, P. 137
McCaffrey, S.C. 39
McIntyre, O 14, 54, 93, 108
McLachlan, C. 27, 132, 178, 182, 185
Misiedjan, D. 48-50, 54-55, 89
Mitchell, A. D., 235-236
monopolies and exclusive service suppliers 40, 201, 215, 216, 222-226
Moynihan, R. 1, 108
Munin, N. 198, 202, 205, 222-223, 229-230, 247, 254, 261
Murillo Chávarro, J. 50, 53, 55, 90

N

national treatment 201, 206, 208, 226-229, 236, 239-242, 260, 262, 268
natural monopoly 12, 222-223

O

Olleta, A. 8, 12, 148
Optional Protocol to the International Covenant on Economic, Social and Cultural Rights 114, 266
Ostrovsky, A. 198, 200, 203-204, 207, 233

P

Palombino, F. M. 54, 114, 132
Paparinskis, M. 134-135
Parisio, V. 231
Petersmann, E.-U. 16
Picone, P. 22, 202
Popa, L. R. 235
privatization of water services 7-12, 15, 18, 36, 102, 103, 127, 128, 138, 148, 172, 194, 197, 203-204, 207, 215, 220, 224, 243n229, 247, 248n255, 263-264, 267-268
Protocol on Water and Health: right to water 64-65

Protocol to the African Charter on Human and Peoples' Rights: right to water 63
public participation: right to water 103
public services: GATS related provisions 242-244; services supplied in the exercise of governmental authority 244-247; procurement for the supply of public services 247-251

R

regional compliance mechanisms 119-120
regional human rights tribunals 114-119
Riedel, E. H. 45
Rieu-Clarke, A. 1, 108
right to an adequate standard of living (Article 11 ICESCR) *see also* right to water 48, 89, 93, 121
right to the highest attainable standard of health (Article 11 ICESCR) *see also* right to water 49, 89, 121, 263, 266
Russell, A. F. S. 75, 106

S

Sadat-Akhavi, S. A. 32
Salman, S. M. A. 45, 107-108
Schortkopf, F. 202
Shore, L. 132, 178,
Simma, B., Kill, T. 27, 128
Singh, N. 2
Smets, H. 54
specific commitments 206, 213-214, 224, 230-233 *see also* market access, national treatment
Speed, R. 198, 200, 203-204, 207, 233
state's regulatory powers: police powers; regulatory autonomy 18-19, 38-40, 125, 128, 131-132, 133-134, 135, 144, 153, 155-158, 159, 166-167, 177-179, 185, 188, 198, 200-201, 204, 214-216, 219, 227-229, 233-234, 235-236, 237-241, 242, 251, 253, 255-257, 261-262, 265, 267-269
Stoll, P.-T. 202
subsidies 215, 216, 220-222, 260-261, 265
subsequent agreement on the interpretation: Article 31(3)(a) 61, 93-95
systemic interpretation: Article 31(3)(c) VCLT 21, 24-28, 37, 39, 130, 132, 182-186, 196, 229, 236, 251, 264
systemic relationships of priority 28-36, 186-190, 252-260, 261

T

Tanzi, A. 7, 14, 65, 100-102, 108-109, 158
teleological interpretation 21, 24-26, 225, 235, 238-239, 264
Thielbörger, P. 48-50, 53-54, 59, 75, 89, 102, 183
Tignino, M. 4, 110
Tully, S -49, 54
Türk, E. 198, 200, 203-204, 207, 225, 233, 238, 244

U

UN human rights bodies 113

V

van Rijswick, H. F. M. W. 2, 45
Vidmar, J. 32-33, 36, 183
Vigorito, A. 72
Viñuales, J. E., 83, 182

W

water grabbing 13
water scarcity 3, 4, 7, 14, 43, 61, 267
Weiniger, M., 132, 178
Winkler, I. T. 47-49, 55, 74, 91, 100-101, 104

World Trade Organization (WTO) 198; dispute resolution 207
WTO Services Sectoral Classification List (W/120) 208-213

Z

Ziegler, A.R. 198, 260

ACKNOWLEDGEMENTS

This book emerged from research that has accompanied me for the past seven years.

During the writing of this manuscript, many persons have assisted me. I would like to start my acknowledgements from Prof. Monica Lugato for her comments on early drafts of the manuscript and, even more, for her guidance in pursuing this career.

I am grateful to Prof. Andreas Ziegler, who supported my book project after being a member of the examining board at my PhD defence. Since then, Prof. Andrea Saccucci has substantially contributed to my professional growth. I must thank him for his understanding and encouragement during the writing of this book.

I am also deeply obliged to Prof. Luigi Daniele, who supervised my PhD thesis, which I used as a basis for this book, and to the memory of Prof. Maria Clelia Ciciriello, who first endorsed my research topic.

I would like to express my gratitude to Prof. Laurence Boisson de Chazournes for her advice on the first draft of my PhD thesis and for having allowed me to join, for some months, the team of the Platform for International Water Law of the University of Geneva, where I enjoyed the stimulating company of Dr Mara Tignino. Likewise, I am thankful to the UNESCO Centre for Water Law, Policy and Science of the University of Dundee for having hosted me as a visiting scholar.

A kind thought goes to my friends and colleagues who have accompanied me along this journey.

Finally, this book would not have been possible without the help of my family. I am greatly indebted to my husband Alessio for having been by my side with love during these years of demanding work, and to my father Luigi, who has always believed in me and strongly encouraged me in the completion of this manuscript.

For Product Safety Concerns and Information please contact our EU representative GPSR@taylorandfrancis.com
Taylor & Francis Verlag GmbH, Kaufingerstraße 24, 80331 München, Germany

www.ingramcontent.com/pod-product-compliance
Lightning Source LLC
LaVergne TN
LVHW011117300926
849160LV00008B/425

* 9 7 8 0 3 6 7 6 1 7 7 1 4 *